A Gallery of Her Own

WOMEN'S HISTORY AND CULTURE
VOLUME 12
GARLAND REFERENCE LIBRARY OF THE HUMANITIES
VOLUME 1414

WOMEN'S HISTORY AND CULTURE

A Gallery of Her Own
An Annotated Bibliography of Women in Victorian Painting

Elree I. Harris
Shirley R. Scott

Garland Publishing, Inc.
New York and London
1997

Library of Congress Cataloging-in-Publication Data

Harris, Elree I.
    A gallery of her own : an annotated bibliography of women in Victorian painting / by Elree I. Harris and Shirley R. Scott.
        p.   cm. — (Women's history and culture ; v. 12) (Garland reference library of the humanities ; vol. 1414)
    Includes indexes.
    ISBN 0-8153-0040-9 (alk. paper)
    1. Painting, Victorian—England—Bibliography.   2. Painting, English—Bibliography.   3. Women painters—England—History—19th century—Bibliography.   I. Scott, Shirley R.   II. Title.   III. Series.   IV. Series: Women's history and culture ; 12.
Z5949.G7H37   1997
[ND467.5.V52]
016.7592'082—dc21   97–13201
                                                                 CIP

Printed on acid-free, 250-year-life paper
Manufactured in the United States of America

To the friends, sisters, daughters,
and foremothers.

CONTENTS

ILLUSTRATIONS

PREFACE

This book is intended as a resource for anyone interested in the artistic contributions and activities of women in nineteenth-century Britain. It is an index as well as an annotated bibliography and provides sources for information about women well known in their own time and about women who were little known then and are forgotten now. Some of the women in these pages exhibited only once or twice and are of interest only to their descendants or to collectors who have happened upon their work and want to know more about the work and the artist. Some of the women in this book are famous because the men who painted their faces and bodies made them icons of the art world. A few of the women in these pages wrote about art, or founded art schools for women, or campaigned for the admission of women to established male academies. Some have left their stories in letters and in diaries; most have left nothing but a few lines in art reviews. All the women in this book deserve to be remembered, and all of them are of interest.

The material for this book has been divided into four chapters. This division is not always distinct because some painters were also models and may be mentioned in both chapters one and three. Citations may include, for example, criticism, exhibition information, and mention of art sales. Nonetheless, the first chapter is concerned with artists who painted during the Victorian period and in some cases up to the times of their deaths in the present century. The second chapter includes many exhibitions at which Victorian women artists exhibited. All venues are not listed; however, major British and international exhibits are noted. We include a chapter about models, and the last chapter is composed of references to general criticism of women's art, contemporary views of the women in art schools, and art as a profession for Victorian women. Following the annotated bibliography is an index of annotations and a biographical listing which includes women who counted themselves as artists in the census and those we identified in our perusal of contemporary publications.

The book is arranged chronologically in each chapter, allowing the reader to follow which artists were painting and exhibiting at the same time as well as to assess an artist's reputation among her contemporaries. This arrangement is also useful in comparing reviews of the same exhibit and in assessing the status of women in the academies and noting sales of their works. Annotations are numbered consecutively throughout, and the index refers to mention of women by annotation number. Included in the annotations are reproductions that have been published, in color or black and white, of paintings, sketches, engravings, portraits, and photographs. A number in the index may refer the reader to an annotation where the name does not appear. In this case the original article named the individual only as "also exhibited" with no other information or commentary. Since the exhibition history of this individual may be of interest to some, we have included the reference.

References examined for this work included books, periodicals, exhibition catalogues and reviews, advertisements, and newspapers. Newspapers and periodicals have not been exhaustively searched; however, contemporary sources include the *London Art Journal, Illustrated London Times, The Athenaeum, Englishwoman's Review, London Times, Magazine of Art, Illustrated London News, St. Nicholas,* and *The Studio.* Further information may be found in art dictionaries, bibliographies, and encyclopedias, and in electronic resources such as the Art Index, RILA, and OCLC databases. Many of the world's library catalogues are also available and accessible through the Internet. Information about the distribution of artists' works in collections is subject to obsolescence, and the user is advised to consult resources listing collections, which will provide a starting point for current information.

Art dictionaries provide much more extensive lists of women in Victorian art than we have listed in our names and dates section. We have listed the names only of women who appear in our annotations. It is important to point out that the annotations are not always representative of their original books, articles, and art reviews. While we tried to reflect the spirit and the tone of each work, an entire annotation may represent only a few lines of the original source. Thus, three pages of a review of a Royal Academy exhibition may contain two lines about a work by a woman--and we ignore the three pages about men and write the entire annotation about one woman. Scholars heading for the original citation may have to thumb through a long biography of a famous male in order to find one or two paragraphs about one female artist or model; our annotation of the work concentrates only on those one or two paragraphs concerning a woman or women of interest.

ACKNOWLEDGMENTS

We thank our long-time friend and colleague, Loretta Rielly of the Oregon State University Libraries, who had the first inspiration for this book, and, before she went on to an even larger bibliographic project, introduced us. We have her to thank for the beginnings of this project and for what has become an excellent working relationship and valuable friendship.

We have also to thank the Interlibrary Loan Departments at the University of Utah and at Oregon State University, especially Doris Tilles, Deborah Campbell, Cynthia Peterson, and Thelma Evans. Oregon State University Librarian Melvin George and Associate University Librarian Karyle Butcher have been patient and supportive colleagues. Thanks also to Mary Francey of the University of Utah Art History Department and Georgiana Donavin of the Westminster College English Department for editing, steady encouragement, and invaluable insights. Dianne Davis' friendship and support may yet inspire an airplane book.

Art historians Jan Marsh, Susan Casteras, and especially Pamela Gerrish Nunn have provided encouragement, bibliographies, lunch, kindness, and willing ears. Their support of this project and interest in it has been of great importance in many ways.

Our student research assistants have been of enormous help in locating sources, organizing material, and taking on the complexities of computer software. Liza Kellogg and Tonya Garreaud of Westminster College of Salt Lake City spent countless hours at work-study wages reading microfilm and dredging through dictionaries, bibliographies, and indexes. Heather Padgen, another Westminster College research assistant, colleague, and friend, tracked down obscure sources and catalogued hundreds of photocopies, proofread the initial drafts of this manuscript, and set up the final manuscript into camera-ready copy. Gregor Firey of the Oregon State University worked through the complexities of the ProCite software and entered over a thousand annotations. Liz Peterson appeared when we needed her to provide last-minute editing and text preparation. Judy Allen-Levanthal of the Westminster College English Department willingly added encouragement and her computer. Jiselle Jones, Julie Rezai, and Craig Des Jardins, all of Westminster College, offered their time and skills for final text preparations.

We are grateful for the financial support that enabled us to travel and to take time off from teaching and librarianship. At Westminster College of Salt Lake City, the Robert F. and Naomi Weyher Summer Grant and the Gore Excellence in Teaching Individual Summer Grant are gratefully acknowledged. Oregon State University Friends of the Library and a Bodleian Library award from William Rieckmann provided critical funding for research and travel.

A GALLERY OF HER OWN

CHAPTER 1

Victorian Women Painters

Escape into Allegory

By the beginning of the twentieth century and with the advent of the Impressionists, Post Impressionists, Cubists, Fauves, Symbolists, Surrealists, and modernism in all its forms, the art of Victorian England had become either a subject of ridicule or a non-subject altogether. Venerable introductory art history texts such as Gardener's *Art Through the Ages* (tenth edition) include Rosa Bonheur as the sole woman artist of the nineteenth century. Only John Everett Millias and Edward Burne-Jones represent English Victorian art as part of the Pre-Raphaelite school, which itself is classified as a type of Realism. With Victorian men given such short shrift in survey texts, it is no wonder that the women became all but forgotten.

Modern popular opinion holds that Victorian women were shamelessly, relentlessly victimized and oppressed by a rigid, prudish social system, held virtual hostages from infancy to old age, and, in short, that they never had any fun. For the most part, women who wanted reform went after reform, and women who wanted to paint managed to pursue their art using whatever resources were available to them. As the most recent scholarship shows, most women enjoyed considerable freedom to study art, to paint, to sculpt and to exhibit their works.[1] Overshadowing their efforts was the antiquated Royal Academy, a bastion of the European Salon system which provided ritualized and rigid training for boys and young men and rewarded their obedience with considerable fanfare at annual public exhibitions where the measure of excellence was the degree of conformity in style and subject matter. In spite of the fact that two women, Mary Moser and Angelica Kauffmann, were founding members, women were excluded from this privileged, if confining Royal

---

[1] Bernard Denvir, "Injustice Collectors," *Artists* 103, (August 1988) , p. 5. Denvir points out the success stories and complains about art historians who dwell on the negative.

Academy training until the Royal Academy was tricked into admitting them in 1861 when Laura Herford submitted as part of her application a drawing signed with only her initials. Even then, women were not allowed full membership in the Royal Academy until 1922. In the intervening years Royal Academy members debated with much gravity the unthinkable possibility of including female members at the annual banquet. Meanwhile, women trained at other art schools and with private instructors showed their works regularly at Royal Academy exhibitions, while the press and the public continued to castigate that most stolid of institutions for its illogical exclusionary behavior.

Another myth about Victorian female artists is that whatever their early training, they married and stopped painting, or they stayed single and stopped painting. Again, modern scholarship shows that while artistic careers, like many other pursuits then and now, took a back seat to the demands of domesticity and children, many women, particularly those who married artists, continued painting and exhibiting. The poet William Allingham wrote enthusiastically to a friend in 1885 that his wife, the painter Helen Allingham, was "happier than ever before in her life, painting out of doors as much as possible." He described the pictures of rural cottages that Helen was painting, remarking that her work was not only beautiful but created a record of a fast-disappearing rural countryside.[2] A letter from author George Eliot congratulating the Allinghams on their new baby expressed her hope that the event would not "greatly hinder Mamma's pencil" and asked if Helen would be willing to provide illustrations for an upcoming edition of Eliot's novel, *Romola.*[3] Henrietta Ward's artist husband was also quite supportive of her work. In her memoirs, she wrote that "Edward was greatly in advance of his age in broadmindedness." She had her own studio, and the household was admonished to respect her work time, although when some "domestic tragedy arose it was she not her husband who was interrupted."[4] With her husband's encouragement, Henrietta Ward walked into a royal Academy lecture even though women were not supposed to attend. "It was distinctly an ordeal," she wrote, "to find myself the only woman present, but I enjoyed the first lecture so much that I am determined to go regularly. . . ." In spite of the efforts of one particularly determined Royal Academy bureaucrat to keep them out, within a short time over thirty women were accompanying Henrietta to the lectures and she no longer felt so conspicuous.[5] Nor were William Allingham and Edward Ward isolated cases of supportive males.

---

[2] William Allingham, *Letters*, Eds., H. Allingham and E. Baumer Williams, (London: Longmans, 1911). Rpt., (New York: AMS Press, 1971). Hereafter cited as Allingham.

[3] Allingham, pp. 177-8.

[4] Mrs. E. M. Ward, *Memories of Ninety Years*, 2nd ed., Ed., Isabel G. McAllister, (London: Hutchinson & Co., 1924), p. 124. Hereafter cited as Ward.

[5] Ward, p. 59.

In a section of his memoirs, artist and designer Henry Holiday wrote of some of his pupils, whom he called "sister-artists." He credited Emily Hayward with "a masterly gift of draughtsmanship" who would have become his "right-hand man" had she not gotten married. He wrote that he lost other pupils for the same reason, although he gave them "sage advice to the contrary." Another promising pupil, Agnes Mortimer, studied with Holiday for several years before leaving for her Yorkshire home "to follow the bad example of others." Jessie Mothersole, another of Holiday's pupils, had been with him for fifteen years at the time he was writing his memoirs. He wrote enthusiastically of her talent with stained glass and decorative art and was obviously proud of her accomplishments, which included a book, *The Isle of Scilly*, which had met with admiration from critics. Holiday announced his intention to leave her his "large stock of cartoons and studies" so that she could use her talent to carry on his work. Presumably, Mothersole had listened to his advice against marriage and had not followed the "bad example of others." One can, of course, sympathize with an artist who spends years training a pupil, only to have her give up her talent and training altogether.

Women who spent much of their early lives training to develop their talent and then were forced to give it up unless they wanted to spend the rest of their lives alone also deserve sympathy. Holiday's disparagement of marriage seems to have been restricted to female artists--immediately after the "sister-artists" section he launched into a lengthy description of his own domestic life; he seemed quite content with his own marriage. A campaigner for the suffrage movement, Holiday saw, too, that domestic duties interfered with art. His own wife, a semi-invalid, spent her days with her embroidery or her piano, though she shared her husband's interest in women's suffrage.[6]

It cannot be denied, given the facts of domestic expectations and the number of women artists who, like Holiday's pupils, disappeared from the art scene after they married, that marriage and careers were incompatible unless the husband was enlightened, the wife determined, and both shared a commitment to art. Ina Taylor wrote about the decline of Georgiana Burne-Jones' artistic endeavors following her marriage to Pre-Raphaelite painter Edward Burne-Jones, who managed to convince Georgiana that her role was in assisting him with his own work and that her talents were too inferior to bother with. Taylor reported that late in his life, Burne-Jones insisted that women artists "don't exist" and "they don't count." She quoted him as saying "I like women when they are good and kind and agreeable objects in the landscape of existence--give life to it and are pleasant to look at and think about."[7] The Burne-Jones marriage is a good example of the importance of mutual support

---

[6] Henry Holiday, *Reminiscences*, (London: Heinermann, 1914), p. 363.
[7] Ina Taylor, *Victorian Sisters*, (Bethesda, Md.: Adler & Adler, 1987), p. 72.

and dedication. Another artist-couple, Henrietta Rae and William Normand, seem to have been successful, although Henrietta's work consistently received more notice in exhibition reviews. Still, her Kensington studio was so frequently visited by famous artists like Frederic Leighton who dropped by to check on her work and give her advice that Rinder suggests that she suffered a "confusion of tongues" and had to move away so that she could develop in her own way.[8]

Many widowed or unmarried women had their own studios and supported themselves and dependents with art lessons and with sales of their works. After the death of her estranged husband, Louise Jopling wrote frankly that "I should, by marrying again, be simply cutting my own throat, as far as my profession goes. . . ." and adds that "with children coming every second year, where would be my time or strength for work?"[9] While she admitted missing some aspects of marriage, she also admitted to "too keen a relish for the bread of independence ever to exchange it for the kickshaws of dependence."[10] Independence not withstanding, Jopling also wrote that "painting is so difficult; it discourages me dreadfully--besides, I hate being a woman. Women never do anything."[11] In spite of these protests, Jopling did marry again and evidently fared better the second time around. Clearly, the issue of marriage vs. career eludes generalities. Jopling could not paint in an unstable marriage; Ward and Rae might not have been able to paint as well if they had been single, or if they had been, like Georgiana Burne-Jones, married to misogynistic husbands.

Unlike Louise Jopling, Anna Lea Merritt remained single. Like Jopling, Merritt saw the incompatibility of the traditional domestic roles and the time, concentration, and hard work demanded of a serious artist. Merritt, who was widowed after a brief marriage, was unencumbered by house, husband, and children, but had parents, siblings, nephews, nieces and friends who made demands of her time. Many single women found they must, as Merritt suggested, "harden their hearts" against those who did not understand that single people, especially those who worked alone in a studio rather than in a public setting, had as many time constraints as married individuals.[12]

While the notion that Victorian women had no freedom is obviously not a blanket truth, this is not to say that they lived in perfect freedom either. Then, as now, choice and success was a class issue, with the privileged accorded the best education and the most opportunities for recognition. Then, as now, women were divided on the subject of women's rights--those who were against reform, those who ignored the subject,

---

[8] Frank Rinder, "'Henrietta Rae': Mrs Normand" *Art Journal* (Oct. 1901) pp. 303-307.

[9] Louise Jopling, *Twenty Years of My Life*, (London: John Lane, 1925), p. 58. Hereafter cited as Jopling.

[10] Jopling, p. 57.

[11] Jopling, p. 64.

[12] Anna Lea Merritt, "A Letter to Artists: Especially Women Artists." *Lippincott's Monthly Magazine*, lxv (March 1900), pp. 363-469.

those who simply complained, and those who actively campaigned. Many talented and educated Victorian women seemed to view the feminist movement with what seems a puzzling ambivalence. The women who had to fight to express themselves in art and literature often deplored the reform proposals which had already helped them and which would only ease their way into the future. The women who objected to reform were almost always comfortably protected by the patriarchy. Elizabeth Thompson Butler, for example, who continued painting on a smaller scale after her marriage to a high-ranking army officer, wrote in her *Autobiography* that although she lost her election as a full member of the Royal Academy by two votes, she thought that "the door has been closed, and wisely."[13] John Oldcastle observed in a *Magazine of Art* article in 1879 that "though never an advocate of women's right to vote or legislate, Miss Thompson . . . always strenuously upheld women's right to work. . . ."[14] The point must be made that many women as well as men feared female emancipation. Henrietta Ward wrote about novelist Eliza Lynn Lynton, who "lived to a good old age and became a strong anti-suffragette." "Having attained to a certain measure of freedom and success herself," Ward wrote, Lynton "seemed anxious to stem the tide by which others of her sex hoped to secure progress."[15] The issues women faced in the nineteenth century were career opportunities and votes; the issues now involve glass ceilings and decent day care. It is thus not quite accurate to picture the Victorian women as victims of a bygone world. Then, as now, women were doing what they wanted to do, sometimes against custom and opportunity, whether the rest of the world approved or not.

Another myth that follows the subject of nineteenth-century women artists is that they painted children and flowers because they could not afford models and because they were not allowed out of the house. In fact, in addition to children and flowers, women painted landscapes, animals, scenes from history and literature, and domestic scenes from their own imaginations. A perusal of any book on Victorian painting will show that men, too, painted these subjects. John Everett Millais' little boy in velvet and lace, titled *Bubbles*, originally titled *A Child's World*, graced the pages of an 1886 issue of *Illustrated London News*, and was for years an advertisement for Pears soap. Millais' picture became an icon for the cult of Victorian childhood. Reviews in the *Art Journal* show that men painted the same subjects that women painted--such as Sir William Zuiller Richardson's popular *Master Baby*, exhibited at the Grosvenor Gallery in 1886. Landseer's animals, Tissot's women in gorgeous gowns, Elizabeth Thompson's military paintings and Henrietta Rae's paintings of female nudes all serve as a caution toward generalizing about gender and genre. Contemporary commentary

---

[13] Elizabeth Thompson Butler, *An Autobiography*, (Boston: Houghton Mifflin, 1923), p. 153.
[14] John Oldcastle, "Elizabeth Butler," *Magazine of Art* 2 (1879), pp. 257-262.
[15] Ward, p. 56.

often criticizes women's lack of skill in rendering the human figure--probably an accurate criticism given women's limited opportunities to attend life classes.

In the last fifteen years, several important studies have revealed not only the sheer number of and public appreciation for professional female artists, but tell much about their training, working conditions, aesthetic theories and personal backgrounds. Rozsika Parker and Griselda Pollock's landmark critical essay titled *Old Mistresses: Women, Art and Ideology* provides important theory for feminist art historians.[16] Jan Marsh and Pamela Gerrish Nunn's *Women Artists in the Pre-Raphaelite Movement*[17] and Marsh's biographical studies of Elizabeth Siddall and Jane Morris[18] open doors to Victorian art history as well as providing insights into the minds and hearts of these enigmatic women. Pamela Gerrish Nunn's *Victorian Women Artists* presents invaluable case histories and critical commentary,[19] and Paula Gillett's *Worlds of Art: Painters in Victorian Society* describes working conditions, provides sales records for paintings, and in two important chapters, focuses specifically on the social status of women artists.[20] Susan Casteras' books and articles provide much-needed critical studies of Victorian art in general and Victorian women painters in particular. Pamela Gerrish Nunn's studies of Rebecca Solomon's paintings are especially valuable as they provide critical studies of the works themselves rather than dwelling on the social conditions under which Solomon worked, treating Solomon's pictures as serious art, and subjecting them to close historical and compositional analysis.[21]

Sadly, most of the paintings by nineteenth-century women have been lost or destroyed; fortunately, contemporary audiences valued them enough to create a market for engravings in magazines and in suitable-for-framing form. Since most Victorians saw Royal Academy pictures in black and white engravings, we have chosen our illustrations in the same spirit. Deborah Cherry has pointed out that paintings by women of domestic scenes frequently portray women and children relaxed and happy with no men present.[22] This fascinating proposal deserves further study. Paintings by Victorian women do seem to avoid melodramatic and morally didactic scenes such as Augustus Egg's sequence of the fate of the fallen wife (*Past and Present*, 1816-1863) or William Holman Hunt's *The Awakening Conscience*

---

[16] Rozsika Parker and Griselda Pollock, *Old Mistresses: Women, Art and Ideology*, (New York: Pantheon, 1981).

[17] Jan Marsh and Pamela Gerrish Nunn, *Women Artists and the Pre-Raphaelite Movement*, (London: Virago, 1989).

[18] Jan Marsh, *The Legend of Elizabeth Siddal*, (New York: Quartet, 1989). Jan Marsh, *Jane and May Morris: A Biographical Story, 1839-1938* (New York: Pandora Press, 1986).

[19] Pamela Gerrish Nunn, *Victorian Women Artists*, (London: The Women's Press, 1987).

[20] Paula Gillett, *Worlds of Art: Painters in Victorian Society*, (New Brunswick, N. J.: Rutgers UP, 1990).

[21] See, for example, "Rebecca Solomon: Painting and Drama," *Theatrephile* Vol. 2, No. 8 (1985), pp. 3-4.

[22] Deborah Cherry, "Picturing the Private Sphere," *Feminist Art News,* 5 (1982), pp. 8-11.

(1854) featuring a woman about to save herself from sin, or like Dante Gabriel Rossetti's *Found* (1853-4) featuring a woman probably beyond saving.

While one must be cautious in reading too much about gender into genre paintings, no art is created in a vacuum and must of necessity reflect forces shaping and surrounding the artist. We chose our illustrations because we liked them, and (with the exception of Rebecca Solomon's *the Fugitive Royalists*) because we had not seen them in modern publications. However, all three pictures seem to possess some elements common to many pictures painted by women; while they fit into the popular domestic genre, they subordinate or do without male figures, they feature or suggest invalid females, and they carry an underlying theme of male oppression.

The engraving of Rebecca Solomon's *The Fugitive Royalists* [fig. 1] appeared on the front page of the 21 June 1862 edition of *The Illustrated London News*. The short paragraph describing it praises the contribution of the feminine element in art and applauds the recent admission of women to the Royal Academy schools. The rest of the article tells the story told in the painting: "A Royalist mother with, perhaps, her fatherless boy. . .has fled in terror from her home, now probably sacked and gutted." The description uses such phrases as "agonized anxiety" and "horrid glories of death or victory" to describe the dilemma of the two women--both torn between their loyalty to each other and with the necessity of protecting themselves and their offspring from outside forces they cannot control. The four figures form a stabilizing pyramid with the shadowy portrait of the uniformed oppressor at the apex. The three women's faces turn inward--the boy dwarfed by his mother's clothing looks outward and the soldier-portrait gazes impassively over the heads of the anxious group. The sleeping girl on the left, a book on her lap, represents the helplessness and passivity, if not the chronic invalidism of the idealized nineteenth-century woman--a strong contrast to the anything-but-indifferent women beside her. Madonna-like, she holds her place in a book, an echo of ages of annunciation scenes, suggesting intelligence and intellectual or religious pursuits as opposed to more domestic pastimes such as embroidery or fancy-work--but she is a picture of helplessness all the same. Of course a man could have painted this picture, but more likely a male artist would confront a male child in a male world as in W. F. Yeam's 1878 *And When Did You Last See Your Father?* That the all-male selection committee saw in this picture its excellence of composition, proportion, human tension and perfect capturing of a dramatic moment is implied in its place in the 1862 Royal Academy exhibition as on the front cover of *The Illustrated London News*.[23]

Laura Alma-Tadema's *Sisters* [fig. 2], another domestic scene without male presence, also celebrates a female relationship, and again includes an invalid female.

---

[23]Roy Strong, *And When Did You Last See Your Father? The Victorian Painter and British History*, (London: Thames and Hudson, 1978).

An article about Alma-Tadema in the November 1883 *Art Journal* included a full-page engraving of this work with the information that the original was exhibited in both the Grosvenor Gallery and the Berlin Academy. As much as the two small girls are dwarfed by their surroundings, the *Art Journal* article made the point that "in the line engraving the relative size of the children has been unavoidably lost."[24] The relationship between children and the enormous adult world, of girls whose only remedies for distress include passivity and flowers, makes a silent statement about female claustrophobia and helplessness, emphasized by the boxed-in composition of vertical and horizontal lines. The upper corner lines converge at a vertical line in the center of the picture which leads directly to the wan little face, to the flowers, along the small visitor's arm, down the streamer on her dress to her small tip-toed feet and along a down-slanting horizontal line to the fallen flower. Perhaps a male artist might have painted this sisterly moment--but consider another sickbed scene, Luke Fildes' 1891 *The Doctor,* in which two men tend a sick child while the mother sits helplessly by with her face buried in her hands. In Alma-Tadema's painting, the relative helplessness of the girls is suggested by their size in relation to the massive furniture, but like the women in Solomon's painting, they are alone with their friendship, and a book waits on a table at the left. Certainly they have not collapsed in a heap of helplessness, and the small flower-bearer is sturdy and determined.

The theme of male oppression is cleverly disguised in Mary L. Gow's 1886 painting *The Willow-Pattern Plate* [fig. 3]. A contemporary *Magazine of Art* review raved about the design, composition and color of this Royal Institute exhibit, while complaining about the triteness of the subject.[25] The story in the willow pattern was familiar to every little girl and every mother, if not to every art reviewer, and neither the familiar story nor Gow's use of it are trite. In the china design, popular in England and the U.S. since the late 1700's, two lovers flee a whip-bearing father across a bridge, escaping his wrath by turning into swallows which wheel in the wind far above the landscape. In Gow's painting, the forms of mother and child lean together in a pyramid with their faces at the apex. They are, like Alma-Tadema's *Sisters,* dwarfed by their surroundings, which seem to cast ominous shadows, making their closeness almost a protective huddle. They are lost together, not in a book, but in a story of another world painted on a plate. The mother points out in the familiar design a story of patriarchal violence and of magical escape and freedom. The child, surrounded by blankets and barely visible under the coverings and pillows on a chaise or small bed, may be an invalid. Certainly helplessness and subordination to external forces are obvious in the story that engrosses them as well as in the looming shadows

---

[24] Alice Meynell, "Laura Alma-Tadema." *Art Journal* (November 1883), pp. 345-347.
[25] "Current Art. II." *Magazine of Art* (1886), pp. 353-359.

1. Rebecca Solomon. *The Fugitive Royalists*, 1862. Engraving. *The Illustrated London News*. Courtesy of the Board of Trustees of the Victoria and Albert Museum.

2. Laura Epps Alma-Tadema. *Sisters*, Exhibited at The Hague, 1883. Engraving, *Art Journal*. Courtesy of the Board of Trustees of the Victoria and Albert Museum.

3. Mary L. Gow. *The Willow Pattern Plate*, 1886. Engraving, *Magazine of Art*.
Courtesy of the Board of Trustees of the Victoria and Albert Museum.

that surround them. Again, a male painter might well have painted such a scene, but the child would more likely be hearing a story of adventure and conquest, if not tragedy, as the fascinated little boy listens to the one-armed soldier in Thomas Robert's 1856 painting *The Empty Sleeve*.

With the end of the nineteenth century came the fruits of the reform efforts of women and men in the art world. The walls of the Royal Academy schools were breached. Training and scholarships for women became available for some women outside of the middle class and of traditional art circles. Economic and social necessity overcame hidebound idealism so that careers and higher education were becoming a possibility for many women. One of the great ironies for women who struggled for recognition in the Victorian age was that the conventional subject matter favored by the public--the genre paintings of domesticity, flowers, gentle landscapes and beautiful children--tended to depict women in just the idealized passivity and helplessness they had to escape. Even the most successful artists were, in effect, painting themselves into a corner. Liberation came at the end of the century with the Arts and Crafts Movement (of which the enlightened Henry Holiday was a part) and in the non-representational directions of twentieth-century painting. Even as modern painting became more and more difficult for the uneducated viewer to relate to, it was less and less necessary for women painters to escape into allegory.

---

1. Summerly, Felix. *A Handbook to Hampton Court*. London: 1842.

    Contains "woodcuts by ladies," but the ladies are not identified.

2. "Grace Aguilar." *The Art Union* (1 November 1847): 378.

    While Grace Aguilar was not, strictly speaking, an artist, her *Home Influences* should be in every house, and *Women of Israel*, her best work, does honor to her Jewish heritage. After fleeing Portugal to escape religious persecution, she and her family made England their home and she supported herself with her literary and artistic pursuits. A kind and intelligent woman, an art lover and friend to many in the art world, her virtuous example should not "pass unnoted down the stream of time."

3. "The Vernon Gallery: The Gallery of British Art of Robert Vernon, Esq., No. 50, Pall-Mall." *Art Union* (1 November 1847): 272-365.

    One of the most extensive art collections in Great Britain is to be donated to the public by its owner, Mr. Vernon. The collection, which represents the donor's years of acquired taste, judgement, and knowledge, contains the best works of the best British artists. The collection includes

Lady and Parrot and *A la Greuze*, by Mrs. Carpenter, and three landscapes by Miss Nasmyth.

4.   Ironside, Robin and J. A. Gere. *Pre-Raphaelite Painters with a Descriptive Catalogue*. New York: Oxford University Press, 1848.

Elizabeth Siddall must have been quite beautiful. Her work is unoriginal but possesses an unusual intensity. She shared her thoughts and feelings with no one; these facts, coupled with her tragic early death create an enigmatic and fascinating figure in the world of art history.

Reproductions (b/w):

Siddall, Elizabeth: *Clerk Saunders*

Rossetti, Dante Gabriel: *Study for Lancelot's Vision* (Elizabeth Siddall as model).

5.   "Society of Arts." *Art Journal* (1 July 1849): 204.

HRH Prince Albert, President of the Institution for the Encouragement of Arts and Manufactures, awarded the most important prizes for this year's achievements. Among the recipients is Miss Catherine Marsh, who received the silver Iris Medal and £2 for her series of wildflower drawings.

6.   "The Book of Ruth." *Art Journal* (1 January 1850): 36.

It is gratifying to see the artistic talents possessed by so many of Britain's female aristocracy put to use in the interest of charitable causes. The superior quality of Lady Cadogan's imagination, drawing and composition enhances the biblical story to make a beautiful and inspirational book. Her illustrations include *The Journeying of Elimelech and His family into Moab; Naomi and Ruth; Ruth Gleaning in the Field of Boaz; Boaz and Ruth; Boaz and the Elders;* and *The Birth of Obed. The Marriage of Boaz and Ruth* is featured as the frontispiece.

7.   "Highland Refugees." *Art Journal* (1 February 1850): 67.

Highland Refugees depicts an aging Scottish couple standing on the French coast, looking toward Scotland with the tragic air of exiles who may never see home again. Fanny MacIan deserves her high reputation as an artist; her works, like this one, use simple eloquence combined with truth, which cannot fail to arouse sympathy for her subjects.

8.   "Miss Biffin [Obituary]." *Art Journal* (1 November 1850): 339-340.

Sarah Biffin, age sixty-six, a famous painter of miniatures, died at her Liverpool home. Biffin, who was born without hands or arms, trained for some years as an indentured servant of the Dukes family. Later, the Earl of Morton took an interest in her work, and saw that she received further training from an eminent miniaturist who helped her develop her talents "to an almost miraculous degree of perfection." The superior quality of her work led to offers to help her relinquish her contract with the Dukes family, who paid her £5 per year, but she remained with them for sixteen years. She painted miniatures of three kings and many members of the royal family and supported herself with her art; however, after the death of the Earl of Morton, she had no one to help her obtain commissions and to sell her work, and she "fell into reduced circumstances." Later, friends took up a collection to provide her with a small income. She left her memoirs, which her family plan to have published.

9. Ruskin, John. *Pre-Raphaelitism and Notes on the Principal Pictures in the Royal Academy, the Society for Painters in Water Colours, Etc.* London: G. Routledge, 1851.

Three flower paintings by Anna Feray Mutrie in the Royal Academy exhibit rate comments from Ruskin. He praises her superb handling of color, but complains that the backgrounds tend to be indistinct. He recommends that she abandon artificial arrangements in favor of flowers in a more natural setting. His advice seems to have been ignored, for both Annie and Martha Mutrie's exhibits for the following year receive the same criticism. Martha Mutrie's *Geraniums* and Annie Mutrie's *Roses* are, Ruskin writes, "nearly as good as simple flower painting can be," but he asks, rather plaintively, "Why not a roadside bank of violets?" Annie Mutrie seems to have sought a compromise, for Ruskin complains that the flowers on a fern bank in her 1857 Royal Academy exhibit, *Royal Flowers,* are too artfully arranged to look natural. She has, Ruskin writes, painted "an unexpected picnic of polite flowers in the country." The 1858 exhibit features Annie Mutrie's *Reynard's Glove* that depicts foxgloves in their natural setting but Ruskin pronounces them too small, and abandons Mutrie's painting for an energetic lecture on foxgloves he has known. Also in the 1856 exhibit is Eliza Turck's *Cinderella After Her Sisters Have Left for the Ball.* Of this painting, Ruskin complains that Cinderella doesn't look like a fairy-tale character, but at the same time he praises the stern realism of Turck's treatment of the story. Anna Blunden's 1858 Royal Academy exhibit, *Past and Present,* is praised for its sincerity and painstaking execution; while the figures in the painting are unsatisfactory, and Blunden's technique lacks strength, the work is of such quality as to make it worth "a long stoop" to look at it. Evidently it was hung very near the floor. Blunden's Royal Academy exhibit for 1859, *God's Gothic*, is perhaps an attempt to correct the lack of strength remarked upon in the previous year. She may have overdone it, because Ruskin seems confused about a harshness of color that he says is nevertheless present in nature. He again praises Blunden's sincerity, but hopes she will try to paint with a gentler hand.

10. Howitt, Anna Mary. *An Art Student in Munich*. London: Longman, 1853.

Anna Mary Howitt's diaries provide a lively and carefully detailed account of her life in Munich and the people she met there. In her preface she credits the men who have helped her in her art career. It is not true, she maintains, "that it is man who thwarts every effort of woman to rise to eminence in the life of Art."

11. "*The Friend in Need*. Miss Solomon, Painter." *Illustrated London News* (23 April 1859): 400.

A charitable woman quietly stays the hand of a pitiless parish beadle about to arrest a poor homeless woman and infant; Solomon's "spirited little picture" is exhibited at the City Gallery.

Reproductions (engraving):

Solomon, Rebecca: *The Friend in Need*.

12. "*The Course at Calcutta*–from a Drawing by Ada Claxton." *Illustrated London Times* (30 July 1859): cover.

In Ada Claxton's cover illustration, an Englishwoman in a black riding habit sits on a handsome horse, both horse and woman quietly observing a crowded procession of Indians and Anglos afoot and in carriages.

13. "*Arrival of Overland Travelers at Point de Galle, Ceylon*. Drawn by Miss Claxton." *Illustrated Times* (31 July 1860): 198.

A black-and-white engraving by Florence Claxton provides the cover illustration. A mustachioed white man in a white suit and pith helmet stands erect and spread-legged, dominating a crowded scene of obsequious Ceylonese (although one dark male gazes at the intruder with a steady look and more real presence than anyone else in the picture). The overdressed Anglo women behind the man in white flutter, cringe, posture and generally look out of place.

Reproductions (b/w engraving):

Claxton, Florence: *Arrival of Overland Travelers at Point de Galle, Ceylon*.

14. "Mrs. Wells [Obituary]." *Art Journal* 23 (1861): 273.

Wells' early work was influenced by the Pre-Raphaelites, but her later work was more conservative. All her work shows "a degree of enthusiasm and well-directed study beyond what is seen in the works of lady artists generally." Her first work to appear in an Academy exhibit was *Elgiva* in 1855. She studied briefly with Coutre in Paris. She met and married Mr. Wells in Rome in 1857. Her painting *The Boy's Crusade* was hung in the Academy in 1860. Her work shows much promise cut off by her death from a fever following childbirth at the age of thirty.

15. "Mrs. Valentine Bartholomew [Obituary]." *Art Journal* (1 October 1862): 206-207.

Anne Charlotte Fayerman Bartholomew was born in Norfolk and raised by her maternal grandfather, a clergyman. Evidence of her artistic ability resulted in her career as a painter of miniatures, still-lifes, and picturesque figures. She married at twenty-seven, and was widowed eleven years later. She published *The Songs of Azreal*, a volume of poetry, and wrote two plays. One, a farce titled *It's Only My Aunt*, achieved much success, especially in America. Eventually, she married Valentine Bartholomew, a noted painter of flowers. They admired and supported each other's art. She was a charitable and caring person, and it is said of her that "the *artist* never forgot the duties of the *woman*."

16. Dafforne, James. "British Artists: Their Style and Character: No. LXXV: Emily Mary Osborn." *Art Journal* 3 (1864): 261-263.

Dafforne feels it is inappropriate to end a ten-year series of biographical sketches of artists without mention of female artists, who "maintain the intellectual honour of their sex" as well as "upholding the high character" of painting. The representative artist is Emily Mary Osborn, whose talent was encouraged by lessons from Mr. Leigh and patronage of William Mitchell; the Queen purchased several of her paintings. Osborn's *Nameless and Friendless* was contributed to the Royal Academy in 1857 where it attracted considerable attention.

Reproductions (b/w engraving):

Osborn, Emily Mary: *Nameless and Friendless; Of Course She said 'Yes'!; The Escape of Lord Nithisdale From the Tower, 1716.*

17. "Historical Picture by Mrs. E. M. Ward." *Art Journal* (1 May 1864): 154.

> Henrietta Ward's historical paintings have been deservedly successful, and her latest work in this genre is equally deserving of praise. Set in the Tower of London, this painting depicts young Edward V, sitting despondently by a table with the future Richard III in the doorway leaning on the young Duke of York. The picture is remarkable for its facial expressions; Edward V's melancholy, the young duke's ingenuousness, and Richard's sinister air are admirably rendered. The princes are dressed in mourning, but royal purples, miniver, tapestry and appointments are remarkable in richness of color and detail. The picture is as ambitious as it is successful, and is "a most conclusive argument as to the justice and necessity of admitting female artists within the ranks...of the Royal Academy."

18. "Fine Arts: Royal Academy." *Athenaeum* (19 May 1866): 675.

> Henrietta Ward's *Palissy the Potter* is honest in its execution, both in technique and subject matter. The painting, the most ambitious of Ward's work so far, is also the best.

19. "Art Politics and Proceedings." *Blackwood's Edinburgh Magazine* (August 1866): 191.

> Henrietta Ward's achievement with *Palissy the Potter* puts her in the forefront of women painters and makes a good case for the recognition of women by the Royal Academy.

20. "Female School of Art." *Art Journal* (1 September 1867): 218.

> Alice Manly received the first of the Queen's gold medals awarded to the best students at the Female School of Art. Manly was recognized for three flower paintings; one of the judges was one of the Mutrie sisters. Manly also won a National Silver Medal from the Department of Science and Art.

21. "Selected Pictures." *Art Journal* 7 (1868): 148-149.

> *God's Acre*, a picture of two little girls braving the bitter winter weather to visit, perhaps, their mother's grave, was exhibited in Pall Mall in 1866. Emily Mary Osborn, who spent much of her time in Germany, often depicted German peasants such as these children in her paintings, showing careful attention to accuracy and detail in dress and setting. The title is from a verse by Longfellow referring to the Saxon name for a burial ground.

Reproductions (b/w engraving):
Osborn, Emily Mary: *God's Acre.*

22. "The Royal Academy." *Art Journal* (1 January 1868): 15.

    The Royal Academy awarded the gold medal for the best historical painting to Louisa Starr. She not only headed the list, but she was the only female to be so honored this year.

23. "Minor Topics of the Month." *Art Journal* (1 April 1868): 58- 59.

    While Mr. Ward will not be exhibiting at the Royal Academy this year, Henrietta Ward will continue to meet the art world's high expectations of her by exhibiting a picture of an incident in the life of Lady Jane Grey.

24. "Selected Pictures. From the Collection of Andrew Holtz, Esq. *Palissy, the Potter.* Mrs. E. M. Ward, Painter. C. W. Sharpe, Engraver." *Art Journal* (1 June 1868): 120-121.

    Henrietta Ward is one of the leading British historical painters, and certainly can be regarded as the best of female artists. Her great work, *Palissy the Potter*, was shown at the Royal Academy in 1866 and was engraved and reproduced in the *Art Journal*. Ward took the scene of her picture from Morley's work, *Life of Palissy*. The passage that inspired her is quoted here. Morley's account describes Palissy's wife as a shrew who had brought his creditors to see the kiln yield the works that would pay their debts, only to berate the artist for whom an accident in the firing had brought failure and utter despair. Ward tempers Morely's narrative, picturing Mrs. Palissy as loving and sympathetic. Ward renders the family disaster with great compassion and artistic skill.

25. Claxton, Adelaide. "*Riddles of Love.* Drawn by Adelaide Claxton. [illustration]." *London Society* (1870): 498-499.

    Adelaide Claxton's drawing of a woman bending over a sick man while a servant fans them illustrates a scene in a serialized story titled "Riddles of Love."

    Reproductions (b/w):
    Claxton, Adelaide: *Riddles of Love.*

26. "Selected Pictures. From the Picture in the Possession of the Publisher. *The Maid of New Orleans.* Mrs. E. M. Ward, Painter. T. Ballin, Engraver." *Art*

Journal (January 1870): frontispiece, 12.

Henrietta Ward depicts a girl Joan of Arc at her domestic duties and looking over her shoulder at a dour and heavily-armed knight taking his rest in her humble cottage. A dog licks his hand, a touching gesture in a work of great skill.

27. "Miss Louisa [sic] Herford [Obituary]." *Art Journal* (March 1871): 80.

Louisa [Laura] Herford's death late last year has been noted, but an additional mention should be made of the fact that she was the first female admitted to the Royal Academy Art Schools. Her application for entry was a drawing signed with only her first initial and surname; the admissions committee assumed that she was male, and she overcame objections by pointing out that the rules of the Royal Academy schools did not expressly forbid women students. As a result of her efforts many women have studied at the Royal Academy.

28. "Selected Pictures. *David Brought Before Saul.* Louisa Starr, Painter. S. S. Smith, Engraver." *Art Journal* (April 1871): 100-101.

Louisa Starr's *David Brought Before Saul,* depicting a young David humbly presenting the head of Goliath to Saul while a young Jonathan peers from behind Saul's throne, received the Royal Academy School's gold medal for "best historical painting" in 1867. Starr's success is proof that the Academy acted wisely in admitting women to its schools, but it remains impossible for women thus trained to become full members in the Academy. Women have distinguished themselves in a great many areas; it seems incongruous that the gates should be closed to them in the field of art.

Reproductions (b/w engraving):
Starr, Louisa: *David Brought Before Saul.*

29. "Miss Pearson [Obituary]." *Art Journal* (June 1871): 166.

Mary Martha Dutton Pearson died on April 15th. She was seventy-two, and while her work is not known by the present generation, at one time her portraits were much admired. She leaves many friends and a loving family.

30. "The Works of Madame Jerichau." *Art Journal* (June 1871): 165.

The works in Elizabeth Jerichau's New Bond Street exhibition reveal an artist skilled in academic discipline seldom seen in a woman's art. A design for an oil painting titled *The Valkyrie* is spirited, and the Valkyrie's horses are "wild and weird." Pictures of women, titled *The Favorite of the*

Hareem; La Penserosa; Homeless, and *Helena, a Young Maiden from Hymentos* are matter-of-fact and avoid prettiness or sentimentality. Jerichau does show feminine sensitivity in her pictures of children titled *O, Sanctissima!; Corn Flowers* and *Little Carin.* Her husband contributes "two charming sculptures" to the exhibit.

31. "Minor Topics of the Month. The Royal Academy." *Art Journal* (January 1872): 29.

Jessie Macgregor has won a "gold medal and books" for her historical painting, deemed the best among this year's work of students of the Royal Academy Schools. Silver medals were awarded to Julia Cecelia Smith and Julia Bracewell Folkard for their drawings from antique casts. The honors awarded to these students make it all the more obvious that the Royal Academy is remiss in not admitting female artists to full membership.

32. "Schools of Art. Female School of Art." *Art Journal* (July 1872): 210.

Enrollment is up at the Female School of Art under Louisa Gann's capable management. Of the ninety national awards available to all 114 art schools, over 20,000 students and over 60,000 art works, four prizes went to students at the Female School. Julia Pocock won the Queen's scholarship; Mary Webb won the Queen's prize medal; Emily Austin won the silver national medal. Gilchrist prizes also went to Mary Webb, Emily Austin, Henrietta Rae and Agnes Ierson.

33. "Crystal Palace School of Art and Science." *Art Journal* (September 1872): 242.

Miss Turner has won a silver medal for a drawing titled *Pompeian Court Interior.* Certificates of merit and commendation are awarded to Flora Teulon, Elizabeth Farquahar and Edith Farquahar.

34. "Selected Pictures. From the Picture in the Collection of Henry McConnel, Esq., Cressbrook, Derbyshire. *The Critics.* Henriette Browne, Painter, C. W. Sharpe, Engraver." *Art Journal* (September 1872): 223-224.

Henriette Browne, one of France's most eminent painters, is well known in England. Her *Le Père Hyacinthe* and *During the War* were exhibited at the Royal Academy in 1870 and 1871. Her best known picture, *Sisters of Charity,* was exhibited at the 1862 International Exhibition and is very popular as an engraving. *Critics*, a painting of two children examining the carcass of a hare, seems to be either an anticipation of a meal or a "mournful contemplation of death." The picture excels in composition and careful rendering.

Reproductions (b/w engraving):

Browne, Henriette: *The Critics.*

35. "Schools of Art. Female School of Art, Bloomsbury." *Art Journal* (November 1872): 302.

Students in 113 art schools competed for prizes and medals this year. Quite a few of the awards have been won by students of Louisa Gann and Miss Wilson at this year's exhibition at the Female School of Art. Alice Blanche Ellis received the Queen's scholarship and a bronze medal for her flower pictures. Ellen Hancock's tempera painting of a passion flower has won her the national silver medal. Also receiving medals, scholarships or special recognition are Emily Selous Fenessey, Julia Pocock, Elizabeth A. Dorrington, Anne Hopkinson, Ellen Ashwell, Louisa Baxter, Elizabeth Hodge, Eleanor Manly, Jennie Moore, Mary Ann Pickering, Edith Tegetmeier, Mary Whiteman Webb, Charlotte Amelia Austen, Susan Ruth Canton, Alice Hanslip and Rosalie Watson.

36. "Obituary. Mrs. Margaret Sarah Carpenter." *Art Journal* (January 1873): 6.

The noted portrait painter Margaret Sarah Geddes Carpenter has died at the age of eighty. She was born at Salisbury and received her early art training there. She moved to London in 1814 and was much in demand as a portrait painter of important people. Her work can be seen in the National Portrait Gallery. She was married to the Keeper of Prints and Drawings for the British Museum, is aunt to author Wilkie Collins, and mother to painters W. Carpenter and Henrietta Carpenter.

37. "Schools of Art. Female School, Queen's Square." *Art Journal* (May 1873): 144.

In the crowded Theatre of the London University, Her Royal Highness the Princess of Wales presented the awards to graduating students of the Female School of Art. Awards were received by Emily Austin, Mrs. E. Finnessey, *née* Selous, Alice B. Ellis, Ellen Hancock and Julia Pocock. Louisa Gann, the school's superintendent, deserves commendation for her leadership and determination which have brought the school through hard times. Living proof of her hard work can be seen in the accomplishments of her students and in the number of awards she herself has won among the heads of art schools. His Royal Highness the Prince of Wales gave a brief address to the students prior to the awarding of prizes.

38. "Paintings by Madame Jerichau." *Art Journal* (August 1873): 254-255.

        Madame Jerichau's exhibition at the Gallery of Messrs. Pilgeram and Lefèvre shows how her work avoids the prettiness that mars the paintings of most female artists. The masculine quality of many of her paintings succeeds because she has confidence to match her skills. Her untitled paintings of women and children are bold and memorable.

39. "Female School of Art." *Art Journal* (December 1873): 378.

        Miss Gann's pupils have the best exhibition yet presented by the Female School. Prizes are awarded to Ellen Hancock for a tempera flower study, Agnes Jerson for watch designs, Emily Austin and Annie E. Hopkinson for watercolor flower studies and Alice Hanslip for a chalk study titled *The Wrestlers*. Winners of scholarships and additional prizes are Jessie Corcoran, Ellen Ashwell, Alice Blanche Ellis, Alice Hanslip, Emily Hentsch, Elizabeth Hodge, Louisa Overbury, Julia Clarke, Hannah Cole, Gertrude Hamilton, Sarah Jones, Jessie Hamilton and Rosalie Watson. Next year's competition for the Gilchrist Scholarship for £15 a year will be open to "all female art students under twenty years of age."

40. Corlett, A. B. "Art and Literature." *Englishwoman's Review* 5 (1874): 293.

        Elizabeth Thompson, the heroine of today's art world, has made two drawings, *Gallop! A Reminiscence of Woolwich* and *Halt! A Reminiscence of Aldershot*. Both drawings are spirited, and figures in *Halt!* are "astonishingly fine in vigour and character."

41. "Art Notes and Minor Topics." *Art Journal* (January 1874): 29.

        Students of the Royal Academy school, including Elizabeth S. Guiness, Janet Archer, and Caroline Nottage have received silver medals. In the National Awards, Louisa Cooper, Emily Fawcett, and Edith Hipkins are silver medalists. Bronze medal winners include Henrietta Meyer, Frederica Moffat, Hilda Montalba, and Constance Philip. Books and Queen's prizes go to Matilda Goodman, Emily Greedish, Kate Hill, Marianne Mansell and Mary Tothill.

42. "Art Notes and Minor Topics. A Series of Drawings." *Art Journal* (February 1874): 61-62.

        Julia Pocock, a medalist and prize winner at several art schools and the daughter of the secretary of the Art Union, has illustrated a translation of German ballads for a work still in private circulation. Pocock's drawings retain "the spirit of the original" and are excellently composed. Her work follows the style of the renowned "Nibelungen."

43. "Art Notes and Minor Topics. The Royal Academy." *Art Journal* (February 1874): 62.

    Silver Medals have been awarded to "Elizabeth Smith Guiness for the best drawing from the antique;" "to Janet Archer for the third best drawing from the antique," and "to Caroline Nottidge for the best restoration of the *Venus de Milo*."

44. "Art Notes and Minor Topics." *Art Journal* (March 1874): 93.

    One hundred and eight candidates have been nominated for membership in the Royal Academy; since there are only two or three vacancies per year, most of these worthy artists, and others equally meritorious but not nominated, have little chance of election. Among the names proposed are Annie Mutrie, Martha Mutrie and Henrietta Ward.

45. "Art Notes and Minor Topics." *Art Journal* (May 1874): 158.

    Clara Montalba is now an associate of the Society of Water Colour Painters. Four other women, Miss Montalba, Mary Harrison, Margaret Gillies, and Mary Ann Criddle are associates.

46. "Banquet at the Royal Academy." *London Times* (4 May 1874): 8.

    At the Royal Academy banquet, HRH the Prince of Wales was cheered by the other guests as he called their attention to *Calling the Roll*. The young lady who painted it deserves admiration and a great future with her art.

47. "The Roll Call." *Art Journal* (June 1874): 191.

    The copyright to Elizabeth Thompson's *The Roll Call* has been purchased "for a very large sum" by J. Dickinson & Co. who plan to "engrave it on a large scale" as soon as the Royal Academy exhibition is over.

48. "Society of Painters in Water Colours." *Art Journal* (June 1874): 167-168.

    Her skill in handling color and light is obvious in Miss Montalba's Venetian scenes; she certainly deserves her recent election as an associate of the Society of Painters in Water Colours.

49. "Art Notes and Minor Topics." *Art Journal* (August 1874): 254-255.

> Students at the Female School of Art have again won prizes, medals, and scholarships under the able tutelage of Louisa Gann, Miss Wilson, Miss de la Belinaye, and Miss Burrell. Anne Elizabeth Hopkinson and Emily Austen have won Queen's prizes. Agnes Ierson has won a bronze medal, and Alice Hanslip has won a Queen's gold medal. Emily Austin has the Queen's scholarship for the second successive year. Martha Lovel, Julia Clarke, Isabella Duff and Jane Duff win "half-studentships." At the University College of Fine Art School, Mr. [sic] Evelyn Pickering wins a Slade Scholarship. Prizes go to Mary Whitehead for a drawing and to Dorothy Tennant for composition.

50. "Miss Eliza Sharpe [Obituary]." *Art Journal* (August 1874): 232.

> On 2 June Eliza Sharpe, figure painter, engraver, and water color painter died. She was a long-time member of the Society of Water-Colour Painters and the aunt of engraver C. W. Sharpe.

51. Scott, William Bell. *Poems, Ballads, Studies from Nature, Sonnets, Etc.* London: Longmans, 1875. Reprint. New York, AMS Press, 1971.

> The poem titled "The Incantation of Hervor" contains an illustration engraved from a painting by Alice Boyd.

52. "Minor Topics." *Art Journal* (January 1875): 29-30.

> At the Female School of Art exhibition, Susan Canton has won the Queen's gold medal for two studies in clay, one titled *The Dying Gladiator*. Alice Hanslip's life studies have won her a £30 scholarship; her study of hands received a national bronze medal. Jessie Corcoran's watercolor of flowers also wins a national bronze medal. For flower studies in oils, Emily Austin, Ellen Hancock and Alice Locke each win a Queen's prize. Emily Austin has won a prize for the best foreground in oils, and Susan Canton won a prize for her illustrations for F. Bennoch's poem "Legends of St. Alban's." Ellen Ashwell and Miss Jerson also contributed designs for the poem. For the Third Grade prizes, Ellen Ashwell, Alice Ellis, Ellen Hancock, Miss Jerson, Alice Hanslip and Charlotte Austin contributed excellent works. Alice Hanslip and Ellen Ashwell have won Vacation prizes for their studies and sketches from nature. Under Louisa Gann's directorship, enrollment at the Female School continues to rise; it is now at a record 194. At the South Kensington Schools of Art, Agatha Lyons and Ellen M. Woods win silver medals. Marianne Mansell and

Louisa E. Poole win bronze medals, Alice E. J. Baker, Emma Greenish, Kate Hill, and Mary D. Tothill win Queen's prizes.

53. "Minor Topics. The Royal Academy." *Art Journal* (February 1875): 61.

The first four lectures on anatomy were, for the first time, open to female students. At the awards ceremony, James Moore [sic] received a prize for the second-best drawing from the antique.

54. "The Water Colour Society's Exhibition, II." *The Nation* XX (18 February 1875): 119-120.

Marie Spartali Stillman's large canvases are almost the only works in the New York exhibition combining a subtle intelligence in the treatment of figures. Her intricate renditions of scenes from Arthurian legends are enhanced by her mastery of color and composition as well as of thought and intellectual depth. Her portraiture contains intelligence and power, and a flower study shows a strong influence of ancient illuminators.

55. "Minor Topics. The Royal Academy." *Art Journal* (April 1875): 125.

Last month's issue announced James Moore as a prize winner for a drawing at the Royal Academy School. The *Art Journal* apologizes for a typographical error. The correct name is Jennie Moore, a former student of the Female School of Art.

56. "Artists of the United Kingdom." *Art Journal* (December 1875): 374.

According to the last census, 1,069 women in the United Kingdom cite their occupations as "painters and artists." The total number of artists listed in the census is 16,562.

57. "A Correspondent Writes." [Mary Harrison obituary]. *Athenaeum* (4 December 1875): 758.

Mary Rossiter Harrison, whose flower paintings richly deserve the recognition they have received in major art exhibitions over her sixty- year career, died on 25 November at age eighty-eight. The sales of Harrison's paintings supported her twelve children and invalid husband. She was one of the first members of the New Society of Painters in Watercolours, where she exhibited until the day of her death. Harrison is unrelated to, and not to be confused with, Maria Harrison, also a flower painter and active member of the Society of Painters in Watercolours.

58. "Obituary. Mrs. Anna Maria Charretie." *Art Journal* (January 1876): 12.

   Anna Maria Charretie died suddenly last October of heart disease. She studied flower painting with Valentine Bartholomew and exhibited at the Royal Academy as an amateur when she was twenty. She continued her art studies after her marriage to Captain John Charretie and after his death supported herself with her oil paintings. Her first Royal Academy picture was *Lady Betty Germain* in 1872; later pictures included *Lady Betty's Maid, Lady Betty Shopping* and this year's *Mistress of Herself, Though China Fall.* She exhibited at other galleries, including the Dudley. Charretie was a kind and sympathetic person who is missed by her many friends.

59. "Obituary. Mrs. Mary Harrison." *Art Journal* (February 1876): 47.

   Mary Harrison, one of the first members of the New Society of Water-Colour Painters, has died suddenly at eighty-eight, just after sending her pictures to the winter exhibition. She supported a large family with her flower and fruit pictures, which she exhibited regularly in the Pall Mall gallery.

60. "Obituary. Miss Adelaide A. Maguire." *Art Journal* (February 1876): 48.

   Adelaide A. Maguire has died at the age of twenty-three after a lingering illness. In spite of poor health she had been active and productive in the art world; she was a member of the Society of Lady Artists and had exhibited at London galleries, including the Royal Academy. She wrote and illustrated a children's book which received good reviews in the *Art Journal.* Maguire was liked by everyone who knew her.

61. "The Royal Academy Prizes." *Art Journal* (March 1876): 87.

   In one of the best student exhibitions ever, Kate May won the first-place medal for her drawing from the antique.

62. "Minor Topics. Miss E. Thompson's *Balaclava.*" *Art Journal* (June 1876): 190.

   Elizabeth Thompson's touching painting of exhausted soldiers and horses after the battle of Balaclava is perhaps her last battle painting. Thompson reportedly will turn her talents toward sacred subjects. *Balaclava* and Thompson's other two famous battle paintings will be engraved by Mr. Stackpoole.

63. "Mrs. E. M. Ward's Picture..." *Art Journal* (October 1876): 319.

Subscriptions from leading artists are already being made for the engraving of Henrietta Ward's *Elizabeth Fry Visiting Newgate*. The picture justifies Ward's reputation as an artist. It is instructional, well composed, and is "among the best productions of British art." It is reported that the Queen herself admires the painting.

64. "Schools of Art Sketching Competition." *Art Journal* (December 1876): 373.

Miss Montalba of the South Kensington Club has won a prize of £3 for her sketch of sculpture titled *Waiting*. Some one hundred works from students of four schools were entered in the competition.

65. Benjamin, S. G. W. *Contemporary Art in Europe*. New York: Harper & Brothers, 1877. Reprint. New York, Garland Publishing, 1976.

Elizabeth Thompson Butler's sudden and surprising success is difficult to assess because critics are likely to be accused either of jealousy or "cruel prejudice against oppressed women." In spite of her popularity, Butler seems willing to accept suggestions for improving the quality of her paintings, but her giant battle scenes lack unity; it would be to Butler's advantage should she take up "sacred subjects."

Reproductions (b/w engravings):

Butler, Elizabeth Thompson: *Missing;* Portrait from her photo.

66. "The Royal Academy." *The Art Journal* (April 1877): 108.

From over a hundred nominations, three new members have been chosen to fill vacancies for membership in the Royal Academy. Not elected, but on the list of nominees, are Annie Mutrie, Martha Mutrie, Elizabeth Thompson and Henrietta Ward.

67. "Minor Topics. Sherwood Forest." *Art Journal* (June 1877): 189.

Mrs. F. Thomas of Sheffield, an artist who has exhibited in London and in provincial galleries, has a series of watercolor drawings resulting from a summer of painting in Sherwood Forest. Little is left of the forest as it used to be, and so Mrs. Thomas' careful records of the trees and plants make them especially valuable in addition to their being excellent as art. Especially noteworthy are *On the Way to Budby School* and *The Old Raff Yard. The Red Drive* and *Simon Foster Oak* are paintings of familiar landmarks of the forest.

68. "*The Shepherd*. From the Picture in the Collection of Henry Wallis, Esq. Rosa Bonheur, Painter. C. Cousen, Engraver." *Art Journal* (June 1877): 176.

One would hardly expect such a model of femininity as Rosa Bonheur to frequent stables and horse yards as she has done in order to paint *The Horse Fair* and other animal paintings. Her picture of a peaceful flock and a pensive shepherd contains truthful representations and "a pleasing and attractive composition."

Reproduction (b/w engraving):

Bonheur, Rosa: *The Shepherd*.

69. "The National Portrait Gallery." *Art Journal* (September 1877): 272.

Among the twenty-four purchases made this year by the National Portrait Gallery is Margaret Geddes Carpenter's portrait of the painter R. P. Bonington.

70. "Minor Topics. The Female School of Art, Queen Square." *Art Journal* (December 1877): 373.

Rhoda Carleton Holmes' life-sized watercolors have won her the Queen's scholarship, and Mary Ann Burnay has won the Gilchrist scholarship for her drawings. Alice Hanslip's drawings from the antique, and Alice E. Hopkinson's drawing of dates and grapes have won them each a national silver medal. On the basis of their drawings, Alice Hanslip, Ida Livering [Lovering] and Catherine Benson have been accepted as students in the Royal Academy School. Five other women at the school have between them two national silver medals, five national bronze medals, and six Queen's prizes. Louise Gann has raised funds for and organized a trip to Rome for six of the advanced pupils.

71. "Alsace. From the Picture in the Possession of Mr. A. H. Marsden. Henriette Browne, Painter. F. Holl, Engraver." *Art Journal* (January 1878): frontispiece, 8.

Henriette Browne's painting *The Critics*, showing children speculating on some dead game, has been featured in this publication, but her most representative work is of scenes from the war between France and Germany. Her study of a Red Cross nurse collecting donations for widows and orphans of French soldiers is titled *Alsace* and an engraving of it is featured as the frontispiece of this issue. The eloquent simplicity of this subject is captured admirably by Browne's skill and sympathy. The picture can be viewed at Mr. Marsden's gallery in King Street, St. James.

Reproductions (b/w):

Browne, Henriette: *Alsace, 1870*.

72. "Schools of Art Prize Drawings." *Art Journal* (October 1878): 206.

    More than 138,000 works from 142 art schools from all over Great Britain were considered for art school prizes and scholarships this year. Dora Bradley of Dublin wins a gold medal for a drawing from life. An oil painting of fruit by Elizabeth Grace of Brighton also wins a gold medal. Miss K. Benson of the Female School of Art in Bloomsbury has won a gold medal and a scholarship. Silver medals go to Margaret Haseler of Birmingham for her watercolor painting and to Miss McLeod of Manchester for her flower painting.

73. Merritt, Henry. *Henry Merritt: Art Criticism and Romance*. London: Kegan Paul, 1879.

    Anna Lea Merritt's biographical sketch of her late husband in volume one reveals that when she met him she was an American studying art in London, working in an ugly studio, and producing "ugly pictures with no truth in them." Under Merritt's patronizing patronage (he referred to her as "little girl," and of himself as her "master," instructing her in proper social manners as well as artistic matters) she was humble and grateful. Her account of his life and her willingness to marry him in the last months of his life before he died of tuberculosis attests to her selflessness. In "Pictures in the International Exhibition" in volume one, Henry Merritt fails to mention English women painters, but his assessment of female artists from the continent is fair, straightforward and without condescension.

74. Oldcastle, John. "Our Living Artists: Elizabeth Butler (née Thompson)." *Magazine of Art* 2 (1879): 257-262.

    The insistence on truth in art has given military and battle scenes a new dignity. Artists specializing in this genre do not glorify war, but take care to show it honestly, with all its pathos and dignity. Foremost among military painters, Elizabeth Thompson Butler has worked hard all her life to perfect her matchless style. Several rejections marked the beginning of her exhibition career, so she is hardly an overnight success, though she is a figure of great fascination and enthusiasm with the public. Her natural talent was nurtured by her parents, who saw that her childhood was unfettered by the usual constraints placed upon girls.

75. "Minor Topics. The Royal Academy." *Art Journal* (January 1879): 18.

    In December the "intermediate year" medals and scholarships were presented to Emma L. Black for her copy of a painting; to Jennie Moore and Ellen Neilson for their drawings of a statue; and to Mary Drew for her drawing from the antique.

76. "Minor Topics. Miss Eliza Turck's Drawings." *Art Journal* (April 1879): 79.

Eliza Turck has just returned from a painting expedition in Brittany: the excellent results of her sojourn can be seen at Mr. Rogers' Maddox Street Gallery. Turck's palette is occasionally too black, but she excels in the use of "tender greys" and a "broad and free" style.

77. "Minor Topics. Society of Painters in Water Colours." *Art Journal* (May 1879): 97.

Helen Coleman Angell has been elected an associate member of the Society of Painters in Water Colours.

78. "Minor Topics. Mrs. E. M. Ward." *Art Journal* (May 1879): 98.

Henrietta Ward, an accomplished painter and teacher, is opening an art school for ladies. Ward has much to offer by way of instruction, as the work of her talented daughters may attest. The school will fill a public need, since the school at South Kensington does not meet the needs of many women who want to study art.

79. "Art Notes from the Provinces. Birmingham." *Art Journal* (June 1879): 111.

The Royal Birmingham Society of Artists has elected Mrs G. J. Whitfield an Honorary Member. She is the first female member in the history of this society to be so chosen.

80. "Female School of Art." *Art Journal* (June 1879): 108.

The Queen's Gold Medal has been awarded to Anne Elizabeth Hopkinson. Students at the Female School of Art have won two National Gold Medals and several scholarships.

81. "Art Publications." *Art Journal* (August 1879): 167.

With her painting *Visit of Elizabeth Fry to Newgate*, Henrietta Ward perpetuates the compassion of Quaker humanitarian Elizabeth Fry. T. L. Atkinson has done an excellent job of engraving Ward's painting, which is dedicated to the Queen. Anna Lea Merritt has collected and published the writings of the late Henry Merritt, critic and art restorer, whose works had previously been printed anonymously.

82. "Minor Topics. Mrs. E. M. Ward." *Art Journal* (August 1879): 165-166.

    The Prime Minister has awarded a Crown pension to Henrietta Ward for her husband's service to art, but of course Mrs. Ward deserves her husband's pension on her own merits. The Queen finds the award "highly satisfactory."

83. "Exhibition at South Kensington of the Prize Drawings and Designs of the National School of Art." *Art Journal* (October 1879): 220.

    One of ten gold medals has been awarded to Mary Denley for a carpet design, and Mary H. Surenne has won a silver medal for a composition drawing. Nearly 14,000 entries were submitted to the competition, out of which 1,100 drawings, paintings, models and designs were selected for exhibition.

84. "Obituary. Mrs. Robertson Christison (Mary Sympson Tovey)." *Art Journal* (October 1879): 217-218.

    Animal painter and portraitist Mary Sympson Tovey met an untimely death on 1 April from fever contracted at her new home in Queensland, Australia. Tovey, who showed an aptitude for art in her early teens, studied at South Kensington and the Royal Academy schools. Her work was exhibited at the Society of Lady Artists, the Bristol Fine Arts Academy and the Royal Academy. Her death is a great loss to the arts and a terrible grief to her husband, family, and friends.

85. "*The Resting Place of the Deer*. Rosa Bonheur, Painter. C. G. Lewis, Engraver." *Art Journal* (December 1879): 264-265.

    Rosa Bonheur's skills can be matched only by the brush of Elizabeth Thompson Butler, who is perhaps superior in that Butler can paint not only animals, but human figures as well.

    Reproduction (b/w):
    Bonheur, Rosa: *The Resting-Place of the Deer*.

86. Koehler, S. R. "The Works of the American Etchers. VIII. Anna Lea Merritt." *American Art Review* (1880): 228-230.

    Few women etchers have a place in art history, and even fewer of those are American. Anna Lea Merritt is the first American female etcher to achieve prominence in this art form. Merritt's apt training came almost entirely from her late husband. Her first attempts at etching furnish illustrations for Henry Merritt's collected works and are not of the fine quality of her most recent efforts. Most are portraits and include two

Portraits of Mary Wollstonecraft, a portrait of *Professor Louis Agassiz*, and a portrait of *Ellen Terry as Ophelia*.

Reproductions (b/w etching):

Merritt, Anna Lea: *Portrait of Sir Gilbert Scott.*

87. Meynell, Wilfrid. "Our Living Artists. Louise Jopling." *Magazine of Art* 3 (1880): 303-308.

Louise Jopling's talent and success are all the more remarkable for the obstacles she has overcome. She faces all the usual obstacles in the path of a woman and unlike most other artistic females she had neither an artist parent nor a privileged childhood. Her career began when, at twenty-three, she took her first lessons in Paris, where she was living with her husband. Within three years she was exhibiting at the Royal Academy. Her second marriage, this time to another artist, enhanced her career opportunities. She paints figure scenes, such as *Five O'Clock Tea*, which shows her interest in things Japanese, and her portraits, such as those of *Miss de Rothschild; Col. the Honorable Charles Hugh Lindsay,* and *Gertrude, Daughter of George Lewis, Esq.*, have brought her deserved recognition. She exhibits regularly in major London exhibitions, and has written articles on literature, art and music for *The Magazine of Art.* The question of how professional artists will make their contribution to motherhood is answered by observing such women as Louise Jopling, Fanny Woodes Fildes, Laura Alma-Tadema and Helen Allingham. Obviously, these women have much more to give their children than the less-criticized women of society and fashion who spend probably even less time with their families.

Reproductions (b/w):

Jopling, Louise: *Five O'Clock Tea; Col. the Hon. Charles Hugh Lindsay*

Photos (b/w):

Louise Jopling.

88. "Minor Topics. The Royal Academy." *Art Journal* (January 1880): 29.

At the annual awards ceremony in December, Edith Savill received a silver medal for a head study from life, and Jane Mary Dealy received a first place silver medal and £10 for drawings of a statue or group.

89. "Art Publications. Miss or Mistress, Jane E. Cook." *Art Journal* (February 1880): 63.

Jane E. Cook's admirable illustrations to Robert Browning's privately printed "The Pied Piper of Hamelin" display excellent drawing and careful attention to detail. While Cook is an amateur artist, her work is of truly professional quality.

90. "Minor Topics. Studies of American Foliage by Mrs. M. F. Butterworth and Miss Stevens." *Art Journal* (February 1880): 62.

Most impressive of the works displayed at their Cadogan Gardens studio are Stevens' paintings on porcelain and on terra cotta, and Butterworth's painting of scarlet poinsettia flowers on satin.

91. *"The Roll Call* and *Quatre Bras* by Elizabeth Thompson (Mrs.Butler)." *Art Journal* (February 1880): 61.

When Elizabeth Thompson's great battle picture, *The Roll Call* was exhibited at the Royal Academy, everyone agreed "that an artist of great and original power had arisen in the land." Thompson's next great picture, *Quatre Bras* attracted as much attention, and justifiably. F. Stackpoole, the engraver, has reproduced both pictures "with great force and truth," capturing minute details and overtones with rare success.

92. "Art Notes. The Prizes..." *Art Journal* (November 1880): 350.

While Mr. Turck attempted to attract "leading artists" to submit Christmas card designs, the best he got were "weak imitations" of well-known artists such as Kate Greenaway.

93. Griffiths, Arthur. "Treasure Houses of Art. The Collection of Mr. C. P. Matthews. II." *Magazine of Art* 4 (1881): 333-337.

Mr. Matthews' art collection includes a great variety of styles and subjects by artists both old and modern. It includes a "gem" by Henriette Browne titled *Turkish Boys Chanting the Koran.*

94. "Art Notes. Royal Academy." *Art Journal* (January 1881): 30- 31.

Among the prize-winning Royal Academy students are Susan Ruth Canton and Theodora F. Noyes. Margaret Hickson was the winner of the keen competition for the Creswick prize. All of the exhibits were better than average.

95. "Art Notes and Reviews. Elections at the Royal Academy." *Art Journal* (March 1881): 94-95.

Even before the recent election at the Royal Academy it was predicted that Elizabeth Thompson Butler would be among the artists not elected, and, as it turned out, she was denied membership.

96. "Art Notes and Reviews. Obituary Notices." *Art Journal* (March 1881): 95.

Among the most notable portraits of the late Thomas Carlyle are those by Helen Allingham, who often painted the philosopher holding a "churchwarden's" clay pipe.

97. "Art Notes. Art Sales." *Art Journal* (April 1881): 128.

At a sale of the collection of the late Charles Kurtz, a sepia titled *Sheep* by Rosa Bonheur sold for £118. A picture by Henriette Browne titled *An Armenian Cap Maker* sold for £232.

98. "Fine Arts: Old Water-Colour Society." *Illustrated London News* (16 April 1881): 379.

The horses in Elizabeth Thompson Butler's depiction of the charge of the Scots Greys at Waterloo are satisfactorily spirited and successfully foreshortened, although perhaps too many of them are off the ground. The sky should be more somber, both to better set off the shouting men and plunging horses, and to be in keeping with historical accuracy. While this painting does not reflect the pathos of *The Roll Call*, or the expression of *Quatre Bras*, it is stirring, spirited and consistent with the quality of Butler's earlier works.

99. "Art Notes and Reviews. Art Notes. The Female School of Art, Bloomsbury." *Art Journal* (May 1881): 158-160.

The Lord Mayor awarded this year's prizes to the competitors from the Female School of Art. Ottilie Bodé and Edith Nisbet received Gilchrist Scholarships, Florence Reason received the Queen's Gold Medal and a scholarship, and Catherine M. Wood has won the Clothworker's Scholarship.

100. "Art Notes and Reviews. Art Sales." *Art Journal* (May 1881): 160.

A chalk drawing by Rosa Bonheur, titled *A Herd of Deer, Fontainebleu*, sold for £115 at a recent sale.

101. "Art Notes and Reviews. Obituary (Jane Bewick)." *Art Journal* (May 1881): 159-160.

Jane Bewick, the daughter of the engraver Thomas Bewick, died on 7 April.

102. "Art Notes and Reviews. Exhibitions. Mrs. Butler's *Scotland Forever!*" *Art Journal* (May 1881): 157-158.

The horses in *Scotland Forever!* are of a heavy Flemish breed, each animal rendered with care that lends individual distinction while at the same time linking it with its fellows to form a powerful and realistic group of chargers suspended in an instant. Their riders, too, are "vividly realized," diverse and distinct. The painting is exhibited at the Egyptian Hall in Piccadilly.

103. "Art Notes and Reviews. New Engraving." *Art Journal* (June 1881): 192.

Rosa Bonheur's 1879 study of a lion's head, titled *An Old Monarch*, has been engraved by W. H. Simmons.

104. "Art Notes and Reviews. Art Exhibitions. Rosa Bonheur's New Pictures." *Art Journal* (July 1881): 222.

At M. Lefévre's King Street Gallery, one can view Rosa Bonheur's excellent and true-to-life pictures titled *On the Alert* and *A Foraging Party*. The animals are rendered to perfection and reveal Bonheur's familiarity and sympathy with wild creatures and their surroundings.

105. "Art Notes and Reviews. Art Sales." *Art Journal* (September 1881): 285-287.

An engraved picture, Elizabeth Butler's *The Battle of Quatre Bras*, has been sold for £745. Henriette Browne's *The Sisters of Charity* has been sold for £519. Rosa Bonheur's *View in Normandy* has sold for £525; her *Les Pâturages* sold at Christie's for £567 and *A Landscape* brought £861. Bonheur's *Le Coup de Canon*, part of a collection of a Glasgow resident, sold for £1501.

106. "Art Notes. A Comeley Volume." *Magazine of Art* 5 (1882): x.

A birthday book designed by HRH the Princess Beatrice contains fourteen pictures in chromo-lithography. Felicia Hemans provided a picture of primroses and violets for the month of March. Adelaide Procter painted pink and white hawthorn for the month of May, and December's design of mistletoe and holly is by Eliza Cook. The book, a quarto volume, is beautifully designed and deserves to be respectfully received.

107. "Art Notes. The Season's Novelties." *Magazine of Art* 5 (1882): xi.

Christmas card publishers have produced some lovely specimens this year, which include lithographs and etchings on white satin. Laura Troubridge uses a novel medium in her *Japanese Designs* with gold and colors on gelatine. Her *Children in Wonderland* is also quite good. Other notable designs include works by Rebecca Coleman, Kate Sadler and Helen Miles.

108. "Art Notes. Miss Greenaway's *Mother Goose.*" *Magazine of Art* 5 (1882): xi.

Kate Greenaway's children in her delightfully illustrated *Mother Goose* are "the dowdiest, dandiest, funniest, tiniest, pleasantest little folk ever seen." Greenaway's distinctively-dressed children reflect the love and feeling she must have for them. The book is certainly one of her best achievements.

109. "Art Notes. Miss Isabella Jay's Copies of Turner's Pictures..." *Magazine of Art* 5 (1882): xxxi.

Critic John Ruskin claims that "many women are now supporting themselves by frivolous and useless art" and he supports Isabella Jay's efforts at making excellent copies of Turner's work because a very good copy of a masterpiece is better than a bad original by an inept artist. Jay's copies at the Dowdeswell Gallery are indeed quite good, but they are copies nonetheless and the art market certainly doesn't need a flood of "desperate reproductions."

110. "Current Art." *Magazine of Art* 5 (1882): 388-395.

Marion Collier's picture of two little girls rehearsing a dance captures the mood of the theatre with excellent technique that demonstrates her hard work and determination to improve. *The Rehearsal* at the Grosvenor Gallery is as good as another of her works, *Coming Tragedian*, in the Royal Academy.

Reproductions (b/w engraving):

Collier, Marion: *The Rehearsal.*

111. "In the Studio. From the Picture by Hénriette Ronner." *Magazine of Art* 5 (1882): 412-413.

Dutch artist Hénriette Ronner has captured the essence of cat in her picture *In the Studio.* The painting, which was exhibited at the Paris International Exhibition, depicts a litter of kittens playing among an artist's palette, brushes, chests, sketchbooks and tubes of paint, while their "demure, matronly, complacent" mother looks on.

112. Barnett, H. V. "Miss Marianne North's Paintings at Kew." *Magazine of Art* 5 (1882): 430-431.

Marianne North has traveled the world sketching and painting plants, flowers, insects and birds; she has given to the nation a collection of over 600 of her works and a building in which to house them at Kew Gardens. North's studies and paintings have scientific as well as artistic value. As colonists and pioneers continue to bring the land under cultivation, many species disappear forever. North's eye for detail, her "surprising accuracy, delicacy, patience and understanding" create valuable records for scientists. As art, North's work has a tendency toward "harshness and coldness," but although no effort is made to rearrange her subjects to please the eye, many of the paintings are quite beautiful.

113. Forbes-Robertson, John. "Rosa Bonheur." *Magazine of Art* 5 (1882): 45-50.

Unrelenting dedication and hard work have characterized Rosa Bonheur's art career and turned her talent into noteworthy achievement. Her first exhibition in the Paris Salon of 1840 was a study of two rabbits; her animal studies continued to receive recognition in France, and her *Horse Fair* brought her fame in England in 1856.

Reproductions (b/w engraving):
Bonheur, Rosa: *A Souvenir of Fontainbleu; Group from the Horse Fair; Ploughing the Nivernais*
Portrait of Rosa Bonheur.

114. Meynell, Wilfrid. "Artists' Homes. Mr. Alma-Tadema's at North Gate, Regent's Park." *Magazine of Art* 5 (1882): 184-188.

The home of the Alma-Tademas has everywhere the touch of the two artist's hands and works. Paintings and busts of Laura Alma-Tadema appear in profusion. Her name and their wedding date appear on a panel of a door. Her studio, located near the front of the house near the conservatory, has compartments in which can be found her "solemn and impressive" painting *Death of the First Born*. She and her husband decorated the piano with designs of antique musical notations. Another compartment has a Spanish motif, and the picturesque conservatory features a white marble Roman fountain as well as yet another bust of Laura Alma-Tadema.

115. "Carlyle in his Eightieth Year." *Art Journal* (January 1882): 7-8 and page facing p.7.

>Helen Allingham "had the privilege of frequent and familiar access" to the late Thomas Carlyle and painted about a dozen portraits of him. Carlyle, an animal lover, liked to be sketched in his garden with his cat, Tib.

116. "Fine Art Gossip." *Athenaeum* (15 April 1882): 482.

>A life-sized family of lions consisting of a magnificent male, his reclining wife, and their spirited children is titled *The Lion at Home* and can be viewed at Mr. Lefevre's Gallery. Rosa Bonheur's style, technique, and sheer artistry have created a picture that would be fit company for a Rubens.

117. "Art Notes. Royal Society of Painters in Water-Colours." *Art Journal* (May 1882): 158-159.

>Constance Phillott is among the five new associate members of the Royal Society of Painters in Water Colours.

118. "Reviews. *On the Alert* and *A Foraging Party*." *Art Journal* (May 1882): 160.

>The strong contrasts of two fine pictures by Rosa Bonheur have lent themselves to unusually large and very skillful engravings by A. Gilbert.

119. "Art Notes. The National Competition." *Art Journal* (September 1882): 285-286.

>Nottingham's Lucy Leavers and Ethel Nisbet of Bloomsbury have won gold medals for their watercolors. The National Competition is an annual event for students of all art schools.

120. "Reviews. *Inkerman*." *Art Journal* (November 1882): 352.

>The engraving of Elizabeth Butler's *The Return from Inkerman* completes the set of her battle pictures, which include *The Roll Call* and *Balaclava*. Of the three pictures, *Inkerman* excels with the understatement that gives it power and lasting interest.

121. Meynell, Alice. "Laura Alma-Tadema." *Art Journal* 22 (1883): 345-347.

>So well does Alma-Tadema depict historically accurate scenes of domestic life in seventeenth-century Holland that her work is exhibited at The Hague. Her careful attention to detail and her cool but richly colorful tints contribute to the excellence of her highly original work.

Reproductions (b/w engravings):
Alma-Tadema, Laura: *The Sisters; May I Come In?; Winter; The Tea Party.*

122. "Art Notes. Royal Academy Schools." *Art Journal* (January 1883): 31.
> At the December ceremony Margaret Dicksee received a silver medal. Mary Drew received a prize of £40 for an allegorical fresco design.

123. "Art Notes. Reviews." *Art Journal* (January 1883): 31.
> Helen Allingham's *Carlyle* is among the works etched for *The Art Journal* by Charles O. Murray.

124. "Purchases of Pictures for the Australian Galleries." *Art Journal* (June 1883): 202.
> The Parliament of South Australia has purchased, among others, a picture by Florence Martin titled *The Student.*

125. "Reviews: New Prints and Books. *An Invitation.*" *Art Journal* (June 1883): 204.
> Not even the excellence of Mary L. Gow's graceful drawings can rescue the weak story of *An Invitation.* Why the publisher chose to put such excellent illustrating and engraving into such a meaningless subject is a mystery.

126. "Angell, Helen Cordelia (obituary notice)." *The Athenaeum* (15 March 1884): 353.
> Helen Cordelia Angell (née Coleman) died on March 8th, age thirty-seven. She began her career as Miss Coleman in 1866 with an exhibit at the Dudley Gallery. A member of the Society of Painters in Water Colours, she was so respected for her fine flower paintings that she was made associate editor in 1879. The exceptional quality of her work more than justified her election.

127. "Art Notes. Obituary (Helen Cordelia Angell)." *Art Journal* (April 1884): 126-127.
> Helen Cordelia Coleman Angell has died suddenly at the height of her career at age thirty-seven. Angell's "crisp and masculine style...stamped out the effeminate and delicate" painting recently in fashion. She was a member of the Institute of Painters in Water-Colours.

128. "Art Notes. The Royal Society of Painters in Water Colours." *Art Journal* (May 1884): 157-158.

Over sixty artists applied for election this year to the Royal Society of Painters in Water Colours. One of the two successful applicants is Mary Forster, whose work is noteworthy for its "delicacy, brightness, and purity of sentiment."

129. "Art Notes. Mrs. Butler's *Quatre Bras*." *Art Journal* (May 1884): 158.

The Museum of Melbourne has paid £1500 for *Quatre Bras*, one of the five works that has made Elizabeth Thompson Butler famous. *The Roll Call* belongs to the Queen, and *The Return from Inkerman* and *The Remnants of an Army* are to be sold at Christie's this month.

130. "*A Dictionary of Artists Who Have Exhibited Works at the Principal London Exhibitions from 1760 to 1880*. Compiled by A. Graves. (Bell and Sons)." *The Athenaeum* (28 June 1884): 830-831.

Graves' book is of considerable use to the art historian who has heretofore had to depend on exhibition catalogues, which frequently list artists by first initial only, and do not indicate name changes. A cross reference of married and maiden names helps to identify female artists. Graves asks for more information to help locate female painters undergoing name changes, so the reviewer offers the information that Mrs. J. Sparkes formerly exhibited as Miss C. A. Edwards, and Miss Coleman of Henley, who specialized in still lifes, now exhibits flower paintings as Mrs. Helen C. Angell. An 1858 Royal Academy exhibit titled *The Hayloft* and signed "Rosarius" can be attributed to Rosa Brett. Graves' book is also a help in sorting out members of family groups and for putting together biographies of artists about whom little is known. The thousands of pictures signed "Anon" are, alas, still unidentifiable.

131. Bacon, Henry. "Rosa Bonheur." *The Forum*, no. 28 (October 1884): 833-840.

A neighbor describes Bonheur's talented family, her stately, animal-rich residence, and her reclusive existence.

Reproductions (b/w):

Photographs: *Crossing a Loch in the Highlands*

Sketches and engravings: *The Studio of Rosa Bonheur; The Home of Rosa Bonheur; The Chateau Court-Yard; The Studio, from the Road.*

132. Merritt, Anna Lea. "A Talk About Painting." *St. Nicholas* XII (December 1884): 85-92.

> Anna Lea Merritt's uncle sparked her interest in painting when he gave her a paintbox when she was three; her interest in portrait painting began when an artist came to her school to make a crayon portrait of her two younger sisters. While the demands of school kept her from pursuing her love of painting and drawing, she never lost interest and began her serious study of art when she was twenty-one. A believer in working from life, Merritt gives some amusing accounts of the difficulties of painting lively child subjects, and describes her experience with two rats who inhabited her studio and which she used as models for the hundreds of rats in her painting of the Pied Piper of Hamelin.
>
> Reproductions (b/w):
> Sketches of children
> Portrait of the grandchildren of Alfred Tennyson (engraving)
> Portrait of Eustace and Percy Loraine (engraving).

133. "Art in June." *Magazine of Art* (1885): xxxiii-xxxvi.

> Mary Forster-Lofthouse has died. She belonged to the Royal Society of Painters in Water-Colours. The Salon features especially good still-lifes this year. *La Place est Prise* by Annie Ayrton is a simple and clever picture of a dog and cat as a kind of still-life; work by Miss Dixwell is also worthy of notice. At the Nineteenth-Century Society's gallery, Alice Miller's simply-colored and "squarely and suggestively brushed" pictures, *Cornfield* and *Quiet Corner,* are among the more competent works.

134. "Art in July." *Magazine of Art* (1885): vii-xl.

> Miss Manly has painted a fan for Princess Beatrice.

135. Chesneau, Ernest. *The English School of Painting.* London: Cassell, 1885.

> Elizabeth Thompson's "second-rate military pictures" lack originality. Kate Greenaway's child pictures are full of surprises and never fail to delight. Her art has "a truly maternal spirit of tenderness."

136. Gow, Mary L. "Design for *April Once More." Magazine of Art* 8 (1885): 253.

> A pair of young lovers in a wood drawn by Mary L. Gow illustrates Edmund Gosse's poem.

137. Havers, Alice. "Design for 'It is the Season.'" *Magazine of Art* 8 (1885): 53.

>   Alice Havers illustrates Robert Louis Stevenson's poem with two children, a young man, a young woman carrying a lamb, and the young man and young woman together as lovers.

138. ---. "Design for 'Swing Song.'" *Magazine of Art* 8 (1885): 300.

>   Alice Havers illustrates a poem by William Allingham. She uses a classical motif--a woman draped in Grecian-style clothing tends a cupid-style child.

139. ---. "Design for 'A Visit from the Sea'." *Magazine of Art* 8 (1885): 21.

>   Alice Havers' seascape, seagulls, and a garden scene with two young women and a cat illuminate Robert Louis Stevenson's poem.

140. Hays, Frances. *Women of the Day*. Philadelphia: Lippincott, 1885.

>   Achievements are carefully listed and marriages barely mentioned in this objectively-written book of biographical sketches. Since this is a contemporary work, many of the articles are incomplete. The entry for Anna Lea Merritt, for example, was written before her masterpiece, *Love Locked Out*, was painted, and before many of Merritt's essays and books were published. Even so, this is a useful, even fascinating, "who's who" of nineteenth-century women.

141. *American Etchers. Reprinted from the Century Magazine for February, 1883, with a Brief Additional Chapter Reprinted in Part from the New York Star, by Mrs. Schuyler Van Rensselaer.* New York: Keppel, 1886.

>   American art has been accused of lacking originality, but the work of Anna Lea Merritt deserves recognition for its "interpretive" quality. Her etchings are mostly portraits, but while her work carefully reproduces the original portrait or painting, she does not simply copy what she sees. A portrait of Sir Gilbert Scott, etched from a painting by a gentleman artist and published in the review, is one of her best.
>
>   Reproductions (b/w etching):
>   Merritt, Anna Lea: *Portrait of Louis Agassiz.*

142. "Art in November." *Magazine of Art* (1886): v-viii.

>   Along with Kate Greenaway's *Little Folks*, this year's best Christmas card and book designs are hunt scenes by Georgina Bowers, Alice Havers' scenes from the stories of Hans Andersen, and pictures by M. E. Edwards.

143. "Art in February." *Magazine of Art* (1886): xvii-xx.

> Martha D. Mutrie, a talented flower and still life painter, has died. Sidney Colvin, who resigned as Slade Professor of Fine Arts at Cambridge, has a long list of achievements and credits, including numbering Jane Harrison among his students. The Glasgow Institute has put together an exhibit of works familiar to Londoners, but new to Glasgow art lovers. Elizabeth Butler's *After the Battle* is part of the exhibit as a work that does not demonstrate technical accomplishment, but is easily understood, even by the most unsophisticated viewer.

144. "Current Art. I." *Magazine of Art* (1886): 345-350.

> Politics at the Grosvenor Gallery rivals that of the Royal Academy, but the pictures are better. Evelyn Pickering's only contribution is hung very near the ceiling. Works by Dorothy Tennant and Louise Jopling are "conspicuously on the line."

145. Havers, Alice. "Design for 'On the River.'" *Magazine of Art* (1886): 521.

> Alice Havers' illustration for J. Arthur Blackie's poem includes an angel looking down on a nymph and a pair of lovers in a sort of gondola.

146. Montalba, Clara. "Design for *Venetian Nocturne*." *Magazine of Art* (1886): 256.

> An engraving of a bridge, buildings, and a canal by Clara Montalba illustrate a small poem by Mary F. Robinson.

147. Rossetti, William Michael, ed. *The Poetical Works of Dante Gabriel Rossetti*. New York: A. L. Burt, 1886.

> The artistically-gifted Elizabeth Siddall was a cutler's daughter with whose body Dante Gabriel Rossetti's poems were temporarily interred.

148. "Art in August." *Magazine of Art* (1887): xli-xliv.

> *Rhymes for the Young* [sic] by William Allingham has just been published by Cassell and Co. with excellent illustrations by Helen Allingham and Kate Greenaway.

149. Allingham, William. *Rhymes for the Young Folk. With Pictures by Helen Allingham, Kate Greenaway, Caroline Paterson, and Harry Furniss.* London: Frederick Warne & Co., 1887.

> Caroline Paterson's illustration for "The Elf Singing" includes an evil-looking two-toed monster and a hungry snake. Greenaway's sketches of children are studies in costume design, while Helen Allingham's

drawings reflect her celebration of nature, plants, and flowers as well as of children and mothers.

Reproductions (b/w):

Allingham, Helen: *Dreaming; Wishing; Sleeping; Nick Spence; A Riddle*

Paterson, Carolina: *The Elf Singing; Jingle Jangle; Here and There; Yes and No?*

Greenaway, Kate: *Ambition*

Reproductions (col):

Allingham, Helen: *The Bird; Amy Margaret; I saw a Little Birdie Fly*

Greenaway, Kate: *The Bubble.*

150. "Saint Cecilia. From a Picture Painted by Mrs. Anna Lea Merritt." *The Studio* II, no. 12 (June 1887): 217-219.

Artists from Cimabue to Rossetti have painted St. Cecilia, whose legend is comprehensively described by Anna Jameson in *The Legendary History of Art*. Anna Lea Merritt's painting of St. Cecilia copies no one, retaining originality while it takes a deserved place in a long artistic tradition. Merritt is commissioned to make an etching of the original.

Reproductions (b/w engraving):

Merritt, Anna Lea: *St. Cecilia.*

151. "A Portrait of Oliver Wendell Holmes by Mrs. Anna Lea Merritt." *Studio* III, no. 2 (August 1887): 39.

Anna Lea Merritt painted the portraits of Oliver Wendell Holmes and James Russell Lowell while all three were in London. Both portraits are very good likenesses, and Merritt has agreed to allow them to be published in *The Studio*.

152. "The Chronicle of Art. Reviews." *Magazine of Art* (1888): xi- xiii.

Among the best of the Christmas books are *Cape Town Dicky*, illustrated by Alice Havers, and *The Star of Bethlehem*, illustrated by Ellen Edwards.

153. "The Chronicle of Art. Engravings and Prints." *Magazine of Art* (1888): xii.

It has become the fashion to collect colored "photogravures" of "celebrated and popular pictures." Although only a few inches square, the pictures are remarkably clear. Alice Havers and Jane Dealy are among the designers in this successful enterprise.

154. "The Chronicle of Art. Obituary." *Magazine of Art* (1888): xvi.

Mrs. Collier, an accomplished amateur who has not exhibited for some years, has died.

155. "The Chronicle of Art. Notabilia." *Magazine of Art* (1888): xxxii.

Edith Martineau has been elected an associate of the Royal Society of Painters in Water Colours.

156. Kitton, Fred G. "Charles Dickens and His Less Familiar Portraits. I." *Magazine of Art* (1888): 284-288.

Dickens first sat for a portrait in 1835 when Rose Emma Drummond, a well-known miniaturist, painted his likeness on ivory as an engagement present to Catherine Hogarth. Margaret Gillies also painted Dickens on ivory in 1844, and this portrait was later made into a steel engraving for a book illustration. Gillies' portrait has been lost--"probably buried in some private collection."

Reproductions (b/w):

Gillies, Margaret: *Portrait of Charles Dickens.*

157. ---. "Charles Dickens and his Less Familiar Portraits. II." *Magazine of Art* (1888): 321-324.

Since the previous article about portraits of Charles Dickens was published, another miniature has surfaced, this one earlier than Rose Emma Drummond's 1835 work, supposed to be the first. Janet Ross Barrow, who was to become a novelist, painted Dickens' portrait in miniature on ivory in 1830, when he was still a reporter and she was only eighteen.

158. "Mrs. Anna Lea Merritt's Portrait of James Russell Lowell." *The Studio* (May 1888): 85.

Anna Lea Merritt's portrait of America's minister to England captures his wise and noble countenance and the scarlet tones of his doctoral gown with "remarkable skill and judgement."

159. "Chronicle of Art. Reviews." *Magazine of Art* (1889): viii.

Among the designers of this year's Christmas cards are artists of established reputation, including Alice Havers and Alice West.

160. "Current Art. The New Gallery." *Magazine of Art* (1889): 289- 295.

Miss Cridland's engraving of a small, grave girl holding a large sleeping baby is reproduced in this article with no commentary. The caption reads "From the Picture by Miss Cridland in the New Gallery."

Reproductions (b/w engraving):

Cridland, Miss: *In the Firelight*.

161. Alexander, Francesca. "Madonina." *Magazine of Art* (1889): 392-393.

Miss Alexander creates pen-and-ink botanical drawings, the like of which, according to John Ruskin in an Oxford lecture, has not been produced "since Leonardo." Alexander is American by birth, but has identified herself entirely with the life and customs of Italy. She also draws Italian peasants; when she draws a saint, she uses an Italian peasant model who has had similar experiences to the saint under consideration. She has agreed to publish nothing without the approval of Ruskin.

Reproductions (b/w):

Alexander, Miss: *Italian Contadina; Madonna*.

162. Howitt, Margaret ed. *Mary Howitt: An Autobiography in Two Volumes*. Boston: Houghton Mifflin, 1889.

In a letter, Mary Howitt recalls that Elizabeth Siddall was interesting, delicate, good for Rossetti, and probably overrated in her artistic talent.

163. Rossetti, William Michael. *Dante Gabriel Rossetti as Designer and Writer*. London: Cassell & Co., 1889.

Elizabeth Siddall appears only in passing and only as she pertains to Dante Gabriel Rossetti's life and art. Their marriage is dealt with in one sentence; in the next sentence the biographer elaborates on a scrapbook acquired at the same time. Siddall's death is described as D. G. Rossetti "suddenly [finding] himself a widower." Siddall's posthumous portrait in Rossetti's painting, *Beata Beatrix*, is treated at more length than the announcement of her death. Some time is spent on Rossetti's suffering the absence of the years of labor tied up in the manuscript collection of the poems he had impulsively placed in her coffin, and Rossetti's "extreme resolution of having them unburied" because of "his reluctance that his light should be permanently hid under a bushel." In any case, William Michael Rossetti is straightforward about his intention to focus on his brother's art and literature rather than on his personal life.

164. —. "The Portraits of Dante Gabriel Rossetti. I." *Magazine of Art* (1889): 21-29.

    Among the known portraits of Dante Gabriel Rossetti is an 1853 or 1854 pen and ink drawing by Elizabeth Siddall in her "simple and sincere" style that is occasionally "deep in invention." Dante Gabriel Rossetti is clearly the model for the handsome, clean-shaven young man "singing to the music of two ...outlandish looking women."

165. ---. "The Portraits of Dante Gabriel Rossetti. II." *Magazine of Art* (1889): 57-60.

    In 1883 the Burlington Club held an exhibition of Dante Gabriel Rossetti's works, including a pen and ink wash dated September 1853, titled *Dante Gabriel Sitting for His Portrait to Miss Siddal*. The actual portrait painted by Miss Siddall unfortunately seems to have been lost, but the author does own another of her works, a very good self portrait.

166. "Chronicle of Art. Art in January. The Royal Academy Schools." *Magazine of Art* (1890): xiii-xvi.

    The fact that ten women were prize winners makes this year's Royal Academy schools competition a memorable one. The work of Alma-Tadema inspired a design for building decoration by Gertrude Hammond. It is so good that she will "have the opportunity of carrying it out."

167. "Chronicle of Art. Art in January. Reviews." *Magazine of Art* (1890): xiii-xvi.

    While she is obviously an amateur, Mrs. E. L. Schute's illustrations of *The Kelfrie's Fiddle Bow* are intelligent and much superior to Mrs. Tom Kelly's book, *Those Were the Days*, which is not worth the printing.

168. "Chronicle of Art. Art in March. Reviews." *Magazine of Art* (1890): xxi-xxiv.

    Joseph Pennell, the author of a recent book on drawing and draughtmanship, has omitted in his work mention of two of the finest artists of all time: Francesca Alexander and Helen Allingham.

169. "Chronicle of Art. Art in March. Obituary [Maude Naftel]." *Magazine of Art* (1890): xxi-xxvi.

    Maude Naftel, a flower and landscape painter of rising reputation, is dead at only twenty-seven. Naftel, the daughter of an instructor at the Slade School of Art, was a member of the Royal Water-Colour Society and had exhibited at the Royal Academy.

170. "The Chronicle of Art. Art in September. Obituary [Alice Havers]." *Magazine of Art* (1890): xlv-xlviii.

> Painter and Illustrator Alice Havers has died suddenly. A student and exhibitor at the Royal Academy, Havers also studied in Paris. She will be remembered for her exceptionally charming, if not technically powerful paintings and for her very fine work in black and white.

171. *"Love's Rubicon." Magazine of Art* (1890): 403.

> Alice Havers' picture of a woman leaning against a tree and gazing pensively at a stream illustrates a poem by Kate Carter.
>
> Reproductions (b/w engraving):
> Havers, Alice: *Love's Rubicon.*

172. Du Maurier, George. "The Illustrating of Books. From the Serious Artist's Point of View. I." *Magazine of Art* (1890): 349- 353.

> When *Cornhill Magazine* printed the novel *Far from the Madding Crowd,* Helen Allingham provided the illustrations. Elizabeth Thompson Butler is among the notable artists who have appeared in *The Graphic.*

173. ---. "The Illustrating of Books. From the Serious Artists's Point of View. II." *Magazine of Art* (1890): 371-375.

> Helen Allingham and Kate Greenaway are among the best artists to have drawn English children.

174. Symons, W. Christian. "Newlyn and the Newlyn School." *Magazine of Art* (1890): 199-205.

> Newlyn, a picturesque Cornish fishing village, is a favorite gathering and working place for a group of artists interested in rendering truthful color, light, and subject. Not to be confused with impressionists, the Newlyn artists celebrate light and simplicity in their work. Among the founding artists of the colony is Elizabeth Armstrong Stanhope Forbes. Marianne Stokes (Mrs. Adrian) is one of the leading artists.
>
> Reproductions (b/w drawing):
> Vos, H.: *Marianne Stokes.*

175. Woolner, Thomas. *"The Wife. Midsummer." Magazine of Art* (1890): 302-303.

> Margaret I. Dicksee's full-page drawings of a young woman show her waiting for her husband outside a cottage; after the husband arrives she serves him tea inside.

Reproductions (b/w engraving):
Dicksee, Margaret I.: *The Wife: Midsummer.*

176. "My Note Book." *The Art Amateur* 23, no. 3 (August 1890): 42.

Not only is Anna Lea Merritt's *Love Locked Out* not the first work by an American to be purchased by the Chantrey Fund, but the *Daily Telegraph* finds it a disappointment because her cupid has a shock of ugly hair that looks as if he has been in a mud fight.

177. "The Chronicle of Art. Art in December. Reviews." *Magazine of Art* (1891): ix-xi.

Since Alice Havers has died, this year's Christmas book, an illustration of Lewis Morris' *Odatis*, will sadly be the last of her charming and graceful works.

178. "The Chronicle of Art. Art in June. Obituary. Mme Juliette Peyrol-Bonheur." *Magazine of Art* (1891): xxxiii-xxxvi.

Juliette Peyrol-Bonheur, the sister of Rosa Bonheur, had a distinguished career that included Salon exhibitions, the Exhibition of 1855, and a bronze medal in 1889. Like her sister, Juliette Peyrol-Bonheur painted animals.

179. "The Chronicle of Art. Art in September. The Pitfalls of Artistic Copyright." *Magazine of Art* (1891): xlv-xlviii.

Mary Harriot Earnshaw gave permission, in a letter, for the newspaper *Queen* to publish her painting titled *On the Threshold. Queen* in turn sold the picture and the copyright to a printer, who registered it, sold the copyright and 55,000 copies of the print to a publisher, and subsequently sued *Queen* for copyright violation. The court found against *Queen,* saying Earnshaw's letter of permission was not a license.

180. Didbin, E. Rimbault. "Lord Armstrong's Collection of Modern Pictures." *Magazine of Art* (1891): 158-165.

Rosa Bonheur's *The Deer Park at Fontainebleu* is the best animal picture in the collection of William George, Baron Armstrong. Bonheur's picture of two deer in a beech forest is "a little poem in colour."

181. Grundy, E. Landseer. "Animal Painters Past and Present." *Magazine of Art* (1891): 388-391.

Rosa Bonheur's *Horse Fair*, considered her best work, was engraved by Tom Landseer. Bonheur's work brings about the same prices as works by another famous animal painter, Sir Edwin Landseer.

182. Hunt, W. S. "Concerning Some *Punch* Artists." *Magazine of Art* (1891): 296-306.

Adelaide Claxton is among the illustrators of the magazine *Punch,* whose pictures included recognizable locales with characters typical of the areas they populated. Georgiana Bowers' hunting scenes appeared in *Punch* some time around 1868.

183. Spielmann, M. H. "A Great Painter of Cats." *Magazine of Art* (1891): 21-30.

The cat is such a difficult and complicated subject that even the most talented of animal painters have avoided drawing or painting it. England's best cat painters cannot equal Henriette Ronner, a Dutchwoman who exhibits her pictures at the Bond Street Fine Art Society and is popular and successful in several countries.

Reproductions (b/w):

Ronner, Henriette: *Studies of Kittens at Rest; Studies of Cats in Action; In the Studio; The Turbulent Family* Portrait of Henriette Ronner.

184. Hare, Augustus J. C. *The Story of Two Noble Lives: Being Memorials of Charlotte, Countess Canning, and Louisa, Marchioness of Waterford.* New York: Anson, D. F. Randolph & Company, 1893.

Stuart's art occupied much of her time and mind, especially later in her life. A chapter titled "The Companionship of Art" contains an extensive catalogue of exhibited drawings and notes (some in French), from her sketchbook. Her subjects consist mostly of women, children, flowers, animals, and biblical scenes.

Reproductions (b/w):

Stuart, Louisa: drawings and sketches.

185. Viccars, S. J. "The Leicester Corporation Art Gallery." *Magazine of Art* (1893): 12-19.

One of the most popular pictures in the Leicester Corporation Art Gallery is Henrietta Ward's *Palissy the Potter*, which was a Royal Academy Exhibit in 1866 and appeared as an engraving in the *Art Journal* in 1868.

186. Walton, William. *Art and Architecture: The Art*. Philadelphia: George Barrie, 1893.

> The American Loan Section includes three paintings by Laura Epps Alma-Tadema. *Battledore and Shuttlecock*, exhibited in 1890 at the New Gallery, is a "rather cold" picture of several young girls at play. *Always Welcome* is much better. Anna Alma-Tadema exhibits an oil portrait and a watercolor of her drawing room. Jessie Macgregor's *Reign of Terror*, exhibited at the Royal Academy in 1891, shows a young woman in an orange-red dress, leaning in fear over her baby's cradle. Macgregor's genre paintings appear frequently at Royal Academy exhibits. Often her subjects are lone women in historical costume. This year's Royal Academy exhibit, *Officers Killed and Wounded on Board the Ajax: None*, is of a girl at a spinning wheel, clasping her hands in relief as she hears the news of the battle of Trafalgar. Macgregor's *Jeptha* appeared in the 1889 Royal Academy exhibit. Kate Dickens Perugini's *Tomboy*, a portrait of a grave girl in a disheveled bonnet and dress, holding an apple, captures a rare moment of stillness in the life of a lively urchin.

187. "The Royal Academy." *The Magazine of Art* XVII (1894): 274.

> The reviewer of Henrietta Rae's *Psyche before the Throne of Venus* finds the composition, drawing, and use of colors to be remarkable, but taken as a whole, the painting lacks a certain conviction necessary for an Olympian scene, a work "hardly expected from a woman."

188. Thwaite, Ann. *Edmund Gosse: A Literary Landscape 1849-1928*. Chicago: University of Chicago Press, 1894.

> This book provides a more complete picture of Nellie Epps and Laura Alma-Tadema's personal lives than can be found in collections of Gosse's letters, but there is little about their artistic endeavors. Nellie's talent is described as "considerable," but her work is not described in any detail.

189. "Art Notes." *Illustrated London News* (21 April 1894): 491.

> Miss Allingham, well known for her attractive paintings of the simple cottages of the poor, has retained her skills but changed subjects in the exhibit of her works at the Fine Art Society's Gallery. She has managed to make the "poverty and thriftlessness" of West Donegal houses into cheerful and attractive exteriors. She has shown a new skill in figure painting; her renditions of dark-complected West Donegal children are beautiful and distinguished.

190. "The Royal Academy: First Choice." *London Times* (5 May 1894): 16.

Henrietta Rae's *Psyche before the Throne of Venus* possesses "clever composition, good drawing, and pleasant colour," but unfortunately the painting lacks the "ferocity" characteristic of Venus in the story. On the whole, however, the painting is worthy of the notice the Academy has paid it.

191. Harding, William M. "A Reminiscence of Mrs. W. M. Rossetti." *Magazine of Art* xviii (1895): 341-346.

After the death of Emma Lucy Madox Brown's mother, Lucy, as she preferred to be called, was educated by an aunt and lived with the Rossetti family for some years after the age of eleven. She began serious art study when she was twenty-four, and the small number of paintings she left show true talent, imagination and sensitivity; her work is weak only where it shows the dominating influence of her father, Ford Madox Brown, and her friend, Dante Gabriel Rossetti. In her short life she exhibited only eight pictures. *The Duet,* a watercolor, was hung in the Royal Academy exhibit of 1870, and all but one of the others were exhibited at the Dudley Gallery. Her art and her life are characterized by keen intelligence and a constant search for truth. She died of consumption at the age of 52.

192. Postlethwaite, Helene. "Some Noted Women Artists." *Magazine of Art* XVIII (1895): 17-22.

While their backgrounds and artistic subjects differ in some ways, Henrietta Rae, Marianne Stokes, Marie Seymour Lucas, Jessie Macgregor, Mary Waller and Anna Lea Merritt have in common their considerable artistic talent and their critical and financial successes. All have exhibited extensively at the Royal Academy; Henrietta Rae made history in becoming its first female member. Short biographical sketches of each woman include lists of major works and exhibits.

Reproductions (b/w):

Marie Seymour Lucas (portrait by her husband)

Macgregor, Jessie: *Self portrait*

Merritt, Anna Lea: *Self portrait*

Henrietta Rae Normand (portrait by her husband)

Reid, Flora: *Self portrait*

Stokes, Marianne: *Self portrait*

Waller, Mary: *Self portrait.*

193. H. H. R. "Art Amongst Women in the Victorian Era." *Englishwoman's Review* 28 (1897): 209-214.

A survey of Victorian art includes almost the whole history of women artists, since so much has been accomplished during that period. Artwork by today's women demonstrates breadth and competence in contrast to work by women fifty years ago where "truth was...sacrificed to prettiness, and force or originality were considered unwomanly." In the present day, artists such as Marie Spartali Stillman paint the beauty of lost golden ages, while Elizabeth Stanhope Forbes paints with truth and realism. Annette Elias and Anna Nordgren paint the unhappy poor in the spirit of modern pessimism. Lucy Kemp-Welch is an unsurpassed painter of horses, and Maude Earl's paintings of dogs are without rival. The achievements and the diversity of women painters is evidence that progress and improvement can go together. The progress of civilization has opened the doors of the art world to women, who have improved culture and brought happiness to many.

194. Neville, Hastings M. *Under a Border Tower: Sketches and Memories of Ford Castle, Northumberland, and its Surroundings with Memoir of Louisa, Marchioness of Waterford.* Newcastle-upon-Tyne: Mawson, Swan and Morgan, 1897.

Children are a favorite theme in Louisa Waterford's exhibition of over 300 paintings at an 1892 London exhibit. The walls of the school she built in a village near her home are decorated with her paintings of Biblical scenes. Her style is bold, her colors bright, and her compositions thoughtful and natural.

Reproductions (b/w):

Louisa, Marchioness of Waterford: Eighteen Biblical scenes from murals at Ford school; *Two Shining Ones; Choristers; The Good Shepherd.*

195. Temple, A. G. *The Art of Painting in the Queen's Reign.* London: Chapman and Hall, 1897.

Helen Allingham's work is so competent that it is an essential part of any good watercolor collection. Laura Alma-Tadema's Dutch domestic scenes owe their excellence to the complimentary quality of figures and scenery, together with "a sound and deliberate method of work." The landscapes and Venetian scenes of Clara Montalba's work are unique in their treatment of light and color. Mrs. Adrian Stokes' paintings are not numerous but are remarkable for their careful study and deliberate precision. The "chaste and sensitive rendering" of Henrietta Rae's *Summer* is typical of the skill of "one of the most gifted and best trained" of female artists. Rae treats her subjects with grace and sensitivity, rendering nature and the human form with singular skill. Elizabeth Butler's fame is well known and well deserved. Her later works have been excellent, although they have not captured the emotions of the public as much as did *The Roll Call*.

Reproductions (b/w):

Butler, Elizabeth Thompson: *Scotland Forever!*

196. Hueffer, Ford Madox. "The Younger Madox Browns: Lucy, Catherine and Oliver." *Artist XIX* (February 1897): 49-56.

The Madox Browns all possessed artistic talent in varying degrees, but with different gifts. Catherine lacked inspiration, but made up for it in perseverance and dedication. Lucy had the most genius, but lacked her sister's patience and discipline. Both learned to paint by helping their artist father in his studio, and both exhibited at the Dudley Gallery in 1869. Some of Lucy's most important work centered around tragic themes-- Margaret Roper receiving the severed head of her father, Thomas More; and *Romeo and Juliet*, which captures the moment of stillness before the final scene of grief and suicide. Lucy might have had a brilliant artistic career had not "the sad, half-grotesque, half-tragic fate that makes the cares of a household an overwhelming benumber of minds turned her thoughts and endeavors to smaller things"; in other words, she married and stopped painting, though she later published a work on Mary Wollstonecraft Shelley. Catherine Madox Brown painted fine portraits of famous people, but, like all her family, she failed in basic technique, especially in brush work. The children's achievements in color did have some influence on the work of their famous father.

Reproduction (b/w):

Rossetti, Lucy Brown: *Romeo and Juliet, Act V, Scene Three; The Duet; The Fair Geraldine*

Hueffer, Catherine Brown: *Industry; Idleness.*

197. Meynell, Wilfrid. "The Life and Work of Lady Butler." *The Art Annual* (1898): 4, 6-7 ff. Reprint. London: The Art Journal Office, 1898.

Years of determined study and relentless work developed Elizabeth Thompson Butler's natural talent and resulted in her being one of the most capable artists of her time. Her careful depictions of soldiers make their deaths and suffering a personal experience for the viewer; thus war is shown in all its stupidity and cruelty. Butler continued her painting after her marriage, in addition to illustrating an edition of her sister's poems and an edition of Thackeray's ballads.

Reproductions (b/w):

Butler, Lady Thompson: *Floreat Etona!; The Cistercian Shepherd and His Flock; The Camel Corps; 'Listed for the Connaught Rangers; Scotland Forever!; Dawn at Waterloo; After the Battle; Halt on a Forced March; "Trot!"; A Quiet Canter in the Long Valley*

Sketches and studies of animals and human figures; photos of Elizabeth Thompson Butler at work; photos of her studios and rooms at Dover Castle.

198. "In the Art World." *New York Times Saturday Review of Books and Art* (15 January 1898): 46.

Anna Lea Merritt's early portraits at the Society of American Artists' exhibit showed talent and promise. Since then she has lived in London, exhibiting regularly at the Royal Academy. Now, after some years she is again exhibiting in the U.S.; three portraits range from satisfactory to "distinctly disappointing." Her subjects are wooden, the backgrounds indistinct. Her portraits of Mrs. Harry Trevor and her two children are "wooden and stiff"; her portrait of the daughter of the Rev. Roderick Terry lacks "a certain indefinable quality of life and verisimilitude." The reviewer suggests Mrs. Merritt would profit from a course of study with New York artists, in particular, Celia Beaux.

199. "Chronicle of Art. Art in December." *Magazine of Art* (1899): ix-xii.

One of the best of the Christmas books is *About Robins*, by Lady Lindsay and published by Routledge. Lady Lindsay collected the material and illustrated the book, which is artistically pleasing, if not scientifically accurate.

200. Rinder, Frank. "Mary F. Raphael." *Art Journal* (1899): 257-259.

Mary Raphael began her art studies at Cooke's studio in London, and received instruction and encouragement from well-known artists, including Simeon J. Solomon. She continued her studies in Paris, and her work since shows her determination to strengthen her own style in her highly competent and original works. Her *Wood Nymph*, an acclaimed Royal Academy exhibit in 1896, shows her talent in painting nude female figures, as well as her real achievement in solving drawing and composition problems. She has shown equal virtuosity in her portraits of women and children. Her portrait of A. E. Woodley Mason will be featured as the frontispiece to his next book.

Reproductions (b/w):

Raphael, Mary F: *Somnia; Miss Eva Leslie Crawford.*

201. Tyler, Sarah. *Modern Painters and Their Paintings.* Boston: Little, Brown and Co., 1899.

Johanna Mary Boyce Wells was born in 1831, exhibited her head study, *Elgiva,* at the Royal Academy when she was twenty-four, and died at age thirty after giving birth to a child. She studied in Rome, exhibited miniatures and genre paintings at London galleries, and has been called the best of all female painters of her time. Henrietta Ward's exceptional technical skills are probably due to her artistic heritage. Margaret Carpenter, who lived to be quite old, achieved considerable success with portrait painting. J. B. (Jane Bewick), the wife of a Scottish college professor, excels in representation of birds and their surroundings. She illustrated the *Book of Birds* and exhibited a painting of firefighters at the Royal Scottish Academy. Martha Mutrie and Annie Mutrie have been exhibiting their fruit and flower pictures at the Royal Academy since 1851. While their work has been criticized for its use of cultivated, rather than wild flowers, it should be remembered that all flowers are worth painting. Rosa Bonheur has "indulged in a thousand eccentricities" in order to pursue her art. She has dressed in men's clothes, lived in herdsmen's huts, and visited friends while wearing paint-spattered clothes. Her work, such as *Ploughing in Nivernois,* proves the success of such single-minded pursuit of art. Henriette Browne is another Frenchwoman whose work is highly esteemed in England as well as on the continent. Browne's *Sick Boy Tended by Sisters of Charity* has been especially admired, and *Saying Grace,* a picture of a black-eyed girl in a white cap, is "innocent and loveable."

202. "New Panels in the Royal Exchange." *Art Journal* (1900): 378- 379.

The late Lord Leighton's suggestion that the grey space of the ambulatory of the Royal Exchange be decorated with frescoes depicting notable scenes in London's history has resulted in some commendable paintings by some noteworthy artists. Henrietta Rae has executed a more human, less dramatic scene than those pictured by her male contemporaries. She has painted London's famous four-times mayor, Sir Richard Whittington, standing in the street in a poor section of London, giving loaves of bread to poor women and children. The affluence of the richly-clad Whittington, his wife, and his servant is contrasted sharply with the poverty of the ragged children and women.

Reproductions (b/w):
Rae, Henrietta: *The Charities of Dick Whittington.*

203. Armstrong, Geneva. *Woman in Art.* n.p.: 1900.

A comprehensive account of European and American women who have contributed significantly to the advancement of art in the past, and continue to influence art in the twentieth century. Eight nineteenth-century British artists receive a careful account of their lives and artistic accomplishments; many other women from many ages and countries are included as well.

Reproductions (b/w):
Bonheur, Rosa: *The Steers*
Butler, Elizabeth Thompson: *Scotland Forever!*

204. Caw, James L. "The Art Work of Mrs. Traquair." *Art Journal* (1900): 143-148.

Truly great mural work in the tradition of the great Renaissance Italian masters is difficult to find in modern times; however, the beautiful and imaginative church decoration of Phoebe Anna Moss Traquair does a creditable job of maintaining the European tradition. Traquair's murals for the Song School of St. Mary's Cathedral, Edinburgh, are a fine example of her technical skill, inspiration, and imaginative interpretation. While there is evidence of Pre-Raphaelite influence, her work is still very much her own. Her crowning achievement to date is the interior decoration of the Catholic Apostolic Church in Edinburgh. She has painted a frieze beginning twenty feet up from the floor. Her designs feature scenes from Christ's life, including Old Testament events. Traquair uses no preliminary sketches, but paints directly on the wall, guided by spontaneity, inner vision, and instinct.

205. Marillier, H. C. "The Romantic Water-Colours of Miss Cameron." *Art Journal* (1900): 148-149.

Art lovers who regret the loss of feeling in modern painting will be pleased with the work of Katherine Cameron, a young Glaswegian whose work has escaped trendy efforts at elegance, " 'impressionism' and slap-dash brilliance" of modern art. Cameron takes her subjects from old ballads and fairy stories, combining skillful drawing and composition with imagination and careful detail. Her flower pictures, miniatures, and portraits reveal the same poetic feeling that mark her competent and original scenes from legends and folklore.

206. Rinder, Frank. "The Royal Academy of 1900." *Art Journal* (1900): 161-183.

Lucy Kemp-Welch, known as an animal painter of some skills, shows a talent for painting water and sunshine in her *Horses Bathing*. Mrs. Young Hunter's painting of Dante and Beatrice shows that the story retains its interest even after six centuries.

Reproductions (b/w):

Hunter, Mary Young: *The Denial: Dante and Beatrice*

Kemp-Welch, Lucy: *Horses Bathing in the Sea.*

207. Ford, Harriet. "The Work of Mrs. Adrian Stokes." *The Studio* 19 (April 1900): 149-156.

Marianne Stokes' highly decorative religious and medieval paintings display a haunting mysticism, probably attributable to her roots in a Roman Catholic country. Years of hard work and study in Munich, Paris and Italy have resulted in a purity of line and color that make her work distinctive, beautiful and memorable.

Reproductions (b/w):

Stokes, Marianne: *Primavera; Light of Light; Saint Elizabeth Spinning for the Poor; Hail Mary; The Queen and the Page; Aucassin & Nicolette; The Passing Train.*

208. Meynell, Wilfrid. "Mr. and Mrs. Adrian Stokes." *Art Journal* (July 1900): 193-198.

Marianne (Preindlsberger) Stokes studied art in Gratz. She began to sell her paintings while she was continuing her studies in Munich. She met her husband in France. They share a fondness of painting Dutch landscape and people. Her paintings of Dutch children reveal her extraordinary skills in drawing and her talent for achieving purity of design and color.

209. "Queen Victoria [Obituary]." *Art Journal* (1901): 97.

Queen Victoria's long career was highlighted by her consistent patronage of the arts. Even more than a patron, however, she was also a painstaking student and gifted amateur. Her watercolors and etchings show a talent that, had it not been sacrificed to the duties of family and country, might have brought her distinction as an artist.

210. Corden, Victor. "The Queen and Painting." *Art Journal* (1901): 99-100.

It is well known that Queen Victoria's firm but delicate sketches and watercolors placed her in the category of a very good amateur artist. She used a "curious cylindrical-shaped paint box with palette attached." At one point in her career, she painted a portrait of the acclaimed portraitist, Winterhalter. Winterhalter, commissioned to paint Victoria, hit on the idea as a way to get her to sit still. Victoria's work, a life-sized head of the famous painter, is considered a good likeness.

211. Fish, Arthur. "Some English Lady Artists." *Harmsworth Magazine* 31 (1901): 329-334.

Although they are still not represented in the Royal Academy membership, women are successfully competing with, and even excelling the work of male exhibitors. The work of Elizabeth Butler, Laura Alma-Tadema, Marie Cornelissen Lucas, Elizabeth Armstrong Forbes, Mary Gow, Margaret Dicksee, Henrietta Rae, Lucy Kemp-Welch and Eleanor Fortesque-Brickdale's is briefly described and appropriately praised as well-known and respected in art circles and much appreciated by the public.

Reproductions (b/w):

Alma-Tadema, Laura: *A Sketch of a Woman*

Dicksee, Margaret: *Sheridan at the Lindley's; The Children of King Charles I*

Forbes, Elizabeth Stanhope: *Dreamland*

Goodman, Maude: *Suspense*

Gow, Mary: *Lady Alma-Tadema; Nothing Venture Nothing Have*

Lucas, Marie Seymour: *We Are But Little Children Weak*

Rae, Henrietta: *Dick Whittington Distributing Alms and Bread to the Poor*

Staples, Mia Edwards: *The Last Kiss*.

212. Meynell, Alice. "Mrs. Adrian Stokes." *The Magazine of Art* xxx (1901): 241-246.

The highly original style of Marianne Prendlsberger Stokes' work came from her careful study and successful adaption of techniques of continental painters of the Middle Ages and of French painting of modern realists. In her pursuit of color she abandoned oils in favor of gesso and tempera. The evolution of her own technique, coupled with honesty, composure, instinct for truth and appreciation for simple things, has put her in the forefront of modern artists, who seek to combine the fresh approach of the twentieth century--avoiding the heavy sentimentality of nineteenth-century painting--without abandoning feeling and thought.

213. Rinder, Frank. "Henrietta Rae: Mrs. Normand." *Art Journal* (October 1901): 303-307.

Although artists have drawn inspiration from classical mythology for thousands of years, the theme is far from exhausted. Henrietta Rae continues the long artistic tradition with her paintings. She began her training by copying from the Elgin marbles in the British Museum while attending a life class at Heatherly's Art School and gradually acquired a Greek artist's appreciation of balance and purity of form. She continued her studies at the Royal Academy Schools for another seven years. She exhibited *Lancelot and Elaine* at the Burlington House Summer Exhibition when she was 21, and has since exhibited yearly in the Royal Academy. She and her husband lived in Kensington for several years, where she was surrounded by famous artists who dropped by regularly to give her advice. Later they moved to another district to escape the "confusion of tongues," and she was able to further develop her own best style: classical scenes and scenes containing high drama.

Reproductions (b/w):

Rae, Henrietta: *Apollo and Daphne; Cephalus and Procris; Doubts; Isabella; Ophelia; Pandora.*

214. Bonheur, Rosa. "Fragments of My Autobiography." *Magazine of Art* 26 (1902): 531-536.

Rosa Bonheur sees her success as the result of talent, determination and hard work. She remembers with gratitude her father's encouragement and instruction, and a kindly butcher's protection as she studied anatomy in a slaughterhouse.

Reproductions (b/w):

Bonheur, Rosa: Sketch for *A Duel; Sketch of a Bear; Sketch of a Leopard; Sketch of a Jackal; A Young Lioness; A Sketch at Fontainbleu; A Spanish Shepherd; Moufflon Sheep; A Sketch of a Horse*; Rosa Bonheur in her studio, 1870.

215. Merritt, Anna Lea. *A Hamlet in Old Hampshire.* London: Kegan Paul, 1902.

Anna Lea Merritt's essays reveal that the artist was a keen and appreciative observer of the plants, animals, birds, insects and people of the England she loved. Her prose style reflects the clarity of her painting and reveals a woman who combined Yankee practicality with a keen intellect, a gentle wit and a generous heart.

Reproductions (col):

Merritt, Anna Lea: *My Garden*

Reproductions (b/w):

Merritt, Anna Lea: *The Village and Beyond; In the Vicar's Garden; The Author's Cottage; The Oldest Cottage; Spring Pasture; June Morning; July Evening; The Pergola; Noon in the Rock Garden; September; Labourer's Cottage; Temptation; A Pond on the Common; The End.*

216. Watson, Walter R. "Miss Jessie M. King and Her Work." *The Studio* 26 (1902): 177-188.

Beautiful illustrations can enhance a good book, rescue a bad one and clarify a confusing one. Jessie King's great sensitivity and tremendous talent have added much to the books she illustrated. Her remarkably individualistic style and her sensitivity to the mysticism of nature have made her illustrations a natural complement, a magical enhancement, and a poetic statement of the essence of the work.

Reproductions (b/w):

King, Jessie: *The Two Corbies; The Princess and the Peacock;* illustration for *The Magic Grammar;* illustration for *La Belle Dame sans Merci;* illustration for Andersen's *Fairy Tales;* frontispiece for *L'Evangelie de l'Enfance; The Little Town by the Sea,* bookplate for William Rowat; *The Romance of the Swan's Nest*

Rowat, M.F.: *Portrait of Miss Jessie King* (book cover design).

217. Dickson, Marian Hepworth. "Miss Lucy Kemp-Welch." *Lady's Realm* 13 (1903): 575-582.

In her Hertfordshire studio, a stone's throw from Lorenz Herkomer's infamous Lululaund, Kemp-Welch practices her "drastic and thorough" methods of painting. The great sensitivity and technical skill with which she painted her favorite subject, horses, led to her being favorably compared to Rosa Bonheur. Her fondness for catching a moment resulted in what she called "snapshots" in oil, and she carried a portable paintbox rather than a camera because she firmly believed in working from life. She felt it was essential for her students to work from life and to avoid the camera altogether. She began exhibiting in her early twenties, had several Academy exhibits to her credit, and her popularity never waned.

Reproductions (b/w):

Kemp-Welch, Lucy: *Sons of the City; The Morning;* "Snapshot" in oils of horses plowing; Two sketches of sea gulls

Photos

Photo of the artist painting in her studio.

218. Rossetti, William Michael. "Dante Rossetti and Elizabeth Siddall. Written by W.M. Rossetti with Facsimiles of Five Unpublished Drawings by Dante Rossetti in the Collection of Mr. Harold Hartley." *Burlington Magazine*, no. 1 (May 1903): 273-295.

Elizabeth Siddall's head is familiar in many paintings and drawings by members of the Pre-Raphaelite circle. She herself was the very model of "maidenly and feminine purity." Her 1853 self- portrait, the best of her own artistic endeavors, is "her very self." She was extravagantly admired and praised by the men who met her; of her own voice, only a few extremely melancholy poems remain. In all, she was an extraordinary woman worthy of marriage to her painter-poet husband.

Reproductions (b/w):

Siddall, Elizabeth: *Self Portrait*

Rossetti, Dante Gabriel: five drawings of Elizabeth Siddall.

219. Clement, Clara Erskine. *Women in the Fine Arts: from the Seventh Century B. C. to the Twentieth Century A. D.* Boston, New York: Houghton Mifflin, Hacker Books, 1904.

Artists are listed in alphabetical order, with short sketches of professional backgrounds, principal works, and notable qualities. It is somewhat subjective for modern scholarship, but a useful overview. Clement interviewed many of the artists herself and sent questionnaires.

220. "Charles John Galloway [obituary]." *London Times* (16 March 1904): 10.

Charles John Galloway, a discriminating patron and collector of art, is remembered as the man who commissioned Elizabeth Thompson Butler's *The Roll Call.* Later, after having to relinquish *The Roll Call* to Queen Victoria, he commissioned Butler to paint *Quatre Bras*, another well-known work he owned for many years.

221. Fish, Arthur. *Henrietta Rae.* London: Cassell, 1905.

Fish's assessment of work by Rae and other women reflects admiration without condescension. He celebrates Rae's marriage in which she and her artist husband share equal footing. Rae's love of Greek and Roman art combined with the challenge of painting flesh tones explains her predilection for painting classical scenes of unclothed females. Although she was admired in the art world (Millais is quoted as having said he would give his left hand for her skill in painting flesh), the public occasionally rumbled that Rae's subject matter would lead to a deterioration of character of her models and viewers.

Reproductions (col):

Rae, Henrietta: *Songs of the Morning; Doubts; Zephyrus Wooing*

Reproductions (b/w):

Rae, Henrietta: *M. Le Curé; Through the Woods; Miss Warman; Lancelot and Elaine; A Bacchante; Val Princep, RA; Eurydice Sinking Back to Hades; Reverie; Ophelia; Apple Blossom; Study of Head in Chalk; La Cigale*; landscape study for *Flowers Plucked and Cast Aside; Memories; Psyche Before the Throne of Venus; Pandora; Apollo and Daphne; Summer; Roses of Youth; Her Eyes Are Homes of Silent Prayer; G.L. Beeforth, Esq.; Lady Newton; The Charities of Sir Richard Whittington; The Marquess of Dufferin and Ava; Sirens; Loot*

Photos:

Henrietta Rae; The Studio at Norwood; Mrs. Normand painting the portrait of the Marquess of Dufferin; Mrs. Normand painting the Royal Exchange panel.

222. Sparrow, Walter Shaw. *Women Painters of the World from the Time of Caterina Vigri 1413-1463 to Rosa Bonheur and the Present Day*, London: Hacker Art Books, 1905. Reprint, New York, 1976

Intended as an overview of 450 years of the work of female artists, the sections on nineteenth-century women can be little more than generalizations and lists of names. The sheer volume of illustrations, however, is noteworthy, even though they are all in black and white.

223. Spielmann, M. H. and Layard, G. S. *Kate Greenaway*. New York: Putnam's, 1905.

While an art student at Heatherley's, Kate Greenaway shared a studio with Elizabeth Thompson. The two habitually bribed the custodian to let them stay to work after hours when the studio doors were locked. Helen Allingham, also a fellow student, remembers that "no one could draw roses" like Greenaway. Her first Royal Academy exhibit, *Musing*, sold for twenty guineas. Greenaway also exhibited at the Dudley Gallery and was a member of the Royal Institute of Painters in Water Colours. Correspondence between Greenaway and John Ruskin reveal their friendship and his admiration for her work. The popularity of *Punch's* "Grinaway Cards," with members of the Royal family and prominent political figures dressed in Greenaway-style clothes, indicate that her influence extended well beyond nursery illustrations.

Reproductions (b/w):

Greenaway, Kate: numerous color plates, black and white illustrations and sketches.

224. Hunt, William Holman. *Pre-Raphaelitism and the Pre-Raphaelite Brotherhood*. London: Macmillan, June 1905.

While Hunt claimed to respect the private lives of others, he managed to slip into light gossip about others while almost completely avoiding the subject of his marriage to Fanny Waugh, her death, and his marriage to her sister, Edith. Hunt's account of the discovery of Eleanor [Elizabeth] Siddall indicates that she first posed for the young woman in Hunt's *Christians Escaping from Persecuting Druids*. Rossetti, Hunt wrote, admired Siddall's beauty at once but didn't express strong feelings for her for over a year. Effie Grey's divorce from Ruskin and her subsequent marriage to Millais was seen as a sort of social inconvenience, and Hunt's sympathies seem to have been with Ruskin.

Reproductions (b/w):

Portraits of Fanny and Edith Holman Hunt.

225. Butler, Elizabeth. *Letters from the Holy Land*. London: Adam and Charles Black, 1906.

Elizabeth Thompson Butler's accounts of her travels in the Middle East are clear, humane, and readable.

Reproductions (col):

Butler, Elizabeth Thompson: *The Start;* Fifteen watercolor landscapes.

226. Allingham, Helen and D. Radford, eds. *William Allingham: A Diary 1824-1889; Introduction by Julius Norwich*, London. New York: Penguin, 1907. Reprint, 1985.

A veritable catalogue of famous Victorians, but Helen Allingham's artwork gets about as much press as her knitting. An amusing account of a churlish Tennyson describes him reluctantly sitting for a portrait as payment for a landscape he asked her to make; another painting episode involves Allingham sitting for hours in the cold to work on a landscape.

227. Muther, Richard. *The History of Modern Painting*, London: Dent, 1907.

When Elizabeth Siddall died after giving birth to a dead child, Dante Gabriel Rossetti, paralyzed with grief, went into seclusion. His poems were instant best-sellers after friends convinced him to retrieve his manuscript from Siddall's coffin, and he was "honored like a god." Marie Spartali Stillman, who lives in Rome and paints with inspiration from Rossetti and Italian masters, is a young member of a group devoted to a style between

Pre-Raphaelitism and classicism. *The Deceitfulness of Riches* by Eleanor Fortescue-Brickdale is one of those works that evolved from the artist's study of ornament and decoration. Clara Montalba paints London port scenes, but excels at Venetian scenes of canals. Her watercolor technique is the type that was once "the chief glory of the English School"; she does not try to compete with oil painting, but "throws [impressions] lightly upon paper."

228. Butler, Elizabeth. *From Sketch-Book and Diary*. London: Adam and Charles Black, 1909.

In the best style of the Victorian travel genre, Butler describes "that heart-piercing contrast between natural beauty and human adversity" she saw in Ireland on her wedding journey. She visited Egypt and Italy with equal social conscience. Her sketches and watercolor illustrations demonstrate a style quite different from her famous oils.

Reproductions (b/w):

Butler, Elizabeth Thompson: Twenty-one sketches

Reproductions (col):

Butler, Elizabeth Thompson: Twenty-eight landscapes.

229. Dick, Stewart. *The Cottage Homes of England*. London: E. Arnold, 1909. Reprint. New York: British Heritage Press, 1984.

This book contains one of the finest collections in print of Helen Allingham's paintings of English cottages. The fine color plates upstage Dick's essays on the history and design of the buildings. The final chapter, "The Cottage in Pictorial Art," contains biographical and critical material on Allingham and her work.

Reproductions (col):

Allingham, Helen: *An Ancient Cottage, I.W.; Cottage near Freshwater, I. W.; Cottage near Tourquay; At Sandhills, Witley, Surrey; Cottage near Oxford; Cottage Children; At Benham, Bucks; Sandhills, Witley (Master Hardy's;) The Old Tucking Mill, Bridgeport, Dorset; At Carlton Kings, Glos.; At a Cottage Door, I.W.; At Bramore, Hants; After Four Centuries; Waxwell Farm, Pinner; Under Hindhead, Surrey; The High Cottage; Old House near Redlynch, Wiltshire; Cottage near Cheltenham; The Dairy Farm, Edenbridge, Kent; At Quidhampton, near Farringford, I.W.; Backs, Godalming; Old Sussex Cottage; Old Farm Near Downton, Wilts; Near Alderly Edge, Cheshire; At Hagbourne, Berks.; Harvest Field Near Westerham, Kent; Downs Near Westerham, Kent; Bluebell Wood, Kent; Feeding the Fowls; The Clothes-Basket; Near Heathfield, Sussex; At West Tarring, Near Worthing; At Toller,*

Dorset; At Paignton, South Devon; By a Devonshire Cottage; At Whittington, Glos.; At a Cottage Gate, Dorset; Cottage Gate, Spring; At Wishford, Wilts.; Hill Farm, Simonsbury, Dorset; Wyldes Farm, North End, Hampstead Heath; The Dairy Farm, Near Crewkerne, Somerset; At Burton Bradstock, Dorset; From Sandhills Common, Witley, Surrey; The Old Malt-House, Brook, Surrey; A Wiltshire Cottage; In a Surrey Garden; A Dorset Garden; Hollyhocks; Watering Flowers; Bluebells; At Granny's; By the Cottage Door, Redlynch, Wilts.; When the Grass is Full of Flowers and the Hedge is Full of Bowers; My Rabbit; Cottage Door, Park Lane, Near Witley; Peacock Cottage, West Horsley; Through the Corn, Downton, Wilts.; Old Surrey Cottage; Michaelmas Daises.

230. Huish, Marcus B., ed. *Happy England as Painted by Helen Allingham, R.W.S.* London: Adam and Charles Black, 1909.

A memoir of sorts interweaves Helen Allingham's life with eighty-one of her paintings of houses, gardens, children, and cottages. Some of the descriptions of the scenes in the paintings are written by Allingham's friends, who appreciated both her art and her personality, and show how the two cannot be seen separately. A chapter titled "Paintresses, Past and Present" gives credit to accomplished female contemporary artists for adding freshness and surprise to the "heavy atmosphere which hung over Art in the later days of the nineteenth century." Allingham's maternal aunt, Laura Hereford, was the first woman to gain admittance to the Royal Academy School and served as an inspiration to her niece as well as to innumerable other women who wanted to study art.

Reproductions (col):

Allingham, Helen: *Minna; In the Farmhouse Garden; The Market Cross, Hagbourne; The Robin; Milton's House, Chalfont St.Giles; The Waller Oak, Coleshill; Apple and Pear Blossom; The Young Customers; The Sand-Martins' Haunt; The Old Men's Gardens, Chelsea Hospital; The Clothes-Line; The Convalescent; The Goat Carriage; The Clothes-Basket; In the Hayloft; The Rabbit Hutch; The Donkey Ride; Witley Lane; Hindhead from Witley Common; In Witley Village; Blackdown from Witley Common; The Fish-Shop, Haselmere; The Children's Tea; The Stile; Pat-a-Cake; Lessons; Bubbles; On the Sands--Sandown, Isle of Wight; Drying Clothes; Her Majesty's Post Office; The Children's Maypole; Spring on the Kentish Downs; Tig Bridge; Spring in the Oakwood; The Cuckoo; The Old Yew Tree; The Hawthorn Valley, Brocket; Ox-Eye Daisies, Near Westerham, Kent; On* the Pilgrims' Way; Night-Jar Lane, Witley; Cherry-Tree Cottage, Chiddingfold; Cottage at Chiddingfold; A Cottage at Hambledon; In Wormley Wood; The Elder Bush, Brook Lane, Witley; The Basket Woman; Cottage at Shottermill, Near Haselmere; Valewood Farm; An Old House at West Tarring; An Old Buckinghamshire House; Duke's Cottage; The Condemned Cottage; On Ide Hill; A Cheshire Cottage, Aderley Edge; The Six Bells; A Kentish Farmyard; Study of a Rose Bush; Wallflowers; A Kentish Garden; Cutting Cabbages; In a Summer Garden; By the Terrace, Brocket Hill; The South Border; Study of Leeks; The Apple Orchard; The House, Farringford; The Kitchen-Garden, Farringford; The Dairy, Farringford; One of Lord Tennyson's Cottages, Farringford; A Garden in October, Aldworth; Hook Hill Farm, Freshwater; At Pound Green, Freshwater; A Cottage at Freshwater Gate; A Cabin at Ballyshannon; The Fairy Bridges; The Church of Sta. Maria della Salute, Venice; A Fruit Stall, Venice

Photos (b/w):
Helen Allingham.

231. Bate, Percy H. *The English Pre-Raphaelite Painters: Their Associates and Successors.* London: G. Bell and Sons, 1910.

The contributions of Dante Gabriel Rossetti and his circle are incalculable; even artists whose aims tend to be in quite different directions occasionally betray the Pre-Raphaelite influence. Lucy Rossetti, Marie Spartali Stillman and Evelyn Pickering (de Morgan) are briefly named as women of talent and influence. Catherine Cameron and Eleanor Brickdale are briefly and favorably mentioned as carrying the tradition into the twentieth century.

Reproductions (b/w):
Brickdale, Eleanor F.: *The Deceitfulness of Riches*
Cameron, Catherine: *Mhari Dhu*
De Morgan, Evelyn Pickering: *Flora; Mercy and Truth*
Siddall, Elizabeth: *Lady Claire*
Rossetti, Lucy: *Romeo and Juliet*
Stillman, Marie Spartali: *Upon a Day Came Sorrow Unto Me; Messer Ansaldo; Showing Donna Dianova His Enchanted Garden.*

232. Merritt, Anna Lea. *An Artist's Garden: Tended, Painted, Described.* London: George Allen, 1910.

Maintaining that "an artist's interest in gardening is to produce pictures without brushes," Anna Lea Merritt offers serious instructions for creating a garden that is as deliberately planted as a picture is painted. Taking up such serious subjects as manures, compost, insects and moles at a time when all gardening was organic, Merritt combines practical instruction, thoughtful observations and brilliant watercolor illustrations.

233. "Chat with a Famous Norwich Artist. Miss Stannard: Eighty-Two and Still Painting." *Eastern Daily Press*, (14 October 1910): 8.

Eloise Stannard's father realized her painting gifts when she was quite young and set her to work painting the flowers and fruit studies which won her recognition for years in the Royal Academy and the British Institute. Now in her eighties and still at her easel, Stannard continues to paint from life rather than from memory or pictures; she feels that an artist must represent the object as it is, untainted by subjectivity or idealism. The advent of color photography has lessened the importance of realistic painting but Stannard still believes in "the ultimate superiority of the human hand."

Reproductions (b/w):
Stannard, Eloise: Detail from a picture of a rabbit
Photos:
Miss Stannard at the age of 82; Miss Stannard at the age of 18.

234. Chester, Austin. "The Art of Anna Lea Merritt." *Windsor Magazine* 38, no. 227 (November 1913): 618.

It seems ironic that the long tradition of austerity among the Quakers would produce a woman whose talent and imagination has richly contributed to art and literature. Born in Philadelphia to a prestigious family, Anna Lea received the same early education afforded to boys, although at the time university education was not possible for women. Most of her art education was from private tutors, as she deplored crowded art schools as detrimental to creativity. She studied in Paris, then in London, was married and widowed in the same year, and has distinguished herself with genre paintings, portraits and murals. Her *Love Locked Out* is in the permanent collection of the National Gallery. A few of her many famous portrait subjects include Oliver Wendell Holmes, James Russell Lowell, Ellen Terry, and Henry James. Studying mural painting techniques, she used Adolph Kleims' method in her murals in St. Martin's Church, Surrey, which have evaded the sad fate of so many other murals in the damp English climate. She has since been influential in reviving mural painting in the United States. She believes women can succeed in art if they remain aloof from domestic demands and if they manage to be less industrious to have more time for quiet contemplation and inspiration. Her book, *A Hamlet in Old Hampshire,* is a delight to read. There is no doubt she could have had as distinguished a career as a writer as she has as a painter.

Reproductions (b/w):

Merritt, Anna Lea: *A Bacchante; Miss Beale, Principal of Cheltenham Ladies' College; Eve; I Will Give You Rest; The Intruder; The Irish Question: A Witness on the Table; James Russell Lowell; Love and the Bachelor Maid; Love Locked Out; The Lure of Fame; Merry Maids; Oliver Wendell Holmes; The Piping Shepard [sic]; Suffer Little Children to Come Unto Me; War; Watchers of the Strait Gate*

Photos:

Anna Lea Merritt.

235. Holiday, Henry. *Reminiscences of My Life.* London: Heinemann, 1914.

In a short section titled "Sister-Artists," Holiday makes passing reference to his pupils Alice Scott, Emily Hayward, Agnes Mortimer and Lilian Wayne. All these women were valued assistants with considerable talent, but their art careers were cut short by death or marriage. Jessie Mothersole, the heiress apparent to Holiday's studio, has avoided both fates. A full-page cartoon by Holiday pleading for female emancipation contains a poem by Mothersole, who, like Holiday, is a suffrage advocate.

236. Morris, May. "William De Morgan. I." *Burlington Magazine* (August 1917): 77-83.

Evelyn Pickering, a pupil and near relation to artist Spencer Stanhope, married De Morgan in 1888. They lived in the famous Chelsea district and were an important part of the art and social scene until 1892, when they moved to Florence, Italy.

237. ---. "William De Morgan (Conclusion)." *Burlington Magazine* (September 1917): 91.

In 1892 when William De Morgan was recovering from illness, Evelyn Pickering De Morgan encouraged his literary efforts. His novel *Joseph Vance* was the result.

238. Badeni, June. *The Slender Tree: A Life of Alice Meynell.* Padstow, Cornwall: Tabb House, 1918.

This biography of Elizabeth Thompson Butler's sister is a colorful picture of the Thompson family. It is an excellent supplement to Elizabeth

Butler's *Autobiography,* a more scholarly and less determinedly optimistic viewpoint of a careful biographer.

239. "Recent Acquisitions by the British Museum and National Gallery." *Burlington Magazine* XXXII, no. CLXXVIII (January 1918): 19-22.

A new collection of prints, drawings and lithographs includes work by E. M. Henderson, D. Woolard and Sylvia Gosse.

240. Stirling, Anna M. D. W. *William De Morgan and His Wife.* New York: Holt, 1922.

Evelyn Pickering De Morgan was a woman of tremendous energy, creativity, and imagination. Her paintings reflect her dream-world of myth and vision. Her marriage to artist William De Morgan benefitted both their careers.

Reproductions (b/w):

De Morgan, Evelyn: *Boreas and the Dying Leaves; The Daughters of the Mist; The Storm Spirits; Aurora Triumphans; Love's Passing; Saint Christina Giving Her Father's Jewels to the Poor; The Little Mermaid; The Five Mermaids; The Valley of Shadows; Queen Eleanor and Fair Rosamund; The Sleeping Earth and the Wakening Moon; The Garden of Opportunity; The Poor Man Who Saved the City; Helen of Troy; The Worship of Mammon; The Moonbeams Dipping into the Sea; In Memoriam*

Photos:

Headstone for the grave of William De Morgan, designed by Evelyn De Morgan; *The Mater Dolorosa,* sculpture by Evelyn De Morgan; Medusa in bronze.

241. Butler, Elizabeth. *An Autobiography.* Boston: Houghton Mifflin, 1923.

Much of this book celebrates and rejoices in such out-of-fashion topics as married life, motherhood, religion, the military, and British imperialism. The combination of an enthusiastic world view, an artist's sharp powers of observation, and a crisp, uncluttered prose style make this book a pleasure to read. It is difficult not to enter into the spirit of one of the most remarkable women of the nineteenth century. Butler's accounts of meeting with Queen Victoria and the poet Tennyson are especially memorable, as is her story of painting *The Roll Call,* and her bemused account of its enthusiastic reception by the Royal Academy and the British public. Her instant fame never seems to interfere with her steady view of the world around her.

Reproductions (b/w):

Butler, Elizabeth Thompson: Drawings of soldiers and horses from Butler's sketch book.

242. Ward, Mrs E. M. *Memories of Ninety Years*. London: Hutchinson & Co., 1924.

Henrietta Mary Ada Ward was the daughter of miniaturist painter Mary Webb. She came from a family with a tradition of distinguished artistic careers. Her husband, Edward Ward, was a successful painter who encouraged and supported her art. Her memories are of many eminent Victorian painters, politicians and writers.

243. Jopling, Louise. *Twenty Years of My Life*. London: John Lane, 1925.

Louise Jopling remembers being deserted by her first husband and having to face life alone, supporting two small children with her painting. She also remembers a brilliant social circle and recalls her tremendous success as a portrait painter and respected royal academician. A firm supporter of women's rights, her independence and spirit seem to have sustained her through difficult times and enabled her to enjoy fully the advantages brought to her through her art.

244. Martineau, Violet. *Gertrude Martineau and Rothiemurchus*. London: Lindsey Press, 1925.

Painter and wood carver Gertrude Martineau spent her happiest years painting landscapes and teaching art classes at the family summer home in Scotland. She counted Barbara Bodichon among her many friends.

245. Adelman, Joseph F. G. *Famous Women: An Outline of Feminine Achievement Through the Ages with Life Stories of Five Hundred Noted Women*. New York: Ellis M. Lonow Co., 1926.

Short biographical and professional achievements with an emphasis on American sculptors, but some of the entries contain interesting comments. For example, Fanny Corbeaux, a self-taught and self-sustaining portrait painter, was also a distinguished biblical scholar. Rosa Bonheur had a particular aversion to her family's business in dressmaking. Kate Greenaway first made her mark in the art world with her Christmas cards.

(b/w):

Rosa Bonheur (artist not identified).

246. Foster, Joshua James. *A Dictionary of Painters of Miniatures (1525-1850)*. London: Philip Allan, 1927.

Sarah Biffin, born without hands or feet, won the Society of Arts medal when she was thirty-seven. She married a man named Wright, exhibited at the Royal Academy in 1850, and died in poverty.

247. "Mrs. Stillman [Obituary]." *The London Times* (8 March 1927): 21.

At her death in her eighty-fourth year, Marie Spartali Stillman was the last of the small circle of women who contributed significantly to the Pre-Raphaelite movement. The daughter of wealthy and educated Anglo-Greek parents, she married W. J. Stillman, a widower with three children. They had three more children together, and while her parental, wifely, and domestic duties did not allow her to pursue her own art with the concentration it deserved, she was an important friend and colleague in the studios and households of Burne-Jones, Morris, Rossetti and others. Her legendary beauty is imperfectly preserved in Dante Gabriel Rossetti's paintings; photographs do not do her justice, either. Her intelligence, charm, sense of humor, and spirit were valued by the many people whose lives she touched.

248. "The Late Mrs. Adrian Stokes." *The Connoisseur* (September 1927): 127.

Marianne Prendlsberger Stokes, born in Graz, Austria, began exhibiting at the Royal Academy in 1884. The following year she was using her husband's name and was professionally known as Mrs. Adrian Stokes. Her figure and "fancy" subjects demonstrated her charm, sensitivity and skill as a painter. She was an Associate of the Royal Society of Painters in Water Colours. She was a pleasant person whose work, with its "curiously subtle appeal, deserves remembrance." She had been ill for some time.

249. Reid, Forrest. *Illustrators of the Eighteen Sixties: An Illustrated Survey of the Work of Fifty-Eight British Artists*. London: Faber & Gwyer, 1928.
Reprint, 1975.

Elizabeth Siddall was named as "a certain young lady" on a list of illustrators that Dante Gabriel Rossetti thought talented enough to provide illustrations for a book of Tennyson's poems. That Siddall's drawings have been lost is hardly a tragedy, since her work is full of "yearning mawkishness" that reflects the weakest aspects of Rossetti's style in a way that is almost a caricature. It is a great mystery that Rossetti didn't recognize this, since he had a keen sense of the ridiculous. Rebecca

Solomon, who was one of her brother Simeon Solomon's most influential teachers, occasionally contributed illustrations to various magazines, but she too had a disastrous ending. Mary Ellen Edwards had great possibilities as an illustrator, but she always drew the same figures in the same way; in the end her work was boring and monotonous. Florence and Adelaide Claxton are "third-rate illustrators."

Reproductions (b/w):

Edwards, Mary Ellen: *That Boy of Norcott's.*

250. "Mrs. Normand [Obituary]." *London Times* (28 March 1928): 11.

Better known by her maiden name, and probably a better painter than her artist husband, Henrietta Rae's female nudes were considered "graceful and poetical" by some, but were ridiculed by others. (One critic called her *Psyche Before the Throne of Venus* a "glorified Christmas card.") Rae also painted portraits of fully-clothed famous men, and was credited by her pupils of both sexes as being a good teacher.

251. "The Late Clara Montalba, R.W.S., 1840-1929." *The Connoisseur* , no. 84 (1929): 263.

Clara Montalba, in her younger years a painter of immense skill and popularity, died in August. She exhibited her first work, an *Interior*, at the Royal Academy in 1866. *St. Mark's*, exhibited in 1881 and *King Carnival*, exhibited in 1887, were her best-known Royal Academy paintings. She was an Associate of the Old Water-Colour Society as well as a member of several art associations on the continent. Born at Cheltenham, Montalba studied with Isabey in Paris, and was best known for her studies of Venetian scenes.

252. Megroz, Rodolphe Louis. *Dante Gabriel Rossetti: Painter Poet of Heaven in Earth*. New York: Scribner, 1929.

While Dante Gabriel Rossetti was hardly blameless in the tragic story of Elizabeth Siddall, her pathological morbidity and her fixation on victimization would have made a stable relationship and a solid marriage impossible.

Reproductions (b/w):

Rossetti, Dante Gabriel: *Lizzie Siddal* (a drawing c. 1855); *Lizzie after Her Marriage in 1860*; a sketch by Rossetti of Lizzie reclining on a pillow.

253. Meynell, Viola. *Alice Meynell: A Memoir*. London: Scribner's, 1929.

> Alice Meynell's daughter writes about her poet mother's acquaintances with famous literary figures, but virtually ignores her more famous painter aunt, Elizabeth Thompson Butler. Meynell does write that her grandmother hated war and found Elizabeth's choice of subject matter to be painful, even though the paintings exposed the evils of war rather than glorifying it.
>
> Reproductions (b/w):
>
> Portrait of Elizabeth and Alice Thompson as children by an unidentified artist.

254. "Mrs. Charles Edward Perugini [Obituary]." *The Connoisseur* 84 (July 1929): 60.

> Kate Dickens Perugini, a Royal Academy exhibitor since 1877, died on 9 May. She was well known as a painter of portraits and genre subjects, including scenes from her father's novels. She was born in 1839 and was married twice, first to Charles Alston Collins and later to Carlo Perugini.

255. "Anna Lea Merritt, Noted Artist, Dies. Member of One of the Oldest Philadelphia Families Stricken in London at 85." *New York Times* (8 April 1930): 26.

> Anna Lea Merritt, whose family came to America with William Penn, died in London, her adopted home. Her *Piping Shepard* [sic] was exhibited in the Philadelphia Academy of Fine Arts in 1899, and was later shown in London. Her *Love Locked Out* was purchased by the Chantry Fund in London. She won medals for exhibits at the Centennial exhibition and received much recognition for a series of works that she began as a memorial after the World War.

256. "Anna Lea Merritt (obituary)." *Art News* (12 April 1930): 14.

> Anna Lea Merritt died on April 7th in London at the age of eighty-five. Merritt's long career included exhibitions at the Philadelphia Centennial, the Chicago Exhibitions, the Pennsylvania Academy of Fine Arts, and the Royal Academy. The high point of her career was the purchase in 1890 of *Love Locked Out* by the Chantry Fund, but she exhibited at the Royal Academy until 1906. She painted a portrait of James Russell Lowell, which hangs in Harvard's Memorial Hall.

257. Charteris, Evan. *The Life and Letters of Sir E. Gosse*. London: Harper Brothers, 1931.

In a letter to his father dated 24 October 1874, Gosse confided his wish to marry Nellie Epps, one of five daughters, of whom four were artists. He spoke to Nellie's aunt, who told him Nellie was determined not to marry, since she wanted to make her own living and intended to secure her independence through diligent application to her art. Gosse persevered, since he was convinced his happiness depended on her marrying him. Gradually, Nellie gave in. Her art career became neither an obstacle nor an issue, since Gosse never mentioned it again.

258. Robertson, W. Graham. *Time Was*. London: Hamish Hamilton, 1931.

The usual Victorian socializing and name-dropping includes Georgiana Burne-Jones, whose wonderful gray eyes Robertson admired very much. He finds Rossetti's fascination with Jane Morris' "mystic beauty" entirely justified, although he saw her as a simple person who was caught in the legend created by her portraits. Marie Spartali Stillman is "Mrs. Morris for beginners." Her classical Greek beauty is more obvious to the untrained eye. Robertson bought Whistler's portrait of artist Rosa Corder and considered it to be one of Whistler's masterpieces; he describes Corder as having a "beautiful stillness." Helen Allingham appears as "the well-known painter of cottages and country lanes" whose kindness, humor and wisdom made her a valued friend. Robertson recalls her sitting with her sketchbook and easel in ditches, nettles and on the walls of pigstys in order to obtain just the right view for painting.

259. Bickley, Francis. *The Pre-Raphaelite Comedy*. London: Constable, 1932.

Elizabeth Siddall seems to have been a different person to each man who knew her; her true identity was lost in the overwhelming presence of a social world alien to the one in which she was raised. Even her paintings and drawings are credited with a genius that, like her beauty, is probably in the minds of the men who created the woman they wanted her to be--as she related to themselves and their lives. Her opposite was Fanny Cornforth, who was as forceful as Siddall was passive, as voluptuous as Siddall was wraith-like, as unabashedly common as Siddall was refined.

260. Hunt, Violet. *The Wife of Rossetti: Her Life and Death*. New York: Dutton, 1932.

Drawing from personal remembrances, family relationships, and life-long acquaintances, Violet Hunt attempts to draw the Pre-Raphaelite men and women out of historical and academic realms and recreate them into whole cloth. The result is chatty, gossipy, bristling with cheerful footnotes and willful non-sequiturs.

Reproductions (b/w):

Boyce, G. P.: *Annie Miller*

Brown, Ford Madox: *Mrs. Ford Madox Brown as Cinderella*

Rossetti, Dante Gabriel: *Elizabeth Eleanor Siddall; Fanny Hughes*

Photos (b/w):

Elizabeth Siddall; Jane Burden; Mrs. Burne-Jones; Mrs. Burne-Jones and 'Pip'; Mrs. William Morris; Fanny Hughes.

261. Larg, David. *Trial by Virgins, Fragment of a Biography.* London: Davies, 1933.

A speculative, somewhat cynical, but hardly clever biography of Dante Gabriel Rossetti that ends with Rossetti placing his poetry manuscript in Elizabeth Siddall's coffin.

262. "Lady Butler [obituary]." *Times* (4 October 1933): 17.

Elizabeth Butler was keenly observant, unfailingly optimistic, and remarkably unworldly. Her success in art never went to her head, and in spite of her "virile talent," she was quite feminine. She loved music, and was an accomplished linguist, but her increasing deafness kept her from being a brilliant conversationalist.

263. "Current Art Notes. Lady Butler." *Connoisseur* 92 (November 1933): 341-342.

While the death of Lady Elizabeth Butler at age eighty-two means little to the modern art world, her great skill at military paintings "exercised a considerable influence on British art" in the last century. Butler, who married in 1877, continued to exhibit "a long series of pictures which established and consolidated her reputation." Butler's success not only revived English military painting, but helped other female artists to achieve recognition.

264. Long, Basil S. "Mrs. Mee, Miniature Painter [obituary]." *Connoisseur* , no. 95 (April 1935): 218-221.

Anne Foldson Mee supported her widowed mother and eight siblings, and later supported her own husband and a half-dozen of her own children with her miniature portraits. Horace Walpole complained that she took too long to deliver several pictures he paid for in advance. After her marriage, her portrait commissions were limited by her husband's injunctions that she paint neither male subjects nor female subjects accompanied by men. Later in life, presumably after his death, she again painted male sitters, first exhibited in the Royal Academy in 1804, and continued her work as a fashionable and recognized miniaturist almost up to the time of her death in 1851 at the age of seventy-six.

Reproductions (b/w):

Mee, Anne Foldson: *Two Portraits of Young Women; Portrait of Lady Anne Adby; Portrait of Miss Elliot; Portrait of Maria Jeanetta Beauclerk, Duchess of St Albans.*

265. Laver, James. *Vulgar Society: The Romantic Career of James Tissot: 1836-1902.* London: Constable, 1936.

Kathleen Newton appears as a mysterious, nameless *grande passion* in this account of artist James Tissot's career. Laver's speculations are drawn from Newton's appearance in Tissot's paintings, and from chance comments of Tissot's acquaintants. Newton's death is attributed not to tuberculosis, as is the generally-accepted version, but to her suicide following a misdirected letter in which Tissot told a friend he was tired of the affair with Newton and wanted out; she reportedly threw herself out of a bedroom window and died of her injuries.

266. Sitwell, Sacheverell. *Dance of the Quick and the Dead.* London: Faber, 1936.

Elizabeth Siddall and Algernon Swinburne were drawn together by his fascination with life and her preoccupation with death. In their beauty, their red hair, and their disregard of convention, they embody the Aesthetic Movement. Using Violet Hunt's imagination and his own poetic license, Sitwell recreates Siddall's last night, her death, and her exhumation nine years later.

267. Troxell, Janet Camp ed. *Three Rossettis: Unpublished Letters to and From Dante Gabriel, Christina, William.* Cambridge: Harvard University Press, 1937.

The correspondence concerning the "ghastly business" of digging up Elizabeth Siddall's body to resurrect Dante Gabriel Rossetti's manuscript is carefully preserved, probably by Rossetti's friend Howells, who was not given to keeping confidences. Rossetti was staying at the home of Alice Boyd when the deed was accomplished.

Reproductions (b/w):

Rossetti, Dante Gabriel: *Lizzie Siddal; Fanny Schott* (Cornforth).

268. Canziana, Estella. *Round About Three, Palace Green.* London: Methuen, 1939.

Estella Canziana remembers her life at Number Three, Palace Green, where she grew up; she credits her mother, Louisa Starr Canziana, with breaking the barrier preventing women from studying at the Royal Academy School. According to Canziana, in 1862 she submitted a drawing signed "L. Starr" with her application, and upon being admitted on the strength of her work, pointed out to the dismayed academicians that no written rule excluded women from Royal Academy schools.

Reproductions (b/w):

Canziani, Louisa Starr: *David with the Head of Goliath before Saul; Self Portrait; The Author's Father; The Author's Grandmother at the age of 18; The Author's Uncle; The Author's Grandmother; The Eternal Door; War News.*

269. Storey, Gladys. *Dickens and Daughter*. London: Muller, 1939.

Just as *Dombey and Son* is more about Dombey than son, *Dickens and Daughter* has more Dickens than daughter. Little time is spent on Kate Dickens Perugini's painting career, but Annie Swynnerton makes a lively appearance in several pages near the end of the book. Swynnerton was irritated at the Royal Academy for waiting until she was seventy-seven to make her the first female associate; after her election she sent paintings that the Academy had once rejected to exhibitions where "they found places on the line." Other useful information: Perugini is pronounced with a soft "g" and Ellen Ternan, Dickens' mistress, pronounced her last name "Ter-*nan*."

270. Lowndes, Mrs.Belloc (Marie Adelaide Belloc). *I, Too, Have Lived in Arcadia; A Record of Love and Childhood*. London: Macmillan, 1941.

Bessie Parkes, author, suffragist and mother of two well-known writers, was a life-long friend of Barbara Bodichon. Parkes' daughter's biography contains recollections and quotes from Bodichon's letters that reveal a blunt, forthright woman and a loyal friend. Parkes and Bodichon were personal friends of Elizabeth Siddall. Parkes, who visited Siddall on the day she died, was convinced her death was accidental.

271. Birkenhead, Sheila. *Against Oblivion: The Life of Joseph Severn*. London: Cassell, 1944.

A somewhat confused chapter titled "Mary" gives glimpses of a woman of spirit and humor. The main support of a family plagued with financial troubles, Mary Severn's great talent for portraits of children led to commissions to paint several of Queen Victoria's offspring. Severn died at thirty-four of measles contracted from a child model.

Reproductions (b/w):

Severn, Mary: *Portrait of Joseph Severn; Self-Portrait*.

272. Burton, Hester. *Barbara Bodichon: 1827-1891*. London: John Murray, 1949.

Details of Bodichon's art and humanitarian efforts are secondary to an affectionate account of her personal life and her warm and lively personality.

Reproductions (b/w):

Bodichon, Barbara: Sketches and drawings

Photo and portrait of Bodichon.

273. Doughty, Oswald. *Dante Gabriel Rossetti: A Victorian Romantic*. New Haven: Yale University Press, 1949.

Barbara Bodichon and Anna Mary Howitt befriended Elizabeth Siddall and were anxious about her health. They took her for walks and found her recuperation cottages. They encouraged Dante Gabriel Rossetti in his relationship with her, doing everything they could to enhance her image. Both Rossetti and Siddall, however, were dogged by unrest and melancholy; their depressions fueled each other, dooming them both to drugs and tragic early deaths.

Reproductions (b/w):

Rossetti, Dante Gabriel: *Beatrice Denying Her Salutation to Dante* (Elizabeth Siddall as model); *Dante Drawing an Angel* (Elizabeth Siddall as model); *Elizabeth Eleanor Siddal* (portrait).

274. Hubbard, Hesketh. *A Hundred Years of British Painting: 1851-1951*. London: Longman's, 1951.

Women artists began to make serious progress in the 1850's after Fanny Corbeaux and a number of her colleagues stormed the lecture room of the Royal Academy and after the Society of Female Artists was established in 1857. A woman was admitted to the Royal Academy schools by mistake in 1860; the Royal Academy closed admission to women until it could build separate facilities for female students. Women artists protested their exclusion in a petition to the House of Commons in 1864. Elizabeth Thompson Butler's battle paintings were popular because of their size and detail. She knew nothing about army life, but was probably coached by her soldier husband. Lucy Kemp-Welch's *Colt-Hunting in New Forest* was purchased by the Chantrey fund for £535; in 1922 she painted the last of the murals in the Royal Exchange. Annie Swynnerton's election in 1922 as a Royal Academy Associate and Laura Knight's service on the Hanging Committee in 1937 are landmarks in Royal Academy history.

Reproductions (b/w):

Knight, Laura: *Spring in Cornwall.*

275. Procter, Ida. "Elizabeth Siddal: The Ghost of an Idea." *The Cornhill Magazine* (December 1951): 368-386.

A careful examination of what is known of Siddall's life reveals a woman whose elusive personality contributed greatly to her contemporary and modern image as enigmatic and remote.

Reproductions (b/w):

Siddall, Elizabeth: *Lady Claire; Lady Affixing Pennon to Knight's Spear.*

276. Woodring, Carl Ray. *Victorian Samplers: William and Mary Howitt.* Lawrence: University of Kansas Press, 1952.

A short biography of William and Mary Howitt, whose many friends included literary and artistic greats, gives short glimpses of their daughter, Anna Mary Howitt, whose patrons included philanthropist Angela Burdett-Coutts. Margaret Gillies and Elizabeth Siddall make brief appearances.

277. Hall, Henry C. *Artists and Sculptors of Nottingham and Nottinghamshire 1750-1950.* Nottingham: Herbert Jones, 1953.

Short biographies of Nottinghamshire artists include eleven women who worked and exhibited in and out of the area, several of whom are represented in the permanent collection of the Nottingam Castle Art Gallery. The ranking list is topped by Kate Greenaway, who is claimed as a native daughter since she had roots and her university education in Nottingham. The women specialized in painting flowers, animals, children, still lifes, and miniatures.

278. Reynolds, Graham. *Painters of the Victorian Scene.* London: Batsford, 1953.

The works of two women artists appear in this compendious volume: Jane Maria Bowkett's *Preparing Tea* is deemed "amateurish." Sophie Anderson's *No Walk Today* is presented without comment.

Reproductions (b/w):

Anderson, Sophie: *No Walk Today*

Bowkett, Jane Maria: *Preparing Tea.*

279. Short, Ernest. *A History of British Painting*. London: Eyre and Spottiswoode, 1953.

While no representative illustrations of women's work are included, chapter eighteen, "Britain's Women Painters," mentions female contributors from fourteenth-century England through the twentieth. Elizabeth Thompson Butler's failure to be admitted to Royal Academy membership is seen as incomprehensible, but later elections of Annie Louisa Swynnerton and Laura Knight begin to close the gap. Lucy Kemp-Welch and Henrietta Rae win brief mention as nineteenth-century achievers.

280. Angeli, Helen Rossetti. *Pre-Raphaelite Twilight: The Story of Charles Augustus Howell*. London: Richards, 1954.

A chapter titled "Rosa Corder" credits Corder not only for her friendship with Howell, Whistler and Rossetti, but for her dedication to her own art and her accomplished pictures of horses. Fanny Cornforth, Jane Morris and Lucy Madox Rossetti's lives cross the pages; Elizabeth Siddall's relationship with Dante Gabriel Rossetti is described as good for neither party. Rossetti's internment of his manuscript with Siddall's body and its subsequent exhumation convey a mood of sympathy and delicacy of feelings on the part of those involved.

Reproductions (b/w):

Whistler, J. M.: *Arrangement in Black and Brown (Rosa Corder)*.

281. "Mrs. H. Sargant-Florence: Painting in a Difficult Medium [Obituary]." *The London Times* (16 December 1954): 10.

Her achievements as a muralist in ancient and modern techniques make the work of Mary Sargant-Florence a challenge to Michelangelo's statement that fresco painting is for men. Her work can be seen in dozens of important buildings throughout Great Britain. Cartoons for two murals, *Suffer the Little Children...* and *Pentecost* were exhibited at the Royal Academy and bought by the Chantrey Bequest Fund in 1933. Her scholarship in researching the techniques of old masters and publication of her book, *Color Coordination*, reflect a keen intellect combined with artistic talent to create a long and highly-productive career.

282. Waugh, Evelyn. "The Only Pre-Raphaelite." *The Spectator* CCV, no. 6903 (14 October 1960): 567.

Fanny Waugh, second wife of Pre-Raphaelite painter Holman Hunt, is accurately portrayed, as Evelyn Waugh remembers her, in Diana Holman-Hunt's novel *My Grandmothers and I*. Evelyn Waugh provides some additional information about Fanny Waugh, but much of her life and personality remain an enigma; certainly she doted on Holman-Hunt, who was, by some accounts, a rather disagreeable and eccentric figure.

283. Fredeman, William E. "Pre-Raphaelites in Caricature: *The Choice of Paris: An Idyll.*" *Burlington Magazine* 102 (November 1960): 523-529.

    The June 1860 issue of *The Illustrated London News* contains a full-page engraving of and accompanying commentary on a detailed parody of Pre-Raphaelite models and subjects. The work itself is far more subtle, sophisticated and detailed than the contemporary description. Adelaide Claxton's biting visual commentary reflects the bitter criticism leveled at the Pre-Raphaelite painters and their aesthetic concepts.

    Reproductions (b/w):

    Claxton, *Florence: The Choice of Paris: An Idyll.*

284. Baldwin, A. W. *The Macdonald Sisters.* London: Peter Davies, 1961.

    The chapter titled "The Burne-Joneses 1860-1920" contains more about Edward than about Georgie. On the whole, this biography is similar to Ina Taylor's *Victorian Sisters*, but is more subjective, and focuses more on the male relatives and acquaintances than on the sisters themselves.

    Reproductions (b/w):

    Portraits of Georgiana Burne-Jones.

285. Birkenhead, Sheila. *Illustrious Friends: The Story of Joseph Severn and His Son Arthur.* New York: William Morrow, 1965.

    The information about Mary Severn is nearly identical to what Birkenhead gives in *Against Oblivion*. New plates include caricatures and a self-portrait by Mary.

    Reproductions (b/w):

    Severn, Mary: *Portrait of Joseph Severn; Self-Portrait.*

286. Knight, Laura. *The Magic of a Line: The Autobiography of Laura Knight.* London: William Kimber, 1965.

    Laura Knight's autobiography reflects the transition from the Victorian to the modern period. She was born in 1877, experienced many of the limitations imposed on female artists of the time, but hard work, determination, a strong sense of adventure and a tremendous interest in life brought her freedom, recognition, and full membership in the Royal Academy.

    Reproductions (b/w):

Knight, Laura: *Boxing; From the Flies; Massine and Karsarvna; The Golden Girl; Elsie on Hassan; Spanish Dancers; A Box at the Folies Bergères; Powder and Paint; A Fair; Hampstead Heath; Girls Climbing to Trapeze; Trio Gymnastique; Beulah's Necklace; The Sick Gypsy; The Jester; Dark Baby; Zebras; Allez-Oop; Hop-Picking; The Wardrobe Room--Stratford upon Avon; Dressing Room; A Shower at Ascot; Ethel; Backstage--Drury Lane; Girl Dressing*

Knight, Harold: *Portrait of Laura Knight at Sixteen*
Photos (b/w):
Laura Knight, 1965.

287. Ormond, Richard. "A Pre-Raphaelite Beauty." *Country Life* 138, no. 30 (30 December 1965): 1780-1781.

Intellectually and artistically gifted, Marie Spartali Stillman studied painting with Rossetti and modeled for Rossetti, Whistler, Burne-Jones and Madox Brown. Her own art shows a decided Pre-Raphaelite influence. Considered by many to be a great beauty, she may also be considered one of the more "intelligently and artistically gifted" of the women in the Pre-Raphaelite circle. By the time of her death in 1927, she was the last member of the group. Her daughter, Lisa Stillman, inherited her mother's artistic talent.

Reproductions (b/w):
Rossetti, Dante Gabriel: *A Vision of Fiametta*
Whistler, James McNeill: *La Princess du Pays de la Porcelaine.*

288. Allingham, Helen and D. Radford, eds. *William Allingham's Diary.* Carbondale, Illinois: Southern Illinois University Press, 1967.

A re-issue of the 1907 edition with some additions, but no new information about Helen Allingham's painting.

289. Bell, Quentin. *Victorian Artists.* Cambridge, Massachusetts: Harvard, 1967.

Henrietta Rae's *Apollo and Daphne* does not depict what Bell considers normal behavior between males and females. He sees Laura Knight's *Flying a Kite* as an early example of British Impressionism. The Pre-Raphaelite's renditions of women, he feels, are exploitative and unrealistic, but he recognizes an effort to be "humane, tender, and delicate."

Reproductions (b/w):
Knight, Laura: *Flying a Kite*
Rae, Henrietta: *Apollo and Daphne.*

290. Day, Harold A. E. *East Anglian Painters. Vol. I*. Eastbourne, Sussex: Sumfield & Day, 1967.

>Emma Smythe, a sister of Ipswich artist E. R. Smythe, taught drawing and painted in watercolors.

291. McCourt, Edward. *Remember Butler: The Story of Sir William Butler*. London: Routledge, 1967.

>Elizabeth's husband hated *The Defense of Rorke's Drift* and *After the Battle* because both depicted what he considered shameful British victories over disadvantaged peoples.

292. Roberts, Jane. *Royal Artists from Mary Queen of Scots to the Present Day*. London: Grafton, 1967.

>An account of the artistic training and talents of members of the British royal family includes detailed discussions of the amateur painting of Queen Victoria and the professional-quality painting and sculpture of her daughter, Princess Louise.

>Reproductions (in col and b/w):

>Queen Victoria and Princess Louise: Sketches and paintings.

293. Ames, Winslow. *Prince Albert and Victorian Taste*. New York: Viking, 1968.

>Even though Prince Albert, and therefore, Queen Victoria, must have known that Effie Grey's marriage to John Ruskin was never consummated, the Queen refused to receive Effie until requested to do so by Effie's dying second husband, John Everett Millais.

294. Cecil, David. *"Visionary and Dreamer: Two Poetic Painters: Samuel Palmer and Edward Burne-Jones."* The A. W. Mellon Lectures in the Fine Arts vol. 15. Bollingen series vol. 35, Princeton: Princeton University Press, 1969.

>Hannah Linell Palmer was a conventional, unimaginative, religious woman, dominated by her autocratic father, and more or less ignored by Samuel Palmer, her reclusive, eccentric artist husband. Georgiana Burne-Jones' talent, power, and presence carried her through her husband's scandalous affair with Marie Zambaco and his more discreet involvements with Mrs. Norton, Mrs. Gaskell, May Morris, and Frances Graham Horner. Georgiana's friendship with William Morris helped her to remain loyal to her husband, while Morris' wife, Jane Burden, became increasingly involved with Dante Gabriel Rossetti, who found solace with Burden after his own wife, Elizabeth Siddall, died of a laudanum overdose.

Reproductions (b/w):

Burne-Jones, Edward: *Portrait of Georgiana Burne-Jones; Portrait Group of Painter's Family: Lady Burne-Jones with Son Philip and Daughter Margaret; Portrait of Frances Horner, née Graham*

Dante, Gabriel Rossetti: *Maria Zambaco née Cassavetti.*

295. Nicoll, John. *The Pre-Raphaelites.* New York: Dutton, 1970.

The chapter on Dante Gabriel Rossetti contains a brief history of Elizabeth Siddall's relationship with him. The text contains four of his portrait sketches of her. Her own work is described as powerful, "dreamlike and idealized" and directly influenced by Rossetti's teaching. Her death is seen as a turning point in his life and in his art. Marie Spartali Stillman is mentioned as Rossetti's model, Ford Madox Brown's pupil, W. J. Stillman's wife, and in her own right, "perhaps the most important American Pre-Raphaelite painter."

Reproductions (b/w):

Siddall, Elizabeth: *Clerk Saunders; Sir Patrick Spens*

Stillman, Marie Spartali: *The Covenant Lily.*

296. Sonstroem, David. *Rossetti and the Fair Lady.* Middletown, Connecticut: Wesleyan University Press, 1970.

Dante Gabriel Rossetti's fantasies about women fall into four categories: mystical, *femme fatale*, fallen prostitute, and victimized woman. He needed Elizabeth Siddall to become a passive Florentine ideal, and she discovered that in order to keep his interest she must be passive and ill. She was possibly, as a result, neurotic, lonely, and given to hysterical rages. She became a *femme fatale*, a kind of Lilith figure who destroys her lover rather than being destroyed by him. People like Ruskin, who were not caught up in the Pre-Raphaelite medieval romanticism, saw her as plain, even homely. When Siddall failed as a Beatrice, becoming the familiar "Guggums" and "Sid," Rossetti turned to Jane Morris, whom he saw as both divine and as a sexual temptress.

Reproductions (b/w):

Rossetti, Dante Gabriel: drawing of Elizabeth Siddall.

297. Allingham, Helen and E. Baumer Williams, eds. *Letters to William Allingham.* 1911. Reprint. New York: AMS Press, 1971.

A letter from George Eliot expresses the hope that the Allingham's new baby will not "greatly hinder Mamma's pencil" and asks if Helen Allingham would be willing to provide illustrations for an upcoming edition of *Romola.* A letter written by Helen Allingham's husband describes her happiness as she works on some paintings of Surrey cottages for a London exhibition. Barbara Bodichon writes of her own love for her art, saying she prefers painting to "long sojourns in stifling rooms with miserable people."

298. Burne-Jones, Georgiana. *Memorials of Edward Burne-Jones.* New York: Benjamin Blom, Inc., 1971.

When Georgiana Burne-Jones met Jane Morris for the first time, she was so struck with her that she dreamed of her the same night. The Morris' housekeeper, a paragon of feminine capability known only as "Red Lion Mary" made clothes for models and embroidered hangings designed by William Morris. Elizabeth Siddall seemed to be always in wretched health.

299. Smith, Christine. "Rosa Bonheur: How She Was Victimized by the (Male) Critics." *Women and Art* (December 1971): 1, 4-6, 20.

The excellence of Rosa Bonheur's work and her choice of subjects and personal dress resulted in some confusion on the part of critics, who either insisted that she was a true paragon of femininity, or, like John Ruskin, suggested that she was famous only because she was female.

Reproductions (b/w):

Bonheur, Rosa: *Sheep on the Pyrenees.*

300. Bodichon, Barbara Leigh Smith. "*An American Diary 1857-8.*" Reed, Joseph W., ed. London: Routledge, 1972.

Barbara Bodichon's sketches and paintings of southern America were exhibited in London in 1861 and received a favorable review from the *Athenaeum.* She also had sketches in an exhibit of British artists that toured major U.S. cities in 1858. Her 2 June 1858 journal records her visit to the exhibit in Boston and her excitement at seeing SOLD on two of her pictures.

301. Knox, Katherine McCook. *The Sharples: Their Portraits of George Washington and His Contemporaries.* New York: Kennedy Graphics, 1972.

Rolinda Sharples' mother's diary records the family's artistic activities in England and the United States. Rolinda's journals are shorter and less descriptive. Her untimely death from cancer in 1838 ended the career of a talented painter of portraits and landscapes.

Reproductions (b/w):
Sharples, Rolinda: *Mrs James Sharples.*

302. Surtees, Virginia ed. *Sublime and Instructive: Letters from John Ruskin to Louisa, Marchioness of Waterford, Anna Blunden and Ellen Heaton.* London: Michael Joseph, 1972.

Surtees prefaces the letters from Ruskin to Anna Blunden with a background sketch describing how Blunden gave up her position as governess and went to London to study art after reading Ruskin's *Modern Painters.* Ruskin's letters to Blunden (there are none from her to him) frequently reflect his irritation at her affection for him and for her persistence in asking his advice. At times he is patient and helpful; more often he is patronizing and appallingly sexist. Critics tend to remark on Blunden's "relentless pursuit" of her hero; that the hero chose to reply to her letters with what often amounts to abuse suggests a curious relationship between the two.

Reproductions (b/w):
Blunden, Anna: *Lakes of Killarney.*

303. Taylor, Gerald. *Centenary Works by Eleanor Fortescue-Brickdale.* Oxford: Ashmolean Museum, 1972.

Eleanor Fortescue-Brickdale studied at the Royal Academy Schools, won medals for her designs, and founded her reputation on works in black and white, several of which were exhibited at the Royal Academy. Her main focus was designs and illustrations for books and bookplates; she illustrated an edition of *Ivanhoe* for Bell & Sons in 1899. Her distinguished career, which began late in the nineteenth century with two oils in the Royal Academy exhibit, was marked by consistent versatility, productivity, recognition, and social and artistic contributions until the late 1930's, when she was still designing stained-glass windows for a major firm. She died in 1945 and is buried in a London cemetery.

304. Hall, Marshall. *Artists of Northumbria.* Newcastle Upon Tyne: Marshall Hall Associates, 1973.

An alphabetical list with biographical sketches and mention of principal works and exhibitions.

305. Staley, Allen. *The Pre-Raphaelite Landscape.* Clarendon: Oxford, 1973.

Anna Blunden is among the artists whose early work reflecting outdoor studies from nature earned praise from John Ruskin. Alice Boyd, who has a watercolor in the British Museum, and Rosa Brett, who also exhibited under the name "Rosarius," are among the amateur Pre-Raphaelite landscape painters who were friends or relatives of the better-known group.

306. Haworth, Helen E. "'A Thing of Beauty is a Joy Forever': Early Illustrated Editions of Keats' Poetry." *Harvard Library Bulletin* 21, no. pt 1 (January 1973): 88-103.

In 1912 the Keats-Shelley Association held a grand fundraiser, the program for which featured drawings and paintings which illustrated Keats' work. Illustrations of "Isabella" that are especially popular include Henrietta Rae's *Isabella: or the Pot of Basil.*

307. Sutton, Denys. "Editorial - The Prisoner." *Apollo* , no. 27 (February 1973): 120-126.

Lizzie Siddall and Jane Morris haunted Dante Gabriel Rossetti in his lifetime, as his work haunts Victorian art now.

308. Spencer, Isobel. "Frances Newberry and the Glasgow Style." *Apollo* (October 1973): 286-293.

Jessie Rowat Newberry, the wife of the head of the Glasgow School of Art, studied and later taught classes in design and embroidery. Her work uses natural forms and a strong linear design. While it is not known if Frances and Margaret Macdonald actually took classes from her, it is certain that Newberry influenced their art.

309. Johnson, Oscar and Peter, Ltd. "Four Oil Paintings by Eloise Harriet Stannard." *Apollo* (December 1973): 52.

The ad features two of Eloise Stannard's oil still-lifes with fruit.
Reproductions (col):
Stannard, Eloise Harriet: *Grapes, Pineapple, Peaches, Plums and Other Fruits; Peaches, Plums and Redcurrants.*

310. Brown, Susan ed. *The Art and Mind of Victorian England: Paintings from the Forbes Magazine Collection.* London: Lund Humphries, 1974.

Sophie Anderson's *Guess Again*, a cheerful portrait of two Italian children, can be considered escapist because of its playful theme, its provincial setting, and the fact that it ignores the struggle for independence taking place in Italy at the time. Edith Hayllar was unusual in her choice of sports scenes, but typical in that she abandoned her art after her marriage. Mrs. Craik's novel *Olive* seems to depict the lives of both Edith and her sister, Jessica. Jessica, who was crippled and never married, continued to paint.

Reproductions (b/w):

Anderson, Sophie: *Guess Again*

Hayllar, Edith: *A Summer Shower*.

311. Dent, Anthony ed. *The Horse Through Fifty Centuries of Civilization*. London: Phaidon, 1974.

Lucy Kemp-Welch worked at a remount depot in 1917 and painted the horses used to move equipment in World War I.

Reproductions (b/w):

Butler, Elizabeth Thompson: *The Charge of the Scots Greys at Waterloo*

Kemp-Welch, Lucy: *Timber-Hauling; Colt Hunting in the New Forest; Forward the Guns*.

312. Ash, Russell. "English Paintings of 1874." *Connoisseur* (January 1974): 33-34.

Some of the best work of the nineteenth century was exhibited at the Royal Academy in 1874. Elizabeth Thompson's *The Roll Call* was by far the most popular. Thompson attached much importance to accuracy, using real soldiers for models and carefully researching details concerning uniforms and equipment.

313. Wood, Christopher. "The Artistic Family Hayllar. Part 2: Jessica, Edith, Mary and Kate." *Connoisseur* (May 1974): 2-9.

All four of the Hayllar sisters exhibited at the Royal Academy. The private instruction received from their painter-father, James Hayllar, enabled them to escape the tradition-bound art schools and resulted in a direct and fresh artistic style. The oldest sister, Edith, is best remembered for her sports subjects. Jessica, who had been crippled in a carriage accident and confined to a wheelchair, painted flowers and interior scenes. Mary gave up painting after her marriage; Kate stayed single and cared for her widowed father. All of the Hayllars stopped painting about 1900 after moving from Castle Priory, whose halls, long windows, arched doorways and spacious rooms seemed to inspire them. Their domestic scenes, using each other as models, are some of the best representations of middle-class Victorian family life.

Reproductions (b/w):

Hayllar, Edith: *Afternoon Tea; Jack Ashore; A Toast; Tommy's School Hamper*

Hayllar, Jessica: *Finishing Touches; Kittens; The Return from Confirmation; Some of the Choir; The Spirit is Willing.*

314. Irwin, David and Francina. *Scottish Painters at Home and Abroad: 1700-1900's.* London: Faber, 1975.

Alice Boyd's friendship with William Bell Scott was intense, long-lasting and not at all improper. The Macdonald sisters' work kept within the themes popular at the end of the nineteenth century, which combined mysticism, religion and nature. Of the Glasgow group, Jessie King's work ranks among the most beautiful, although its scope is limited to medieval themes. The Scottish painter Alexander Nasmyth had seven daughters; he trained each of them so they could teach at his popular art school. They also joined him in a boycott of the Edinburgh Art Society. Nasmyth's later paintings were done mostly by his daughters with enough of his own work imposed to enable him to sign them. Charlotte Nasmyth is the subject of a National Gallery portrait by Andrew Geddes. Queen Victoria, a competent amateur artist, did much to promote and to encourage Scottish artists.

Reproductions (b/w):

King, Jessie M: *Pelléas et Mélisande*

Macdonald, Frances: *Ill Omen.*

315. Munsterberg, Hugo. *A History of Women Artists.* New York, NY: Clarkson N. Potter, 1975.

Rosa Bonheur's status as the best-known female artist of her day may have led to her work being somewhat over-rated. Two of her female contemporaries, Mary Cassatt and Berthe Morisot, were probably better artists. Kate Greenaway is the first and one of the best female printmakers. A solid education at the South Kensington Art School and Slade School at Oxford, exhibitions at the Dudley Gallery and membership in the Institute of Painters of Watercolors attest to her talent and versatility.

Reproductions (b/w):

Bonheur, Rosa: *The Horse Fair*

Greenaway, Kate: *Polly put the Kettle on; Tom, Tom, the Piper's Son.*

316. Reynolds, Jan. *The Williams Family of Painters.* Woodbridge, Suffolk: Antique Collector's Club, 1975.

Caroline Williams exhibited her landscapes with the Society of Lady Artists and the Society of British Artists. Sales from her paintings supported her artist-father in his old age. Since she signed her work "C.F. Williams" some of her paintings have been attributed to Charles Frederick Williams, but the styles of the two painters are quite different, especially in Caroline Williams' bold use of color. A list of "Works in Public Collections and Exhibitions" indicates a career active from 1858 to 1890. Kate Elizabeth Williams Gilbert's landscapes show good handling of color and strong influence by her father.

Reproductions (b/w):

Gilbert, Kate: *Landscape, Isle of Wight; Morning on the South Devon Coast*

Williams, Caroline Fanny: *River Landscape; Night on the Beach.*

317. Messum, David. *The Life and Work of Lucy Kemp-Welch.* Woodbridge: Suffolk: Baron, 1976.

Single-minded dedication, considerable talent, and a passion for animals made Lucy Kemp-Welch one of the foremost animal painters in art history. A protegé of the British artist Herkomer, she took over his school when he became too ill to run it, becoming a sought-after art teacher in her own right. In addition to thirty-three Royal Academy exhibitions, she painted posters for the government during World War I and was president of the Society of Animal Painters for many years.

Reproductions (col):

Kemp-Welch, Lucy: *The Gypsy Horse Drovers; Colt Hunting in the New Forest; The Riders; Stag's Head; Forward the Guns; Women's Work in the Great War; Elephants and the Big Top; Behind the Scenes; Hunters in the Orchard at Bushey with 'Trust'; Study of the Head of a Bay Horse; Waiting in the Shade; Study of Ducks Bathing in a Pond; Horse's Head Against the Skyline; White Carthorse; Seagulls and the Incoming Tide; Going Strong; The Hay Wagon; Donkey and Foal in Bluebells; In the Sunset; Ponies on the Moor; In the Shadow; Waiting their Turn; Ambling Home*

Reproductions (b/w):

Kemp-Welch, Lucy: *In Sight! Lord Dundonald's Dash on Ladysmith; Foam Horses; Timber Hauling in the New Forest; The Waterway; The Straw Ride; Launching the Lifeboat; The Joy of Life; 'For Life' Exmoor; Timber Hauling at Ironshill, New Forest; Turning at the Cliff's Edge; Above the Cove; Bay Mare and Foal at Bushey; On the Other Side: Horses Grazing on the River Bank; The Gipsy Camp and Donkeys; A Dapple Grey in Sunlight; Queen of the Elephants; Head of White Horse with Colored Bridle; Bushey Church and Pond; Circus*

Ponies in their Stalls; Ploughing on the Downs; On the Sunset Cliff; The End of the Day; Head of a Carthorse Wearing a Yoke; Head of a Bay; Bay Tethered Under a Tree; Goats Grazing on the Purbeck Hills; The Cow Byre; Chestnut Horse Exercising; The Starting Post, Goodwood; Tired Out; Early Morning Ride at Russley; Forward to Victory--Enlist Now!; Bringing up the Guns; Exhausted: Troops and Horses in the Midday Shade; Driving the Gun Team; A New Forest Foal; Foals Grazing; A Short Rest: Study of Horses Drinking; Bluebells in the New Forest; A Jubilee Arch, Bushey; The Ford; Launching the Lifeboat; The Horse Drovers; The Blacksmith; The Afternoon Ride; St. Ives Harbour; The Passing Train; In the Pond; Sheep and Lambs Grazing; An Alsatian Dog; Head of a Hound; Lucem Spero; Study of a Boy Leading Horses; Study of Grey Shire Horse; New Forest Yearling; The White Pony; Study of White Horse; Patience: The Carthorse; Swimming About; Swans at Ipswich; Mare and Foal on the Moors; Horses and Soldiers Resting; Horses Wading in a Pond; Carthorses on the Track; Sketches and studies

Photos (b/w):

Photos of Lucy Kemp-Welch, friends, family, houses.

318. Edwards, Marion R. "Elizabeth Eleanor Siddall: the Age Problem." *Burlington Magazine* 119 (1977): 112.

According to her birth certificate, Elizabeth Siddall was born on 25 July 1829, making her twenty-one when she met Dante Gabriel Rossetti, thirty-one when she married him, and thirty-two when she died. It cannot be known whether it was from error or deception that census records list her as younger than she really was, but the discovery of the birth certificate clears up a long debated question.

319. Johnson, Peter and Ernle Money. *The Nasmyth Family of Painters.* Leigh-on-Sea, England: F. Lewis, 1977.

A chapter titled "The Nasmyth Daughters" includes biographical sketches of the six daughters whose landscape paintings were known and exhibited through most of the nineteenth century. An appendix provides titles, exhibitions, exhibition dates, and some sales figures.

Reproductions (b/w photos):

Nasmyth, Jane: *Landscape; Loch Katrine; A View of the Isle of Arran from the Ayrshire Coast; Scottish Landscape*

Nasmyth, Margaret: *Lake Scene; View of Kinfauns Castle; Perthshire; The Water of Leigh; The Falls of Clyde*

Nasmyth, Elizabeth: *Scottish Landscape*

Nasmyth (Mrs.Bennet), Anne Gibson: *Scottish Landscape; Windsor; Garden Scene*

Nasmyth, Charlotte: *Highland Pass; Hampstead Heath; Musselburgh; Landscape with Figures.*

320. Swanson, Vern. *Alma-Tadema: The Painter of the Victorian Vision of the Ancient World.* New York: Scribner's, 1977.

Lawrence Alma-Tadema married his pupil, Laura Theresa Epps, when she was seventeen. She raised Anna and Laurence, his daughters from his first marriage. Her paintings of Dutch-genre family scenes did not receive the prices or the recognition of his classical-genre paintings. She appears in many of his works, as do his daughters. Anna and Laurence received £100 each when he died; the Royal Academy received over £58,000. Both daughters died unmarried and in poverty.

Reproductions (col):

Alma-Tadema, Anna: *The Drawing Room; Townsend House*

Roman-genre paintings with Laura, Anna, and Laurence as models

Reproductions (b/w):

Alma-Tadema, Laura: *Self-Help* (detail); portraits of Laura, Anna, Laurence, and Alma-Tadema's first wife, Marie de Boisgirard.

321. Houfe, Simon. *The Dictionary of British Book Illustrators and Caricaturists, 1800-1914.* Woodbridge, Suffolk: The Antique Collectors' Club, 1978.

Alphabetical listings include dates, publications, exhibitions, society memberships and bibliographies. Many illustrators were also painters who exhibited regularly at the Royal Academy and major galleries.

Reproductions (col):

Greenaway, Kate: *A Gaudy Flower*

French, Annie: *A Garlanded Wedding*

Reproductions (b/w):

Kemp-Welch, Lucy: Original drawing for an illustration

Holden, Evelyn B. Illustration to *The House that Jack Built*

King, Jessie M. *Percival and the Damsel*

Benham, Jane E. Illustration to Longfellow's "Evangeline"

Edwards, Kate: *June Dream; Five Minutes Late!*

Holden, Evelyn: *Binnorie O Binnorie*

322. Lewis, Robert C. and Mark Samuels Lasner, eds. *Poems and Drawings of Elizabeth Siddall.* Wolfville, Nova Scotia: Wombat Press, 1978.

Sixteen poems, all about abandonment, death, and dying, suggest that Elizabeth Siddall was a very depressed person. A chronology of her short life, as well as a short preface, complement the poems and drawings.

Reproductions (col):

Siddall, Elizabeth: *Self Portrait; The Holy Family*

Reproductions (b/w):

Siddall, Elizabeth: *MacBeth; The Vanishing of Arthur; Eve of St. Agnes; Lady of Shalott; The Nativity; Two Marys at the Sepulchre; Sir Patrick Spens; Clerk Saunders* [two versions]; *Landscape; Design for a Capital; Portrait of the Artist's Sister; Clara Siddall; Self-Portrait, Seated.*

323. "*Ophelia:* Original Etching by Anna Lea Merritt." In *American Art and American Art Collections*, n.p., ed. Walter Montgomery. New York: Garland, 1978.

The painting that originated this engraving of Ophelia was exhibited at the Royal Academy. Merritt studied the faces of inmates of a mental institution in order to capture Ophelia's distracted state.

Reproductions (b/w etching):

Merritt, Anna Lea: *Ophelia.*

324. Nunn, Pamela Gerrish. "The Case History of a Woman Artist: Henrietta Ward." *Art History (U.K.)* vol. 1 pt. 3 (September 1978): 293-308.

Henrietta Ward's life and career serve as a case history of nineteenth-century women who followed artistic careers. Her parents encouraged her studies, she married an artist, had eight children, and steadfastly continued to paint and exhibit in the face of opposition and condescension from the art world. Critics discuss art by women in a separate category, as if gender, not talent, were the basis on which art is to be judged. Genre subjects, too, are thought to be allocated according to social notions of gender sensibilities: men receive commissions to paint powerful political figures and important state events; women, regardless of the scope of their capabilities, are commissioned to paint children and other women. Henrietta Ward, for example, painted the royal children, but public and state commissions went to her male colleagues.

325. Bauer, Carol and Lawrence Ritt. *Free and Ennobled: Source Readings in the Development of Victorian Feminism.* New York: Pergamon, 1979.

Barbara Bodichon's political self emerges without mention of her artistic achievements. She is given credit for being a talented artist, but emphasis is on her considerable achievement and efforts in establishing women's rights and women's education.

326. Callen, Anthea. *Women Artists of the Arts and Crafts Movement: 1870-1914*. New York: Pantheon, 1979.

The Arts and Crafts Movement was a social and economic movement as well as an artistic one. Women in all phases of design formed the backbone of an art movement that had tremendous impact on art history and on female opportunities in fine and applied arts.

Reproductions (b/w):

Morris, Jane and Burden, Elizabeth: Three embroidered panels based on Chaucer's "Illustrious Women"

Morris, May and Theodosia, Middlemore: *Orchard* potiére; Left half of an embroidered frieze

Traquair, Phoebe: Embroidered panels

Macdonald, Margaret: Design for menu of Mrs. Cranston's; "White Cockade" Exhibition Cafes

Macdonald, Margaret or Frances: Design for embroidery "Fledglings"

Macdonald, Margaret or Frances and MacNair, Herbert: Poster for the Glasgow Institute of Fine Art

King, Jessie: *Sorrow; She Threw Her Hair Backward*

French, Annie: *The Lace Train*

Levetus, Celia: Bookplate design

Fortescue-Brickdale, Eleanor: *The Lover's World*

Green, Elizabeth Shippen: *"Poor Little One!"*

Raeburn, Agnes: Poster for Glasgow Lecture Association

Smith, Jessie Wilcox: *Tom Reached and Clawed...*

Photos (b/w):

Group photo of Morris and Burne-Jones Families, 1874

Georgiana Burne-Jones reading, 1880

Morris and Burne-Jones children in a tree, 1874

Jane Morris holding May Morris, c. 1865

Jenny Morris c. 1890

May Morris c.1890

May Morris c.1886

May Morris c.1865

Margaret Macdonald c.1900

Fran and Jessie Newberry c. 1900.

327. Warner, Marina. *Queen Victoria's Sketchbook*. New York: Crown, 1979.

Victoria's childhood and adult life, both public and private, were recorded in lively detail with sketches and paintings which serve here to illustrate an informal account of her education, marriage, and travels. Victoria's watercolors are typical of the Victorian amateur who succeeded in capturing elusive moments with admirable talent and imagination.

Reproductions:

Queen Victoria: sketches, drawings and paintings in color and black and white.

328. Edwards, Marion R. "This Modestly Educated Girl from Southwark: The Family and Background of Elizabeth Siddall." *Family History*, no. 10 (April 1979): 189-198.

Census records, the *Post Office London Directory*, church records, workhouse and infirmary records provide names, dates, addresses and occupations not only for Elizabeth Siddall, but for her parents, siblings, and their descendants. Although the Siddall family name died out with the death of her childless brothers in 1908 and 1912, two of her sisters, Ann and Lydia, married and had children. Elizabeth Siddall's sister Clara was certified insane and died in an asylum in 1902. Her mother and brother James were both buried at Nunhead Cemetery, but their graves are no longer identifiable.

329. Larner, Gerald and Celia Larner. "Child-like Vision of an Artist." *Weekender: Glasgow Herald* (27 October 1979): 9.

Jessie King's book cover designs won a gold medal at the Turin exhibition, but her versatility made her one of the best-known and loved of the turn-of-the-century Glasgow artists. She worked on over 100 books, studied architecture in Paris, and, with her husband, developed an original design known as the Kirkcudbright Style, which is simpler and more versatile than the Art Nouveau from which it is derived. King designed simple pottery paintings later in life. She may be considered the last of the Glasgow-style artists.

330. Hobson, Anthony. *The Life and Art of J.W. Waterhouse, R.A.: 1849-1917*. London: Christie's, 1980.

Henrietta Rae's 1910 Academy picture, *Hylas and Nymphs*, a "mawkish" and "feeble" work, shamelessly plagiarizes Waterhouse's painting of the same title and composition.

331. North, Marianne. *A Vision of Eden. The Life and Work of Marianne North*. New York: Holt, Rinehart, 1980.

Marianne North was an independent woman of independent means with a passion for painting and plants. Her travels in search of exotic flora made her one of the most peripatetic of Victorian women. She gave London's Kew Gardens over eight hundred of her paintings and a building to put them in. Several species of plants and one genus are named after her.

Reproductions (col):

North, Marianne: Over 100 color plates of plants and landscapes from North and South America, the East, Europe and Africa.

Photos (b/w):

Marianne North at her easel; the Marianne North Gallery at Kew Gardens.

332. Ashton, Dore. *Rosa Bonheur: A Life and a Legend*. New York: Viking, 1981.

Well-illustrated with black and white photos, this informal biography of one of the most famous women in art attempts to reflect her independence, originality, talent, sensitivity, and tremendous intelligence.

333. Merritt, Anna Lea. *Love Locked Out: The Memoirs of Anna Lea Merritt with a Checklist of Her Works*, ed. Galina Gorokhoff. Boston: Museum of Fine Arts, 1981.

Portrait painters, wrote Anna Lea Merritt, must not only possess technical skill, they must also be able to engage the mind of the sitter in order to capture a particular expression that makes a portrait more than a mere likeness. Children are especially difficult because they must be made to hold still without their being aware of it. A work of art must "convey thought or emotion from one human mind to another." The same story-telling skills that must have kept her subjects still and attentive are evident in Merritt's memoirs as she relates key events in her life and career as one of the most sought-after painters in England and America.

Reproductions (b/w):

Merritt, Anna Lea: *Jacqueline and Isaura Loraine; Miss Mildred Carter; Grandmother's Boa; Little Quakeress; The Shipley Sisters; Gwen; Marion Lea; Dorothea Beale; Mrs. William Henry Rawle; The Three Sons of Horace Howard Furness; Joseph Leidy; James Russell Lowell; General John Adams Dix; Horace Howard Furness; Sir William Boxall in Later Life with His Dog, Garibaldi; Watchers of the Straight Gate; Love Locked Out; A Patrician Mother; War; The Helping Hand;*

The Happy Valley; When the World was Young; Merry Maids; The Limes; Phlox and Nicotiana at Moonstoke House

Reproductions (col):

Merritt, Anna Lea: *Marion Lea with Violin; Josephine Low; From Hurstbourne Hill; Sheep Approaching Fill the Road*

Photos (b/w):

Anna Lea Merritt, 1885 and 1913.

334. Crabbe, John. "An Artist Divided." *Apollo* 113, no. 231 (May 1981): 311-313.

Barbara Leigh Smith Bodichon's paintings are primarily landscapes, rarely containing figures or buildings. She delighted in capturing clouds, storms, water, trees and rugged coasts, mountains and cliffs. While she studied with many influential artists, her style is very much her own. She first exhibited at the Royal Academy at age twenty-three; several other well-established galleries and societies exhibited her work and in 1857-58 some of her drawings of the Louisiana landscape were exhibited in Washington. Her work as a social reformer kept her from achieving her full potential as an artist, but the power and skill evident in her pictures may yet gain her deserved recognition.

Reproduction (b/w):

Bodichon, Barbara Leigh Smith: *Trees with Haystacks; Hastings Beach with Fishing Boats*

Photos (b/w):

Photo of Barbara Bodichon.

335. McKerrow, Mary. *The Faeds: A Biography*. Edinburgh: Canongate, 1982.

The story of Susan Bell Faed, artist-sister of painters John, James and Thomas Faed, is sadly typical of many artistically-gifted women. The only daughter of a large family, she remained at home and unmarried in order to care for her mother, while her brothers pursued their respective careers. Her 1866 painting, *The Country Lass*, was exhibited at the Royal Academy, followed by *Rose Bradwardine* in 1867 and *Remember the Sweeper* in 1868. She also exhibited five pictures in the Royal Scottish Academy between 1867 and 1868, and two more in 1883 and 1884. Her brother James felt she would have had an eminent place in the art world had she applied herself, and found it wonderful that "she could do such good things with studying so little."

Reproductions (b/w):

Faed, Susan Bell: *Rose Bradwardine*
Portrait of Susan Bell Faed by James Faed.

336. Nunn, Pamela Gerrish. *The Mid-Victorian Woman Artist, 1850- 1879*. Ph.D. diss., University College, London: 1982.

An edited version of this comprehensive work is published as *Victorian Women Artists*. Scholars can benefit from the copious notes and expanded commentaries in this original version.

Reproductions (b/w):

Alldridge, Emily (Mrs. Crawford): *In the Nursery*

Allingham, Helen Paterson: *Will the Ice Bear?*; *Innocent*; *Thomas Carlyle*; *Dolorosa*

Anderson, Sophie: *Foundling Girls in Chapel*; *Tambourine*; *Neapolitan Girl*; *The Children's Story Book*; *No Walk Today*; *A Foundling*; *Red Riding Hood*; *On the Tiptoe of Expectation*; *The Studio*; *Elaine*; *Wait for Me*; *Ladybird, Ladybird*

Anonymous: *A Royal Artist, the Princess Louise*; *Art Students Exult over Mafkeing*; *Art Students Copying Pictures at the Louvre, Paris*; *The North London School of Drawing and Modeling, Camden Town Lunch Time*; *Correcting Pupil Work*; *Let Us Join the Ladies*; *Henrietta Ward and Princess Alice, Mixed Antique Class*; *Slade School*

Backhouse, Margaret: *Self-satisfied*; *Children Minding Their Mother's Stall*

Barker, Lucette (LEB): *'Come Forth, O Ye Children of Gladness'*

Blackburn, Jemima (Wedderburn): *Can the Leopard Change His Spots?*; *Sir Robert Peel Showing His Pictures*; *Water Ousel, Grey and Red Wagtails*

Blunden, Anna: *For One Short Hour*

Bodichon, Barbara: *Near Land's End*; *Arab Tomb near Algiers*; *Afternoon, a Sketch*; *An Aquaduct*; *untitled watercolors*; *Venice*; *detail of Venice*; *Barn at Rottingdean*; *Untitled, after Carot*; *Untitled, after Barbazon, Sold Goupil*; *The Sea at Hastings*; *Untitled, 1876*; *Stone Pine*; *Cedar Forest in the Snow*; *Arab Market, Blidah*; *Sketch for Kabyle Parliament*

Bonheur, Rosa: *The Horse Fair*; *Labourage in the Nivernais*

Bowkett, Jane: *Preparing for Tea*; *Afternoon in the Nursery*; *In an Ornamental Garden*; *Lucy Ashton at the Mermaiden's Fountain*; *Young Lady in a Conservatory*; *Promenade at Brighton*

Boyce, Joanna: *La Veneziana*; *The Child's Crusade*; *sketches*; *Leveret*; *Shanklin*; *untitled sketches*; *Sidney*; *untitled study*; *Peep-bo!*;

The Heathergather, Hindhead; The Babbacombe Boy; Bird of God; Vanessa; Italian Boy; Do I Like Butter?; No Joy the Blowing Season Brings (The Outcast); Sketches for Gretchen; *Undine;* untitled sketch; *Elgiva; Rowena Carrying the Cup of Voltigern; Sybil;* sketches for *Peep-Bo!*

Brett, John: Rosa Brett

Brett, Rosa: *Chicks; The Hayloft; Near the Sheep Wash; Oaks, Farnhurst; The Artist's Mother; Thistles;* untitled; *The Old House at Fairleigh; Study of a Turnip Field; Barming, Kent*

Brown, Catherine Madox: *Idleness in Industry*

Brown, Lucy Madox: *Romeo and Juliet; Margaret Roper*

Browne, Henriette: *An Eastern Beauty*

Brownlow, Emma: *Left in Charge; Cottage Interior, or the Baby Brother; Baby's First Shoes; A Skein of Worsted; The Foundling Restored to its Mother; The Sick Room; The Christening; Taking Leave; A Foundling Girl at Christmas Dinner; On Thoughts of Charity Intent; By the Gate;* sketches including *Hetty and the Squire; A 'Special' Taking Leave of His Family; The Lecturer; The Drawing Room and the Street; The Fashion of the Day; Vaccination by the Parish;* untitled; *Evangeline; Hammer; The Conscript's Departure; Lobesgang at Berne; Riverside at Quimper*

Burgess, Adelaide: *Girls Begging*

Burr, Margareta Higford: *Interior of the Arena Chapel in 1306*

Carpenter, Margaret: *John Gibson; Richard P. Bonington, The Sisters (the Artist's Daughters); Mother and Two Children; The Love Letter; Sir John Mordaunt; Archbishop Sumner; Augusta Thelusson*

Charretie, Anna: *What Shall Be My Song Tonight?*

Claxton, Adelaide: *Academy Belles; The First Monday at the Royal Academy Exhibition; At the Academy; The Good Time That's Coming; Ritualistic Enthusiasts; The 'Fancy' of the 'Fair'; The Grass Widow; Come unto These Yellow Sands; Ten Shillings a Night; A Romance in a Boarding House; Christmas Belles; The Daily Governess; I Cannot Sing the Old Songs; Miss Leslie's Song; Seeing; Smelling; Tasting; Riddles of Love; Feeling; Hearing*

Claxton, Florence and Adelaide: *One O'Clock: Supper Time and the Nursery Dinner; Two O'Clock: Sitting up for Mistress and the Penny Steam-Boat; Three O'Clock: Burglars and Shopping in Oxford Street; Four O'Clock: Up with the Lark and Washerwoman's Tea; Five O'Clock: Overworked and Rotten-Row; Six O'Clock: The First up in the Morning* and Home from Business; Seven O'Clock: Morning Toilet and Inspection; Eight O'Clock: Morning Post and Coffee; Nine O'Clock: Going to Business and Waiting for Doctor; Eleven O'Clock: The Gordian Knot and the Last Will and Testament; Twelve O'Clock: Liberty, Equality and Fraternity and The Obstinate Juryman

Claxton, Florence: *Governesses Here, Want of Governesses There; Daughters Here, Sons There; Needlewomen Here, A Modiste There; Servants Here, Servants There; Partners Here, Partners There; A Spinster Here, a Bachelor There; Kiss-in-the Ring; Innocence and Guilt; Twenty-four Hours of the Season, By My Lady's Watch; A Conversazione at Willis's Rooms; The Artists' and Amateurs' Valentine's Day*

Coleman, Helen (Angell): *Azaleas*

Colket, Victoria (Hine): *St. Peter Mancroft Church*

Corbaux, Fanny: *Children of J. Thornton; The Pennant Children; The Carrier Pigeon*

Dixon, Annie: *Elizabeth, Lady Stuart de Rothesay; Alfred, Lord Tennyson; Louisa, Marchioness of Waterford; Reading Prayers at Highcliffe; At a Window in Ford Castle*

Duffield, Mary (Mrs. William): *Summer Flowers; The Geranium*

Dunn, Edith: *A Sketch in 'The Garden of England,' The Two Valentines*

E. V. B.: *Lady Waterford in the Last Days; A Children's Summer; Fairy Tales of Hans Christian Anderson; Beauty and the Beast; The Redbreast Pays His Annual Visit*

Eastlake, Caroline: *A Child's Nosegay*

Edwards, Kate: *An Autumn Reverie*

Edwards, Mary Ellen: *The Princess of Wales Distributing the Prizes...; Female School of Art; At the Royal Academy; Forgiveness; The Rival Blues; Watching at Sea and Waiting at Home; On Christmas Day in the Morning; A Legend of Saint Valentine; Catherine Glover and the Glee Maiden; A Good Show of Flowers; A Friendly Talk; That Boy of Norcott's; Patriotism, Time of the Spanish Armada; A Friend in Need; Flight of French Peasants from Bazeilles; St. Denis: Arrival of the Wives' Train from Paris; The Communist Prisoners in the Orangerie, Versailles: the Visiting Hour; A Game of Chess; St Valentine's Day; Rosalind and Celia*

Egerton, Jane: *On the Terrace*

Farmer, Emily: *In Mischief, Out of Mischief; Kitty's Breakfast; In Doubt; The Alphabet Lesson*

Fellowes, Caroline: *The Prince Consort as a Boy*

Fox, Elizabeth Bridell: *William Fox; Gretchen; The Returned Loveletters*

Gastineau, Maria: *Conway Castle*

Geefs, Fanny: *The Young Mother*

Gillies, Margaret: *Richard Hengist Horne; James Leigh Hunt, Trust.*

Gouldsmith, Harriet: *Queen Victoria and Her Children in the Grounds of Buckingham Palace*

Gow, Mary: *Fairy Tales*

Harrison, Mary: *Flowers in an Upturned Basket; Flowers on a Stone Ledge*

Hay, Jane Benham: *Evangeline; April*

Henrietta Ward (anonymous photo)

Herford, Laura: *Elizabeth Garrett, L.S.A.*

Howitt, Anna M.: *The Angels Appearing to Joan of Arc*

Hunter, Elizabeth: *Little Charlotte's Writing Lesson*

Jay, Isabella : *Untitled, after T.M. Rooke*

J. M.: *The Female School of Art*

Jerichau, Elisabeth: *A Wounded Danish Soldier and His Betrothed; Shipwrecked*

Jopling, Louise: *Mrs. Geoffrey (Susan) Cockell; Self-Portrait; Five O'clock Tea; Song of the Shirt; Weary Waiting; Elaine*

Laird, Alice: *Fastening Her Bow*

Lamonti, Elish: *Lady Dufferin; The Duchess of Dowager of Manchester and Her Daughter*

Lane, Clara: *Edward W. Lane*

Lingren, Amalia: *Girl Tending Cattle; Dalecarlia, Sweden*

Louisa, Lady Waterford: *Jesus with the Doctors; The Virgin, St. Anne and Jesus; Samuel; David; Cain and Abel; Isaac and Abraham; Joshua; Daniel; Jacob and Esau and Joseph; Moses and Miriam; Samuel; The Education of the Virgin; The Sleeping Disciples; Feed My Lambs; The Stairs of Life; The Fates; Sweetest Eyes Were Ever Seen; Autumn with a Sieve; Looking out to Sea; Mentone Fisherman; Ford, Standard One*

Macgregor, Jessie: *An Act of Mercy*

Marrable, Madeline: *Isola Bella, Lago Maggiore*

Martineau, Edith: *Woods at Aviemore; Balkan Tribesman; The Potato Harvest*

Mearns, Lois: *The Conference*

Montalba, Clara: *St. Mark's, Venice; Early Morning*

Murray, Elizabeth: *Beggars at a Church Door in Rome; Two Little Monkeys; Pfifferari Playing to the Virgin-Scene in Rome; Rivals for Church Patronage; Woman in a Mantilla*

Mutrie, Annie: *Flowers; My First Bouquet*

Mutrie, Martha: *Camellias; Roses*

Nasmyth, Anne: *Alpine Lake Scene*

Nasmyth, Jane: *Furness Abbey*

Nasmyth, Margaret: *London from Twickenham*

North, Marianne: *Doum Palms and Date Palms*

Oliver, Emma (Mrs.William): *Vale of Dedham*

Osborn, Emily: *The Escape of Lord Nithisdale; Lost; Home Thoughts; Christmas Time; Nameless and Friendless; Mrs Sturgis and Her Children; Madame Bodichon; Our Widowed Queen; The Christmas Tree; Bâl Maidens on Their Way to Work; Of Course, She Said 'Yes'!; Sunday Morning, Betzingen; God's Acre; For the Last Time; The Golden Daydream; The Visitation*

Pasmore, Mrs. J. F.: *The Flower-Seller*

Paton, Amelia (Hill): *David Livingston; Dinah Craik, Née Mulock*

Perugini, Kate Dickens: *A Little Woman; Multiplication*

Photograph of Emma Brownlow

Photograph of Emma Brownlow in 1904 with her daughters Emma and Dora and grandson

Pusey, Clara: *Dr. Pusey and His Family at Breakfast, Christchurch, Oxford*

Rayner, Louise: *Foregate, Chester, Market Place, Lambrow*

Rosenberg, E. (Mrs. J. D. Harris): *Flowers*

Sandys, Emma: *Viola; Lady in a Yellow Dress; Adeline or Saxon Princess; Mariana in the Moated Grange*

Setchel, Sarah: *The Momentus Question; And Ye Shall Walk in Silk Attire*

Severn, Mary: *Peleus and Thetis, from the Camirus Vase*

Sharpe, Eliza: *Portrait of a Lady; Phoebe Mayflower*

Sharples, Rolinda: *The Artist and Her Mother*

Siddall, Elizabeth: *Pippa Passes; A Design; Sir Patrick Spens; Lady Affixing Pennant to Knight's Spear; The Woeful Victory*

Solomon, Rebecca: *The Fugitive Royalists; Self-Portraits; Pet Woffington's Visit to Triplet; The Friend in Need; The Governess; The Gamester; Love's Labour Lost; Love's Disguise; A Fashionable Couple*

Stannard, Eloise: *Summer Fruits; By the Old Garden Wall; Fruit Painted from Nature; Cottage Fruit*

Starr, Louisa (Canziani): *David Before Saul; Brian H. Hodgson; Sintram; Hardly Earned; Imogen*

Swift, Kate: *Cross Purposes; A Stitch in Time Saves Nine; Saying Grace; Où Est Mon Père? or Sweet My Child, I Live for Thee; The Orphans*

Taylor, Rose: *Eating Air on the Maidan*

Tekusch, Margaret: *Disraeli; The Countess of Granville; The Ambassador of Austro-Hungary*

Thompson, Elizabeth: *Quatre Bras; Reading the Roll Call after a Battle in the Crimea; Missing*

Thornycroft, Mary and Thomas: *Queen Boadicea; Alfred the Great and His Mother*

Thornycroft, Mary: *Princess Alice; The Cradle; Plenty* (Princess Louise); *Peace* (Princess Helena); *Princess Alexandra; The Princess Royal; The Skipping Girl*

Walker, Alice: *Wounded Feelings*

Ward, Henrietta: *The Young May Queen; Queen Mary Quitting Stirling Castle; Scene from the Childhood of Joan of Arc; Sion House 1553; The First Step; The Crown of the Feast; Palissy the Potter; Elizabeth Fry Visiting Newgate (Newgate 1818); An English Rosebud; God Save the Queen; Chatterton; The Queen's Lodge, Windsor, in 1872; The Princess Royal; Chelsea Church Gardens*

Warren, Sophy: *Benhill Wood, Sutton; Pond and Trees, Sunset; Old Mill at Evesham; Port on the Shore*

Williams, Caroline: *On the Thames; A Night on the Beach*

Withers, Augusta Innes: *Partridges.*

337. Matthews, Jacquie. "Barbara Bodichon: Integrity in Diversity." In *Theorists: Three Centuries of Key Women Thinkers*, Dale Spender ed. New York: Pantheon, 1983.

Bodichon's personal wealth and progressive education made her acutely conscious of deprivation and exploitation of women of all classes. Best remembered for her distinguished art career, the proceeds of which went to found Girton College, Cambridge, she was an energetic and imaginative leader in women's suffrage. She realized that achieving female emancipation meant changing social attitudes toward women as well as achieving legal, education, and economic reforms. Many of her significant contributions have been attributed to others.

338. Wood, Christopher. *The Pre-Raphaelites*. London: Wiedenfeld and Nicholson, 1983.

Marie Spartali Stillman studied with Ford Madox Brown, but her work shows a strong influence of Rossetti. Evelyn De Morgan's work is both Pre-Raphaelite and symbolist. The versatility of Eleanor Fortescue-Brickdale is evident in her book illustrations, oils and watercolors. Stillman and model Alexa Wilding appear in Rossetti's *The Bower Meadow*, and Wilding is given credit for her appearance in Rossetti's *Veronica Veronese*. Elizabeth Siddall receives mention, and of course she appears in several of Rossetti's paintings, but none of her works are represented.

Reproductions (col):

Fortescue-Brickdale, Eleanor: *The Wise Virgins*

De Morgan, Evelyn Pickering: *Hope in the Prison of Despair*

Stillman, Marie Spartali: *Messer Alesandro Showing Madonna Dianova His Enchanted Garden.*

339. Lalumia, Matthew. "Lady Elizabeth Thompson Butler in the 1870's." *Women's Art Journal* (March 1983): 9-14.

The liberal mood of the country and the demands of the middle class for individual rights and recognition explains the popularity of Butler's military paintings. A critical analysis of *The Roll Call*, *The Return from Inkerman*, and *Balaclava* reveals that Butler's work falls into the category of British Social Realism. Like other artists who championed the underclass with realistic and careful depictions of their living conditions, Butler shows the reality of war and the toll on the common soldier. Her paintings are thus an appeal for reform rather than a glorification of war.

Reproductions (b/w):

Butler, Lady Elizabeth Thompson: *The Roll Call; Balaclava; Inkerman.*

340. Ferens Art Gallery. *Trial and Innocence: Victorian Works from the Ferens*. Hull, England: Ferens Art Gallery, 1984.

Elizabeth Thompson Butler's military paintings were influenced partly by French war painters, but unlike them, she painted to show the harsh realities of war. More idealistic was Sir Frederic Leighton, whose *Farewell* uses as a model Hetty Dene, sister of Dorothy Dene, his favorite model. Leighton apparently regarded the Denes as "adopted daughters" whose company he found relaxing.

Reproductions (b/w):

Butler, Elizabeth Thompson: *Inkerman*

Leighton, Frederick: *Farewell* (Hetty Dene as model).

341. Moore, Helena. *Trial and Innocence: Victorian Works from the Ferens. Exhibition Catalogue: 8 September-21 October, 1984.* Hull, England: Ferens Art Gallery, 1984.

Elizabeth Thompson Butler's military paintings distinguish themselves by avoiding sentiment and jingoism. They are straightforward and serious, anticipating the realistic attitudes of those who experienced the great tragedy of World War I many years later. Butler's early work recalled the Crimean War, but she was still painting into the first quarter of the twentieth century. Frederic Leighton's friends Hetty and Dorothy Dene modeled for his classical paintings.

Reproductions (b/w):

Butler, Elizabeth Thompson: *Inkerman*.

342. Christian, John. "Marie Spartali: Pre-Raphaelite Beauty." *The Antique Collector* (March 1984): 42-47.

The renewed interest in Pre-Raphaelite paintings has sparked interest in Marie Spartali, whose work is still available to the collector at reasonable prices. Spartali, whose beauty was much admired by poets and painters, modeled for many leading artists. Although she studied art with Ford Madox Brown, her work shows Rossetti's strong influence. She showed her paintings at major London galleries as well as at the Royal Academy. She continued to paint even after her marriage, and in spite of the responsibilities of a large family. Her sister, Christine, was the model for Whistler's *Princesse du Pays de la Porcelaine*, a central painting in his celebrated Peacock room.

Reproductions (b/w):

Stillman, Marie Spartali: *Sir Tristram and La Belle Iseult; Beatrice; Kelmscott Manor; By a Dear Well, Within a Little Field*

Photo of Marie Spartali by Julia Margaret Cameron; head study of Marie Spartali by Rossetti; Marie Spartali in a Burne-Jones painting.

343. Nunn, Pamela Gerrish. "Rosa Brett, Pre-Raphaelite." *Burlington Magazine* CXXVI, no. 979 (October 1984): 630-635.

Plagued by ill health and isolated from other artists except for her mentor brother, Rosa Brett produced highly accomplished landscapes, still lifes, and nature studies. Some of her work appeared at the Royal Academy and smaller exhibitions; she preferred to use the pseudonym "Rosarius."

Her brother's Pre-Raphaelite friends greatly admired *The Hayloft,* which appeared at the 1858 Royal Academy exhibition. This article lists Brett's known works, as well as those dated, undated and untraced.

Reproductions (b/w):

Brett, Rosa: *The Hayloft; Detling Church; Turnip Field with Barns Beyond; Study of Trees.*

344. Allnutt, Gillian. *Lizzie Siddall: Her Journal (1862).* Warwick: Greville Press, 1985.

A fictional poem reflects Siddall's voicelessness and the struggle between her own identity and the persona given to her by Rossetti's relentless efforts to re-shape her face, her life, and her past.

Reproductions (b/w):

Rossetti, Dante Gabriel: *Rossetti's Vision of Lizzie Siddall*
Siddall, Elizabeth: *Self-Portrait.*

345. Fox, Caroline. *Painting in Newlyn, 1900's-1930.* Penzance, Cornwall: Newlyn Orion, 1985.

The Newlyn School was named after the Cornish fishing village where a group of artists went to paint the people and scenery between the years 1880-1900's. Elizabeth Armstrong Forbes, one of the original group, receives some mention in the biographical sketch of her husband; however, none of her paintings are represented here.

346. Herstein, Sheila R. *A Mid-Victorian Feminist, Barbara Leigh Smith Bodichon.* New Haven: Yale University Press, 1985.

Encouraged by John Ruskin and Dante Gabriel Rossetti, Barbara Bodichon had shows in London in 1859 and 1861; however, her talent for painting and her enthusiasm for art took second place to her work in social reform. Her friendship with Dante Gabriel Rossetti and her concern for Elizabeth Siddall's health are indicative of her ties with the art world as well as of her generous and compassionate nature. As the title indicates, this book concerns Bodichon's humanitarian efforts; only a few pages deal with her work as an artist.

347. Marsh, Jan. *The Pre-Raphaelite Sisterhood.* New York: St. Martin's, 1985.

The lives of Emma Madox Brown, Elizabeth Siddall, Annie Miller, Fanny Cornforth, Jane Morris, and Georgiana Burne-Jones are examined in a readable and successful attempt to see them in the context of the period in which they lived. The Pre-Raphaelite models have been both glorified and diminished by artists and viewers who see them as mythical figures in a kind of art-world melodrama. Extensive background on social and economic conditions contribute to the study of women's history.

Reproductions (col):

Siddall, Elizabeth: *Self-Portrait; Lovers Listening to Egyptian Girls; The Ladies' Lament.*

348. Nunn, Pamela Gerrish. "Rebecca Solomon: Painting and Drama." *Theatrephile* 2, no. 8 (1985): 3-4.

Three of Rebecca Solomon's paintings reflect a combination of interest in the theatre and commitment to social consciousness that is not found in other nineteenth-century painting. *Behind the Curtain* (1858) depicts a family group of players grouped around an ailing actor/son; *The Arrest of a Deserter* (1861) deals with the on-stage arrest of a soldier for whom the lure of the theatre proved stronger than devotion to the military. A third painting, *Peg Woffington's Visit to Triplet* (1860), brings actor and artist together in a scene where the famous eighteenth-century actress leaves her followers to visit the home of an ailing, poverty-stricken artist. Solomon's theater pictures typically use interior settings with three walls which place the viewer in the position of an audience viewing a stage production.

Reproductions (b/w):

Solomon, Rebecca: *Behind the Curtain.*

349. Reynolds, Simon. *The Vision of Simeon Solomon.* Slad, Gloucester (England): Catalpa Press, 1985.

Brief mention of Rebecca Solomon includes the information that she was eight years older than her brother Simeon, and taught him much of what she learned from her assistantship to Millais. Like her brother, she suffered from alcoholism. She died after being run over in the street by a carriage. She modeled for her brother and appears in many of his paintings.

Reproductions (b/w):

Solomon, Simeon: (Rebecca Solomon as model) *The Painter's Pleasurance; Shadrach Meshach and Abendnego; The Japanese Fan.*

350. Barr, John. *Illustrated Children's Books.* London: The British Library, 1986.

The popularity of Kate Greenaway's old-fashioned children owed much to the reaction against industrial sprawl and urban pollution. Beatrix Potter's careful renderings of detail from nature was influenced by her admiration of the Pre-Raphaelite painters.

Reproductions (color):

Greenaway, Kate: *A, Apple Pie; Marigold Garden; Under the Window*

Upton, Florence: *The Adventures of Two Dutch Dolls and a Golliwog*

Potter, Beatrix: *The Tale of Peter Rabbit.*

351. Hook, Philip and Mark Poltimore. *Popular 19th Century Painting: A Dictionary of European Genre Painters*. Westbridge, Suffolk, England: Antique Collectors Club Ltd., 1986.

Elizabeth Thompson, Lady Butler's artistic accomplishments are notable in a time when it was difficult for women to compete successfully with men, especially because she achieved considerable success in the masculine genre of battle painting. Numerous other female artists are listed without commentary.

Reproductions (b/w):

Anderson, Sophie: *A Spring Beauty*

Butler, Elizabeth Thompson: *The Roll Call*

Earl, Maude: *The Lap of Luxury*

Hamburger, Helen Augusta: *Feline Exploration*

Perugini, Kate: *A Little Woman*

Sutcliffe, Harriette: *Gathering Plums*

Waller, Mary Lemon: *Gladys, Daughter of Major Lutley Jordan*

Wilmot, Florence: *Freeman.*

352. Marsh, Jan. *Jane and May Morris: A Biographical Story 1839- 1938*. London: Pandora, 1986.

This is an engrossing biography of Jane Burden Morris, wife of designer William Morris, and model for some of Rossetti's most famous paintings. Marsh's solid knowledge of Victorian social conditions and her sympathy with Jane, her sister Bessie, and Jane's daughter, May, uncover fascinating personalities and give credit to their contributions to the burgeoning arts and crafts movement. This book fills the gap left by Morris' biographers, who ignore, dismiss, or misinterpret these women.

Reproductions (b/w):

Illustrations: family portraits and photos

Morris, May: embroidery.

353. Morris, Jane. *Jane Morris to Wilfred Scawen Blunt*. Peter Faulkner, ed. Exeter, Devon: Exeter University Publications, 1986.

Jane Morris' letters to Wilfred Blunt begin in 1883 and end in 1913. Relevant passages from his diaries, some previously unpublished, provide explanations and insights. Their affair was a brief part of a long friendship in which they shared their interests in poetry, politics, and friends. Taken as a whole, Morris' letters are poignant glimpses into the nineteenth-century female world of enforced idleness, suffocating boredom, and no central heating, conditions which in Morris' case found an outlet in preoccupation with health problems and the weather.

354. North, Marianne. *Some Recollections of a Happy Life: Marianne North in Australia & New Zealand*, Helen Vellacott ed. Baltimore: Edward Arnold, 1986.

Charles Darwin told Marianne North that as a botanical painter she simply must go to Australia. Of course she immediately packed her paints and set off, traveling through Australia, Tasmania and New Zealand, recording her adventures in her diaries and her botanical finds in her paintings.

Reproductions (col):

North, Marianne: *Evening Glow over 'The Range'; An Old Currajong Tree, New South Wales; View from Collaroy, New South Wales, Looking towards the Liverpool Downs; Possum up a Gum Tree; View of Melbourne, from the Botanic Gardens; Musk Tree and Background of Evergreen 'Beech'; A West Australian Banksia; Foliage, Flowers, and Seed Vessels of a Rare West Australian Shrub; Fernshaw, Victoria; A New Zealand Dracophyllum; New Zealand Flowers and Fruits; Blue Gum Trees, Silver Wattle, and Sassafras on the Huon Road, Tasmania; View of Lake Wakatipe, New Zealand; Fishbone Tree and the Parson Bird of New Zealand; View of the Otira Gorge, New Zealand; Castle Hill, with Beech Forest, New Zealand*

Reproductions (b/w):

Photo of Marianne North taken by Julia Cameron

Marianne North on the doorstep of her home at Alderly.

355. Usherwood, Paul. "Elizabeth Thompson Butler: The Consequences of Marriage." *Woman's Art Journal* (March 1986): 30- 34.

Thompson's marriage to Major William Butler contributed to the demise of her successful career, since her role of military wife and mother of six children kept her away from the London art world. The political climate shifted from domestic reform to jingoistic imperialism. Her paintings reminded the public of episodes they wanted to forget. While her marriage provided her with horses and military models, her work did not sell well after 1881; male painters who could witness battles firsthand superseded her in the genre.

Reproductions (b/w):

Butler, Elizabeth Thompson: *'Listed for the Connaught Rangers', After the Battle*; *Evicted*; *The Colours.*

356. Cherry, Deborah. *Painting Women: Victorian Women Artists.* Rochdale, England: Rochdale Gallery, 1987.

At its best, a Marxist-feminist critical approach offers new ways of seeing, and this exhibition catalogue is an important compilation of information about women who contributed much to the Victorian art world. Ironically, however, the political rhetoric occasionally overpowers or even subverts the work that was in its own time overwhelmed by condescension and misogyny. Cherry claims that, in the same way art by nineteenth-century women participates in or reflects the exploitation of the poor and the working classes by the bourgeois, women artists submit to or reflect the oppressive power-hungry patriarchy.

Reproductions (b/w):

Allingham, Laura: *Under Hindhead, Surrey*

Alma-Tadema, Laura Epps: *Always Welcome*

Blunden, Anna: *The Seamstress*

Bodichon, Barbara Leigh Smith: *Ye Newe Generation*

Bosanquet, Charlotte: *The Rev. E. Bosanquet's Cottage at Denham*

Boyce (Wells), Joanna Mary: Drawing of women attending an anatomy lecture; Drawing of woman student attending the ladies classes at the studio of Thomas Couture in Paris; Study of woman servant descending stairs

Bowkett, Jane Marie: *Preparing Tea; An Afternoon in the Nursery; A Young Lady in a Conservatory*

Brown, Lucy Madox: *The Magic Mirror*

Butler, Elizabeth Thompson: *Balaclava*

Childers, Milly: *Self Portrait*

Dacre, Isabel Susan: *Lydia Becker*

De Morgan, Evelyn Pickering: *Medea*

Forbes, Elizabeth Armstrong: *A Game of Old Maid*

Gillies, Margaret: *Mary and William Howitt; Trust*

Harris, Elizabeth Louisa Rosenberg: *Flowers with a Bird's Nest*

Havers, Alice: *The End of Her Journey; The Belle of the Village*

Hayllar, Edith: *Feeding the Swans; A Summer Shower*

Hayllar, Jessica: *Finishing Touches; A Coming Event*

Macgregor, Jessie: *In the Reign of Terror*

Merritt, Anna Lea: *War*

Mutrie, Annie Feray: *Azaleas*

Offord, Gertrude Elizabeth: *Interior of the Old School of Art, Norwich*

Osborn, Emily Mary: *Nameless and Friendless; The Bâl Maidens; The Escape of Lord Nithisdale from the Tower, 1716*

Rae, Henrietta: *Psyche Before the Throne of Venus*

Rayner, Louise: *Tolsey Lane, Tewkesbury*

Setchell, Sara: *The Momentous Question*

Severn, Anna Mary: *Self Portrait*

Siddall, Elizabeth: *Madonna and Child with an Angel*

Solomon, Rebecca: *The Governess; The Fugitive Royalists*

Stannard, Eloise Harriet: *Strawberries in a Cabbage Leaf with Flower Pot Behind*

Stillman, Louise Spartali: *Fiametta Singing*

Swynnerton, Anna Louisa Robinson: *Susan Isabel Dacre*

Walker, Alice: *Wounded Feelings*

Ward, Henrietta: *God Save the Queen; Queen Mary Quitted Stirling Castle on the Morning of Wednesday, April 23*

Webb, M.D. (Robinson): *Three Fisher Wives; A Volunteer for the Lifeboat*

Wells, Augusta: *Drawing of a Woman Servant Washing Dishes*

Whitaker, Frances Mathilda (Fanny McIan): *After the Battle of Prestonpans.*

357. Newall, Christopher. *Victorian Watercolours*. London: Phaidon, 1987.

A study of watercolor painting during the nineteenth century includes women who worked in the medium and who contributed to its development and progress.

Reproductions (col):

Allingham, Helen: *Young Customers; South Country Cottage*

Alma-Tadema, Anna: *Eton College Chapel*

Bodichon, Barbara: *Isle of Wight*

Boyle, Eleanor Vere: *And a Neglected Looking Glass...*

De Morgan, Evelyn: *Deianira*

Fortescue-Brickdale, Eleanor: *In the Spring Time*

Greenaway, Kate: *Study of Rock, Moss and Ivy; Misses.*

358. Nunn, Pamela Gerrish. *Victorian Women Artists*. London: The Women's Press, 1987.

Victorian women challenged the middle-class notion that intense dedication and professional achievement were improper, if not impossible for females. Case histories of six artists, and an examination of worlds and traditions of nineteenth-century art schools and exhibitions, reveal a complex and fascinating network of challenges and obstacles, and introduce accomplished figures ignored by art historians.

Reproductions (col):

Brett, Rosa: *The Old House at Fairleigh*

Brownlow, Emma: *The Foundling Restored to Its Mother; The Christening; The Sick Room; Taking Leave*

Louisa, Lady Waterford: *Mentone Fisherman; Sweetest Eyes Were Ever Seen*

Sharples, Rolinda: *The Artist with Her Mother* (cover)

Ward, Henrietta: *Chatterton*

Wells, Joanna Boyce: *Elgiva; Sidney; The Heathergatherer; The Child's Crusade*

Reproductions (b/w):

Boyle, Eleanor Vere: *A Children's Summer*

Brett, Rosa: *The Hayloft; Detling Church; Two Ladies; Sketchbook*

Brownlow, Emma: *The Drawing-Room and the Street; The Fashion of the Day; The Vaccination; Left in Charge*

Butler, Elizabeth Thompson: *Calling the Roll*

Carpenter, Margaret: *The Sisters*

De Morgan, Evelyn Pickering: *Aurora Triumphans*

Edwards, Mary Ellen: *At the Royal Academy*

Greenaway, Kate: *Little Loves*

Merritt, Anna Lea: *Love Locked Out*

Osborn, Emily Mary: *The Escape of Lord Nithisdale; Lost*

Sharples, Rolinda: *The Song*

Ward, Henrietta: *Queen Mary Quitting Stirling Castle; Sion House; Palissy the Potter*

Wells, Joanna Boyce: *La Veneziana; Gretchen.*

359. Taylor, Ina. *Victorian Sisters*. Bethesda, Maryland: Adler & Adler, 1987.

Georgiana Macdonald Burne-Jones is best remembered as the wife and model of painter Edward Burne-Jones. She was also a close friend of George Eliot, and was devoted to improving conditions for women and the working classes. Her sister Alice was Rudyard Kipling's mother, her sister Agnes married the painter John Poynter, and her sister Louisa was mother of prime minister Stanley Baldwin. Taylor's biography of the Macdonald sisters explores the family and ethnic heritage that produced so many remarkable people.

360. Usherwood, Paul and Jenny Spencer-Smith. *Lady Butler, Battle Artist: 1846-1933*. London: National Army Museum, 1987.

Elizabeth Thompson Butler's career spanned over fifty years and included numerous exhibitions and publications. Her husband, an outspoken British Army officer, championed oppressed groups and lost causes; her own work reflected a keen eye for detail and deep human sympathy.

Reproductions (col):

Butler, Elizabeth Thompson: *The Roll Call; The 28th Regiment at Quatre Bras; Balaclava; Return From Inkerman; 'Listed For Connaught Rangers; The Remnants of an Army; The Defense of Rourke's Drift; Scotland Forever!; "Floreat Etona!"; After the Battle; To The Front; Evicted; Halt on a Forced March; Dawn of Waterloo; "Steady the Drums and Fifes!"; On the Morrow of Talavera; The Colours: Advance of the Scots Guards; Yeomantry Scouts on the Veldt; Within the Sound of the Guns; Rescue of the Wounded; The Dorset Yeoman at Agagia, 26th Feb. 1916; In the Retreat from Mons: The Royal Horse Guards; A Detachment of Cavalry in Flanders*

Reproductions (b/w):

Butler, Elizabeth Thompson: *Lady Butler Painting at Dover Castle; Elizabeth Thompson, 1874; Thomas James Thompson, c. 1850; William Butler, San Francisco, 1873;* Photograph of the Artist, c. 1893; Photograph of Lady Butler with her eldest son Patrick; *Soldiers Watering Horses; Missing; Quatre Bras; Studies of Garibaldini;* Four drawings of British and Yankee Volunteers; *English Guardsmen; Military Types; Sketches of Prussian People; Female Students at the South Kensington School of Art; Bavarian Artillery Going into Action; A Mercenary in Period Armour; Self- Portrait; Mimi Thompson; Ploughing in the Fields near Florence; 10th Bengal Lancers Tent-Pegging,* study for *Waiting for* the Colonel; Waiting for the Colonel; Chasseur Vedette; Study of a Wounded Guardsman; The Roll Call; studies for the Front Rank of the Square in *Quatre Bras; A Quiet Canter in the Long Valley, Aldershot; Italian Boy; Balaclava; The Return from Inkerman;* study for *'Listed for the Connaught Rangers; 'Listed for the Connaught Rangers; The Remnants of an Army; Jellalabad, January 13th, 1842;* studies for *The Defense of Rorke's Drift; The Defense of Rorke's Drift; A Vedette of the Scot's Greys;* study for the composition of *Scotland Forever!; Scotland Forever!;* a German version of *Scotland Forever!; "Floreat Etona!"; Studies of the Cameron Highlanders; Piper, Cameron Highlanders; Private, Cameron Highlanders; After the Battle: Arrival of Lord Wolseley and Staff; Study of a British Soldier and Two Camels; Breton Boy Leaning on a Stick; A "Lament" in the Desert; To the Front; Evicted; Plymouth Sound; Patrick Butler, Aged Seven; Eileen and Elizabeth Butler, the Artist's Daughters; On the Terrace at Shepherd's Hotel, Cairo; The Fostât Becalmed; At Philae; Zouave Teaching a Dog to Beg; Threshing Corn in Brittany; Monavoe Delgany, Co. Wicklow;* study for *A Halt on a Forced March; Halt on a Forced March: Peninsular War; The Camel Corps;* study for the bugler and central group of *Dawn of Waterloo; Dawn of Waterloo; "Steady the Drums and Fifes!"; On the Morrow of Talavera; The Flag;* study of *The Colours; The Colours: Advance of the Scots Guards at the Alma; Sketchbook, 1890;* vignettes for the 'head' and 'tail' of *From Sketch-Book and Diary; Goats in Egypt; Friday Afternoon on the Mahmoudieh Canal; Well in the Nile Delta; The Egyptian Donkey Barber; The Start; Royal Horse Artillery Halt!; Sketchbook 1874; The Return of the Coldstreams; Trooper, Life Guards; "Right Wheel!"; "Bravo!"; Lieutenant-General Sir William Butler KCB; A Radical General: Yeomanry Scouts on the Veldt; Dispatch Rider; Rescue of the Wounded, Afghanistan; Off to the Paar!; A Corner of Our Garden at Rosebank; Bersaglieri at the Fountain, Perugia; Bringing in the Grapes; The Quirinal Palace, Rome; Croagh Patrick, Clew Bay; Patrick, Au Revoir!; Kettledrummer, 18th Hussars; A "V.C." of the Irish Guards; A "V.C." of the Lancashire "Fusiliers"; A "V.C." of the Seaforths; A London Irish at Loos; "Eyes Right!"; "Action Front!"; Trooper of the Lancashire Hussars Yeomantry; The Dorset Yeoman at Agagia, 26 Feb. 1916; The Charge of the Warwickshire and Worchestershire Yeomanry; A Man of Kent; Back to His Land; Sailor; In Retreat from Mons: The Royal Horse Guards; A Detachment of Cavalry in Flanders; Eileen, Vicountess Gormanston.*

361. Borzello, Frances. "*Jane and May Morris: A Biographical Story 1839-1938.*" *Crafts* , no. 8562 (6 May 1987): 52.

Although a lack of solid information about her subjects makes it necessary for her to be "forever supposing and surmising," Jan Marsh's biography of the Morris women is a brilliant success. Her treatment of Jane's intriguing transition from lower-class working girl to a solid presence in Victorian art circles is both plausible and sensitive.

362. Spurling, John. "Recorder of Collective Murder. *Lady Butler: Battle Artis.* National Army Museum, London..." *New Statesman* 113 (25 June 1987): 29-30.

The excellent exhibition of Elizabeth Thompson Butler's works celebrates a talented, if not first-rate, artist who excelled at documenting the grim reality of war.

363. Usherwood, Paul. "Lady Butler's Irish Pictures." *Irish Arts Review* (December 1987): 47-49.

Elizabeth Thompson Butler's Irish sympathies are implied in paintings inspired by visits to Ireland with her Irish husband. British viewers, who did not share her compassion, saw *'Listed for the Connaught Rangers* as a recruitment scene, an appendix of sorts of the battle scenes which had made her famous. *Evicted!* provided no such easy explanation. It was dismissed as "melodramatic," admired for its scenic qualities, and remained unsold.

Reproductions (b/w):

Butler, Elizabeth Thompson: *'Listed for the Connaught Rangers; Evicted!*

364. Daniels, Morna. *Victorian Book Illustration*. London: The British Library, 1988.

A publisher discovered Kate Greenaway's drawings in the Grosvenor Gallery; Eleanor Vere Boyle was married to Queen Victoria's chaplain. Boyle is the most important female illustrator of the 1860's.

Reproductions (color):

Boyle, Eleanor Vere: *A Golden Boat on a Great, Great Water*
Greenaway, Kate: *The Quiver of Love*.

365. Fine, Elsa Honig. *Women and Art: A History of Women Painters and Sculptors from the Renaissance to the 20th Century.* Montclair, New Jersey: Allanheld and Schram, 1988.

   The section titled "The English School Portraiture" contains brief biographical sketches of Victorians.

366. Marsh, Jan. "Imagining Elizabeth Siddall." *History Workshop Journal*, no. 25 (March 1988): 64-82.

   The perception of Elizabeth Siddall's life and person correspond with the artistic, political, and social viewpoints of the eras following her brief life. Seen as a paragon of purity and passivity by late Victorians, she became a menace of frigidity in the more liberated 1920's. Her addiction to laudanum makes her a hero for the drop-out drug cult of the 1960's, the feminists of the 1980's adopt her as a female victim of the masculine power structure, while current trends endeavor to establish an identity for her that is separate from Dante Gabriel Rossetti's life, work and influence.

   Reproductions (b/w):

   Siddall, Elizabeth: *Self-Portrait*

   Rossetti, Dante Gabriel: *Elizabeth Siddall Reading; Portrait of Elizabeth Siddall*

   Photos (b/w):

   Elizabeth Siddall.

367. Shefer, Elaine. "Elizabeth Siddall's *Lady of Shalott*." *Women's Art Journal* (March 1988): 21-29.

   While William Michael Rossetti's accounts of Siddall's educational and artistic training are condescending and based on conjecture, Dante Gabriel Rossetti appears to have been enthusiastic about her talents. A comparison of William Holman Hunt's *Lady of Shalott* with Siddall's version of it reveals a sharp contrast between the private female world and the more public male world; Siddall depicts her subject as object rather than artist, a "dabbler" lacking the focused intensity of a serious artist. Her low opinion of her artistic talents may be attributed to Ruskin's condescending attitude toward women artists. The design of Siddall's dresses reveals a tension between freedom and spiritual imprisonment.

368. Nunn, Pamela Gerrish. "Rebecca Solomon's *A Young Teacher*." *Burlington Magazine* CXXX, no. 1027 (October 1988): 769-770.

   Three new works by Rebecca Solomon were discovered as a result of the Geoffrye Museum's 1985-86 exhibition of the work of Rebecca Solomon and her two brothers. The original painting of *Behind the*

Curtain and a replica of *Peg Woffington's Visit to Triplet* were extant in engraving and original form respectively. The third work, an oil titled *A Young Teacher*, which sold originally for £84, is medium sized, with an arched top. It shows a young girl and a baby seated behind a small table with a dark-skinned woman wearing a middle-Eastern-style shawl over a Victorian-style dress. The woman is seen by contemporary reviewers as receiving instruction from the Anglo child. This racially-prejudiced interpretation is probably consistent with Solomon's own; but a modern, less biased reviewer could see the dark woman as the *ayah*, or teacher, of the children.

Reproductions (b/w):

Solomon, Rebecca: *Behind the Curtain; A Young Teacher*.

369. Treble, Rosemary. "The Royal Academy's Victorian Paintings." *Apollo* (October 1988): 264-269, 297-300.

Since 1768, every artist admitted to full membership in the Royal Academy must donate a "diploma piece" to the academy's permanent art collection. The portrait collection includes Margaret Carpenter's painting of her brother-in-law, *William Collins*. Carpenter deserves to be better known; during her lifetime she received a pension from Queen Victoria, who admired her work. Anna Lea Merritt's portrait of *Sir William Boxall and His Dog Garibaldi* is "charmingly Hogarthian." These two paintings are the only works by women in the Academy's Victorian collection.

370. Christian, John. *The Last Romantics: The Romantic Tradition in British Art: Burne-Jones to Stanley Spencer*. London: Lund Humphries and Barbican Art Gallery, 1989.

Mary Sargant Florence and Phoebe Anna Moss Traquair are credited for their contributions to mural painting. Marie Spartali Stillman, whose beauty and artistic talent gained her fame as both model and artist, rates a short biographical sketch and color reproductions of two of her paintings. The versatility of painter, illustrator and muralist Kate Bunce made a substantial addition to the Birmingham art scene. The so-called "academic painters" include Marianne Prendlsberger Stokes, Elizabeth Adela Armstrong Stanhope Forbes and Eleanor Fortescue-Brickdale. The turn of the century Celtic, or Scottish, school owes much to the extreme versatility of Phoebe Anna Moss Traquair and Margaret Macdonald (Mackintosh), who both contributed much to the Arts and Crafts Movement. Jessie Marion King was also a major figure in the decorative arts, although she evolved a highly independent and personal style.

Reproductions (col):

Fortescue-Brickdale, Eleanor: *The Lover's World; The Little Foot-Page*

De Morgan, Evelyn: *Flora*

Stillman, Marie Spartali: *By a Clear Well; The Enchanted Garden*

Traquair, Phoebe Anna Moss: Illuminated manuscript from *Sonnets from the Portuguese.*

371. Hemming, Charles. *British Landscape Painters: A History and Gazetteer.* London: Gollancz, 1989.

Helen Allingham's "myopis nostalgia" called attention to the beauty and fragility of old country settings. Her paintings helped perpetuate the myth of the idyllic countryside for materialistic urban industrialists.

Reproductions (b/w):

Allingham, Helen: *Old Cottage at Pinner.*

372. Marsh, Jan. *The Legend of Elizabeth Siddall.* New York: Quartet Books, 1989.

The accounts of the life and personality of Elizabeth Siddall change with the times in which they are written, vary with the purposes of the writers, and shape the myths that explain this silent, enigmatic figure. Writing a responsible account of her life calls for insightful untangling of a bewildering variety of stories, which include fictional accounts and film versions. Every age seems to view Siddall through its own political and social values. Identifying the information that seems consistent and factual, both old and recently discovered, provides a biographical account that satisfies the demands of modern objective and substantiated scholarship. Siddall's work merits and gets careful criticism that places her in her rightful place as an artist and a poet.

Reproductions (b/w):

Siddall, Elizabeth: *Lady of Shalott; Lady at Loom; Jeptha's Daughter; Self Portrait; St. Cecelia Sketch; Sir Galahad and the Holy Grail; Sketch for Sir Galahad; Lovers Listening to Music; Pippa Passing Loose Women; MacBeth; Give me the Daggers; Woeful Victory; Before the Battle; The Ladies' Lament*

Photos (b/w):

Photo of Elizabeth Siddall.

373. Vincent, Adrian. *One Hundred Years of Traditional British Painting.* London: Newton Abbot, 1989.

Helen Allingham's timeless paintings of country houses have lasting appeal but are now priced out of sight for most of her admirers. Her illustrations for the *Graphic* and her connection with the Pre-Raphaelite circle added to the success gained from her painting. Mary Elizabeth Duffield is known for her flower paintings, ten of which appeared in Royal Academy exhibitions; and for her 1856 book, *The Art of Flower Painting.* Jessey Fairfax Bates exhibited her first Royal Academy painting, *A Corner of the Studio*, in 1896.

Reproductions (col):

Allingham, Helen: *Valewood Farm; Under Blackdown, Surrey*
Duffield, Mary Elizabeth: *Roses Blairie*
Bates, Jessey Fairfax: *Geraniums.*

374. White, Colin. *The Enchanted World of Jessie M. King.* Edinburgh: Canongate, 1989.

Jessie King is one of the best, if lesser known, of the brilliant artists of the Glasgow School. While her illustrations and designs for books are among her most remarkable contributions, her distinctive style and versatility touched nearly every phase of design, including wall panels, greeting cards, and jewelry. Her style reflects the best of the elegant Art Nouveau of Beardsley and Toorop and is touched with the mystery and medievalism of the Celtic tradition and the Pre-Raphaelites.

375. Atwood, Philip. "The Stillmans and the Morrises." *Journal of the William Morris Society* ix, no. 1 (1990): 23-28.

Marie Spartali married William Stillman in 1871. He had three children from his first marriage and he and Marie had a daughter and two sons; one son died when an infant. The Stillman family moved to Florence, but Marie often went back to London to visit the Morris family. One daughter, Lisa, came back to England to study art, and had a close relationship with the Morris family. Illness in the Stillman family brought about the loan of Morris' country home, Kelmscott Manor, for recuperation purposes. When Marie Spartali Stillman and Jane Burden Morris were widowed they continued their close friendship.

Reproductions (b/w):

Stillman, Lisa: *Sketches of the Family Cat.*

376. Burkhauser, Jude. *Glasgow Girls: Women in Art and Design 1880-1920.* Edinburgh: Canongate, 1990.

The "Glasgow Girls" worked and studied alongside the "Glasgow Boys" to create the backbone of the Art Nouveau movement in Great

Britain, as well as to exert considerable influence on the movement in Europe and the United States. Biographical sketches, historical and critical essays by a number of contributors furnish a readable, scholarly, and indispensable background for studying the painting, design and crafts of this period.

Reproductions (b/w):

Hundreds of photos, drawings, paintings, and designs in color and black and white.

377. Casteras, Susan P. *English Pre-Raphaelitism and its Reception in America in the Nineteenth Century*. Rutherford, N. J.: Fairleigh Dickinson University Press, 1990.

A study of nineteenth-century America's reactions to British art contains only brief mention of Sophie Anderson's *Lending a Deaf Ear* as "overdone...second rate Pre-Raphaelitism." Barbara Bodichon's landscapes were thought to contain promise, but Elizabeth Siddall's *Clerk Saunders* was generally seen as "childish."

Reproductions (b/w):

Anderson, Sophie: *No Walk Today*

Osborn, Emily: *Nameless and Friendless; Home Thoughts; The Cornish Bâl; Maidens Going to Work in the Mines*

Solomon, Rebecca: *The Governess*

Stillman, Marie Spartali: *The Covenant Lily*.

378. ---. *"Malleus Malificarum* or *The Witch's Hammer*: Victorian Visions of Female Sorceresses." In *Victorian Sages and Cultural Discourse: Renegotiating Gender and Power*, Thais E. Morgan ed. New Brunswick, N. J.: Rutgers University Press, 1990.

The supernatural female in Victorian painting is the antithesis of the submissive ideal woman. The witch or sorceress is generally depicted as menacing, distorted, and disturbed. Evelyn Pickering de Morgan's *Medea* is, however, calm and contemplative, an exception to the half-crazed Medeas painted by de Morgan's contemporaries. Maria Zambaco modeled for Vivien in Burne-Jones' *The Beguiling of Merlin* and modeled for Circe in another Burne-Jones painting. Zambaco thus doubles as sorceress and seductress, since Burne-Jones, who was married, was emotionally involved with her.

Reproductions:

De Morgan, Evelyn Pickering: *Medea*

Burne-Jones, Edward: *The Beguiling of Merlin* (Marie Zambaco models for Vivien).

379. Chadwick, Whitney. "Sex, Class, and Power in Victorian England." In *Women, Art and Society*, 165-190. London: Thames and Hudson, 1990.

While Victorian women were breaking into the art world during a time of intense demand for emancipation, their work, for the most part, pictures middle-class domestic idealism. Some social protest can be seen in Elizabeth Thompson Butler's refusal to confine herself to domestic scenes, in Anna Blunden and Rebecca Solomon's paintings of governesses and seamstresses, in Lucy Madox Brown Rossetti and Henrietta Ward's historical incidents showing brave and resourceful women, and in Evelyn Pickering de Morgan's depiction of Medea as beautiful and powerful rather than evil and vengeful. Caught between the idealized passivity and domesticity of the Victorian world and the intense demands of artistic excellence, female artists often found a kind of middle ground allowing for inner expression and outer conformity.

380. Mallalieu, H. L. *The Dictionary of British Watercolour Artists up to 1920.* Woodbridge, Suffolk: Antique Collector's Club, 1990.

Dates, comments and other information accompany many of the illustrations.

Reproductions (b/w):

Allingham, Helen: *The Fields in May*

Arden, Margaret Elizabeth: *A White Throat*

Barret, Harriet: *Dead Birds*

Barton, Rose: *Piccadilly*

Blake, Fanny: *The Bearer of Sad Tidings*

Bowditch, Sarah: *A Chub*

Boyle, Eleanor Vere: *The Sunbeam Stole in to Kiss Him*

Butler, Mildred Anne: *A Lady Painting*

Byrne, Anne Frances: *Wild Flowers*

Cameron, Katherine: *The Legend of Christmas Rose*

Forbes, Elizabeth Stanhope: *Mother and Child*

Fortescue, Henrietta Anne: *Geneva*

Gastineau, Maria: *On the Antrim Coast*

Gordon, Julia Isabella Levinia: *On a French River*

Lawrence, Mary: *Still Life of Wild Flowers*

Palmer, Hannah: *A Rocky Stream*

Potter, Beatrix: *Linyphia Triangularis; Yus, Yus, They Eat and They Do Eat*

Princep, Emily Rebecca: *A Lady Sketching*

Rayner, Louise J: *Haddon Hall*

Rayner, Margaret: *Playing by the Front*

Rushout, Anne: *Flower Study*

Scott, Caroline Lucy: *The Lion Gate, Hampton Court*

Smirke, Mary: *On the Thames near Barnes; The Thames at Twickenham*

Stillman, Maria: *Antigone Burying Polyneices*

Turck, Eliza: *The Garden Path*

Waterford, Louisa Anne: *Children Fording a Stream; Children Gathering Faggots*

Youngman, Annie Mary: *Dandelions.*

381. Robins, Anna Gretzner. "British Impressionism: The Magic and Poetry of Life Around Them." In *World Impressionism: the International Movement 1860-1920*, 71-113. ed.Norma Broude. New York: Abrams, 1990.

Encouraged by Fred Brown, a Slade School professor with a following of women art students, Ethel Walker adopted the ideas and techniques of Impressionism, exhibiting a number of *plein air* paintings at the New English Art Club, formed to exhibit Impressionist paintings rejected by the Royal Academy. By the 1890's the Royal Academy had relented; Laura Knight's Impressionist-influenced *Flying a Kite* was hung in the Royal Academy exhibit of 1910.

Reproductions (col):

Knight, Laura: *Flying a Kite*

Walker, Ethel: *The Garden.*

382. Rossetti, William Michael. *The Pre-Raphaelite Diaries and Letters*. London: Hurst and Blackett, 1990.

Dante Gabriel Rossetti writes to Madox Brown that Elizabeth Siddall's self-portrait, "a perfect wonder," is to be exhibited at the Winter Exhibition and that she is painting a scene from Tennyson's "Lady of Shalott," intended for the Royal Academy. Anna Mary Howitt's painting *Gretchen at the Fountain* is creating tremendous interest and enthusiasm at the Portland Gallery. William Rossetti regards Barbara Bodichon as a gifted landscape painter.

383. Marsh, Jan. "The Woeful Muse." *The Antique Collector* (April 1990): 58-63.

In addition to her dramatic personal involvement with the Pre-Raphaelite Movement, Elizabeth Siddall was also a serious artist who studied with Rossetti and at the Sheffield Art School. Her work can be found in such art galleries as the Tate and the Ashmolean.

Reproductions (b/w):

Siddall, Elizabeth: *Pippa Passing the Loose Women; Study for the Woeful Victory; Self Portrait.*

384. Bettencourt, Michael. "A Victorian Painter of Moments." *Christian Science Monitor* (2 April 1990): 16.

Marriage to a famous historical painter provided Laura Alma-Tadema with an artistic partnership that enhanced, rather than stifled, her career. She rejected her husband's lavish classical subject matter as well as the academic format of her other famous teacher, Ford Madox Brown, in favor of informal scenes of children, mothers, and lovers. Her preference for domestic scenes has led art historians to categorize her in the Dutch genre.

Reproductions (col):

Alma-Tadema, Laura: *A Knock at the Door.*

385. "Maas Gallery [Advertisement] *Head of Elizabeth Siddall.*" *Apollo* (June 1990): 10.

Reproductions (b/w):

Head of Elizabeth Siddall.

386. Usherwood, Paul. "Elizabeth Thompson Butler: A Case of Tokenism." *Woman's Art Journal* 11, no. 2 (September 1990): 14-18.

During the mid-1870's the Royal Academy was pressured by the public to reform its exhibition and membership practices. Elizabeth Thompson Butler served as an ideal token symbol of academy liberalism because she painted large attention-getting canvasses with a subject--military heroism--that flattered the male image. The academy's ploy backfired, however, when Thompson came within two votes of admission to full academy membership, a crisis which resulted in rule changes specifically excluding women from serving on the council or attending banquets, since no other changes resulted from Butler's career, she cannot be seen as a catalyst breaking the way for other female artists.

Reproductions (b/w):

Butler, Elizabeth Thompson: *Scotland Forever!*

387. Casteras, Susan P. "William Maw Egley's *The Talking Oak.*" *Detroit Institute of Arts Bulletin* (December 1990): 27-41.

Alfred, Lord Tennyson's poem "The Talking Oak" inspired William Maw Egley's painting of the same title, with Polly Egley serving as the model. Tennyson's poem also inspired Sophie Anderson.

388. Vincent, Adrian. *A Companion to Victorian and Edwardian Artists*. Hong Kong: David & Charles, 1991.

This is a good source for names, dates and brief biographical sketches of a few Victorian women artists, including reproductions of some of their lesser-known works.

Reproductions (col):
Allingham, Helen: *A Cottage at Shere*
Barton, Rose: *Grandpa's Garden*
Bayfield, Fanny Jane: *A Bunch of Roses*
Coleman, Helen Cordelia: *Mignonette and Azalea in China Bowl*
Dealy, Jane M: *The Sisters*
Dell, Etheldin Eva: *Mother and Family Outside Their Cottage*
Duffield, Mary Elizabeth: *Geraniums, Fuchsias and Daisies*
Erichson, Nelly: *Golden Hair*
Goodman, Maude: *The Music Lesson*
Hadden, Nellie: *A Bird Fancier*
Hatton, Helen Howard: *Before Bedtime*
Hayllar, Kate: *Eastern Presents*
Moberly, Mariquita Jenny: *Attentive Admirers*
Naftel, Maude: *Mrs. Birch's Garden; Betws-y-Coed*
Paterson, Caroline: *The Garden Path*
Rayner, Louise: *Foregate Street, Chester*
Sainsbury, Grace: *Telling the Time*
Smith, Edith Heckstall: *The Young Match Seller*
Stannard, Emily: *A Still Life with Game*
Sutcliffe, Harriet: *Gathering Plums*
Thompson, Isa: *Springtime*
Waller, Marry: *Portrait of Nancy Tooth*.

389. Waller, Susan. *Women Artists in the Modern Era: A Documentary History*. Metuchen, N. J.: Scarecrow, 1991.

Women's experiences in art history and their progress in the art world is charted from memoirs, journals, letters and public records from the eighteenth century through the twentieth. Anna Jameson observes women artists, Anna Mary Howitt describes her experiences as *An Art Student in*

Munich, and Elizabeth Thompson Butler and Henrietta Ward lend diaries and memoirs.

390. Faxon, Alicia Craig. *"The Legend of Elizabeth Siddall,* by Jan Marsh, *Women Artists and the Pre-Raphaelite Movement,* by Jan Marsh and Pamela Gerrish Nunn; *Worlds of Art: Painters in Victorian Society,* by Paula Gillett. Book Review." *Woman's Art Journal* 12, no. 2 (September 1991): 34-35.

Jan Marsh's book explores the changes in Elizabeth Siddall's image over the decades, and offers explanations for each of the widely varying interpretations of her life and the roles she played in the lives of others. Solid scholarship offers an opportunity to view Siddall as she was, not as others saw her. Marsh and Nunn's collaborative work offers not only considerable information about Victorian women artists as individuals, but makes a solid case for including women in any study of the Pre-Raphaelite movement. Gillett's *Worlds of Art* provides an invaluable social and cultural overview of Victorian artists; she balances the male and female experience to provide a uniquely comprehensive picture.

Reproductions (b/w):

Bunce, Kate: *Melody (Musica)*.

391. Casteras, Susan P. "Gender and Discourse in Victorian Literature and Art." In *The Necessity of a Name. Portrayals and Betrayals of Victorian Women Artists,* 207-232. Antony H. Harrison ed. Dekalb: Northern Illinois University Press, 1992.

Female artists seldom depicted themselves at work. They tended to follow male traditions in subject matter with the usual scenes of motherhood and domesticity. Two exceptions include Florence Claxton's allegorical *Woman's Work: A Medley,* and Emily Mary Osborn's *The Governess.*

Reproductions (b/w):

Claxton, Florence: *Woman's Work: A Medley*

Knight, Laura: *Self-Portrait of the Artist with Nude Model*

Osborn, Emily Mary: *Nameless and Friendless; The Governess*.

392. Jay, Eileen, Mary Noble and Ann Stevenson Hobbs. *A Victorian Naturalist: Beatrix Potter's Drawings from the Armitt Collection.* London: Penguin, 1992.

A self-taught naturalist and an accomplished mycologist, Beatrix Potter endured condescension and even rudeness from "experts" at the National History Museum and Kew Gardens. Her correspondence with a Scottish friend and fellow naturalist reveals the extent of her knowledge and interest; her drawings and paintings of mosses and fungi reveal astonishing technical skill as well as keen observation and painstaking accuracy.

Reproductions (b/w):

Potter, Beatrix: paintings and drawings of mosses, fungi, grasses, birds, animals and archaeological artifacts.

393. Londraville, Janis. "May Morris' Editing of 'So Many Stories Written Here.'" *Journal of the William Morris Society* X, no. 1 (1992): 31-33.

For eight years May Morris was in love with John Quinn, an American who influenced her while she was editing the collected works of her father, William Morris. Biographers tend to omit mention of May Morris' relationship with Quinn because he wished it kept private and most of his letters to her have not survived. William Morris' papers included a love poem called "So Many Stories Written Here," which his daughter copied out and sent to Quinn without comment. Reading the poem with this knowledge makes the poem more meaningful as a statement of May Morris' feelings.

394. Helland, Janice. "Review of Colin White's *The Enchanted World of Jessie King.*" *Woman's Art Journal* 13, no. 2 (September 1992): 46-47.

Colin White's book ignores Jessie King's political views, her relationships with her female contemporaries at the Glasgow School of Art, and it fails to address several fundamental questions that rise from a study of King's prolific and successful art career. Further, in maintaining that decorative art, such as King's, is, of necessity, "superficial," White imprisons King and her work in male-imposed stereotypes.

Reproductions (b/w):

King, Jessie M: *And Gave the Naked Shield.*

395. Birkett, Dea . "A Victorian Painter of Exotic Flora." *The New York Times* (22 November 1992): 30.

The Marianne North Gallery in the Royal Botanic Gardens at Kew has recently been renovated, and is as popular now as it was when it opened in 1882. The exhibit contains 832 of her landscapes and botanical paintings. The brilliance and intensity of North's work makes it an important contribution to art; that many of the forests and plants she painted no longer exist makes her work a vital record of natural history. North began traveling the world and painting after the death of her invalid father when she was forty. She worked and traveled for the rest of her life, pausing in 1882 to help organize the opening of her gallery at Kew. She is still considered a leading botanical artist.

396. Cherry, Deborah. *Painting Women: Victorian Women Artists.* New York: Routledge, 1993.

Biographical sketches of individual women fit with the larger context of social history, with women's relationships with each other, with their work, and with the social system of which they were a part. Notes, bibliography, a checklist of artists with their dates, professional associations, and areas of specialty.

Reproductions (b/w):

Allingham, Helen: *Near Witley, Surrey*

Barker, Lucette: *Lavender Sweep, Wycliffe and 'Liebe Nurse'*

Barker, Lucette: *Laura Taylor and Her Son Wycliffe*

Blunden, Anna: *For Only One Short Hour*

Bodichon, Barbara: *"Ye Newe Generation"*

Bosanquet, Charlotte: *Drawing Room at Meesdenbury, March 1843*

Bowkett, Jane: *Preparing Tea; An Afternoon in the Nursery*

Boyce, Joanna (Wells): *Peep Bo; Gretchen*

Brett, Rosa: *Study of a Turnip Field, Barns and Houses*

Cameron, Catherine: *Roses*

Childers, Milly: *Self-Portrait*

Dacre, Susan Isabel: *Lydia Becker*

De Morgan, Evelyn: *Aurora Triumphans*

Forbes, Elizabeth Armstrong: *School is Out*

Gosse, Ellen: *Torcross, Devon*

Havers, Alice: *The End of Her Journey; The Belle of the Village*

Hayllar, Edith: *Feeding the Swans*

Hayllar, Jessica: *Finishing Touches; Fresh from the Altar*

Jopling, Louise: *Weary Waiting*

Macdonald, Frances: *Ill Omen*

Merritt, Anna Lea: *War*

Neale, Maude *Hall: Two Women in an Aesthetic Interior*

Offord, Gertrude: *Interior of the Old School of Art, Norwich*

Osborn, Emily Mary: *Nameless and Friendless; Barbara Leigh Smith Bodichon; Our Widowed Queen*

Rae, Henrietta: *Psyche at the Throne of Venus*

Richards, Emma: *Self-Portrait*

Severn, Mary: *A Woman of the Petre Dawkins Family; Self-Portrait*

Siddall, Elizabeth: *Self-Portrait; Pippa Passes; The Lady of Shalott*

Solomon, Rebecca: *A Young Teacher; The Governess; The Fugitive Royalists*

Spartali, Marie: *The Lady Prays Desire; Fiammetta Singing*

Stannard, Eloise: *Strawberries on a Cabbage Leaf with a Flower Pot Behind*

Swynnerton, Annie: *Susan Isabel Dacre*

Walker, Alice: *Wounded Feelings*

Ward, Henrietta: *God Save the Queen; Queen Mary Quitted Sterling Castle...*

397. Slatkin, Wendy. *The Voices of Women Artists*. Englewood Cliffs, N. J.: Prentice Hall, 1993.

Since being famous and writing autobiographies each cross the line of social propriety for women, what famous women write about themselves bears careful reading and a different sort of interpretation. Because the voices of women have not been included in the mainstream of literature about art, a compilation of writings by women with opinions about femininity and their place in the art world holds particular interest. Rosa Bonheur is defensive about her short hair and trousers; Anna Howitt calls on women to use their brains and talents, then she marries and never paints again; Louise Jopling firmly asserts her total satisfaction in her single state before she marries for the third time; Elizabeth Thompson Butler keeps her clear vision through fame, marriage, and the horrors of war; and Anna Lea Merritt stays single and maintains that women artists cannot be successful unless they have wives.

Reproductions (b/w):

Butler, Elizabeth Thompson: *The Roll Call*

Merritt, Anna Lea: *Love Locked Out.*

398. Helland, Janice. "Frances Macdonald: The Self as Fin-de-Siècle Woman." *Woman's Art Journal* 14, no. 1 (March 1993): 15-22.

Frances Macdonald's early highly-stylized female forms can be seen as challenging conventional representations of women as either angels or vamps. Later in her career, her representations of female figures seem to reconcile the traditional roles with a wish for independence. Isolation is a familiar theme in her paintings; it is possible to view her work in the light of her own position of woman and artist at the turn of the century when women's roles as well as art styles were changing.

Reproductions (b/w):

Macdonald, Frances: *Girl in the East Wind; A Pond; Spring; Man Makes the Beads of Life but Woman Must Thread Them; Prudence and Desire.*

399. Tarbell, Bethany. "Rosa Bonheur's Menagerie." *Arts and Antiques* (November 1993): 58-64.

While Bonheur's paintings made her one of the best-known artists of the nineteenth century, modern feminist critics see her works as statements of budding independence and power. One critic speculates that Bonheur included self-portraits in men's clothing and short hair in several of her paintings, including the great *Horse Fair.*

Reproductions (col):

Bonheur, Rosa: *The Horse Fair; Plowing the Nivernais; Haymaking in the Auverne; Royalty at Home; Gathering for the Hunt*

Photographs (b/w):

Engraved Portrait of Rosa Bonheur c. 1857

Rosa Bonheur and Nattalie Micas c. 1882

Rosa Bonheur with her lioness c. 1885

Bonheur at Château de By c. 1885

Rosa Bonheur and Anna Klumpke.

400. Marsh, Jan. *Christina Rossetti: A Literary Biography.* London: Jonathan Cape, 1994.

Since, as Jan Marsh remarks, London artists and authors were often acquainted, this biography of the poet Christina Rossetti contains insights as well as glimpses of many women involved in Victorian art, including, of course, Elizabeth Siddall.

401. Carr, Carolyn K. and Webster, Sally. "Mary Cassatt and Mary Fairchild MacMonnies: The Search for Their 1893 Murals." *American Art* 8, no. 1 (December 1994): 52-69.

Some of the murals from the 1893 Chicago Exhibition were saved; Mary MacMonnies' *Primitive Woman* was exhibited in 1906 at the Société Nationale des Beaux Arts, in 1911 at an exhibition in St. Louis, Missouri, and from 1911 at least until 1912 above the grand staircase of the Chicago Art Institute. MacMonnies' mural, and Mary Cassatt's mural, *Modern Woman*, were offered to the University of Notre Dame in 1911, but there is no further record of them. Other works from the exhibition were sent to Midwestern colleges and museums, leaving a possibility that these and other art works from the Women's Exhibition may yet be found.

Reproductions (b/w):

Cassatt, Mary: *Modern Woman; Portrait de Mlle S. H.* (Sara Tyson Halloway)

MacMonnies, Mary Fairchild: *Primitive Woman.*

402. Hirsch, Pam. "Barbara Leigh Smith Bodichon: Artist and Activist." In *Women in the Victorian Art World*, 167-186. ed. Clarissa Campbell Orr. New York: Manchester University Press, 1995.

One of the most influential and successful of feminist reformers, Barbara Leigh Smith Bodichon, was also recognized as an accomplished landscape painter. Much of the money she donated to found Girton College, Cambridge, came from sales of her paintings. Bodichon's family background, friends, education, eclectic reading habits and travel opportunities contributed to her artistic as well as to her political vision, both of which reflect a strong influence of Romanticism.

Reproductions (b/w):

Bodichon, Barbara: sketch from 1846-51 sketchbook; *Eruption of Vesuvius from Naples, May 1855; Trieste--Vienna Road; Solitude; Louisiana Swamp*

Laurence, Samuel: *Head Study of Barbara Leigh Smith Bodichon.*

403. Irwin, Francina. "Amusement or Instruction? Watercolour Manuals and the Woman Amateur." In *Women in the Victorian Art World*, 149-166. ed. Clarissa Campbell Orr. New York: Manchester University Press, 1995.

Nineteenth-century "how to" manuals were widely available resources for amateur painters. Queen Victoria kept *Ackermann's Manual of Colours* tucked in her paintbox, even though she had no shortage of famous and competent painter-teachers. These manuals, which encouraged close observation to nature as well as careful use of line and color, were especially useful to amateur botanical painters.

Reproductions (b/w):

Gartside, Mary: *Ornamental Groups Descriptive of Flowers, Birds, Shells, Fruit, Insects, etc.*

Irvine, Anna Forbes: *Ballochbuie Forest, Braemar.*

404. Marsh, Jan. "Art, Ambition and Sisterhood in the 1850's." In *Women in the Victorian Art World*, 33-48. ed. Clarissa Campbell Orr. New York: Manchester University Press, 1995.

The deeply-ingrained proscription against "calling attention to oneself" proved a serious obstacle to women artists. Madame de Staël's novel *Corinne* provided an independent, talented, self-reliant heroine who played a major part in liberating the image of the nineteenth-century British female. Many women found support for themselves and their art in friendships, societies, schools and exhibitions. Still, lack of opportunity and the pressure to keep a low profile took its toll among many gifted female artists.

CHAPTER 2
Exhibitions
Going Public

Leafing through the annotations in this section, one cannot help but be struck by the number of exhibitions and the number of female exhibitors. Both can be attributed to the importance in the nineteenth century of sketching and painting as an essential part of middle- and upper-class education. Boys as well as girls grew to adulthood with art as an interest, hobby, or vocation. Since photography was still in its early, awkward stages, one captured "Kodak moments" in sketchbooks and travel diaries, especially as travel became easier and cheaper. Painting, especially in ladylike pastels and watercolors, was as important a part of a young woman's repertoire as her needlework and her musical accomplishments. Women who wanted to get serious with oil paints and art schools discovered that the leap from art for casual amusement to serious profession involved much more than a change of attitude. All the arts demand time, concentration, self-absorption, hard work, and relentless dedication--all qualities that were considered unladylike in a time when creatures like David Copperfield's flighty Dora and his devoted Agnes were feminine ideals. The Doras were encouraged to be childlike ornaments and the Agnesses were trained to be selfless and self-effacing.

A middle-class education taught the rules of perspective, proportion and color in an art tradition that was entirely representational and thus easily understood even by the untutored. Art galleries were plentiful, accessible, and convenient social gathering places, crowded with paintings and spectators. Exhibitors and spectators were undeterred by the galleries' practice of crowding every available inch of wall space with pictures, where a picture placed at eye level, or "hung on the line" gave it particular prestige. Art reviewers often complained that small paintings placed too high to be seen often deserved better, and that pictures "on the line" should have been placed someplace less conspicuous. It should be remembered that these were exhibits of contemporary art, and that galleries were privately owned. Art museums were certainly as well or better attended than they are now, but the popular appeal of art in the nineteenth century is hard to imagine in today's world when private galleries are small and struggling and the successful galleries tend to be intimidating and to cater to the wealthy and well educated. Indeed, most people today have never been in a private art gallery, and when they do wander in, they often feel bewildered or bored. Modern art has freed itself from the fetters of sentimentality and the insistence on realism and the limitations of realism, but schools have not educated the public to keep the pace.

Of course, popularity has a price. Victorian art was plagued with amateurs and dilettantes of both sexes in huge numbers. The problem was furthered by the number of women who needed to support themselves and painting was one of the few possibilities, since it was considered fairly respectable and since higher education and professions were not yet open to women. A good painting gives pleasure, and pleasing others was a Victorian woman's highest calling. The poet William Allingham, writing of his wife Helen Allingham's work, remarked in a letter to a friend that making art was "a good lot, to feel the truest pleasure in one's work and at the same time. . . one is providing for the pleasure of others."[1] William Allingham took his wife's work quite seriously, but his mention of the altruistic side of her work was followed by a statement of its practicality: her paintings preserved a record of old rural cottages falling into abandonment and disrepair with the population migration to the cities. Helen Allingham's painting's were ideal not in themselves but in the pleasure they gave and in their historical value. If a woman needed justification to pursue serious art, these two served admirably.

Since serious training was available to only a few wealthy women, the combination of women painting for fun and women who painted seriously but not always skillfully led to too many paintings, most of them mediocre or just plain bad. The reviewers constantly complained about the poor quality of work by female exhibitors. Even supportive publications like *The Art Journal* and *The Magazine of Art* seem to condescend even when occasionally surprised by excellence. Critical reviews were too brief, too patronizing, and as Pamela Gerrish Nunn points out, too male.[2] Constructive, specific criticism by professionals is a crucial tool for a serious artist. Reviewers usually mentioned women's exhibits briefly, at the end of long articles focusing on the probably better-executed works by better-known male artists. The women occasionally merited a sentence or two, with congratulations for a "vital,

---

[1] William Allingham, *Letters*, Eds., H. Allingham and E. Baumer Williams, (London: Longmans, 1911), Rpt., N. Y.: AMS Press, 1971.

[2] Pamela Gerrish Nunn, "Critically Speaking," *Women in the Victorian Art World*, Ed., Clarissa Campbell Orr, (New York: Manchester UP, 1995), pp. 107-124. Nunn points out that art criticism was a male voice with a male point of view and thus not always an appropriate assessment of women's art. Thus, women's diaries, letters, and personal records deserve critical attention and assessment.

graceful" work or a "touching subject"; sometimes only a string of names appeared with a "works deserving mention" comment. Just as unhelpful and even more discouraging were assessments of paintings "too vigorous for a lady" or "too refined" or "bland" or "poorly drawn." Searching a nineteenth-century art review for mention of women is now, as it must have been then, an invitation to eye strain and frustration. The annotations in this book will not mislead if one remembers that an article consisting of six pages of fine print in narrow columns may or may not contain a few brief sentences about paintings by women.

On the more positive side, however, were the art societies that welcomed women as full members and who held quality, juried exhibitions. The Royal Academy may have been the most prestigious, but it was far from the only option.[3] The watercolor societies, for example, for the most part supported successful artists such as Helen Allingham, the Montalba sisters, Helen Angell, Mary Ann Duffield and Mary L. Gow. Regional art societies outside of London such as those in Birmingham, Manchester and Liverpool also encouraged such excellent artists as Louise Rayner, Edith Martineau, Emily Mary Osborn, Louise Jopling and Alice Havers, who in turn must have been an inspiration for professionalism and excellence. Articles in the London art journals mentioned women working with fine arts societies in Ireland and Scotland, although little has been written about them. Exhibits of The Irish Fine Arts Society, The Royal Scottish Academy and the Glasgow Institute of Fine Arts, among others, featured Irish and Scottish women artists and frequently English women artists as well.

In a class by itself and certainly one of the most fascinating of art societies was the controversial Society of Lady Artists, founded in 1857. If offered physical space and convenient communication for women in the arts, and predictably created controversy. Its exhibitions were accessible for amateurs and provided a good marketplace for professional artists of lesser standing, and for buyers who could not afford Royal Academy prices. This advantage carried with it the penalty of lesser standing so that established artists tended to avoid it for fear of damaging reputations earned by hard fighting and intense competition in male-dominated exhibitions. Anna Lea Merritt, who contributed significantly to the art in the Women's Building of the 1893 Chicago Exhibition, warned in a *Lippincott's Monthly Magazine* article of 1900 that a lower competitive level resulted in lower quality and diminished progress.[4]

---

[3] For comprehensive discussions of the history and workings of the various art schools and societies open to women, see Pamela Gerrish Nunn's *Victorian Women Artists* and Paula Gillett's *Worlds of Art: Painters in Victorian Society.*

[4] Anna Lea Merritt, "A Letter to Artists: Especially Women Artists," in *Love Locked Out: The Memoirs of Anna Lea Merritt*, Ed., Galina Gorokhoff, (Boston: Museum of Fine Arts, 1981), pp. 233-238.

The reviews of Society of Lady Artists exhibitions are often odd, such as the one in an 1889 *Magazine of Art* article which called the Society an institution of neither school nor creed with little to justify it, since the quality of exhibits are poor and since women have always been well treated in traditional galleries and societies.[5] An 1853 review praised the society's seventh exhibition as its best yet, calling it "one of the most useful" of art organizations.[6] An 1881 *Magazine of Art* review commented that the society's current exhibition ranked with "any minor exhibition. . . where the artist has, so to say, no sex."[7] "No sex" in this case is praise--the reviewer meant that the women's painting, if not exactly good, was at least starting to look more like what the men were producing for the mainstream exhibitions. An earlier 1883 *Magazine of Art* review mentioned the society's lack of skill and seriousness but praised the obvious efforts of its exhibitors to improve their work.[8] The *Art Journal* was consistently less querulous and more encouraging. An 1858 *Art Journal* review remarked on the limitations imposed on women of talent who had no access to instruction in drawing human models from life.[9] Over the years the *Art Journal* continued to encourage the society with lengthy reviews, positive comments, and an effort at specific and constructive criticism. An 1875 review chastised successful artists who neglected the women's exhibit once their work achieved recognition elsewhere. Elizabeth Butler, Henrietta Ward, Louise Jopling, Eloise Stannard and Barbara Bodichon were praised for their continued support of the women's society.[10] The question of whether women should exhibit their work in their own space or continue to compete with men was still an issue in 1893 when art submissions to The Women's Building of the Chicago Exhibition were definitely inferior to the ones sent to the main art exhibition building. Even Elizabeth Butler, who sent *To The Front* to the women's building, was represented in the Fine Arts Building by *The Roll Call*,[11] perhaps the most famous of nineteenth-century British paintings. Ironically, the American press virtually ignored it. It probably would have been better noticed in the Women's Building.

Susan Casteras writes of the many friendships among Victorian women artists, of the ways they supported each other through "matronage" of buyers and mentors, of the diversity of backgrounds and skill-levels and of the determination, dedication, and independence of these women at work.[12] Her scholarship points out the

---

[5] "The Chronicle of Art. Exhibitions of the Month," *Magazine of Art*, (1889), pp. xxix-xxxi.

[6] "The Society of Female Artists," *Art Journal*, (1 May 1853), p. 95.

[7] "Art Notes," *Magazine of Art* 4 (1881), pp. i-xlviii.

[8] "Art in April," *Magazine of Art*, (1883), pp. xxv-xxxiii.

[9] "The Society of Female Artists," *Art Journal*, (1 May 1858), pp. 143-144.

[10] "The Society of Female Artists," *Art Journal*, (1 June 1875), pp. 186-187.

[11] Jeanne Madeline Weimann, *The Fair Women*, (Chicago: Academy Chicago, 1981).

[12] Susan Casteras, "From 'Safe Havens' to 'A Wide Sea of Notoriety,'" *A Struggle for Fame: Victorian Women Artists and Authors*, (New Haven: Yale Center for British Art, 1994).

importance of further study, of avoiding generalizations about an oppressed body of women, and for seeing these Victorian artists as a courageous group who did as much to change the art world as any of the male schools which so pointedly ignored or disparaged them. These women were fascinating, alive, and are still very much with us in their work and in the statements they made with their lifestyles, with their writing, and with their painting.

---

405. "Exhibition of the Royal Academy: The Seventy-Ninth: 1847." *The Art Union* (1 June 1847): 185-199.

This year's exhibition is one of the best in the history of the Academy, particularly because of the contributions of the younger members, a reminder that reform from within the institution is crucial to its health and progress. The "liberal men members" have had some of their reforms thwarted, but recognition of the need for change would only benefit the academy and the progress of art. Only a few of the 700 pictures in the exhibit can be mentioned specifically. Margaret Carpenter has two paintings worthy of mention: *Mother and Child,* which features life-sized figures, and *John Turner, Esq.,* a successful portrait of a thoughtful subject. Miss F. S. Day's *Portrait of a Lady* exemplifies brilliant handling of flesh tones. Fanny Geep's *Mrs. George Brooke* is a brilliantly painted portrait; *Mrs. John Palmer* is a graceful likeness, and the draperies are painted remarkably well. Miss M. Townsend's *A Portrait,* a study of an elderly person, is agreeable and natural. *The Slave's Dream,* a picture of a female slave in chains, holding her child and dreaming of her husband, herself and their child together, is well drawn and admirably composed, but the artist, Mrs. McIan, usually paints with more color: the picture is certainly not finished. Miss E. Cole has painted Portia with energy and boldness, even if the figure of Portia "is wanting in becoming expression." Rosamund Vertue has submitted *Study from Nature*, a head study well drawn and colored. Miss M.A. Cole's *Ave Maria* is "judiciously composed." In the Drawings and Miniatures section, Alicia Laird's *Madame Yturregui*, Margaret Gillies' *Charles Walpole, Esq.*, Mrs. G. R. Ward's *Portrait of a Lady*, and Mrs. W. Carpenter's *Children of George Eyre* are done with the skill and care that is typical of their work.

406. "The Society of Painters in Water Colours: The Forty-Third Exhibition: 1847." *Art Union* (1 June 1847): 201-202.

Eliza Sharpe has taken great care with *The Ten Virgins,* one of the few figure-paintings in the exhibit. Three flower pieces, *Camelias; A Jar of*

Flowers; and *Spring Flowers,* show Maria Harrison's great skill in imitating nature.

407. "The British Institution Exhibition: 1848." *Art Union* (1 March 1848): 81-84.
A poorly-managed exhibition of works without genius contains only a few paintings worthy of mention. *Roses*, painted by Mrs. Harrison, displays her usual freshness, knowledge, and skill, and Mrs. Carpenter's *A Child and Kitten* is lifelike, but carelessly finished.

408. "The Free Exhibition: First Exhibition--1848. Hyde Park Corner." *Art Union* (1 May 1848): 142-144.
A well-organized exhibit of high standards in a room with ideal light deserves to be recognized and encouraged, especially as it makes room for fresh talent ignored by the Royal Academy. Fanny McIan has two noteworthy works: *The Lesson* pictures a medieval lady receiving archery instruction from a Friar Tuck figure. *The Little Sick Scholar* is taken from a scene in Dickens' *Old Curiosity Shop*. Ann Paulson has painted *Fruit* and *The Upset Basket* with "power and truth." Emma Oliver has several landscapes, including *Richmond, in Yorkshire*, and *On the Muse*. Nancy Rayner's *The Retainer's Gallery, Knowle*, is "almost too vigorous for a lady." Mrs. Robertson's *Moses* is a literal representation of the Old Testament account of baby Moses' rescue from the river. *The Virgin Mary*, a life-sized painting, is not as carefully finished as one is used to seeing in Robertson's work.

409. "New Society of Painters in Water-Colours: Fourteenth Exhibition: 1848." *Art Union* (1 May 1848): 141-142.
The Society continues to progress in quality and influence. The many meritorious works in this year's exhibit are from some of Britain's most distinguished artists. Unfortunately, only a few can be mentioned here. It is a pleasure to see work by Sarah Setchel, who has not exhibited for several seasons. Her subject, *An Ye Shall Walk in Silk Attire*, is taken from a Scotch ballad, and while it has some excellent aspects, it is unfortunately like a painting by Wilke. Also of note are Mary Harrison's elegant and lifelike *Fruit and Flowers*. Fanny Corbaux's *Leah*, picturing an Old Testament theme, is reminiscent of the old school of painting, and her *Rachel* is a good companion piece. Mrs. Margetts' *Bacchanalian Cup*, a still-life of grapes and flowers, is brilliant, charming, elegant, and marvelous. *Vivia Perpetua*, by Jane Sophia Egerton, takes a story from church history and depicts it with extraordinary force.

410. "The Society of British Artists: Twenty-Fifth Exhibition: 1848." *Art Union* (1 May 1848): 138-141.

In a disappointing exhibit with few pictures worthy of mention, Mrs. Harrison's *Fruit* is painted with admirable attention to freshness and texture. The watercolor room has the best exhibits, and among the fine examples are *Lover's Quarrel*, by Miss M.A. Nichols; *Fruit*, by Miss M. Harrison; *Gerard Dow*, by Anne Brimmer; *Case of Bracelet Miniatures*, by Mrs. V. Bartholomew; and *The Rustic Nosegay*, by Jane Amelia Burgess.

411. "Exhibition of the Society of Painters in Water-Colours." *Art Union* (1 June 1848): 181-182.

The forty-fourth exhibition is unfortunately redundant; it features the same old landscape scenes. Figure paintings would add interest and variety. The older members, especially, seem unambitious and uninterested in challenges. The society needs new members. Maria Harrison's *Roses* shows careful study and considerable knowledge.

412. "The Free Exhibition: Hyde Park Corner." *Art Union* (1 June 1848): 198.

Space limitations in last month's review of this exhibit meant omitting works that deserved mention. Several are mentioned now, among them the still-lifes of Mrs. Paulson. Her careful arrangements are painted with skill and freedom that must make her a good teacher as well as a consummate painter in this genre.

413. "The Royal Academy. The Eightieth Exhibition: 1848." *Art Union* (1 June 1848): 165-180.

This year's exhibition opened with the usual dinner, congratulations, and private viewing, but an undignified throng rushed in to view the exhibit when it was opened to the public. The noise, crowds and heat made it impossible to contemplate the paintings with care. The Royal Academy really ought to do something. Among those works exhibited were Mary Dear's *Studies*, similar to Jane Benham's *Studies from Nature*, painted with great skill unworthy of the humble subject. Both Dear and Benham are capable of better work. Mrs. Carpenter's *A Lace-Maker* is agreeable and competent. Her *Lady Jones* is also excellent; the color and vigor found in this fine figure painting is unexcelled by "even the most distinguished professors of this genre." In Eliza Goodall's *The Idle Nurse*, a cottage scene of a young woman by a cradle, the handling of color could set an example for much more experienced artists. A reading woman, the subject of Miss M.A. Cole's *Meditation* is painted gracefully and tastefully. The subject of *The Echo of the Waves*, by Miss E. Acraman, is children on the sea shore, a scene taken from Wordsworth's "Excursion." The painting deserves to be better placed. Mrs. Arnold painted the landscape and T. Uwins painted the figures in *Dorothea Surprised by Cardeno, the Curate, and the Barber*. The story has been done too often to offer anything new, and in this rendition the figures are small, the landscape sweeping and romantic. Among the drawings and miniatures, Mrs. J. H. Carter has carefully drawn the head and bust of *Mrs. Charles Harrison* and colored it agreeably. Miss M.A. Nichols' *The Portrait of Shakespeare* is a good imitation of a cameo and a recognizable portrait of the famous subject. Mrs. J. H. Carter's head and bust of *Mrs. John Hare* features remarkably good color. Mrs. V. Bartholomew (Fitz James) has created a tiny portrait with remarkable resemblance and excellent color in *A Bracelet Miniature of Jones Hall Pope, Esq.* She captures childhood delicacy in *A Bracelet Miniature of Master Howard*. Mrs. A. Cole has managed remarkable color in *Portrait of a Belgian Lady*. Picture and portrait are combined with great success in Clara E. F. Kettle's *The Misses Soulsby*. A miniature in oil of *Mrs. Charles Walpole*, by Miss M. Gillies contains good finish with depth. Mrs. H. Moseley has drawn the head of Miss Henrietta Ward that shows off the young lady's animation. About 1,500 pictures were rejected this year, several artists of high repute were among the disappointed. Clearly, larger facilities are in order.

414. "The British Institution: Exhibition 1849." *Art Union* (1 March 1849): 78.

The British Institution exhibition this year contains 504 pictures displaying technical skill but not much intellect, even from painters who possess the genius to challenge themselves. A few pictures display skill, including *Summer Amusement*, a seascape with a child and toy boat, painted by Mrs. Carpenter. Miss J. MacLeod's figures are well drawn and skillfully painted in *The Interior of the Fisher's Cottage*, which depicts a young woman mourning over a young fisherman.

415. "The Exhibition of the Society of British Artists." *Art Journal* (1 May 1849): 145-146.

The exhibits this year are limited so that no pictures were hung too high to be seen, and works of non-members are exhibited on an equal basis with works of members. The exhibits number over 600, of which only a few can be mentioned. *The Future Artist* is poetical and pastoral, as it shows a farmer's boy, who may represent Gainesborough, sitting with a sketch book. The picture is a credit to its painter, Miss Fox. *Near*

Penryn--North Wales is small and its subject insignificant but Charlotte Nasmyth's treatment gives it importance. Mrs. Hurlstone's *Helping Pa* and Anne Bartholomew's portraits also merit mention as important pieces.

416. "The Hyde Park Gallery." *Art Journal* (1 May 1849): 47.

An earlier review was written before the catalogue and exhibition were completed; a few works are so exemplary as to merit mention here, among them Mrs. Robertson's *Little Red Riding Hood*, which shows a forceful style. Fanny MacIan's *Soldier's Wives Waiting the Result of a Battle* shows great skill and originality. The figures wear eighteenth-century costumes painted with careful detail. The painting, in all respects, is "masterly."

417. "Exhibition of the Society of Painters in Water-Colours." *Art Journal* (1 June 1849): 177-178.

The 28 April private review of the Society of Painters in Water-Colours showed no large works, as water color is not suited to a large scale. The 365 paintings are some of the best exhibited by this society in years. One work, *Nature and Art* by Mary Ann Criddle, shows a woman and child sitting near a sketch of "suffer the little children," and combines the sacred and secular in natural proximity. Maria Harrison's *Basket of Roses* contains "great spirit and natural freshness of hue."

418. "Exhibition of Paintings and Drawings by Amateur Artists." *Art Journal* (1 June 1849): 199.

An exhibition to raise funds for London charity schools features mostly works by women from the aristocracy. The paintings and drawings are of superior quality, demonstrating not only talent, but knowledge of art that can only enhance and encourage the work of other artists and appreciation by the public. By far the best of the exhibit is *Rest of the Weary* by Miss Blake; her picture of an Italian peasant woman with her child resting on the steps of a church shows skill in composition that would do credit to a professional. Miss Blake has also contributed *Walnut Gathering on Lake Lucerne: Amsterdam;* and the *Valley of the Linth.* Other works deserving special mention are Miss Sneyd's *Crown of Thorns* and *Interior;* Lady E. Finch's *Interior;* the Marchioness of Waterford's *The Return of Tobias;* Miss Houlton's *Study of a Young Girl;* Mrs. Davidson's *The Chateau de Valere* and *Venice;* Lady C. Palmer's *A Study of Heads;* Hon. Eleanor Stanley's *The Castle of Risti;* and Viscountess Canning's *View in the Campagna, Rome.* Woodcut artists are well represented by Miss Harriet Ludlow Clarke, whose woodcuts of old works of old masters have appeared in the *Art Journal*. Her sister, Miss Clarke has contributed a head study of a Scotch terrier. Other female contributors include the Countess Somers; Viscountess Combermere; the Ladies Dacre; M.A. Legge; C. Legge; Grenville H. Clive; E. and F. Finch; A. and H. Cadogan; M.A. Alford; S. H. Williams; E. Butler; Talbot; E. Stanley, and Grey. Untitled contributors include Jemima Wedderburne; Miss Gordon; F. Boothby; E. and M. E. Sneyd; Swinburne; and F. Cust.

419. "The New Society of Painters in Water-Colours." *Art Journal* (1 June 1849): 178-179.

Mary Margett's *Flowers and Fruit* is a still-life painted with truth and skill. Other works exhibited by this artist are of equal merit. *Hagar* by Fanny Corbaux depicts a scene from Genesis. Meritorious drawings in the exhibit include Fanny Steer's *Ludlow, Shropshire; Bank of Primroses* by Mary Harrison; *Margaret* by Jane Egerton; and *A Portrait* by Sarah Setchel. The exhibit contains mostly landscapes and some very good figure drawings. On the whole, the exhibit lacks range, but presents less melodrama and sentiment than usual.

420. "The Royal Academy. The Eighty-First Exhibition: 1849." *Art Journal* (1 June 1849): 165-178.

The eighty-first exhibition of the Royal Academy is just like all the others: the academy is so locked into its past and so resistant to reform that it cannot serve the needs of the artists struggling for recognition and who have something to contribute to the advancement of art. To compound the problem, the old artists have stayed with their old habits. Of the 1,341 works (145 sculptures), some works possess merit and deserve favorable mention. Mary Harrison's *Fruit*, a painting of black grapes and other items, is executed with great feeling. Margaret Carpenter's *Mrs. John Walton*, a portrait of a lady dressed in crimson, is equal of much of the best works in the exhibit, and her portrait of *The Children of George Smith, Esq.* is painted with her usual excellence. Jessie MacLeod's *A Village Genius*, a picture of a boy playing a violin for an admiring audience of relatives, is painted with good color and composition. Eliza Goodall's *Interior* of a highland cottage, made from sketches on the spot, is a small picture of considerable quality. Harriet Arnold's *The Farm Yard* is a faithful and skillful rendition of its subject. *Plough Horses Startled by a Railway Engine*, by Jemima Wedderburne, is an "extraordinary subject for a lady, but painted with skill and spirit." Edith Acraman has painted *A Vase of Flowers* with a red curtain with care and good taste. Among the miniatures, Margaret Gillies has painted a child and a woman in black, titled simply, *Portraits*. Anne Bartholomew has painted brooch miniatures of *Georgina Flint and Emily Montague--Niece and Daughter of the Hon. Mrs. Spencer Montague*. The heads of the two children are painted with remarkable delicacy, color, and finesse. Other works of interest include Maria Moseley's *A Portrait* and Mary Anne Nichols' imitation cameos.

421. "Exhibition of the Prize Pictures of the Art Union." *Art Journal* (1 September 1849): 272.

The exhibition of prize paintings of the British Artists affords advantages for both artist and public; fewer paintings mean better positions on the wall to the advantage of the painting and the ease of the spectator. Among the noteworthy exhibits are Fanny McIan's *Soldiers' Wives Waiting the Result of Battle,* which received favorable comment at the Free Exhibition; its "judicious grouping and good color" are more evident in this less-crowded exhibit. *Hagar,* a watercolor by Fanny Corbaux is among the pictures cited as having considerable merit.

422. "The British Institution. Exhibition 1850." *Art Journal* (1 March 1850): 89-92.

Most of the exhibits can be described as only mediocre, but in any case, they are an improvement over the last three years. The hanging arrangement is better, and many artists seem to be trying to improve. Not all the works can be mentioned, but focus is on younger artists who show promise. Among these is Mrs. Philips. Her *The Interior of the Chapel of St. Erasmus, Westminster Abbey* is an accurate study done on the spot. *The Gleaner's Child* by Margaret Carpenter is a small, but firmly-painted head study. An ambitious and praiseworthy work by Jessie MacLeod, *The Return of the Prodigal Son*, deserves mention, as does Mary Harrison's careful rendition of a vase of flowers, titled simply, *Roses*.

423. "Royal Scottish Academy." *Art Journal* (1 April 1850): 101- 102.

The work of Scottish painters is easily as good as that of their London counterparts. Many works of younger artists especially show genius and promise. Frances Stoddart has contributed one of the best landscapes in *Head of Ullswater--Cumberland*. The light on water, hills and trees creates a pleasing effect. Another agreeable scene appears in Jane Nasmyth's *Furness Abbey;* she has done especially well with the group of thorns in the foreground. Worthy of mention among the painters of miniatures are Mrs. Dewar and Mary Anne Nichols.

424. "Society of British Artists: Twenty-Seventh Exhibition--1850." *Art Journal* (1 May 1850): 136-138.

The 735 paintings, sculptures, and miniatures in this exhibit show a few meritorious works, but little in the way of incoming new talent or progressing older talent. Bad management and stiff competition seem to be bringing about the decline of this society. Noteworthy watercolors include *Sketch of Miss Mowatt, the American Actress* by Miss Fox; *Brooch Miniatures* by Anne Bartholomew; and *Cleopatra* by Clara E. F. Kettle.

425. "The New Society of Painters in Water-Colours." *Art Journal* (1 June 1850): 179-180.

While this sixteenth exhibition of 329 works shows few subjects of real merit, the figure compositions are of excellent quality. Mary Harrison's *Garden Shed* is "a celebration of brilliant hues and tender textures" of flowers and fruit. *The Convalescent*, a picture of a pale girl with a lingering illness being tended by a cheerful, healthy, affectionate sister, is one of Fanny Corbaux' best works as yet. Her *Doubts* also merits mention. Mary Margett's *Roses and Fruit* shows "temptingly real" grapes. Emma Oliver's *At Lambedr--North Wales* is "picturesque" and effectively drawn. Sarah Setchel's *Jessie and Colin* illustrates a scene from *Crabbe's Tales* in which Colin Grey's mother "suggests he should procure the license." Setchel does not exhibit often, but when she does, her works are always, like this one, extraordinary. Mary Harrison's *Lilac* and Fanny Harris' *Study from Nature* also deserve praise.

426. "The Royal Academy. The Eighty-Second Exhibition: 1850." *Art Journal* (1 June 1850): 165-178.

The refusal of the Royal Academy to take advice or admit change has resulted in loss of support from the government and the public; the Royal Academy has lost funding and space. All this amounts to a tremendous loss to the art world. One concession this year has been an invitation to journalists for a private preview. The 1,456 paintings, miniatures and sculptures are mostly satisfactory. Mrs. Carpenter is represented by several works of excellence: *Portrait of Mrs. Simpson* shows a graceful woman in white; *Children of Rev. G. Barnes, Northcote*, shows a boy, a girl, and a kitten; and *A Lady Sketching* shows a woman standing in profile against a tree. All exhibit Carpenter's firm touch and fresh color, and the last reminds one of "the more sketchy style of the English school." Eliza Goodall's *A Farmhouse Kitchen* is a fine example of her tasteful interiors. *A Study of a Factory Child* by Miss Fox is a delicate head study, but is so poorly placed as to make closer observation difficult. Henrietta Ward's "clean decided touch" can be seen in *Result of Antwerp Marketing*, a composition of basket, pheasant, fruit and other items. Margaret Gillies' *Miss Annie Finlaison*, an elegant portrait of a woman in white, and A. Cole's *Portrait of Mrs. Charles Salaman* are simple and tasteful. Mrs. Carpenter's *Portrait of Mrs. Wigan*, a watercolor sketch, and a head study by Fanny Corbaux, show skill in touch and color.

427. "The British Institution, Exhibition 1851." *Art Journal* (1 March 1851): 72-75.

The 538 exhibits of painting and sculpture are generally below average; little imaginative effort seems to have been expended, even by the best-known artists. The reviewer suspects that, unfortunately, few paintings were rejected. Jessie MacLeod has painted a number of figures, some with especially well-done heads, in *A Village School tittled--Arrival of a Poor Irish Scholar*. The scene is from a story by Mrs. S. C. Hall (wife of the *Art Journal* editor). Eliza Goodall's *Cottage Children* is a commendable scene with several children; it is as good a work as any of Goodall's paintings so far.

428. "The National Institution. The Third Exhibition." *Art Journal* (1 May 1851): 138-140.

This is an excellent exhibition of 449 works marked by an effort to meet new challenges. Emma Oliver's *Coniston Lake, Westmoreland* is up to her usual excellence in its firmness and truthful color. Miss L. Gillies is among those singled out for honorable mention in the watercolors and chalk drawings.

429. "The Society of British Artists. Twenty-Eighth Exhibition--1851." *Art Journal* (1 May 1851): 136-138.

The Society's efforts to encourage new talent and to improve the work of established members has resulted in an excellent exhibition. Charlotte Nasmyth's *Near Ballington, Cheshire*, a picture of three oaks, is so light that it is flat, but the trees are well done. Mary Harrison's *Roses* display the talents of a mature and observant artist. Eliza Turck's *Study of a Head* is life-like and life-sized. Concerning the watercolor room, there is not much space to comment, but several works deserve mention. Clara E. F. Kettle has sent two charming miniatures, *The Sisters* and *Portrait of a Lady*. Anne C. F. Bartholomew's *Portrait of Miss Glyn* is "a miniature of exquisite softness and finish." Mrs. Merrifield's *Portrait of Lady Crompton* and Miss Scott's *The Wandering Minstrel* also deserve recognition.

430. "The British Institution: Exhibition, 1852." *Art Journal* (1 March 1852): 69-74.

This year's exhibition of the British Institution follows the tradition of the last few years of producing second-rate exhibitions by second-rate artists. The most talented and well- known artists avoid it because of bad practices of the British Institution in earlier years. In its favor, it may be said that there are some improvements in the hanging practices, and that the exhibition of 531 paintings is no worse than in earlier years. All of the exhibits are reviewed here. Eliza Goodall's cottage interior, showing a mother and child at lessons, is titled *La Leçon Religieuse*. It is an excellent piece of work in all respects. Her *Irish Mother*, another study of a mother and child is sensitively drawn and colored. *Hush!*, by Margaret Carpenter is a lively headstudy of a child. A small *Study from Nature, a Girl of Audernach*, by Jessie MacLeod, is distinguished by its quality.

431. "The Exhibitions." *Illustrated London News* (1 May 1852): 343.

Fanny McIan's *Highlands, 1852* is one of the best pictures in a fine selection at the National Institution of the Fine Arts. Simply titled, the picture contains tremendous emotional appeal-- poor emigrants taking a last painful look at their beloved homeland. The picture is powerful, truthful, and must provoke thoughtful consideration by the viewer.

432. "The Royal Scottish Academy, 1852. The Twenty-Sixth." *Art Journal* (1 May 1852): 133-138.

Scotland has contributed some of its finest artists to English academies, and as usual, the Scottish Exhibition reflects that tradition of excellence. Among those deserving mention in the collection of almost 700 works are watercolors by Mary Harrison titled *Spring Flowers and Camellias;* Anne Bartholomew's *The Sisters;* a graceful and brilliantly colored miniature titled *Portrait of a Lady* by Clara Kettle; *An Autumn Group* by Julia Childs; and *Hollyhocks* by Mary Ann Duffield.

433. "The British Institution: Exhibition, 1853." *Art Journal* (1 March 1853): 84-88.

Small paintings of landscape and marine subjects predominate in this fine exhibit of almost 600 paintings. The few scenes from poetical subjects are, for the most part, not remarkable. Margaret Gillies' *From the Ballad of Auld Robin Gray* is done with her usual care. Mrs. W. Carpenter's *I Know My Lesson*, a head study of a little girl, is done with Carpenter's usual "natural colour and firm touch." Eliza Goodall's *A French Market Place* shows such careful attention to detail that it creates a "perfectly French" atmosphere. Mrs. G. E. Hering shows the influence of her teacher in *From a Sketch Near Spezzia*, but the effect has charm, and the color is brilliant.

434. "The Society of Female Artists." *Art Journal* (1 May 1853): 95.

The seventh exhibition of "one of the most useful...institutions" promoting fine art makes a successful transition through "the perils of infancy" to a stable and recognized school. Between two- and three-hundred works were rejected; the result is the best exhibition yet from this institution. The usual flowers, fruit and still-life compositions at which women excel are much in evidence, but the real test of an artist is figure drawing, and this exhibition has some fine examples of that genre as well. In the past, works by French women have been featured in this exhibition; this year only two, Madame Jerichau's *Britannia Rules the Waves* and Madame Lundgren's portraits of the Brothers Grimm represent French contributions. Margaret Gillies' touching *Awakened Sorrows--Old Letters* shows a young girl comforting an older female companion. The close relationship of the two is obvious. The drapery alone makes this a work of considerable merit. Margaret Backhouse has sent four or five drawings mostly of heads of children. *Only a Half-Penny* depicts a little girl selling flowers. *Bringing Home the Dinner* is a picture of a small girl carrying a dish of meat and potatoes. In *Borrowed Plumes*, a girl tries on her employer's cap. All are well colored and well drawn. Mrs. Robertson Blaine has outdone herself with a landscape, *The Town of Le Puy, etc*. Another much warmer composition depicts what is perhaps a suburb of Toledo. Margaret Carpenter has painted a quite successful portrait of the sculptor, *Mr. Gibson*. Emma Oliver's *Savoy* is "a rich and sunny landscape." Other of her paintings in this collection are equally successful. Miss Williams has contributed two small pictures, both titled *Burnham Beeches*. Adelaide Burgess' *A Dutch Maid* is a powerful picture, all the more remarkable because it is done in watercolor. Emma Walter's *Flower and Fruit, Fresh Gathered* is a forceful painting of a usually tame subject. Even better is her *Winter Fruits and Stone Ware*. Mrs. Follingsby's landscape *Die Hohe Campe* is a wild Bavarian scene "painted with a feeling for surface and substance that would do credit even to distinguished masters in landscape art." Ellen Partridge's *The Ballad* depicts a country girl sitting on a bank. Figure paintings by Kate Swift are *Saying Grace* and *The Bee and the Butterfly*. Also distinguishing herself is Georgiana Swift with *The Tangled Walk*. Agnes Bouvier's *The Picture Book*, a richly-executed painting of a girl reading to a child, is accompanied by some carefully done and well-colored head studies. Mrs. Keating, who is successful with paintings of animals, has contributed a *Brace of*

Woodcocks; a *Brace of Pheasants;* a *Skye Terrier* and a *Ratter,* all painted in the highest degree of excellence. Florence Peel's *Gems of the Ocean,* a watercolor of a mackerel and a mullet, is powerful and richly colored. These and other works deserve enthusiastic support from the public.

435. "The Eighty-Fifth Exhibition of the Royal Academy, 1853." *Art Journal* (1 June 1853): 141-152.

An absence of the old established names and of more than a handful of promising new ones again marks the lack of progress of the Royal Academy. New blood and innovation are badly needed if this indispensable institution is to be preserved. Not all the exhibits can be mentioned here, but Mrs. W. Carpenter represents female artists with *Mrs. Frewin and Her Infant Son* which is so well done that it may be her best work to date.

436. "The British Institution Exhibition: 1854." *Art Journal* (1 March 1854): 61-65.

Miss E. Well's *View in Norfolk* is a small but effective composition of cottage and trees. Jessie MacLeod's *Scene from the Bride of Lammermoor* in which Lucy Ashton is asked to identify her handwriting, contains numerous figures, some of which are successfully done. The five-hundred-seventy-two pictures are mostly genre and landscape subjects. It is obvious that the artists are traveling but not reading and thinking. A lack of figure compositions is understandable, since figure painting takes considerable time, labor and expense. Small pictures take less time and money to produce, and there is always a market for them.

437. "The National Institution Exhibition 1854." *Art Journal* (1 April 1854): 105-107.

Anna Mary Howitt's *Margaret Returning from the Fountain* illustrates a sad Margaret from the *Faust* legend. The picture exhibits Pre-Raphaelite propensities in its tremendous force of light, color, and composition. As the first painting of a young female artist, the picture is even more commendable, but no allowances need to be made for her age and sex; the picture would honor any artist and promises a distinguished career for Howitt.

438. "Royal Academy Exhibition." *Illustrated London News Supplement* (6 May 1854): 423-426.

This year's Royal Academy exhibition was attended by Queen Victoria herself. The general feeling is one of good humor and of work done well. Among the many fine paintings deserving special attention is Rebecca Solomon's *The Governess,* Annie Mutrie's *Orchids and Other Flowers,*

Martha Mutrie's *Spring Flowers*, and Henrietta Ward's *Scene from the Camp at Chobham*.

439. "Exhibition of the Scottish Academy. The Twenty-Eighth." *Art Journal* (1 June 1854): 108-112.

The collection of works by northern artists is one of the best in years; in addition, almost all the pictures are hung at eye level and in good light. Among the works worth special notice is *Paris: A Newfoundland Dog* by Jessie MacLeod. The picture is done with force and truth, but since the dog is all black, the addition of a bit of color would make the picture even better.

440. "The New Society of Painters in Water-Colours." *Art Journal* (1 June 1854): 175-176.

The 367 works in a wide variety of subjects do not create a remarkable exhibit. The best quality is in the smaller pictures. Jan Egerton's *Nourmahal* is a well-executed study of an oriental figure spoiled by the bad attitude of the model. *Dead Game* by Mary Margetts is a composition of dead pheasants, carefully drawn and colored to create a very true-to-life study. Fanny Corbaux's *After the Ball*, represents an exhausted and contemplative woman in the best of Corbaux's figure studies thus far. *Portrait of Henry Cooke, Esq.*, is so full of expression, color, truth and artistic skill that many people familiar with Sarah Setchell's works must regret that so few are exhibited. Fanny Stier's *Woodland Scene* deserves mention for its composition and color.

441. "The Old Water-Colour Society." *Art Journal* (1 June 1854): 173-175.

In the fifteen years since the Old Water-Colour Society has been holding exhibitions, its artists have made remarkable progress from soft washes and tints to a solid, powerful effect that can easily compete with oils. This collection of 356 drawings includes figure compositions of considerable excellence. Margaret Gillies' *The Mourner*, inspired by lines from Tennyson, shows a group of well-drawn figures whose features are "a triumph in one of the most difficult acquisitions of art." Maria Harrison's *Fruit*, a composition of black grapes, white grapes, melons and other fruit, exemplifies truthful color and accurate drawing.

442. "The Royal Academy. The Exhibition, 1854." *Art Journal* (1 June 1854): 157-171.

As usual, the Royal Academy exhibit is marked by complacency and lack of progress. The after-dinner speeches at the opening banquet were boring and contained no new or noteworthy ideas. Inviting professors of literature to converse with the artists might produce some element of thought and perhaps genius. Over 2,000 pictures were rejected; of the 1,531 exhibited, many were hung out of sight, or even in dark stairwells. The visible pictures worth mentioning include Mrs. W. Carpenter's *Portrait of a Lady*, which is graceful and feminine. Louisa Rayner's *An Old Kitchen, Sussex*, features a careful drawing of a carved sixteenth-century chimney. *Interior of Etchingham Church* tackles and overcomes some remarkably difficult challenges. Mrs. G. E. Hering's *From a Sketch in the Isle of Arran*, a small painting of a mountain and sunset, is charming and poetic. Jessica Hayllar's *Lady Mynzondie*, a head study, is perhaps too shaded, and has a distracting light reflection in the eyes. Rebecca Solomon's *The Governess* tells two stories at once--the privileged young woman enjoys a suitor and a piano; the less fortunate young governess has only a boring lesson to give a boring pupil. Both stories are told with truth and insight. Martha Mutrie's *Spring Flowers* is remarkable in its color, strength of composition and drawing. Annie Mutrie's *Orchids and Other Flowers* is equally well done. The works are all the more remarkable in that they represent so much talent in one family. Miss Fox's *Eva and Lilly*, head studies of two children, are accurately drawn and painted. Eliza Goodall's *Le Déjeuner*, a family group of French peasants, is painted with rare insight that makes it "a production of striking sweetness." *Scene from the Camp at Chobham*, by Henrietta Ward, shows women and men in a military camp. It is artistically sound and intellectually powerful and mature. It is safe to predict more and even better work from this artist. Lack of space prevents a review of all the miniatures in the exhibition, but among those of unusual excellence are *Orange Blossoms* by Elizabeth Murray, showing a crown of these flowers held in a bride's hand. Margaret Gillies' study of *Mrs. William Gladstone* shows a successful treatment of expression. Maria Moseley's *A Portrait* of a woman in black is sweet and lifelike. Anne Charlotte Bartholomew's tiny *A Bracelet Miniature of Miss Rogers* is skillfully painted. Also deserving mention is Miss L. Caron's *Portrait of Miss D. Laing*.

443. "The British Institution Exhibition, 1855." *Art Journal* (1 March 1855): 69-72.
Little in the way of originality and continuity of subject characterizes this exhibit of 543 paintings. Eloise Stannard's *Fruit from Nature* is "a dessert of the fruits usually served up on canvas." Annie Mutrie's study of red, white, yellow and damask *Roses* is delicate and truthful.

444. "The Society of British Artists. Thirty-Second Exhibition--1855." *Art Journal* (1 April 1855): 138-140.

The Society of British Artists exhibits over 800 oils, watercolors and miniatures, most of which lack vigor and inspiration, perhaps because so many spirits are dampened by the trials of the Crimean War. Clara E. F. Kettle has two works worthy of mention: *The Three Pets*, a miniature of a child captured with color and expression; and *The Daughter of Babylon*, which is equally successful. Anne Charlotte Fayerman Bartholomew's *Fruit* is remarkably truthful and lifelike. Worthy of mention, though space forbids comment, are Louisa Roberts' *Portrait of a Lady*; Mrs. Withers' *Study of Fruit*; and Mary Ann Duffield's *Roses, Etc.*

445. "The Society of Painters in Water Colours." *Art Journal* (1 May 1855): 185-186.

This exhibit of 322 works is perhaps the best the society has presented so far, with particular strength in figure paintings, from life-sized to miniatures. Margaret Gillies has three works in the exhibit. *Looking Back at the Old Home* shows two women and a child admirably done, but the expressions on their faces don't seem to relate to the sentiment in the title. Perhaps the best of Gillies' work to date is *The Past and the Future*, a beautifully-colored picture of an older woman and a younger woman with surpassingly expressive faces. Also worth special mention is her *Portia Planning the Defense of Antonio*. Mary Ann Criddle's *Thoughts Elsewhere* is a profile head study of a thoughtful girl. Maria Harrison's *Camellias; Fruit and Flowers;* and *Entrance to the Conservatory* are all meritorious.

446. "The Royal Academy. The Eighty-Seventh Exhibition, 1855." *Art Journal* (1 June 1855): 169-183.

As usual, the effort to exhibit some 1,500 paintings results in most of them being hung to disadvantage or even placed out of sight. Unfortunately, some of the best works are in the worst places, and vice versa. Only the best works can be mentioned here. Emily Osborn's *My Cottage Door* is a small picture of a girl entering a vine-framed door. The Mutrie sisters are represented with Annie's *Azaleas* and *Orchids;* Martha has contributed *Primula and Rhododendron*. The flowers in all these paintings are perfectly done, although the exotic orchids are not as poetic and appealing as the more familiar blooms. Emma Walters' *Just Shot* is a rendition of a bird dying in some holly and weeds. The plants are well done, but this hardly excuses the inappropriate subject for a lady. Mrs. W.

Carpenter's *Absence* is a picture of a richly dressed but grief-stricken woman. In the miniatures room, Hannah Essex' *An Enamel Group of Flowers* is brilliantly painted with "microscopic nicety" and *Mrs. Cowling*, a portrait by Maria Mosely, is excellent. Clara E. F. Kettle's *A Portrait* has considerable merit, as does Anne Charlotte Bartholomew's *A Girl Reading*. Space does not permit comment on other deserving works, such as Margaret Gillies' *Mrs. Kelsall;* Eliza Sharpe's *Portrait of a Lady;* Miss Raimbach's two portraits, *The Infant Daughter of the Hon. Mr. and Mrs. Melville,* and *Captain and Mrs. Wigram;* Annie Dixon's *Miss and Mr. T. Sherwood;* Kate Salaman's *Ella, Second Daughter of Phineas Abraham, Esq.;* Marianna Sykes' *L.R. Sykes, Esq.;* and Jane Masters Rodgers' *Portrait of a Lady.*

447. "The British Pictures and Works in Sculpture in the Great French Exhibition." *Art Journal* (1 July 1855): 128-129.

Fench artists ignorant of British artistic achievements will be surprised and enlightened by this exhibition and hereafter accord British art and artists with due respect. Artists are listed alphabetically. Included in the exhibit are Mrs. W. Carpenter's *Portrait of an Old Lady;* Margaret Gillies' *Study of the Head of a Young Girl,* and *The Mourner;* two works both titled *Flowers* by Miss Mutrie; Fanny Corbeaux's *Leah-Rachel;* Mary Harrison's *Fruit and Flowers;* and Mary Margetts' *Still-Life.*

448. "The Royal Academy. Exhibition. The Eighty-Eighth. 1856." *Art Journal* (1 June 1856): 161-174.

Overcrowded as usual, with too few landscapes and too much of the influence of the Pre-Raphaelite heresy, this year's exhibition does contain some good examples of male portraits. Not all exhibits are mentioned. Margaret Carpenter has submitted *Lady Fitz-Wigram.* The subject is in a commendably relaxed pose, with her head leaning on her left hand. In *Children,* life-sized head studies of a boy and a girl, the boy is especially well done. *Dr. Neil-Arnott, M.D., FRS* is a good head study. Anna E. Blunden has sent *A Sister of Mercy* in which the figure tending to a poor ill woman is accurately drawn. Anna and Martha Mutrie's *Geraniums and Roses* is "exquisitely well done... with an accuracy that rivals nature." Anna Mutrie's *Orchids* and *Primulas* are delicately painted and brilliantly colored. M. E. Dear's *Marietta* is an excellent head study of a child. M. H. Stannard's *Winter* is a picture of a dead bullfinch near some lifelike bunches of holly. Henrietta Ward is represented by one of the best works in the exhibition, which takes up a challenging subject: lively children in a cluttered drawing room. Ward has painted the details with care. Her picture *The May Queen* depicts a scene from a Tennyson poem. The great success of the picture is Ward's treatment of light, which cannot be too highly praised. *Primroses*, by Mrs. Harrison, lacks elegance but is carefully and accurately painted. Mrs. J. H. Carter's *Arthur, Youngest Son of Charles Baring Young, Esq.* is a fine example of portraiture, as is Elish LaMonte's miniature of *The Late Earl of Belfast*. E. Weigall's *Mrs. George H. Virtue* is brilliantly colored and "most conscientiously worked out." Clara E. F. Kettle's *Miss Mortimer* and *Mrs. Talbot Baker* "are distinguished by excellent quality." Ellen Partridge's *S.T. Partridge, Esq. M.D.* deserves mention, as does Anne Charlotte Bartholomew's *Autumn Fruit*.

449. "The Society of Female Artists." *English Women's Domestic Magazine* 6 (1857): 90-93.

   Many of the works gathered from all over England for the first exhibit of the Society of Female Artists show considerable promise. Women artists have been dismally limited in training and subject matter, but next year's exhibit deserves support and interest that will encourage still better quality.

450. "The British Institution. Exhibition, 1857." *Art Journal* (1 March 1857): 69-72.

   Lack of taste on the part of the public rather than lack of talent on the part of the artists results in an uninspiring exhibit of 565 paintings. The smallest pictures are the best ones, some of which "present heart-breaking instances of microscopic manipulation." Not all pictures are reviewed. Among those mentioned are Miss Mutrie's *Cactus* with its brilliant overpowering color out-doing nature. Emma Brownlow's *The Mother's Grave* is painted with assurance, but the drawing is poor.

451. "The Exhibition of the New Society of Painters in Water Colours." *Art Journal* (1 June 1857): 179-180.

   Fanny Harris' red and white *Camelias*, her *Roses*, and *The Chosen Blooms* are well-drawn and brilliantly colored. Mary Margetts' *Bacchanalian Cup, Grapes, Etc.* is unusually lively for this genre, and the colors are beautiful. Although ladies do not generally paint dead birds, Margetts' *Pheasants* show that a woman can handle the subject and the close detail required. Honorable mention goes to Louisa Corbeaux' drawing *The Trial*. On the whole, this exhibition of 354 works lacks innovation.

452. "The Exhibition of the Royal Academy." *Art Journal* (1 June 1857): 165-176.

If Reynolds and other early "greats" in the eighty-nine year history of the academy could view this exhibit, "they would say that art in England is ruined." The landscapes are ugly, the portraits ordinary, and the Pre-Raphaelitism bad and extravagant. This disappointing exhibit does contain some small works worth mentioning. Instead of a title, a quote from Shakespeare captions *"Tis better to be lowly born/And range with lowly lovers in content/Than to be perked up in glistening grief/And wear a golden sorrow."* These lines serve as a title to a picture of an unfortunate gentleman of the Restoration period who is depressed over his gambling losses. His wife, standing near him, is equally unhappy. Rebecca Solomon's message is clear and her painting well executed. Mrs. W. Carpenter's *Portrait of a Lady* is clearly-colored and well drawn. The subject, posed in profile, looks natural and relaxed. Henrietta Ward's family portrait of small children singing for a woman at a piano is titled *God Save the Queen*. It is one of the best works in the collection, distinguished by its execution and composition. Margaret Robbinson's painting from *Faust* of two girls gossiping at a fountain is executed with considerable power and "masculine vigor." *Margaret and Lizzy with Pitchers at the Fountain* is the work of an experienced and knowledgeable student of art. Eliza Turck has substituted a quotation for a title for her painting of a country woman sitting under a tree. The plants are well done in this painting, captioned, *"I'll sit me down and must/Beneath yon shady tree...."* Annie Mutrie's *Orchids* and the mossy bank that serves as a background make a nice picture together. Her *Roses* is a brilliant and original work. *Nameless and Friendless* by Emily Osborn is more firmly composed and drawn than the works of most women. Osborn has put much emotion in the picture of a poor young woman hoping to sell her painting to an art dealer who makes a good living by the hard work of others. The rainy weather adds to the pathos of the scene.

453. "Foreign Art: The Exhibitions of the British and French Paintings in New York." *The New York Times* (7 November 1857): 2.

The problem with this exhibit is not that Britain and France were impertinent to send an art exhibit when America was in a "dismal world of protested notes and insolvent banks." American art, with no historical school of its own, can profit by exposure to matured concepts, theories and techniques. The poor quality of the exhibit, however, makes it useless and even insulting to Americans seeking education and refinement. One of the worst examples of the inadequacy of the exhibit is Elizabeth Siddall's *Clerk Saunders*.

454. "The English and French Exhibitions." *Evening Post (New York)* (14 November 1857): 2.

Of the French portion of this exhibition, Rosa Bonheur's work is cold, unfeeling and academic, but it is saved by the joyous vitality of the animals she paints. Of the English exhibits, Elizabeth Siddall's *Clerk Saunders* numbers among "childish vagaries" hardly worth the time and trouble it took to send the whole exhibit overseas.

455. "The Society of Female Artists." *The English Woman's Journal* (1858): 205-209.

It is neither fair nor practical for women to exhibit with men as long as women's artistic studies are so limited and their lives are burdened with domestic responsibilities. The Society of Female Artists' exhibition gives women's work a chance to be evaluated in terms of women's progress toward a newly-opened career choice. Separate exhibitions for women encourage new students without overwhelming or discouraging them. Artists such as the Mutrie sisters, who compete successfully in the male institutions, would do well to exhibit in the women's exhibitions to enhance and encourage the work of their female contemporaries.

456. "The British Institution for Promoting the Fine Arts of the United Kingdom." *Art Journal* (1 March 1858): 77-80.

This is an encouraging exhibition of 574 paintings and drawings of younger artists striving to improve. While established artists are not challenging themselves, contributions are nonetheless valuable. There is however, much evidence of shameful favoritism in the selection, rejection and hanging that is discouraging to young artists and detrimental to the advancement of art. Among the best works in one exhibit are Louisa Rimer's brilliant red and white *Camelias;* in Eloise Stannard's *Fruit Painted from Nature,* the fruit is well done but the background detrimental to the whole. Annie Mutrie has rendered *Honeysuckle* with her usual remarkable skill that combines both force and delicacy.

457. "The Society of British Artists." *Art Journal* (1 April 1858): 141-142.

Of the 919 works exhibited, nearly all seem to aspire to mediocrity in order "to paint down to the comprehension of the buyers" and thus to sell pictures. Very few of the exhibits deserve mention. *Padlocked* by Jessie MacLeod pictures a young woman by a garden gate; the work is artistically successful, but it is not clear what story is being told.

458. "The Society of Female Artists." *English Women's Journal* (May 1858): 205-208.

The *Athenaeum* says "we must not look for a Michael Angelo among the ladies"; however, at this time there doesn't appear to be Michael Angelo among the men either. Women are painting the same "portraits, landscapes, scenes from Shakespeare, old houses, animals and fruit" as the men are painting. In any case, women can't compete with men until they have the same training.

459. "The Society of Female Artists." *Art Journal* (1 May 1858): 143-144.

When the works of over 500 women are brought together, it becomes obvious that a tremendous amount of talent deserves recognition. Many of the works are still lifes and fruit because these women had not had access to schools with life model classes, but they have obviously worked hard at painting "with their best instructress--nature." Miss Margitson's *Fruit*, featuring white grapes, a cut melon, and plums, is a good example of such work. Ellen Cole's *Meditation* is a frontal head study of an old man. Mary Linnell's landscape, *A Farm Road*, shows a road with trees and a bank on the right, and a pool on the left. The picture is a "triumph" because its treatment gives much interest to an ordinary scene. Charlotte Hardcastle's *Autumn* errs in the stiff arrangement of such natural plants as ferns, ivy, weeds, and wildflowers. The foreground in Mrs. W. J. Brown's *A Welsh Spring* is carefully painted, if a bit "cold," but the two groups of trees in the picture are painted with great care and patience. *Gleaners,* by Kate Swift, pictures two sisters at a stile. The younger plays with a goat; the face of the elder sister is not as well-painted as her sister's. Mrs. Chisholm Anstey has obviously worked hard at a truthful rendering of *Evening Study in an Italian Vineyard*. The grieving girl in Emma Blunden's *The Emigrant* is well done, but her dress is the same color as the ship she leans against--a grave error, especially since the figure has her back to the viewer. Anna Blunden's *The Daguerreotype* features two sisters, both well done, but the background behind the younger is distracting. Sarah Linnell's *The Gipsie's* [sic] *Haunt* is a good landscape treatment with "powerful" color. The figure of Hagar at prayer in the foreground is emphasized by the background in Mary Ann Cole's *Hagar and Ishmael*. The flowers are brilliant and well-drawn in Louisa Serena Rimer's *Rhododendrons*. While some of the drapery in Alice Walker's *Evening Rest* is realistic, the composition of this picture of a Turkish family could be improved. Roses and ivy in Eliza Mill's *Love and Friendship* are quite competent. Henrietta Ward's *The Bath* is an example of the fine results that knowledge and hard work can produce in "the most earnest students of the opposite sex." The subject is a nurse about to bathe a little boy--the subjects are not remarkable, but Ward's technique is. *Flora--a Nursery Sketch*, another of Ward's child portraits, features a little girl on a hobby horse. Frances Stoddart has contributed two landscapes; *Banks of the Tummel at Faskally, Perthshire,* and *Nidpath Castle, on the Tweed*. Both works "embody some of the very best principles of landscape art." Eliza Fox has produced a lifelike and pleasant resemblance in her *Portrait of W. J. Fox., Esq., M. P.*, and in her *Portrait of Miss Dorah Roberts,* a frontal chalk study that shows knowledge of drawing. *The Ruined Temple of Kom Ombos, Egypt,* is a realistic rendering of sands and ruins by Mrs. Robertson Blaine. Margaret Carpenter's *The Little Boat Builder,* a portrait of a small boy by the seashore, is a lifelike and apparently effortless rendering. She has also contributed *Portrait of Dr. Neil Arnott, F.R.S.*, a three-quarter chalk portrait. Mrs. A. Shirley has painted *Cart-Horses Belonging to the Lion Brewery, Lambeth,* a careful rendering of an unusually unsentimental subject. She also exhibits *Shetland Ponies,* the property of Her Majesty. Margaret Robbinson shows "a firm masculine style tempered by infinite sweetness" in a half-length portrait of a wandering mother carrying a child on her back. Titled *Ballad Singer of Connemara, Ireland,* the picture features an unlikely combination of ripe apples and blooming lilacs; the staring doll behind the sleeping child is distracting. Mrs. Stuart's *Fruit,* Mrs. Davis Cooper's *Study of Fruit and Flowers,* Miss Burrows' *A Study From Nature,* Emma Walter's *Flowers,* and Mrs. Withers' *Lilies and Roses* and *Winter Berries* are all careful studies and are true to nature. The title *The Flooded Meadows* is affixed to several works by Florence Peel, some of which are oils and some are drawings; all have merit. Miss Yetts' *A Woody Slope* is "somewhat hard," but hard work and much study will certainly result in more successful work. Mary Ann Coles' *The Love Letter* is a carefully composed small figure study. Mrs. T. J. Thompson's *Lane Brocham, Surrey;* Mrs. Mallison's *Sunset at Ventor;* Miss Sewell's *The Cowgate, Edinburgh;* M.A. Carrington's *On the Tay, Near Dunkeld,* Mrs. Grote's *Burnham Beeches* and *Gatehouse of Boarstall, Bucks.*; and Mrs. E. Stanley's *Lake of Lucerne* are commendable landscapes exhibiting care in the rendering and faithfulness to the subjects. Picturesque architectural studies appear in the works of Mrs. Hemming (*Rue des Lazettes, Honfleur*), Mrs. Higford Burr (*Cathedral, Florence*), Miss Blake (*Florence, from the Church of San Miniato*). Maria Moseley's miniature, *Bertie,* is of a little boy in blue velvet. Moseley has achieved textures truly remarkable in oil paint. She has also contributed *Edith,* a life-like crayon portrait of a little girl. Anna Mary

Howitt's *From a Window* is an evening landscape of a lawn, trees, a vine-framed window, and in the room, careful details. The whole effect is too elaborate, and the subject somewhat gloomy, but Howitt's work is accomplished and has evidence of "genius and power." Emma Oliver has sent *Braubach on the Moselle* and *Namur on the Meuse;* both works show truthful rendering and skillful drawing. *The Morning Star of Memory* by Margaret Backhouse, is a tasteful drawing of an elegant woman in white with a crescent and star gem on her forehead. Backhouse's *The Orphan* is a head and bust study of a little girl whose expression is so sad that the work hardly requires its title. A light and agreeable drawing by Margaret Tekusch is titled *Portraits of Mrs. Edward Lewin and Mrs. J.C. Lees.* Adelaide Burgess' *A Poacher in Embryo* is a painting of a boy holding a bird's nest. More sentimental in mood is her *The Last Dream* in which a dying girl dreams of angels by her bedside. It is "a work of surpassing sweetness." Elizabeth Murray's *The Best in the Market* is "brilliant" and a *Shepherd Boy of the Campagna of Rome* shows a boy with character in his face and posture that perfectly suits his rustic and picturesque costume, complete with a peacock feather in his hat. Eliza Dundas Murray's *Bangorough Castle, Northumberland* is as well painted as her picturesque *Entrance to Seaham Harbour on the Estate of the Marchioness of Londonderry.* Lady Belcher's *Blarney Castle, County Cork* is "bold and effective," and *Sunset Effect--Valley and Round Tower of Glendalough, County Wicklow* does especially well with its treatment of distance. *Hawthornden, Once the Residence of Drummond the Poet,* by Marianne Stone, is a view up the river Dean from a bridge. The trees, and especially the details in the foreground, are most successful. Stone's *Scotch Cottage Home, Loch Lomond* pictures a poor hovel with a magnificent view; also successful are her *The Tweed--Eidon Hills;* and *English Cottage Home.* Emily Macirone's *The First Meeting of Florizel and Perdita,* a scene from Shakespeare's *Winter's Tale* has some originality. Anne Charlotte Fayerman Bartholomew's *A Marseilles Minstrel* is a good study of "one of those French female peripatetic professors of the hurdy-gurdy."

460. "The New Society of Painters in Water-Colours." *Art Journal* (1 June 1858): 174-175.

Mrs. Margett's *Fruit and Flowers,* a composition of a vase with a grapes, peaches, etc. is "rich and brilliant." Fanny Harris' *Hollyhocks* is brightly painted and natural, since the flowers are growing in a garden rather than being arranged in a bouquet. Emily Farmer's *His Own*

Trumpeteer, a study of a boy with a toy trumpet, is clearly colored, but the child's eyes need more shade.

461. "The Royal Academy." *Art Journal* (1 June 1858): 161-172.

The hangers of this year's exhibition "have covered the walls like a Chinese puzzle" and poor works are hung well while good pictures are nearly out of sight. A Jockey Club member with some spare time might have done a better job, and to cap it off, the favorite picture of the undiscerning public is Frith's vulgar *Derby Day.* Of the works deserving mention, Annie Mutrie's *Azaleas* has intense color, but is not up to her usual standards. Henrietta Ward's *Howard's Farewell to England* is one of her most important pictures to date. The subject, the philanthropist Howard, surrounded by his wife and children sitting in his garden saying goodbye to his tenants, is rendered with force, truth, and skill in composition and execution. In short, "it leaves nothing to be desired." Three well-done figures and a carefully-worked landscape in Margaret Robbinson's *Straw-Rope Twisting in the Highlands* results in a "minutely worked out" picture. Anna Blunden has pictured the past and the present in a picture of two flower-gathering children near an old ruin. The careful detail of both foreground and background is not possible, but Blunden carries it off with "finesse" and the total picture is "marvelous in execution."

462. "The Society of Painters in Water Colours." *Art Journal* (1 June 1858): 174-175.

Better quality than in former years can be seen in the 329 exhibits. Inspired by a scene from the "Faerie Queene," Margaret Gillies sends *Una and the Red Cross Knight in the Caverns of Despair*, containing an unprecedented example of a suit of armor painted by a lady. Maria Harrison's *Field Flowers* is an excellent work deserving mention.

463. "The Royal Academy Exhibition: The Ninety-First, 1859." *Art Journal* (1 June 1859): 161-172.

The Pre-Raphaelite influence is probably responsible for efforts that artists are putting into representing minute details in their painting at the expense of originality and a certain freedom of style and touch. As usual, too many good works have been hung in places where they are nearly impossible to see. The best places are reserved for the academy members, whether deserved or not. One example of the hanger's folly is *An Incident in the Life of Frederick the Great of Prussia*, a small picture of Henrietta Ward's, which although unquestionably one of the best works in the exhibit, has been placed near the floor, "where it will have a continual coating of dust." The two children in the scene, playing at soldiers, are forcefully and truthfully rendered; color, composition and finish are uncompromising. Jane Benham Hay, who now lives in Italy, and who, as "Miss Benham" established a reputation with her illustrations of the works of Longfellow, has sent *England and Italy*, two boys and a landscape, in which both figures and scenery are well rendered. Hay's past work is evident in that she is capable of more powerful subjects, but she is obviously striving for higher art and is certainly succeeding. In the portrait genre, Margaret Geddes Carpenter's head and bust of *W.H. Carpenter, Esq. F.S.A.* is not only "bright" and "animated" but "will go farther than a volume of argument to compel the Royal Academy to acknowledge 'the rights of women,' which they have been always disposed to ignore." Ellen Partridge has submitted a fresh and natural head and bust study of *Miss Eliza Partridge. Olivia and Sophia in their Sunday Finery* is typical of the fine quality that entitles Margaret Robbinson to be recognized as one of the best of professional artists. Olivia is having her hair done in flowers by Sophia; the textures of the laces and material of their clothing, as well as the excellence of the head studies are the work of an accomplished professional. The usual stiffness of arrangement in flower painting makes Martha Mutrie's *Garden Flowers* a welcome relief, with its firmness, naturalness, and power of color handling. Annie Mutrie's *Traveller's Joy* may be even better; "both works are of surpassing excellence."

464. "Society of Painters in Water Colours." *Art Journal* (1 June 1859): 173.

The work of Margaret Gillies stands out in this very fine exhibition, one of the best ever seen. *The Highland Emigrant's Last Look at Loch Lomond* depicts an aged, mournful Scot sitting on a mountainside; Gillies has combined force and sentiment in this work. *Father and Daughter* is a picture of two mourners gazing at a portrait of their dear departed. The face of the daughter suggests a confidence in the hereafter.

465. "The British Institution." *Art Journal* (1 March 1860): 77- 80.

People with houses large enough to accommodate large pictures have generally inherited large canvasses of old masters and have ceased to be art patrons; modern artists, therefore, tend to paint small pictures to accommodate small houses, and the scope and subject of the older school has diminished accordingly. Eloise Harriet Stannard exhibits a still life redundantly titled *Fruit, Painted from Nature*. It is like every other still life, and fruit must be painted from nature, in any case.

466. "The Royal Academy Exhibition: The Ninety-Second, 1860." *Art Journal* (1 June 1860): 161-172.

As usual, the reformers in the Royal Academy are out-voted by the *status quo*, and the quality of an artist's work does not, as it should, make him eligible for membership. Since well over 2,000 works were rejected this year, the accepted pictures are not hanging all the way up to the ceiling as in past years. This year's exhibition contains better quality and more thought and diplomacy than in previous years. Unknowns and non-members have been hung "on the line" along with the works of better known and more privileged artists. One of the Mutries has contributed a work titled *Fungus*, an arrangement of fungi, mosses, and grasses, but the effect is not natural. *Where the Bee Sucks* gives brilliance to a humble subject; Annie Mutrie's composition of limestone, moss, gorse and wildflowers is close to nature in both subject and composition. Miss Mutrie's *Heather*, another study from nature, shows bright flowers on a summer mountainside. *Hyacinths* is "rich and brilliant." Mrs. Carpenter has achieved "firm extension and mellow color" in *Miss Durant*, a portrait that is unfortunately hung too high to be seen to advantage. Elizabeth Jerichau-Bauman's *Italy* is "perilously political," with her subject matter, a young man in hopeless despair over the conditions in his country. One would expect, rather, nymphs or glorious landscapes from a beginning lady painter. Rebecca Solomon's *Peg Woffington's Visit to Triplet* carries such power and skillful execution that it is difficult to accept it as the work of a lady. The work is thoughtful and intelligent, original and powerful, and Solomon must be counted among the "great women of the age."

467. "The Society of Painters in Water-Colours." *Art Journal* (1 June 1860): 173-175.

A wide range of subjects and well-placed works characterize this year's exhibit. Margaret Gillies' head and bust study of a small girl with a happy expression is titled *An Arran Girl Herding*. Another of her works, titled *The Merry Days When We Were Young* takes its subject from Wordsworth. Young people making music for a wistful older woman conveys both merriment and sentiment, and Gillies' technique is "ingenious and elegant." The cool classicism of draperies and the chaste composition balance the eloquent sentiment of *Imogene After the Departure of Posthumus*.

468. "The Royal Academy." *Saturday Review* (2 June 1860): 709-710.

Few works by women appear in this year's Royal Academy Exhibition, but those few are "very creditable." Henrietta Ward's "clever little picture" of a child taking its first steps has already been mentioned, but Rebecca Solomon's scene from the life of Peg Woffington also deserves mention. Both pictures have faults in the use of color; Ward's is too hard and is too heavy with reds and yellows. Solomon's colors are too dark, and need "force." Solomon's composition, however, and Ward's expressions are most praiseworthy. Mrs. Well's *Departure--an Episode in the Children's Crusade, 12th Century* is a refreshing change from the usual scenes from Shakespeare and other poets. The picture is unfortunately not well hung, so a more careful criticism is not possible, but the excellence of expression on the faces of the subjects is "forcible and natural." Margaret Robbinson's *What We Still See in Chelsea Gardens* is too much like the style of D. Maclise in use of color, and too little like it in the drawing. Robbinson's figures are not badly drawn, but the limbs could be better, especially the left arm of the woman in the picture who is talking to an old man. *The Governess* by Emily Mary Osborn is the equal of any work in the exhibit. The subject is "hackneyed," the governess "tall, graceful, and refined," the mother "stout, ill-tempered" and the children "ugly and malevolent-looking little demons" but the drawing is forceful and the color excellent. Also worth mention is *Asleep among the Ruins--Rome* by Eliza Florence Bridell. This painting of a little girl is tasteful, simple and well done.

469. "Society of Female Artists." *Art Journal* (1 January 1861): 72.

This exhibition has made steady improvement over the years; the artists are especially to be commended for relying on their own ideas for their works, rather than making copies of famous works by famous male painters. Elizabeth Murray has submitted *Lost and Won: Gamblers in the Campagna of Rome*, a picture of two boys and a girl from the country. The boys have been gambling; one celebrates his wins while the other mourns his losses. Murray's *A Spanish Scribe Reading the Gypsy's Love Letter* is a large painting with a picturesque group of an old, poor, but spirited scribe with a black boy eating an orange. The treatment is independent, dashing and spirited. *A Neapolitan Going to the Festival* is one of Murray's most successful pictures. The subject is a joyous young woman dancing and playing the tambourine. Also by Elizabeth Murray are *Two Little Monkeys* and two portraits: *Temple, the Son of H. J. Murray, Esq., H.B.M. Consul at Portland, U.S.;* and a life drawing titled *Garibaldi.* Murray's works add significantly to this exhibition. Margaret Gillies' *An Arran Reaper*, a picture of a country girl in a picturesque sunbonnet, is a beautiful and interesting exploration of the country aspect. Edith and Major Bennenden are pictured in profile watching from the battlements of a castle as the soldiers approach. The intensity of their features add much to the picture. Also contributed by Gillies are *A Gypsy Girl* and *At the Spring*. Some of the best watercolors ever seen by the reviewer are studies of poor children by Margaret Backhouse. *Deux Sous la Pièce* depicts a child selling plums; *For our Pie* shows a small girl carrying large stalks of rhubarb whose leaves cover her head. *Nanny;* and *Patient Waiting* complete Backhouse's contributions. Mrs. Robertson Blaine shows "vigorous, masculine decision of manner" in her works, particularly in *Tombs at Gadara--The Snowy Hermon in the Distance,* a desert scene which captures ruggedness and solitude. Emma Oliver shows her command of both oil and watercolor in her exhibits, including *Near Pheffers, Switzerland;* and *On the Rhine*. Small subjects become powerful pictures in the skillful hands of Mrs. J. T. Linnell; she exhibits *Sheaves,* and *Margin of Wood*. *The Gleaner* by Ellen Partridge is a picture of a child, and is Partridge's best work to date. Florence Peel shows great versatility in her several exhibits. Her best is a watercolor, *A Dead Wood Pigeon,* but also worth mention are an oil, *Aram Lilies,* and a chalk drawing, *Portrait of Mr. Hewitt. Winter Berries* and *Lilies and Roses* by Mrs. Withers display "sweetness of feeling." Miss Walters has sent true-to-nature flower compositions: *Spring Flowers; Apple Blossoms and Nest;* and *Pomonas Gifts*. Miss Lances' *Fruit* is remarkable in its treatment of color and its "ease of manner." Mrs. E. D. Murray has sent landscapes including *Scarborough; A Calm;* and *The South Stack Lighthouse*. Lady Belcher sends three drawings: *Furness Abbey, Marinella;* and *Hereford Cathedral*. Emma Brownlow's *La Benedicite,* a picture of a mother teaching a child to pray, is a competent work, but not Brownlow's best. A long-time contributor, Anne Charlotte Bartholomew, has sent two drawings, *The Pet of the Family;* and the *Basket of Eggs*. The reviewer looks for the competent work of Mrs. Higford in these exhibitions; *Vespers in the Chapel of Sacro Speco* is up to her usual high quality. Louise Rayner's *A Street View in Salisbury* is too "opaque" but well drawn. Mrs. Lee Bridell tells the story of the martyr Vivia Perpetua in *Saint Perpetua and Saint Felicitas;* she has also contributed a very good head study in chalk. Miss Wilkinson's *Old Houses, Sorrento* and *A View from Santa Lucia, Naples* are drawn with decision and show much promise. Adelaide Burgess exhibits two interesting drawings, *Please Remember the Grotto;* and *Snowdrop,* while Mrs. Col. Keating sends some extremely good still lifes. Fanny Hoseason Hall's *My First Model,* a small picture of a little Welsh girl is well done for a "first model" and Miss Hewitt's *The Bird Finder* is a very good drawing. Two interesting contributions by Mrs. Sturch are *Golden Wealth;* and *Vesuvius from the Strada Nuova*. Placed on a pedestal are "highly wrought" miniatures by Clara E.F. Kettle and Alicia Laird. Kettle's brilliant miniatures have been noted before. Miss Fraser has sent two exquisite drawings, *The Burning of Rhodes House* and *Standing to Be Photographed*. Several French women, including Madame Juliette Bonheur Peyrol, Louise Eudes de Guimard, and Madame Lelour, have contributed meritorious works. Exhibitions by institutions such as these will aid in calling attention to "the powers of women in art," which are reaching a maturity that will place them on an equal footing with works by men.

470. "Exhibition of the Royal Academy." *The Art Journal* (1 June 1861): 161-172.

Martha and Annie Mutrie both paint fruit and flowers with skill, rich color and great truth. It is difficult to give precedence to either, since both paint in the same genre with such consummate skill; however, *Hollyhocks*, by Martha Mutrie, with its deep color, its combination of soft petals and angular spikes of the flower, is superior in some ways to the less dramatic *Orchids* of Annie Mutrie. Both sisters, however, surpass any work done by other flower painters. Emily Osborn's *The Escape of Lord Nithisdale from the Tower, 1716* is an unusual subject for a lady and executed with more boldness than one would expect from a woman. The work is clever and well painted and Osborn has used her particular genius in the "extraordinary intensity" of Lord Nithisdale's expression.

471. "The Society of Painters in Water-Colours." *Art Journal* (1 June 1861): 173-174.

The excellence and virtuosity evident in the exhibition of the fifty-seventh year of the Old Water-Colour Society makes it clear that Turner's joke about "paper stainers" no longer has any truth to it. Among the 295 paintings, Margaret Gillies' *Beyond* deserves mention. This drawing of two women, one with a "face full of cheerful hope, Christian endurance and affectionate care," encourages her companion, who, lacking these qualities, seems discouraged and unconvinced. This is Gillies' most successful work yet. No other artist can match her almost classical style. Also exhibited by Miss Gillies are *Selling Fish--Arran* and *An Orphan Fisher Boy, Corrie, Isle of Arran*.

472. "Exhibition of the Royal Academy." *Art Journal* (1 July 1861): 193-198.

On the whole, quality in this exhibition is poor, the best spaces having been given to academy members, displacing better work by lesser known or unknown artists. *Fruit Fragments* by I. Inglis is a small picture, but the reality of the slices of apple make it one of the best pictures in the exhibition. Mrs. Collinson's *Flowers* and *Colmslie Castle* are worth notice. Rebecca Solomon's *The Arrest of a Deserter* is quite good, but not as good as her last year's *Peg Woofington*. Rosarius, "whoever he might be" [he is Rosa Brett] has painted *Thistles;* they are as true to nature as painting can get them, but "they are only thistles after all" and hardly worth the close attention the artist gives them.

473. "Fine Arts. The Winter Exhibition." *Athenaeum* (23 November 1861): 692-693.

On the whole, the pictures exhibited at this ninth exhibition are very bad. The best pictures, among them Benham Hay's *Tobias: Patriasa Oculos Currans*, have been exhibited before, and are worth seeing again so that they may be more closely studied. *Tobias* lacks vigor. It displays some lack of proportion in its drawing, but the design is clever and color treatment shows considerable promise. Benham Hay's style is developing well; careful study may place her in the highest ranks. Henrietta Ward's *Fetch It* has "spirit and elegance," and *Baby Going for a Ride*, showing a composition of three figures, is too opaque, but is vital, graceful and nicely composed. Rebecca Solomon exhibits two works, *A Young Teacher* and *The Appointment*. The first lacks color, but shows great improvement over Solomon's earlier paintings; the second has good expression and is "credible." Mrs. Robbinson has successfully imitated the worst qualities of Maclise's style in *The Love Birds*. The lower bedecked child is supposed to be lively, but instead is stiffly drawn, and the color is hard. The lace on the child's dress looks like cut-out paper, and the background greenery looks like stamped metal. There is evidence, however of some "careful as well as powerful handling." Ellen Edwards' *La Belle Jardinère*, a picture of a child watering flowers, is flimsy, but shows considerable promise in the treatment of color, which "if cultivated carefully with an eye to nature, may come to something notable." *Lobesang at Berne* by Emma Brownlow is "heavy and coarse," but has considerable merit in the grouping and expression of the figures.

474. "The Society of Painters in Water-Colours." *Art Journal* (1 January 1862): 16-17.

This "Winter Exhibition of Sketches and Studies by the Members" is an experimental exhibition of 465 works. One of Margaret Gillies' exhibits is *Study of a Tuscan Woman;* it possesses great dignity and presence.

475. "Fine Arts. Royal Academy." *Athenaeum* , no. 1803 (17 May 1862): 667-668.

Annie Mutrie's *Cottage Nosegay* is "a delightful study of common blooms" and one of the most deserving works in the exhibit. Dorothy Solomon's *The Fugitive Royalists* is to her credit, especially in her delicate treatment of the boy in the picture. Solomon's treatment of color and expression continues to improve. Mrs. Wells' head study of a winged child is titled *The Bird of God* and "displays her powers to a fine pitch." Mr. Wells' portraits of his deceased wife reading out loud is not well done—the colors are harsh and the pose stiff. Henrietta Ward should never abandon the painting of children since she has a genius at making them live on canvas. Her first historical painting titled *Despair of Henrietta Maria on Hearing of Charles the First's Execution* excels in expression and color, but there is room for improvement in the composition.

476. "Exhibition of the Royal Academy." *The Builder* [London] (24 May 1862): 367-368.

Easily the best historical painting in the exhibition is Henrietta Ward's *Scene at the Louvre in 1649--the Despair of Henrietta Maria at the Death of Her Husband, Charles I.* The picture would be a great credit to any artist, but considering the demands placed upon women and their lack of opportunities, it is extraordinary that a female could accomplish so much. Indeed, judging from Rebecca Solomon's *Fugitive Royalists*, the reviewer can only conclude that women are better at overcoming adversity or that they are better managers of time than male artists. Jane Benham Hay's *The Reception of the Prodigal Son* not only shows improvement over her earlier exhibits, but reflects her seriousness and determination to improve. Emily Osborn has contributed two excellent pictures of German domesticity: *Die Erwartung* and *Der Lebensmai*. Annie and Martha Mutrie's flower pictures look so fresh and real that one can almost imagine their scent.

477. "The Royal Academy. Concluding Notice." *The Saturday Review* [London] (24 May 1862): 592-594.

Rebecca Solomon's *Fugitive Royalists* has "masculine force of colour" but the drawing requires "greater firmness and decision." The picture is by far the best work by a female artist to appear for quite some time. Jane Benham Hay also demonstrates ambition and "great power of colour" in *The Prodigal Son,* but the work leans toward the conventional tone of "the Etty school." Henrietta Ward "enters... upon the domain of her husband" with her painting of Henrietta Maria learning of her husband's execution. The queen has a "demoniac countenance" rather than a despairing one, however, and the picture, titled *Scene at the Louvre in*

1649, is uninteresting, historically inaccurate, and not "at all fitted for a lady's pencil." Mrs. Ward is better off painting children than queens. Annie Mutrie's *A Cottage Nosegay* is a study of flowers in a jar next to a pincushion and thimble. This picture and another titled *Dahlias* demonstrate Miss Mutrie's skillful handling of color.

478. "Exhibition of the Royal Academy (Third Notice)." *Illustrated London News* (31 May 1862): 564.

Henrietta Ward's *A Scene at the Louvre, 1649* is the best of her work so far. Ward's drawing, color, text interpretations and technical skills are excellent. Jane Hay's *Tobit: The Reception of the Prodigal* demonstrates a steady improvement, especially in her drawing skills. The subject is a good one that will never become tiresome. Rebecca Solomon's skills are also improving, as evidenced by *The Fugitive Royalist.* The subject is a most suitable one for a woman. Emily Mary Osborne's illustrations of German peasants, especially *Für den Christgarten*, are pleasing, if not on the scale of her *Escape of Lord Nithisdale.* Finally, a "small tenderly-painted head" of a child in wings and white has "melancholy interest" in that it is the last work of the late Joanna Mary Boyce Wells.

479. "The Royal Academy. Exhibition, 1862." *Art Journal* (1 June 1862): 129-134.

The absence of the more notable painters is not only conspicuous, but also leaves little with which to compare the works of the younger painters. Henrietta Ward has contributed an important work in *Scene at the Louvre in 1649--the Despair of Henrietta Maria at the Death of Her Husband Charles I.* Ward has used the text with wisdom and sensitivity.

480. *"The Fugitive Royalists* by Miss Solomon." *Illustrated London News* (21 June 1862): 641.

This year's Royal Academy exhibition contains numerous worthwhile pictures by women. This fact is not remarkable, since art itself contains much of such feminine graces as elegance, feeling, and tenderness and its purpose is to embellish life. Rebecca Solomon's *The Fugitive Royalists* shows that her work has made tremendous progress. Its subject, two mothers with their respective children caught between political terrorism and the stronger bonds of sisterhood, is probably the best told and most touching in the exhibition.

Reproductions (b/w):

Solomon, Rebecca: *The Fugitive Royalists.*

481. "The Royal Academy." *Art Journal* (1 June 1863): 105-116.

A royal commission is at present evaluating the administration and management of the Royal Academy, which can only benefit from such a review. In this exhibition, for example, can be seen the very bad practice of hanging the pictures of the forty members on the line, regardless of quality. This "cruel monopoly" fails to serve the interests of art or of the country. The rest of the exhibit lacks coherence, so pictures are mentioned here according to genre. Under historical subjects, Henrietta Ward exhibits *An Episode in the Life of Mary Queen of Scots.* The beautiful queen, dressed in black, stands before the cradle containing her infant son, whose care she is giving to the Earl of Mar. The cradle in the painting is one in which the real infant slept, and many details of the picture are painted with equal attention to detail and historical fidelity. The figure of the queen is painted with simplicity that gives it considerable power by avoiding the usual trap of sentimentality. Mary Severn Newton's portrait *Mrs. Charles Newton* deserves note for its exceptional treatment of color. The sitter's blue dress and the background of emerald green are harmonized by intermingled play of intermediate tones. Elizabeth Maria Anna Jerichau-Bauman's portrait of her husband, *Jerichau, the Sculptor of Copenhagen* is vigorous in spite of some crudeness in color and roughness in execution. Emily Mary Osborne's *Good Night* deserves "express commendation." Fruits and flowers often are ignored for more dramatic subjects, but in the right hands can show the brilliance of the artist. Martha Mutrie's *Foxgloves* in a bed of ferns, and Annie Mutrie's *Autumn*, with heather, ferns, and wildflowers, are among the most brilliant in the exhibition. Eloise Stannard's *Fruit* is well composed and colored. The grapes are "translucent and purple," the leaves the color of autumn, and a silver dish "casts radiant lustre."

482. "The Society of Painters in Water-Colours." *Art Journal* (1 January 1864): 4.
Among the exhibitors of this second annual exhibition, "Miss Gillies is a liberal contributor of picturesque figures."

483. "British Institution. Exhibition of Works by Living Artists. 1864." *Art Journal* (1 March 1864): 87-89.
The quality of this year's 633 pictures is better than in former years. Kate Swift's Dutch-style interior, *Das Festkleid, a Schevening Girl, Buying her Wedding Dress*, is deservedly hung on the line. The figures in the shop possess considerable character; the picture displays much care with detail and finish, although the color and execution could be improved. Eloise Stannard's *Autumn*, a still-life grouping of fruit, has good color, but lacks light and composition.

484. "Exhibition of the Society of Female Artists." *Art Journal* (1 April 1864): 97-98.

Mrs. Robertson Blaine exemplifies a new aspect of this exhibition with two oil studies from life: one, a small head study, and the other, a picture of an old religious recluse. Both studies are "touched with much spirit." Blaine has also contributed two desert scenes, admirable in the soft treatment of the desolate subjects with their unforgiving distances. One is *Caravan Arriving at a Well Near Thebes, Upper Egypt*. The other, *Jebel esh Sheik--Syria as Seen from Gadara at Early Morning* is especially admirable with its "silent expanse of twilight desert" bounded by remote mountains just touched by early sunlight. The result conveys considerable depth, especially remarkable given the lack of detail in the actual scenery. Helen Hoppner Coode's two life-sized heads in oil also exemplify the advantages of life study made possible by the society. Both studies are vigorous and rendered with "substance and decision." Miss Gillies' *The Romance* is a watercolor characterized by elaborate finish and more depth and color than is her usual work. The picture of a woman in medieval costume engrossed in her reading admirably overcomes technical difficulties. Gillies' *Desolation* is an oil painting of a broken-hearted figure in a loose white dress; her pose and expression clearly convey her hopelessness. Margaret Backhouse's watercolor, *The Sandringham Gipsy*, displays accomplished brushwork in the lively head study of a child. Indeed, the firmness of her treatment is equal to the best work of a male painter. Backhouse has also contributed several portraits. *Montague, Malcolm, and Henry, with a Story Book--the Three Little Kittens; Beggars; Berlin Wool;* and *The Broken Lily,* works by Adelaide Burgess, are as good as any of her earlier exhibits; the figure in *Berlin Wool* is especially good. Kate Swift's *Das Trauerkleid* shows a scene in which a fisherman's widow buys mourning clothes; *Alice* is a carefully done life-sized portrait. Ellen Partridge's *Now We are Seven* is in watercolor, and *A Portrait* is done in oil. Both works show care in execution. *On Thoughts of Charity Intent*, a picture of a little French peasant girl searching her pocket for money to donate to the poor; *Orphans;* and *The Baby Brother,* all by Emma Brownlow, "are distinguished by an energetic readiness of touch rarely met with in the productions of ladies." Georgina Swift's *Dutch Fisherwoman Mending Nets* captures a familiar type. Miss Lefroy shows a sure touch in drawing and spirit in painting what might be thought "a difficult subject for a lady," but *The Floodless Wilds Pour Forth Their Brown Inhabitants,* a herd of deer traveling over a snowy field, is a successful work. Eliza Dundas Murray's *Baja, from Pausilippo* is a charming and accurate Italian landscape. Miss Rayner's drawings capture bits of interesting scenery and architecture in a way that helps the observer see what might be otherwise missed. She makes considerable and quite effective use of color; the results titled *Market Day, Chippenham; Street View, Salisbury; Leith Harbour; Wells Cathedral, from the Vicar's Chapel;* and *Porch, Lichfield Cathedral* are all successfully executed with a competent hand. Margaret Rayner has contributed three pictures; one is titled *Old Watermill, Chester.* Julliette Bonheur Peyrol's *Hen and Chickens* would seem a dull subject, and though painted with soft lines and low tones, the picture of spotted chicks and their mother is surprisingly lively. Among the landscapes, Miss J. W. Brown's *In North Wales* stands out, as do her smaller pictures, *Snowdon* and *Scottish Wildflowers.* Maria Gastineau's *On the Lake of Llanberis, North Wales;* Miss Warren's *View from Matlock, Derbyshire* and *A Composition;* and Carolina F. Williams' *An Old Mill and Cottage* all deserve mention. *English Kingfishers* and *Snap--a Portrait* are two of several meritorious works contributed by Agnes Dundas. Miss M. Clemones has sent *Crookholme Mill, Rade, with Bell Bridge House;* and *Sebergham Bridge, Looking towards Carrick Fell, Cumberland.* Clara Mitchell's *Ruins at Rome;* and Emma Oliver's *A Gipsy Girl;* Sarah Wilkes' *A Rivulet at Llangolen, North Wales,* and Madame du Gue's *Spring* are notable in the landscape category. Etchings are often uninteresting next to paintings, but Annie Fraser's *Six Illustrations for Hans Andersen's Fairytales* possess beauty and delicacy "which only very rare endowments and accomplishments could impart." Flower and fruit paintings continue to improve because so many compete in this genre. Emma Walters' *Greenfinches and Flowers* and *Grapes and Vase* are fresh and brilliant; Mrs. Withers' delicate *Grapes* and *Magnolia Grandiflora;* as well as works by Anna Maria Fitz James and Miss James are all excellent artistic achievements. The exhibit as a whole is "a remarkable advance" over exhibits of the past.

485. "The Royal Academy." *Art Journal* (1 June 1864): 157-158.

A good exhibition of works by a number of notable contributors, as well as by some promising amateurs marks this year's exhibition. Henrietta Ward's *Princes in the Tower* is a fine historical painting. An evil- looking Richard III has brought the two unfortunate princes into a gloomy prison cell. The detail and care that Ward has put into this painting is unsurpassed; the monotony of the preponderance of browns in the dungeon scene could, perhaps, have been tempered by shades of grey. *For*

The Last Time, a sad picture of two sisters about to say their final farewells to a dead parent is a credit to Emily Mary Osborn's talent for pathos. The work could have benefitted from more careful painting. Eliza Fox Bridell's *Love Letters* is weak in composition and too strong in execution, but the picture itself has power and character. Emma Brownlow's *Repentance and Faith*, by contrast, is so refined it is "little short of sickly." The picture still has merit in its emotion and sensitivity. Miss M. Redgrave's small but cheerful and carefully painted *The Whortleberry Gatherer* deserves mention, as does Anna Blunden's *Mullion Cove, near the Lizard*. This picture is rather severe, but the fault might lie in the scene rather than with Blunden's technique. Martha Mutrie's *Primulas in a Pot* is an exception to the sisters' usual practice of painting wild flowers in a natural setting. The result is nature every bit as natural as in its domesticated state. The sisters excel themselves in *Spring Flowers* and *Souvenir*. Eloise Stannard has not succeeded so well with *By the Old Garden Wall*, a good composition of simple fruit spoiled by the addition of an ostentatious Greek temple in the background.

486. "Institute of Painters in Water Colours. The Thirty-First Exhibition." *Art Journal* (1 March 1865): 175-176.

This year's exhibition is competent, but lacks any truly outstanding worth. *Ave Maria* by Elizabeth Murray is unconvincing, "showy" and "cheap," with its model in studio costume, eyes turned toward the heavens. Emily Farmer's *The Bird's Nest*, however, is difficult to fault. The simple subject, a simply-dressed and happy child with a simple treasure, is "painted to perfection."

487. "The Society of Painters in Water Colours. The Sixty-first Exhibition." *Art Journal* (1 March 1865): 173-175.

While this society is generally acknowledged to represent the best in the art profession, this year's exhibition, because of unavoidable mischance, lacks its usual perfection. It continues, however, to provide a variety of new techniques and improved methods in watercolor painting. Margaret Gillies' *Youth and Age* is a careful and truthful head study of an elderly man.

488. "The Society of Female Artists." *Art Journal* (1 March 1865): 68.

While the Society has done much good by bringing more notice to familiar artists and bringing new artists to the public's attention, all the exhibitors must continue to improve, especially in the area of figure compositions. Those who do not choose to work in this difficult area can still excel in landscape painting. An especially novel, and therefore most commendable work is Margaret Gillies' *A Young Knight*. The figure is dressed in a complete suit of armor, and the subject is certainly an unusual one for a lady. The picture is well done and carefully detailed. An artist who identifies herself only as E. V. B. has contributed three excellent etchings. *Arcadia* pictures a young reveler in a shower of fruit; *Fragments* features young Christ; and *A Dream* is as thoughtful as the other two. *Fragments* might well make a good painting, but the quality of the etching makes the work sufficient as it is. *Beatrice Mary Florence* and *The Young Archer* are mature and accomplished portraits of children by Mrs. E. Maynard. Miss Swift, who prefers humble subjects, has submitted *Two Heads are Better Than One*, and *A Stitch in Time Saves Nine*, both improvements over her exhibits of last year. Margaret Backhouse's *A Little Gleaner* excels in both the figure and the background; the picture is the best she has done thus far. The work of a foreign exhibitor, Mrs. Nils Möller's *Instruction* seems to be quite good, but is hung too high to be carefully examined. Emma Brownlow exhibits *The First Born*, and *Anxious Moments--a Ray of Hope*. The latter work, a scene of a physician with a sick child, has more emotion than the former picture. Both pictures have good qualities but are a bit "hard" in their treatment. Georgina Swift's *Returning from Covent Garden* doesn't look finished. Clara E. F. Kettle's *Cleopatra taking the Asp from Charmain*, a large, ambitious picture on ivory, is very carefully done. Adelaide Burgess' best work yet is *A French Flower Girl*, a very lifelike head study. She also exhibits *The May Wreath* and *Cat's Cradle,* which show real improvement over last year's work. Sarah F. Hewitt exhibits *The Jew's Harp* and *Shade in a Hop Garden*. The latter is a very difficult subject. Agnes Bouvier's *Kiss Little Sister* handles color well, but is deficient in feeling. Alicia Laird's *Miniature Portrait* of a young lady is very beautiful. Mrs. L. Goodman has sent several oil portraits: *Mrs. H. Thurburn; The Late James Fadaile, Esq.;* and *Lady Flora,* exhibited by Miss A. L. Oakley. Emma Landseer Mackenzie has sent *The Path Through the Woods*. Louise Rayner's *Durham, from Below Framwell Gate Bridge* is a careful rendition of a favorite scene of artists. Her *Black Gate, Newcastle* and *Old Houses of Elyet Bridge, Durham* show skill but are too dark. Several other works and their artists deserve mention. They are *Near Lugano;* and *Lago Murrano on the Luino Road* by Clara Mitchell; *Chelsea, From Below the Old Bridge* by Elizabeth Dundas Murray; *Lying to in Warfleet Creek, Dartmouth* by Harriette Anne Seymour; *Loch Katrine* and *Oaks at Ampthill Park, Beds.* by Mrs. Wilson Eustace; works by Maria Gastineau and Miss Bradshaw Smith; *From the Common, Richmond,* by Palacia E. Fahey; *Sketches at Folkestone* by Mrs. Hussey; *Great Mongeham, Kent,* by Bessie Parkes; *The First Sketch,* by Rochat; *Noon, Near Horsemonden, Kent* by Carolina F. Williams; *Rue St. John, Beauvais* by Mrs. Hemming, and *Uncertain Ground,* by Miss Lefroy. Flower painters too, excel in this exhibition. Worthy of special attention are *Fruits and Flowers* and *Fresh Flowers Gathered* by Emma Walter; *Dorsetshire Growth; Cinerarias;* and *Summer Briar Roses* by Mrs. Pfeiffer; *Apple and Holly* by Anna Maria Bartholomew Fitz James; *Grapes and Apples;* and *Hazel Nut and Bramble* by Helen Coleman; *Wild Roses* by Ellen Catelo; *Disarranged Roses* by Harriet Harrison; and *Fruit* by Mrs. Nixon. Agnes Dundas excels in both still life and animal painting. This exhibition shows much talent in flower and landscape painting, but not much progress in the narrative genre.

489. "The Royal Academy." *Art Journal* (1 June 1865): 161-172.

A separate section in this review decries the lack of quality of the works of female exhibitors. Rebecca Solomon has sent two pictures, both "slovenly." Emily Mary Osborn's picture is "careless." Exceptions are Eliza Fox Bridell's *Little Ellie,* a scene from Elizabeth Barrett Browning's "Romance of the Swan's Nest." *Little Ellie* is Bridell's best work thus far; she has done a fine job with the leaves on the trees and the drapery on the figures. Mary Ellen Edward's *The Last Kiss* provides another pleasing exception. This picture of a woman who has dug a grave in a flower garden for her pet bird and is kissing the little bundle goodbye is overwhelmingly sentimental, and by the way, well painted and nicely composed.

490. "The Exhibition of the Society of Female Artists." *Art Journal* (1 January 1866): 56.

The reviewer, however sympathetic, has often been hard-pressed at these exhibitions to find positive words without stretching the truth. This year's exhibition is happily different, with such marked improvement that many of the pictures could easily find a place in larger more prestigious exhibits. Moreover, the spirit of the society lends its own character to its exhibition in that amateurs and professionals exhibit side by side, and both benefit. In this exhibition, 150 members exhibit 400 works; not all can be mentioned. Sophy S. Warren's *Eton College* is typical of her numerous contributions in her skillful drawing and handling of color; her trees are a kind of hallmark. Maria Gastineau's watercolor, *West Coast of Scotland,* is characteristic in its combination of grey tones and the transparent handling of color characteristic of her family tradition. Better is her *In the Pass of Glen Coe*, which shows promise, but still lacks that careful finish that many women seem unable to give their work. Harriette Anne Seymour's *An Old Craft Under Repair* successfully tackles such problems as detail and foreshortening to produce a painting of "much pluck and power." Although it has a more grandiose subject, Lady Sophia Dunbar's *The Bay of Algiers* is less successful in artistic skill. Barbara Bodichon's *Trees* in a storm is infused with too much energy for such a simple subject. With so much exuberance, Bodichon might be better suited to painting heroic scenes, such as the storm in *King Lear*. M. E. A. (Eva E.) Pynne's *Sketch from Nature*, considerably more subdued, excels in its peaceful blend of grey-green tones. For the most part, the works in oil lack professionalism, "as if the material did not conform itself agreeably to female use," but a few artists prove the exception. Mrs. J. F. Herring's *Homestead* and Carolina F. Williams' *On the Thames Near Wallingford*, and *Near Cookham;* Mrs. Robertson Blaine's *Jungfrau*, and *The Tombs Near Cairo* show talent with landscape. Agnes Dundas' talent with dog portraits is evident in *The Pomeranian Dog* and *Skye Terrier*, and she shows talent with birds as well in *A Snipe*. Mrs. Goodman has painted two rather bad portraits which deserve notice because of the subjects, a dilemma faced by the National Portrait Gallery. She has painted *Miss Bessie Parkes* and *Madame Bodichon*. Kate Swift, who has more potential than she shows in *The Sister's Lesson*, needs to work on using color. Her *Train up a Child in the Way It Should Go* seems unduly influenced by Dyckmann's *The Blind Beggar*. In the watercolor category, Margaret Backhouse's *The Pet* shows too much force, and *Whom Love First Touched with Other's Woe* suffers from too little study of anatomy. Agnes Beresford Bouvier's lack of figure drawing training is obvious in *Children of the Campagna*. Miss Beresford's *A Tyrolese Girl Returning from a Pilgrimage* has good points, but color is not well handled. Adelaide Burgess' *Two Boulogne Fisher Girls* and *A Boulogne Shrimper* make use of striking contrast between the figures and the sky, but the technique is a common one and the result is somewhat ordinary. Rose Rayner has contributed a good figure study that needs variety from the green background in her sketch of *A Wandering Russian Pole*. The three best works in the exhibition are two drawings by Miss Royal and one drawing by Florence Claxton. Royal's *La Brunette* and *La Blonde* are idealized and romanticized head studies, the tones and colors clear and natural. Claxton has assembled five drawings in one frame, all satires of female hypocrisy. They are titled *The Chapel; The Oratory; The Synagogue; The Friends'*

Meeting; and *St. George's, Hanover Square.* Three members of the Rayner family exhibit studies of buildings and street scenes, subjects that seem, for some reason, to appeal to female artists. The *Church at Hastings* by Margaret Rayner is truly rendered, but Louise Rayner has carried truth too far in her unpleasantly overcrowded street scene, *Market at Chester.* She has failed in her artistic duty to render less desirable situations in a way more restful to the senses. Fanny Rayner's *The Chapel of the Virgin, Dieppe* is more consistent with the artistic practice of her family. In the fruits and flowers category, Mrs. H. Harrison paints in harmonious autumn colors, while Emma Walter escapes harmony altogether in her exuberant and overdone hues. Charlotte Jones achieves reality, peace, naturalness and careful perspective in her excellent flowers and fruits. Anna Maria Fitz James and others paint realistic birds' nests. Several amateurs deserve mention; Mrs. Mitchell's *The Pope's Palace, Avignon* is remarkable in drawing and original handling of color. Miss Townsend's sketches of scenes at Southsea and Southampton possess a beautiful blend of strong color and delicacy. Charlotte Babb's Shakespeare studies reveal the need for more instruction, and J.H. Humphrey's *Helena* is a good head study with too much contrast. Mrs. W. Hannay's *Beatrice* is a beautiful and carefully-rendered head study; Isabella Jones' street scenes show skill in color and proportion in her work, *La Petite Fille Bretonne,* but the features of this head study are well handled. *Étude d'Accessoires* demonstrates solid artistry. The shortcomings of the works in the exhibition must be weighed against the possibility that painting is one of the few suitable occupations available to ladies. Art is a much loftier pursuit than the "inanity and drudgery" of needlework which has been forced upon women whose spirits and intellects have suffered "torture and degradation." Women deserve the rewards and honors afforded by successful artistic pursuits. Bessie Parkes and others deserve praise for their support.

491. "Exhibition of the Royal Academy." *London Times* (22 May 1866): 12.

    The weakness in Henrietta Ward's *Palissy the Potter* is in the overstatement of grief of the potter and his wife and the emaciation of two of the children. The painting is redeemed, however, by the central group of touchingly tearful children.

492. "Institute of Painters in Water Colours. Thirty-Second Exhibition." *Art Journal* (1 June 1866): 175-176.

    In this mediocre exhibition of 329 works, Elizabeth Murray has sent a drawing, *The Cheat Detected--a Scene from Spanish Life,* which, viewed from a distance, is commendable in its treatment of composition, figures, and color. Closer inspection, however, reveals problems that could be overcome with professional instruction. Still, this work shows improvement over Murray's exhibit of last year. Emily Farmer's drawings *The Magic Swan* and *The Passing Cloud* deserve praise for everything but her handling of color.

493. "The Royal Academy." *Art Journal* (1 June 1866): 161-172.

A Parliamentary mandate forces the Royal Academy into sorely-needed reforms. This year's exhibition is, as a result, under closer scrutiny than in the past. Henrietta Ward's *Palissy the Potter* is a monumental work, but badly placed. The tragedy of the scene, where Palissy surveys his ruined work while his sick and starving family watches in despair, is relieved by touches of beauty in the children's faces. Considerable skill in color and composition makes this picture "truthful and picturesque, earnest and heartfelt." Susan Bell Faed's *The Country Lass* deserves mention, as do the several works of Elizabeth Maria Anna Jerichau-Bauman, a Danish artist who has four fine works in this exhibition. A. Farmer's *The Remedy Worse than the Disease* is worked with obvious care, but lacks color and texture. A small, carefully-worked picture with a six-line title shows Kate Swift's talent. Margaret Robbinson's *Happy Idleness* has too much emphasis on drapery and not enough on the figures beneath it; Mary Ellen Edwards' *Evening* is too much like her last year's submission, but is still commendable in the care in which it is done.

494. "Exhibition of the Society of Female Artists, 9, Conduit Street." *Englishwoman's Review* 2 (1867): 136-138.

In the eleven years since the Society of Female Artists has been holding exhibits, the steady efforts of the artists resulted in a creditable exhibition. Women seem to be especially talented at painting pictures of beautiful rural scenes which give such pleasure to those who must live and work in the towns.

495. "Institute of Painters in Water Colours. Thirty-Third Exhibition." *Art Journal* (1 June 1867): 147-148.

Elizabeth Murray's *The Spanish Milk Stall* has everything but composition, which could be improved with closer attention to detail. Emily Farmer's work has not improved over last year's exhibit. This year's picture, *The Primrose Seller*, is pleasing, but not memorable. The society has decided to admit foreign artists as honorary members so that visitors can enjoy Henrietta Browne's sketch, *A Sister of Mercy*, and Rosa Bonheur's *The Highland Lake*.

496. "Institute of Painters in Water-Colours" *Art Journal* (1 May 1868): 111-112.

The former New Water Colour Society has changed its name to the Institute of Painters in Water-Colours, admitted some new members, and created an honorary membership to include foreign artists, including Henriette Browne and Rosa Bonheur. Bonheur exhibits a rather disappointing replica of her famous *Deer--Fountainbleau*. Among British members, Emily Farmer also does less than expected. Elizabeth Murray's *Gipsy Forge at Seville*, while it has power, is too overdone to be successful. Murray's subject and her treatment of it are too complex; she would do well to stay within her abilities and pay more attention to nature.

497. "The Royal Academy." *Art Journal* (1 June 1867): 137-146.

An above-average exhibition this year speaks of the freedom and independence of England and her artists. Henrietta Ward's *Scene from the Childhood of Joan of Arc* is as interesting as it is skillful in execution. In the scene, a weary soldier in armor asks the young Joan for news of the war, while a kindly dog licking his hand and soldiers waiting outside in the sunshine balance the otherwise somber mood; the picture needs nothing to improve it. Louisa Starr exhibits a good head study, *La Penserosa*, and a scene from the *Taming of the Shrew* which handles color and composition well, but needs more force. Emily Mary Osborne's small *Morning--Bavaria* is somewhat overdone, but has evidence of refinement and care in the rendering. Anna Blunden's *Tintagel* rescues the reviewer from the fear that Blunden was "going the way of all Pre-Raphaelites," but this small work shows careful study and deserves praise. Landscapes by Mrs. Luker and flowers by Anna and Martha Mutrie are commendable.

498. "Royal Academy." *Art Journal* (1 June 1868): 101-110.

The one-hundredth anniversary of the Royal Academy exhibition is marked by the usual "respectable mediocrity" but the academy has opened its doors to new members and the public can expect more interesting exhibitions in the future. Henrietta Ward's *Sion House* is a brilliant treatment of the scene where the reluctant Lady Jane Gray is told that she is to be queen. In Ward's picture, the princess' "Puritanical features" are "pained and perplexed" while political plotters huddle in the hall. Ward has captured apprehension, reluctance, and victimization in the face of the unhappy princess, but at the same time, a direct simplicity saves the picture from sentimentality. The painting has been rightfully well received, and is well hung. Louisa Starr's *David before Saul* deserves recognition; it is painted with the skill one expects of a much older artist. Eliza Fox Bridell's portrait of Barbara Bodichon is forceful and understated; Louise B. Swift's portrait of *Miss Alice Judd* displays the skill of a recognized artist of accomplishment. Elizabeth Maria Anna Jerichau-Bauman's *Martyr* transcends the "low naturalism" affected by Danish painters, and is especially noteworthy for its skillful treatment of drapery. Margaret Robbinson has not done well with *First-Born*, which ignores form for eye-catching color. *Red Roses*, by Miss Freer, overdoes the drapery of the figure. Though the picture has some good qualities of composition, it is somewhat affected. Miss Banks' *The Day Dream* is "praiseworthy." A study by Miss Thornycroft deserves honorable mention.

499. "Institute of Painters in Water Colours. Third Exhibition of Sketches and Studies." *Art Journal* (1 January 1869): 27.

The high standards of the Institute are much in evidence. Emily Farmer's *The Girl Reading* is tasteful, elegant, and truthful. The artist has made such progress that the picture found a buyer on the first day. Mary Ann Duffield deserves mention for her excellent flower pieces.

500. "The Royal Academy. One Hundred and First Exhibition." *Art Journal* (1 June 1869): 161-172.

A tasteful new building with excellent lighting does justice to the 912 pictures in the exhibit. Over 3,000 works were turned away, dashing the hopes of many artists, but maintaining the high standards of the academy. In Gallery IV, Henrietta Ward exhibits *Scene from the Childhood of the Old Pretender,* in which the six- year-old prince, about to get into a coach, stops to speak to some humble, but sympathetic subjects. As is typical of Ward's paintings it avoids sentimentality while provoking sympathy and reflection. Elizabeth Maria Anna Jerichau-Bauman's *The Dying Pole* lacks refinement, but *After Sunset--Italian Girl Spinning* is not only vigorous, it is one of Jerichau's best works. Anne Escombe is evidently a new exhibitor. Her picture of a too-elegant dressing gown is titled *Drapery;* the picture is "clever, but outrageous" and scandalous in its lack of seriousness. Rosa Bonheur sends a small *Moutons Ecossais*, and another sheep picture, *Mouton des Pyrénées.* They are not as good as her usual work; the blue is overdone and the sheep lack definition. Overall, this picture by a deserving and always-welcome artist lacks her usual high quality. Annie F. Mutrie's *Qui Si Vendono Fiori* is a profusion of flowers commemorating her recent trip to Italy.

501. "The Dudley Gallery. The Third Winter Exhibition." *Art Journal* (December 1869): 369.

Quality and number of exhibits continues to decline at the Dudley as well as most other galleries. Alyce Thornycroft's *The Old Path* shows promise. Louisa Starr's *Wandering Thoughts* has power, but is too dark and looks unfinished.

502. "Institute of Painters in Water-Colours. The Fourth Exhibition of Sketches and Studies." *Art Journal* (January 1870): 26.

Mary Ann Duffield and Mary Harrison's fruit and flowers redeem the "disappointing" exhibits of the female members. Emily Farmer's work is bland; her *Music* is "too pretty"; her *Saying Grace* is "too proper." Honorary member Rosa Bonheur does not exhibit.

503. "Society of Female Artists." *Art Journal* (March 1870): 89.

Nearly 500 works by over 200 artists indicates the popularity of this exhibition; the largest obstacle for all-female exhibits is the failure to attract artists who can successfully compete with men in other exhibitions. Rosa Bonheur and Jane Benham Hay's work in this exhibit is testimony to women's capacity to achieve genius. Hay contributes four pictures, including *A Ravine Near Florence; The Florentine Procession;* and *Study of a Head* which show the skill and knowledge women can achieve with good training. *Little Sunbeam*, a head study by Margaret Backhouse; *Checkmated* by Emily Ryder; *A Study of a Head* and *Wandering Thoughts* by Julia Pocock show skill, competence and talent. Good finish and color mark E. Percy's *Queen Elizabeth in the Sanctuary;* Rebecca Coleman's *Day Dreams in the South of France* and Harriette A. Seymour's *The British Floating Harbour* should be noted. *Venetian Water Carriers* by Agnes Bouvier demonstrates "a refined waxy idealism." The *Punch* artist, Georgiana Bowers, exhibits a spirited pen-and-ink drawing titled *Tally-Ho! Back!* and another illustrator, Florence Claxton sends *Dances, Past and Present*. Lucette Elizabeth Barker exhibits *Baby Sketches, from Life,* which captures childish characteristics "to the very life," but Claxton's *The Tiff* is more interesting, and equal to any work in the exhibit. Among the landscapes, Madeline Marrable's trees and foreground are unusually good in *An Avenue of Fir Trees in Bramshill Park*. Sophy Warren's moonlight is "sicklied over by silvery sentiment." F. Kempson's *Lago Maggiore* is artificial, and *Peace on Earth* is good except for its title--it is not a religious painting, but an ordinary sunset. *Summit of the Bernina Pass* by Maria Gastineau proves that female artists are not too proud to borrow from well-known male relatives. Barbara Bodichon's *Effect of Fog, Hastings*, is up to her usual competency. Jane Deakins' coastal scene is sketchy and careless, a lesser evil than the "feeble finish" too common in this exhibition. Margaret Rayner captures the "color, texture and time-worn surface" of *Isfield Church, Sussex*. Flower and fruit paintings are predictably good; especially noteworthy exhibitors in this genre are Anna Maria Bartholomew Fitz James, C. James, Miss Lane Emma Walter, E. A. Manby and Mary Harrison. Among the animal painters, the names are more noteworthy than the paintings. Rosa Bonheur's *St. Hubert's Stag*, a blue chalk drawing of a stag with a cross between his antlers is "finely modeled," but "more strange than pleasing." Bonheur's sister, Madame Peyrol Bonheur's best work is *Poultry. One of the Lions of St. John's Wood* is Jessica Landseer's drawing of one of her father's models for the Trafalgar Square lions. Alyce Thornycroft's skill is evident in her oils, *My Grandmamma* and *A Prelude*. Alberta Brown, a beginning artist, deserves encouragement for the promise evident in *An Anxious Moment*, but Anna Maria Charritie's head study is less successful. Mrs. J. F. Herring's exhibit suggests that she should not sacrifice form for effect. *Roman Cattle* by Miss Jenkyll is immense, and Eloise Stannard's fruit studies are splendid as always. The benefits of training in German landscape techniques are evident in Miss Kernig's *A Landscape, the Bavarian Alps*. Elizabeth Bridell's spirited figure paintings, *Morgiana Dancing* and *Swift* deserve notice. All in all, the work of the society deserves credit for the persistence which has won for it "growing success and widening sphere of usefulness."

504. "Institute of Painters in Water-Colours. Thirty-Sixth Exhibition." *Art Journal* (June 1870): 175-176.

Too many bad paintings characterize this year's exhibit of 283 pictures, eight of which are by female members. Mary Ann Duffield's *Flowers* deserves mention. *The Little Brother's Peace Offering* by Elizabeth Murray has "texture, colour, but not drawing."

505. "The Royal Academy. One Hundred and Second Exhibition." *Art Journal* (1 June 1870): 161-172.

Over 1,200 works can be seen at this year's exhibition, and over a thousand of them are sent by artists who are not members of the Royal Academy. No one picture stands out this year. Louisa Starr's *J.E. Pfeiffer, Esq.* is the best portrait. Color is "superb" and laid on with a firm but subtle hand. Less successful is her picture titled *Undine*, which is neither close to nature nor to the original; the face is beautiful, however, and the figure drawing knowledgeable. The Mutrie sisters paint the best flowers. Annie F. Mutrie's *Japanese Chrysanthemums* "present pleasant novelty."

A head study by Anna Maria Charretie and *A Venetian Girl* by Margaret Robbinson deserve special mention, as do the drawings by Miss Riviére and Agnes MacWhirter. The term "female artist" is "now a term of contempt"; women win their space in exhibitions through merit, not political maneuvering. Emily Osborn's *Lost* is a good example. It excels in composition, drawing and story-telling, though the detail might be more delicately rendered. Osborn has been studying in Munich and her work reflects the influence of the Piloty school. The subject of Sophie Anderson's *Elaine* is over-used but the canvas is "large and effective" if not quite managed. "The moral is preferable to the art" in Mary Ellen Freer's *Renounced*, which is "somewhat muddled and thick."

506. "Institute of Painters in Water-Colours. Sketches and Studies." *Art Journal* (February 1871): 43.

Modesty by Emily Farmer has the charm associated with her work. Louisa Corbeaux, who seldom exhibits, has sent a cat study. Mary Ann Duffield's *Sketches of Fungi* avoids the sameness often associated with flower pictures.

507. "Exhibition of the Society of Female Artists." *Art Journal* (March 1871): 90-91.

It is difficult for women exhibiting solely with the Society of Female Artists to establish a reputation, since the best women artists leave to exhibit "where they can enter into rivalry with the opposite sex." The supporters thus deserve extra credit for putting together a very good exhibition. Louise Bisschop's work has improved since she married a Dutch painter; her *L'Espoir de la Fouile* reflects his style. Although the color is weak and the background too strong, the drawing and shadows make this work the best in the room. Helen Thornycroft's drawing and expression are good, although the color and background are not succ~ sful in her picture of a Turk titled *Study*. Julia Pocock knows her limits, which many female artists do not. Her *Die Haustochter* is a good life study. Louise Stern shows promise in her study of a boy with a book. Rebecca Coleman deserves encouragement for *A Child's Message to Headquarters*. Florence Claxton deserves praise for *Juliet;* Margaret Backhouse's *A Girl at Crochet* and *The Little Blonde* show considerable competence. Agnes Bouvier's *A Goldfinch* is an indicator of her abilities in nature study. She will meet with success if she is faithful to realism. E. V. B. submits five black-and-white drawings with considerable power. Henrietta Ward's *Going to Market--Picardy* was exhibited at the Royal Academy. Her drawing, *A First Step in Life*, demonstrates her superiority in nursery pictures. Her daughters Eva and Flora Ward are talented and quite promising artists. Most of the landscapes are mediocre, but deserve some commendation, such as *Old Eastbourne and Low Tide, Lynmouth* by Marian Croft. Croft's handling of light and color have quite pleasing results. Ten drawings by Madeline Marrable demonstrate high standards and talent suitable for any exhibition. Sophy Warren's *Near Benhill Wood, Surrey* is her best landscape so far. Catherine Nichols' *The Brook* is a careful and promising work. Miss Kempson has fallen into the triteness trap common to female artists in her mountain scene titled *Solitude*. Jane Deakin's pleasing picture titled *Low Tide* shows the careful attention to nature that most women artists seem to scorn. Miss Morice's *On the Norfolk Coast* has "truth and force." Emily Crawford has sent several small paintings that are "earnest and sound" and of the type that "are loved in English homes." Crawford's careful study and thoughtfulness are obvious in these pictures representing the seasons and the qualities such as *Industry* and *Idleness.* Among the flower pictures, special commendation must go to Charlotte James for *A Gathering in Autumn;* to Teresa Hegg for *Periwinkle;* and to Miss Lane, Miss Webb, Emma Walter and Anna Maria Fitz James. Elizabeth Eastlake has unfortunately deserted the Society of Female Artist's exhibition for the Dudley Gallery. Ellen Partridge's portrait of *Professor MacDonald*, and Anna Maria Charretie's portrait titled *Alan and Linda* deserve recognition. Louise B. Swift paints dogs better than she paints people, as is obvious in *Guard it Well* and *Feeding Time.* Fanny Assenbaum's *Sunrise on the Jungfrau* is "startling by reason of the wide expanse of white snow fields," but it is weak in detail. Jane Benham Hay's *Italian Studies* are "clever and brilliant in light." Morning on the *Banks of the Medway* by Carolina F. Williams is one of the "most artistic" landscapes in the exhibition. Eloise Stannard has exhibited her still-lifes of fruit at the British Institution. *Apricots* and *Hambros* are worthy of her exceptional skill. Louisa Starr's *Sketch* demonstrates her talent. Alyce Thornycroft's scene of an anxious mother finding her lost child is titled *Found at Last* and may be "the most remarkable work among the oils." Thornycroft needs to work on color and technical skills to do justice to her concepts in subjects. The Society of Lady Artists serves an important purpose in giving aspiring talent a place to exhibit and the public a good place to view and to appreciate art.

508. "Institute of Painters in Water-Colours. The Thirty-Seventh Exhibition." *Art Journal* (June 1871): 155-156.

Among the flowers and fruit, two works deserving mention are Fanny Harris' *Clematis, Gladiolus, etc.* and Mary Ann Duffield's *Flowers and Fruit.*

509. "The Royal Academy. One Hundred and Third Exhibition." *Art Journal* (June 1871): 149-154.

The Royal Academy has a new building, but no innovations or reform. The quality of this year's exhibition is much the same as it has always been. Henrietta Ward's picture of little Frederick the Great having his palm read and his destiny predicted is titled *The Fortunes of Little Fritz.* It deserves its place on the line. Rosa Brett's *A Spring Afternoon* is "a fresh study from nature." Frances Redgrave sends a pleasing study of resting sheep. It is titled *A Wotton Glebe.* Emily Osborn's head study, *Isolde,* of a beautiful woman decked with jewels and peacock feathers shows a foreign influence and lacks the power and finish of which Osborn is capable. The advantage of lengthy study in Germany may reflect itself in her future work. *Arab Marriage,* while hanging too high, shows Eliza Bridell's work in Algeria to good effect in its skillful drapery and truthful colors. Worthy of commendation are Sarah Beale's *The Pleasures of Art* and Annie Mutrie's *The Balcony.*

510. "Society of Painters in Water-Colours. Sixty-Seventh Exhibition." *Art Journal* (June 1871): 154-155.

Margaret Gillies' *The Escape* "has obtained commendation."

511. "The Royal Academy. The One Hundred and Third Exhibition. Second Notice." *Art Journal* (July 1871): 173-180.

The Mutrie sisters always paint delightful flower pictures. In this exhibition, Annie Mutrie's *Balcony* is brilliant. *Le Père Hyacinthe* by Henriette Browne is a good and truthful portrait, but as do many of Browne's pictures, it "wants color and transparency." Emily Osborn paints charming, playful children in *Hay Boat,* a scene on a Bavarian Lake. *The Knight's Guerdon* by Mary Ann Edwards is "refined" and "poetic." Deserving special notice are Sophie Anderson's *London Street Flowers;* Constance Phillott's *A Study;* and Edith Martineau's *A Head from Life.*

512. "Schools of Art. Female." *Art Journal* (February 1872): 57.

Julia Pocock has won the Queen's scholarship of £30 per annum for her work at the Female School of Art. At the school's January exhibition, Pocock's oil head study; a full-length sculpture, *Hero Listening;* a life-sized bust; a copy of the *Dying Gladiator;* and drawings from *Paradise and the*

Peri all deserve recognition. Miss Selous' *Water Carrier,* a drawing of a girl with a water jar should be noted, as should drawings of Miss Lamb's from *Lallah Rookh* and by Miss Hanslip from *Ingoldsby Legends.* Miss Wise's drawing is also clever. Mary B. Webb's still-life of a hare, pigeons and vegetables has won her the Queen's gold medal. Emily Austin's flower paintings gain her a silver medal. Alice B. Ellis' designs for fans has attracted the particular attention of Princess Louise. Ellis and Miss Hopkinson have made some dessert-service designs. The school superintendent, Miss Gann, and her assistants have much to be proud of.

513. "Society of Female Artists." *Art Journal* (March 1872): 89- 90.

This year's exhibition contains 421 paintings and drawings and six sculptures. *The Princes in the Tower* by Henrietta Ward and *The Danish Fisherman* by Elizabeth Jerichau-Bauman are the most noteworthy oil paintings. Ward's picture is one of her most careful works; Jerichau's painting of a fisherman sheltering his child is "one of the many evidences that women are advancing indisputable claims to advances in art." She sends five others, including a study of children titled *The Danish Vicar's Birthday.* Also deserving mention are Caroline F. Williams' *Winter's Evening* and *Near Hastings;* Louise Swift's *The Casual Ward;* Alberta Brown's *The Orphan;* Hortense Wood's *Sunset;* Miss Southernden Thompson's *Children of St. Francis;* Louisa Bridell Fox's *Before Minerva's Temple;* and two paintings by Alice Thornycroft. All in all, the quality of the oil paintings is quite average. The watercolors are much better and would in many cases hold their own in any exhibition. The flower pictures of Miss Ashworth and Teresa Hegg are, however, typical of this section of the exhibition, lacking imagination and life. Frances Key's *Moonlight on the Lakes, Capel Curig* is solid and avoids sensationalism. Madeline Marrable's work, including *The Yew-Tree Walk, Clifden* are "bright and very pleasant." Miss Freeman Kempson's scene of "silvery sundown over ... gray waters" titled *At Evening Time It Shall be Light* has simplicity and charm. Adelaide Maguire's two pictures suggest that she may be a good artist if she is willing to study nature. Louise Rayner's pictures, *Walk in Front of Eton College; Bridge Street, Chester; City of Durham* and *The Cloister, Eton College* are excellent and "display good conscientious work, as does Victoria Colkett's *St. John's College, Cambridge* and C. E. Bishop's "humble little picture." Architectural studies of Knole by Flora and Eva Ward are a testimony to their mother's genius and training. Julia Pocock's work is not of the quality one has come to expect from her. The best picture in the exhibition is Margaret Backhouse's study of a little girl titled *Our Postman in the Country.* Sophy

Warren's *Evening* and Ellen Partridge's *Calculations* are excellent. A thoughtful and careful treatment of nature is evident in Clara McKenzie Kettle's *Morning in the Valley of the Rhone*. Most original and striking are scenes of Siam by a resident, Palacia E. Alabasta. Other excellent works are *Monk's Road, Lincoln* by Marian Croft; and *Avenue at Souton* by Marian Edwards. Established artists such as Henrietta Ward and Elizabeth Jerichau-Bauman exhibit works here, but too many other talented women do not. It is one of the women's handicaps that their quickness and intuition bring them easily to a certain level, but they do not advance, not having been taught that real accomplishment comes only after enormous hard work and drudgery. It is all very well to keep a woman "a schoolgirl till her hair is grey," but schooling will not take the place of patient effort.

514. "Crystal Palace." *Art Journal* (May 1872): 166.

  Henrietta Ward has won a silver medal for her historical painting titled *Going to Market, Picardy*, in the Crystal Palace Exhibition. Her painting is titled *Going to Market, Picardy*. Margaret Robbinson's *A Summer Evening at Strawberry Hill* has won a bronze medal in the same category.

515. "The Royal Academy. The One Hundred and Fourth Exhibition." *Art Journal* (June 1872): 149-156.

  Henriette Browne, a French painter, sends two grief-filled historical pictures, *1870* and *During the War*.

516. "The Royal Academy. The One Hundred and Fourth Exhibition." *Art Journal* (July 1872): 181-186, 201-203.

  Louisa Starr's *Scene from the Merchant of Venice* in which Portia remarks on Bassanio's pale cheek fails in its weak treatment and in a stippling that hides the entire painting. Starr's portraits, *B. H. Hodgson, Esq.* and *Mrs. J.E. Pfeiffer* are much more successful. Hodgson's portrait is animated and brightly colored. *The Queen's Lodge, Windsor*, a portrait of George III, his wife, daughters, and some visitors, is one of Henrietta Ward's best achievements and a superb "representation of royal social life." Augusta Wells' painting of a game of "follow the leader" is inappropriately titled *Oranges and Lemons*. Miss Lane's portrait of *Helen Faucit (Mrs. Theodore Martin)* accurately preserves its subject's amiable disposition. Louise Rayner's *The Butter Market, Windsor* and Annie Dixon's miniatures deserve notice.

517. "The International Exhibition. English and Foreign Pictures." *Art Journal* (September 1872): 237.

Nearly a thousand paintings, mostly by British Artists, comprise this year's collection at London's International Exhibition. *Scene from the Childhood of the Old Pretender* by Henrietta Ward is one of the popular paintings in the British collection. In the French collection, Browne's *Au Printemps* deserves recognition.

518. "Society of Lady Artists." *Art Journal* (April 1873): 104.

The exhibition of the Society of Lady Artists at the Conduit Street Gallery has 409 oil and watercolor paintings. While some pictures of flowers, fruit and animals are excellent, a marked deficiency in figure painting is evident. Many artists stop with the head, avoiding the more difficult bits. Elizabeth Thompson's *Salutations, Rome*, a curious picture of a soldier saluting ("with the wrong hand") a cardinal is only a sketch but shows promise of turning into something much more developed. Mrs. Paul Naftel's *The Lily of the Valley* lacks firmness, and Margaret Backhouse's *A Child of the South* lacks sparkle. Backhouse's other exhibit *Jour de Fête*, has some of the brilliance of color one associates with her work. Helen Thornycroft manages a tasteful handling of ancient costume in *A Venetian Musical Party;* A.L.'s *The Dream of Kriemhilde* is a difficult subject far beyond the artist's skills. Henrietta Ward's *Winter* is a "little shivering embodiment." Flora Ward's *The Legion of Honour* and Eva Ward's *The Queen Beech, Knole* are clever pictures which, with their mother's work, show considerable imagination and talent for one family. Adelaide Claxton's *Little Nell* is almost too intense to suit its namesake. Three heads, titled *Morning; Noon;* and *Night* by Florence Claxton are expressive but hard. Rebecca Coleman's *A Devonshire Haymaker* is not up to her usual work. Eliza Sharp sends three copies of old masters. Four head studies, *Far from Home* by A. E. Burrow; *A Portrait*, and *Bessie, Daughter of Henry Dunning McLeod, Esq.* by Susan C. Domett; and *Sunshine* by S. M. Louisa Taylor deserve notice. The landscape collection is not distinguished, but Madeline Cockburn Marrable's thirteen drawings are quite distinctive. Worth mention are Miss Kempson's *Twilight, Near Oban;* Ann Ashley Hall's *An Ancient Palace in Venice;* Charlotte J. James' *Red, Purple, and White Grapes;* Anna Maria Fitz James' *Fruit and Greengages and Grapes;* Emma Walter's *Canaries;* Jane Benham Hay's *Entrance to the Monastery of Santa Caterina-Lago Maggiore;* Louisa B. Swift's *My Pets;* Alyce Thornycroft's portrait of *Mrs. Thornycroft;* Mrs. W. Burgess' *The Gipsy;* Elizabeth Hunter's *Do I Like Butter?;* Mrs. J. F. Herring's *The Farm Yard;* and Eloise Stannard's *Fruits*. Artists worthy of notice are Mrs. J. W. Brown, Emma Brownlow King, Mrs. G. Frank, Ellen

Partridge, Maria Gastineau, Adelaide A. Maguire, Mrs. Withers, Miss Lane, E. Lane, and Mary Harrison. Barbara Bodichon's seascape, *Tea, Hastings,* lacks realistic treatment of the water. Teresa Hegg's *Begonia* is a skillful and elegant flower picture; her other pictures are also well done. Louise Rayner's interior view of *St. George's Chapel, Windsor* is "elaborate and highly successful." *Marshal MacMahon* is a well executed-portrait of a dog by Lady Coleridge. It deserves to be placed in a more favorable place in the exhibition.

519. "Exhibition of the Royal Academy." *Art Journal* (June 1873): 165-170.

Annie Mutrie's *In the Garden* contains the feeling and the power that takes a flower painting beyond botanical study into the realm of art.

520. "The Institute of Painters in Water-Colours." *Art Journal* (June 1873): 174-175.

Honorable mention among the 273 drawings in this year's exhibition includes Mary Margett's *Hollyhocks* and Mary Ann Rosenberg Duffield's *Flowers.*

521. "Exhibition of Royal Academy." *Art Journal* (July 1873): 197- 203.

Louisa Starr's *Imogen* shows improvement in "technical accomplishment" at the expense of originality and imagination. The picture becomes less a work of art than an illustration; Starr should beware of sacrificing her talent for the sake of poor workmanship. Laura Alma-Tadema's *Mamma's Chair* and Miss Martineau's *A Portrait* deserve mention for clever handling of color. Also deserving of mention are Louise Romer's *Bribery* and Ellen Montalba's portrait titled *Mrs Frances Lowther.* Mary Ellen Edwards' *Sweet Success* demonstrates skill in handling color and light, although the subject is not really the best.

522. "Exhibition of the Royal Academy." *Art Journal* (August 1873): 236-241.

A Norwegian artist, Miss Ribbins, exhibits two portraits, *Baron Hochschild* and *Baroness Hochschild;* both pictures are thoughtfully and firmly painted. *Undine* by E. Sandys, shows careful drawing but the color is coarse. Rosa Brett's *A Winter Afternoon in Kent* merits attention. Louise Romer demonstrates her skill with color in a portrait titled *Miss Elmore.* Last year's academy medal winner, Jessie Macgregor, sends a picture of a grief-stricken woman with her hands clasped over her head. The picture is titled *And the Veil of Thine Head Shall Be Grief, and the Crown Shall Be Pain.* The subject requires a more experienced hand then Macgregor's, but her talent is still evident. *Hero Worship in the Eighteenth Century* by Emily Osborn is a scene from Boswell's biography where Samuel Johnson looks up from his writing at two young women who come in vain to worship at his feet. Composition and drawing are good, but Ward needs to work more on handling color. Miss Martineau distinguishes herself in strength, form and color in her *Head of a Girl*. Colors are confused and overly warm in spite of Marie Spartali Stillman's obvious sense of harmony in two scenes from *Morte d'Arthur* titled *The Finding of Sir Lancelot Disguised as a Fool* and *Sir Tristram and La Belle Fonde*. Both pictures possess "the true spirit of romantic luxuriance" in their imagination, detail, and beauty. Two excellent portraits are Lady Coleridge's *Miss Coleridge;* and Ellen G. Hill's *John Scott, Esq.*

523. "Royal Scottish Academy. Forty-Eighth Exhibition." *Art Journal* (April 1874): 103-104.

In an exhibition of mostly Scottish artists, the work is excellent. Anna Charretie needs to use less pink and white if she is to achieve more realistic flesh tones, but *Belle Bouquetière* and *Happy Thoughts* are thoughtful and graceful. In Christina Ross' *The Winter's Tale*, two girls react realistically to the appearance of ghost. *Tito*, Constance Phillott's classical head study, is a success, as are Miss Johnston's *Rowans* and *Apple Blossom*. Jessy Frier's *Loch Earn* is commendable and Agnes MacWhirter's still lifes are effectively arranged and colored.

524. "Birmingham Society of Artists." *Art Journal* (May 1874): 146.

General good quality and a plethora of watercolors characterize the spring exhibition of the Birmingham Society of Artists. Contributing members of the society include Mary Ann Duffield, Emma Oliver, Gertrude Martineau, Constance Phillott, Lucy Madox Brown, Louise Rayner and others.

525. "Society of Lady Artists, Great Marlborough Street." *Art Journal* (May 1874): 146.

While male artists tend to have technical training and "mechanical excellences" they often lack imagination and refinement in their work, even sinking to vulgarity upon occasion. Female artists generally lack the technical skills, but bring to art "graceful taste and refined thought" and in this exhibition, while no outstanding example of any mechanical skill emerges, neither is there vulgarity. Elizabeth Thompson's work contains "a superior vigour" in *Tent-Pegging*, a picture of horsemen endeavoring to spear a peg from horseback. Thompson avoids idealism or decorative qualities and aims for expression, and in this respect her work is perfect. Emma Sandy's *Fair Rosamond* is powerful and thoughtful; few pictures in the gallery can match it for composition, harmony, and expression. Louise Jopling's picture of a "lady at her toilette" shows an understanding of tone and color. Also praiseworthy are figure paintings by Anna Maria Charretie, *A Roman Peasant* by Rebecca Solomon, and *Written on Sand* by Mary Ellen Edwards. Landscapes by Barbara Bodichon and Alyce Thornycroft, Clara Montalba (who has just been made an associate of the Society of Painters in Water-Colors) E. V. B. and Rebecca Coleman deserve notice and praise. The new gallery at Great Marlborough Street is more spacious and better lit than the old Conduit Street Gallery.

526. "Exhibition of the Royal Academy." *London Times* (2 May 1874): 12.

Calling the Roll is, of all the pictures exhibited this year, the one most likely to be remembered. In its compassionate rendering of human suffering, it neither exaggerates with sensationalism nor offends with sentimentality. Thompson's earlier paintings were unfairly treated, but with the success of this painting her future works will be assured of a good place.

527. "The Royal Academy Exhibition: Second Notice." *Illustrated London News* (9 May 1874): 446.

Elizabeth Thompson's *Calling the Roll after an Engagement, Crimea* is an astonishing success at capturing the terrible realities of human suffering caused by war. Thompson avoids sentimentality in an uncompromising detail that is almost harsh. The strength achieved in this painting is all the more astonishing given Thompson's youth and inexperience. It is, in short, a surprise.

528. "The Royal Academy: (Third Notice)." *The Athenaeum* (16 May 1874): 670.

Elizabeth Thompson's *Calling the Roll* is commendable for its intense drama and excellent execution. It is a credit to the artist.

529. "Exhibition of the Royal Academy: Second Notice." *London Times* (26 May 1874): 6.

Without Elizabeth Thompson's *The Roll Call*, the Royal Academy Exhibit this year would have fallen far below its usual high level of quality.

530. "The Royal Academy." *Art Journal* (June 1874): 161-166.

The picture receiving the most attention this year is Elizabeth Thompson's *Calling the Roll after an Engagement--Crimea*. Thompson has worked very hard at her art and has already received mention in the *Art Journal* this year for her skills in animation and design in a drawing exhibited at the Society of Lady Artists. Much of the power of *Calling the Roll* is derived from its superb understatement; Thompson avoids sentiment and sensationalism to achieve "terrible quietude and passionless severity of absolute fact." Beyond its popularity, Thompson's painting is unquestionably art. Louisa Starr handles tones of brown and gold extremely well in her portrait *Miss Denison* and Louise Jopling's *La Japonaise* demonstrates cleverness of color. Ellen Montalba's portrait *My Sister* deserves mention. Jessie Macgregor is an artist of proven merit and she rightly strives for higher achievement; however, in *Orpheus and Eurydice* she has reached too far and the picture unfortunately fails.

531. "The Royal Academy. Second Notice." *Art Journal* (July 1874): 197-201.

Five O'Clock Tea is Louise Jopling's best work thus far and is also the best of many paintings in the exhibition with a Japanese theme. Jopling's skill in composition and tone is exceptional. Henrietta Ward's sense of drama gives her paintings mass appeal, which perhaps compensates for lack of high artistic skill. In *The Defense of Latham House*, Ward captures a moment when a shell bursts in the dining room of the Countess of Derby while she and her daughters remain at their dinner, unmoved by the excitement. Two excellent portraits deserving mention are S. Ribbing's *Mrs. Charles G. Barclay* and Mary Backhouse's *A Venetian Girl*. Miss Mutrie sends a very good painting of azaleas and a camellia. Ellen Stone's *A Map of the War* and Laura Epps' *My Doll's Picnic* both deserve attention.

532. "Black and White Exhibition." *Art Journal* (August 1874): 232.

Elizabeth Thompson's military subjects are among the works of prominent artists exhibiting studies of "pure form and light and shade."

533. "The Royal Academy. Concluding Notice." *Art Journal* (August 1874): 225-229.

Annie Mutrie's *Poppies*, Henrietta Ward's *My Pet*, Louisa Starr's *The Story of the Spanish Gypsy* and Flora Ward's *The Bridal Morn* are worthy of notice. Among the portraits, a chalk drawing by E. Sandys of *The Duchess of St. Albans* is very good, and Ellen Hill's spirited portrait of

Arthur Hill, Esq. is a "masterly piece of drawing." Mdme. Cazin's landscape *A Market Garden in London* is hanging near the ceiling, thanks to lack of intelligence of the hanging committee. Mdme. Cazin's works are well known and at least this painting is accompanied by other excellent works, also placed at an inconvenient height.

534. "Art Notes from the Provinces. Cork." *Art Journal* (February 1875): 61.

The School of Art in Cork, an institution known for training artists of high reputation, recently held an exhibition of paintings and drawings to which people of many social classes contributed. Lady H. Newenham's *The Newsboy* is a "clever impersonation."

535. "Institute of Painters in Water-Colours." *Art Journal* (February 1875): 58-59.

Elizabeth Thompson is one of the few artists in this exhibition who avoids "smallness and pettiness." Her sketch of a figure from last year's picture, *Tent Pegging*, shows a man on horseback at full gallop; the expressions on the faces of the man and the horse compliment each other and the drawing is "roughly and boldly executed." Her other picture, *Charge of the Life Guards at Wimbledon* is too detailed and lacks clarity.

536. "Society of British Artists." *Art Journal* (February 1875): 59.

In a collection of almost 900 pictures, most of them worthless, a few deserve mention. Ellen Wilkinson's *Rest* is a "graceful composition" of two figures under a tree. Mary Backhouse's *Bothered* also deserves notice.

537. "The Dudley Water-Colour Exhibition." *Art Journal* (March 1875): 93.

The Dudley's prestigious exhibition displays some 600 works, having rejected almost a thousand. Figure painting is one of the weak areas, but some are worth mentioning. *Saint Sebastian* by Helen Thornycroft, and a picture of a young girl by Edith Martineau are two such examples. Flowers are a popular subject; some good examples are exhibited by Miss E. Cooper, Miss J. Samworth, Susannah Soden, Helen Coleman, Marie Spartali Stillman and Mrs. Pratten. Agnes MacWhirter makes her debut with a promising still life.

538. "The Water-Colour Society. Winter Exhibition." *Art Journal* (March 1875): 92.

Clara Montalba's paintings prove that she deserves her recent election as a member of the Water-Colour Society. While *The Thames at Limehouse* is not altogether successful in treatment of atmosphere, Montalba amply displays her skill with color with her rendering of a crimson bed in an interior study. *A Rainy Day at Venice* is "one of the best studies of the effect of weather to be found in the gallery."

539. "Glasgow Institute of Fine Arts." *Art Journal* (May 1875): 155-156.

The Queen has loaned Emily Osborne's painting *The Governess* to this fourteenth exhibition of the Glasgow Institute. Louisa Starr manages the cold greys of the sea and sky very well in *Break! Break!*, but the expression on the face of the mourner in the painting is too stern.

540. "Minor Topics." *Art Journal* (May 1875): 157-158.

Helen Allingham is a new associate of the Society of Water- Colour Painters. The Institute of Water-Colour Painters has added three women to its membership; they are Mary Gow, Marian Chase, and Miss Coleman.

541. "Royal Scottish Academy." *Art Journal* (May 1875): 154-155.

The faces of the old woman and her small pupil in I. Scott Lauder's *The Knitting Lesson* are extremely well done. Lauder's *The Italian Fruit Seller* also deserves mention. The forty-ninth exhibition of the Royal Scottish Academy boasts over a thousand works. The overall quality is much better than the average.

542. "The Society of Lady Artists." *Art Journal* (June 1875): 186-187.

The Society of Lady Artists is a good place for beginning artists to exhibit their work, but as they gain skill and notoriety they tend to move to other societies. Those women who fit that category and are not represented in this exhibition might want to remember to send pictures here. Elizabeth Thompson is one whose work was first noticed here. She sends a life-sized picture of an Italian dressed in fur that was painted for this exhibition. She also loans a painting titled *Roman Shepherds Playing at Morra.* Mary Backhouse sends *Lucretia* and Ellen Partridge sends *Ironside;* both pictures are life sized. Henrietta Ward's reputation was made at other galleries, but she always supports the Society of Lady Artists by sending a picture. Her picture of a chubby baby is titled *Innocence.* Other well-known artists are Mary S. Tovey, who sends *Ruth and Boaz;* Alyce Thornycroft, who sends *In an Orchard;* and Louise Jopling, whose picture is titled *Through the Looking Glass.* Eloise Stannard represents near perfection in fruit painting, and Louise B. Swift shows her skill with dog portraits in *Oscar and His Friends.* Other notable still life studies are *Still Life* by Minna Nixon and *Oriental Jar* by Maria Brooks. Worth noticing are *Friesland Girl Knitting* by Georgiana Swift; *Chequered Shade* by Mrs. B. L. Hindes; and *Grandmamma's Treasures* by Alice

Renshaw. In the watercolor section, Mary Harrison demonstrates her skill at color and drawing in *Hollyhocks*. Teresa Hegg's work is not as "broad and dashing" as Harrison's, but her wildflower studies are refined, delicate and accurate. Fruit and flower pictures deserving praise are sent by Emma Walters, Rose Emily Stanton and F. Corbett. Anna Maria Guerin sends *Study of Goldfinches*, which is typical of her dainty bird studies. Emma Cooper paints like Guerin in her *Nest and May*, but her style is "larger and broader" in *Hie! Lost*, a life-size partridge lying dead in a turnip field. Anna Maria Charretie's figure study, *Priscilla* is more finished than her *Gretchen*. Two good head studies are Helen Thornycroft's *Study of a Head* picturing a "hooded Italian looking from under his hand-shaded brow" and Elizabeth Westbrook's *Lillian, Wife of the Rev. Godfrey Thring of Hambleton Rectory*. Two portraits by Julia Pocock, and a portrait of *Professor Ruskin* by Mrs. F. Nixon excel in their category. *Windsor Castle Interior* and *Old Homestead, Bucks* by Flora E. S. Ward are proof that this young artist continues to progress. Mrs. P. Naftel has been recently elected to the society, and *Pretty Polly* shows that she deserves the honour. Maria Gastineau's *Castle Rock, Vale of St. John, Cumberland* excels in atmosphere. Worthy of notice are *Ayesha of Algiers* and *Dream of Ancient Egypt* by A. Lenox. Charlotte Babb's drawing of *Charmain* from *Antony and Cleopatra* is "splendid" and Madeline Marrable's work in her scenes of Venice and the Tyrol is "as industrious as ever." Other artists whose names are well known and who send work to this exhibition are Barbara Bodichon, F. Maud Allridge, Clara Montalba, Margaret Backhouse, Alice Percival Smith, and Emily Partridge.

543. "Society of British Artists." *Art Journal* (June 1875): 187-188.

Charlotte Babb paints in the style of Mr. Leighton in her picture of anxious women watching a battle. *On Troy Walls*, as Leighton would undoubtedly tell her, is too ambitious a subject. Isabel Bennett's *The Young Royalists* and *Near Chingford, Essex* are placed too low to be easily noticed. Mary S. Tovey has sent a very good portrait, and Ann Marie Charretie's *Lady Betty at Home* shows her excellence in figure painting. Also worthy of notice among some 900 pictures is Ellen Gilbert's *Pamela about to Deposit Her Letters in the Concerted Hiding-Place by the Sunflower;* Miss Claxton's *Moonshine;* J. A. Edwards' *Breakfast Time;* Katherine Scott's *Foxgloves;* and H. F. A. Miles' *Spring.*

544. "The Institute of Painters in Water-Colours." *Art Journal* (July 1875): 214-215.

The Institute of Painters in Water-Colours reflects its innovative attitude in an exhibition full of life and vitality. The Institute was the first to invite foreign artists, which include Rosa Bonheur and Henriette Browne, and of the British members, Marian Chase and Mary L. Gow are its newest associates. Chase sends a picture of foxgloves and roses titled *Summer-Time;* Gow's picture is titled *Enid's Wedding Morning.* Both pictures fully justify the artists' election to the Institute. Flower paintings of note include Mary Harrison's *Dark Roses,* Mary Margetts' *Spring Flowers;* and *Cabbage Roses and Sweet Peas* by Mary Ann Duffield. Helen Cordelia Coleman-Angell's painting is also commendable. Emma Oliver sends some good scenes from Scotland and Italy. Elizabeth Thompson's *Trooper of the Scots Greys* will attract attention and interest from her many admirers.

545. "The Royal Academy Exhibition." *Art Journal* (July 1875): 216-220.

Over 1,000 oil paintings, watercolors, crayon sketches and miniatures can be seen in this year's exhibition. Against many predictions of failure Elizabeth Thompson has painted a picture the equal of her tremendous work of last year. *The 28th Regiment at Quatre Bras* shows a range of emotion from "the hysterical defiance of inexperienced boyhood to the settled iron resolution of bearded men"; she has rendered her figures with "decision and certitude" that can only be called genius. The only criticism is that the faces of the men do not show the grime and smoke of the battle, but that is a small detail which can easily be fixed. What Thompson needs now is to be allowed to get on with her work without interference of "injudicious friends and fussy patrons." Eva Ward sends two pictures of young women, one of them life-sized. They are titled *The Bouquet Stall* and *Absent* and show skill in handling color and expressing sentiment. Mary Ellen Staples' clever picture of two tree-carving lovers is titled *The Record.* Henriette Browne's picture *Pet Goldfinch* shows a little girl distracted from her studies. Mary S. Tovey's picture is titled *Mrs. Llewellyn.* Louise Jopling sends *Modern Cinderella.* Anna M. Lea's two pictures, *St. Cecila* and *Baccante* are both worth attention. Also commendable is an untitled work by Maria Burnham Brook; Rosa Brett's *Doubtful Greeting;* Maria Brooks' portrait *Mrs. Montague Cookson;* Blanche Jenkins' *Merry Christmas Time;* Miss Tiddeman's *From the Sunny South, Wild Roses,* and *Veni, Vedi, Vici;* Alice Manly's *A Bit of Glen Scenery, Aber, Carnavonshire;* and M. Stuart Wortley's portrait of *The Right Hon. James Stuart Wortley, Q.C.* Wortley's countenance can be seen in this exhibit in a portrait by A. Stuart Wortley.

546. "The Royal Academy." *Art Journal* (August 1875): 247-252.

Henrietta Ward's gentle scene of two highland lovers, *The Poet's First Love*, shows her skill and her artistic calling. She can do no better than to continue the work she is doing where "humanity and nature are in perfect harmony." Theresa Thornycroft's competent work, *Design from the Parable of the Ten Virgins*, is well drawn and has classical serenity. Women on a rooftop pouring water on the heads of pedestrians is the subject of *The Montevidean Carnival* by Alice Havers. Gold-medalist Louisa Starr shows remarkably able handling of color in her picture of a tired governess titled *Hardly Earned*. Anna Maria Charretie's clever picture of a woman, a girl, and a kneeling servant has as its title only a quotation from the Pope. Maria Brooks sends *Little Nell at the Window*, and Mary Ellen Staples sends *Loves Me--Loves Me Not?* Martha Mutrie's *Cottage Window* deserves notice, as does Louise Rayner's *Fair Day, South Petherton, Somersetshire;* Clara Montalba's *La Salute Venice;* Edith Martineau's portrait *Emmeline, Daughter of R. Smith, Esq. of Goldings;* and Kate Bisschop's drawing *Good Night.* Marie Spartali Stillman's *Mona Lisa* carries roses and displays originality and fine handling of color. Augusta Wells copies George Leslie's handling of tone in her picture *Courtyard of a Dairy Farm.*

547. "The Royal Academy Exhibition." *Art Journal* (September 1875): 263-264.

Lady Coleridge's two excellent chalk drawings are a picture of a boy, titled *Nineteen;* and a portrait of the *Very Rev. John Henry Newman, D.D.* The miniature collection includes work by Mrs. Dixon, Miss Dixon, Mrs. E. Barrett, Margaret Tekusch, and Maria E. Burt. Louisa Steele creates enamel portraits on gold, work that was much in demand in France until recently. This little-understood art is not only beautiful, but also "imperishable." Her exhibitions are titled *J. Steele, Esq.* and *Mrs. J. Steele.*

548. "The Autumn Exhibition at the Royal Institution, Manchester." *Art Journal* (November 1875): 349-350.

Limited space prohibits anything but the names of some of the best-known artists in this exhibition, including Emily Mary Olson, Laura Alma-Tadema and Clara Montalba.

549. "Exhibition of the Society of British Artists, Suffolk Street." *Art Journal* (February 1876): 59-60.

The best Winter Exhibition ever of the Society of British Artists contains over 700 pictures. Exceptional works have been contributed by

Margaret Backhouse, Hilda Montalba, Kate Greenaway, Helen Thornycroft and Grace H. Hastie.

550. "Winter Exhibition of the Water-Colour Society." *Art Journal* (February 1876): 58.

Two burglars are dramatically thwarted in Clara Montalba's *Sketch of Knowle House*. The subject is enhanced by dark and gloomy tones. Two outdoors scenes, *Storm at Sea* and *Brow of the Hill* show Montalba's versatility. Two other pictures, *Thames Mudlarks* and *Blackfriars Bridge at Early Morning* are undramatic scenes which gain interest with her painting techniques. Helen Allingham exhibits an excellent portrait of *Thomas Carlyle* in a garden. Pictures by Maria Harrison, Margaret Gillies and Mary Ann Criddle are up to these artist's usual high standards.

551. "Winter Exhibition of the Institute of Painters in Water- Colours." *Art Journal* (February 1876): 58-59.

One of the honorary foreign members, Rosa Bonheur, sends a watercolor titled *Meadow at Fontainebleau*, a picture of cows in a meadow. *Hollyhocks* and some other flower studies by Helen C. Coleman-Angell; three *Studies of Flowers* by Mary Ann Duffield; and *May Blossoms* by Marian Chase are clever representations of their genre. Elizabeth Thompson has abandoned the battlefield for an Italian *Wine Press*. Mary Ann Duffield's *Head Study* is placed near the door. The late Mary Harrison's works, *Dark Roses* and *Cabbage Roses* are not rendered as the paintings of her youth, but they are especially remarkable for their "softness, richness of color, and largeness of treatment," because Harrison was eighty when she painted them.

552. "The Picture Gallery at the Royal Aquarium, Westminster." *Art Journal* (March 1876): 93.

More than 3,000 pictures from various galleries were judged by a committee, and some 1,000 paintings in this exhibition represent the best. Louise Jopling's *The Five Sisters of New York* illustrates a scene from *Nicholas Nickleby*. Juliana José sends *An Arab at his Devotions*. Other excellent works represent Elizabeth Jerichau, Miss Westbrook, M. Claxton, Alice Thornycroft, Grace Fenton, Marie Spartali Stillman, Mary Ellen Staples, Eleanor Manley, Clara Montalba, Florence Tiddeman, Mrs. F. Hueffer, and J. Simpson.

553. "Society of Lady Artists, Great Marlborough Street." *Art Journal* (April 1876): 125.

Quality continues to improve and the Society of Lady Artists continues to thrive, although of the 666 drawings and paintings there is still a great disparity in degrees of excellence. In the still-life category, *Snipe* by Charlotte Forbes-Cockburn and *A Brace of Partridges* by Emma Cooper are quite good. In flower and fruit paintings, Emma Walter provides excellence in *Group of Orchids* and a bullfinch with grapes titled *Monarch of All She Surveys*. Also good in this category are *Nature and Art*, a collection of fruit with a shell by F. Davis; *Golden Hambros* and *Black Hambros* by Eloise Stannard; and *Nancy* by Mary S. Tovey. Teresa Hegg's flowers are of a high enough standard to be exhibited anywhere. Sophy S. Warren and Madeline Marrable display their usual excellence in landscapes. Marrable's pictures include *Sunset on the Pitz Roseg* and *Looking Towards Como from Tremezzo*. Barbara Bodichon's *Cornfield After a Storm* and Miss Kempson's *Castle Rock;* Kate Macaulay's *Welsh Moors;* Marianne Foster's *Bradford-upon-Avon;* Mrs. Hines *Rock House;* Mrs. P. J. Naftel's *On the Llugwy, Capel Curig,* and Fanny Assenbaum's *A Peep through the Wood* all deserve notice. Excelling in animal painting are Alice Dundas with her *Head of Terrier;* a life-sized *Study of a Pair of Oxen* by Miss Kirschener; and Louise B. Swift's picture of a white bulldog. Margaret Backhouse's figure painting of an Italian shepherd and F. Maud Allridge's head in brown tones and a head by Helen Thornycroft are among the best of the figure paintings. Eliza Bridell Fox sends *When Will the Kettle Boil?* and Emily Crawford's white-capped French girl titled *Net Mender* and her *Idlers* are excellent. Mary Eley's pipe-smoking pensioner, *Disappointed Hero* is a bit hard but "well studied and full of character." Also pleasing is C. Pierrepont's *Necklace of Roses*. If the fabric of the Italian girl's shawl in *Brown Study* is an indicator, A. Lenox has remarkable skills in rendering texture. With more consistency, this picture could have been the best in the room. Also worth noting are a seascape by L. Wren and *Loch on Eilan* by Sophia Dunbar. Among the most famous exhibitors are Elizabeth Thompson who "signifies her presence and good wishes" with *In a Florentine Farmyard* and *Chapel of a Country House, Near Florence*, two small studies. Jane Benham Hay sends *Entrance to the Monastery of Sancta Caterina, Lago Maggiore* and a small picture of rocks and houses. Louise Jopling reflects the teaching of her French master in *Labour of Love*. Henrietta Montalba sends a sketch of two girls playing, and Hilda Montalba sends *Far Away*, a picture of a girl mending nets and looking out to sea. It is one of the best pictures in the gallery and qualifies her as one of the best female artists.

554. "Minor topics. The Crystal Palace Picture Gallery." *Art Journal* (June 1876): 190.

> For this year's exhibition at the Crystal Palace gallery, Sophy S. Warren has won a silver medal for *Sunset on the Way*.

555. "The Great Exhibition: What Women Have Done For It." *New York Times* (4 June 1876): 1.

> Too many pictures crowd the art exhibit of the Women's Pavilion, but among the excellent works that attract large crowds is *The Patrician Mother* by Anna M. Lea, a Philadelphia native now living in London. The three-quarter figure of a woman holding a child is well drawn; the antique drapery is heavy but enhances the figure without "mock modesty." A prominent German critic has pronounced this work one of the best in the exhibit. Lea's work is firm and purposeful; she is a woman who "knows just what she wants to do, and does it without doubt or hesitation." Her picture of St. Genevieve sitting in a forest holding a child attempting to pet a fawn is also well done, popular, and "appeals directly and forcibly even to the untaught and unpracticed eye." Ellen Hale's picture of a boy reading is also popular and deserves mention.

556. "Exhibition of the Society of Painters in Water Colours." *Art Journal* (July 1876): 209-210.

> Among the 250 works in this collection, Mary Ann Duffield's *Irises and Scarlet Geranium* and her five other flower pictures deserve recognition. Marian Chase's *Red Currants; Raspberries;* and *The Chapel of the St. Vierge, the Cathedral of Notre Dame, Chartres* also merit notice. Emma Oliver's best work is *Near Aberarder, Inverness*. Elizabeth's Murray's Roman scene, titled *The Best in the Market* and a woman with a fish titled *An Eastern Jewess* were sent from the British Consulate in Portland, Maine. Fanny Corbeaux sends *We Always Make Ourselves Comfortable*, a small drawing. Helen C. Angell sends two flower pictures and a very good drawing titled *Apples*. Mary L. Gow's *Elaine* illustrates the medieval subject in Tennyson's poem. *Out of Date* pictures a young woman taking an old-fashioned bonnet out of a chest. Both pictures prove Gow's skill at color, tone, and subject.

557. "The Royal Academy Exhibition." *Art Journal* (July 1876): 213-216.

> Henrietta Ward renders a grim subject in inspiring terms in one of her best pictures for some time. *Mrs. Fry Conducting Her Young Friend Mary Sanderson for the First Time to Visit the Female Prisoners in*

Newgate shows the Quaker philanthropist in her bonnet and shawl carrying a crimson Bible. The picture is carefully detailed and contains a fine lesson in morality.

558. "The Royal Academy Exhibition. Second Notice." *Art Journal* (August 1876): 229-232.

Ellen Montalba's portrait of a grey-haired woman is exceptional, and Louise Jopling's *Alsace* captures the mood of mourning very well. *Miss Mischief,* Maria Brook's little girl in black, is one of the best child portraits in the exhibition. M. Stuart Wortley's portrait of the *Hon. Mrs. J. Stuart Wortley* is excellent, but the artist must attend to research when representing coats-of-arms; the one in the background is not accurate. A sick child with a red geranium manages to avoid mournfulness in F. Tiddeman's *Between Two Worlds.* A portrait of G. R. Ward, Esq. represents one of the best known names in English art. Ward is son and nephew to famous artists, but his "greatest family honor" is being the father of Henrietta Ward.

559. "The Fine Arts at the Centennial VIII: The American Pictures." *The American Architect and Building News* (19 August 1876): 269-270.

The exhibit of paintings by American artists is poorly organized, badly hung, and lacks originality and distinction. Several portraits by Anna Lea Merritt are more English than American and lack strength and color, but are excellent in refinement and character.

560. "The Royal Academy Exhibition. Concluding Notice." *Art Journal* (September 1876): 261-264.

Garden Lily is one of Martha Mutrie's best, and Annie Mutrie equals her sister in *Evening Primrose. Garden Lily* has a bank of flowers in the background, *Evening Primrose* has an old brick house. The Mutries are unexcelled in their genre. Elizabeth Dawson's *Fruit* deserves mention, as does a portrait by Janet Archer. Other pictures "marked for approbation" include Jessie Macgregor's *The Gardener's Daughter;* Ada Hanbury's *Shellfish* and Eleanor Stuart Wood's *Fruit. Mrs. Henry S. King,* a portrait by Louisa Starr of a woman at a desk with a plaid blanket over her lap shows cleverness and continued improvement, especially in her color techniques.

561. "Minor Topics. The Female School of Art Prize Exhibition, Queen's Square." *Art Journal* (December 1876): 373.

Over 200 students attend the Female School of Art; the last exhibition was the best in its history. Its graduates are beginning to establish themselves as professionals in painting and design. Among this year's prize winners, the National Silver Medal and The Queen's Gold Medal were awarded to Ida Lovering for a female head-study in chalk. The National Silver Medal is competed for on a nationwide basis, while the Queen's Gold Medal is an award in individual schools. Florence Reason wins the National Silver Medal and the National Gilchrist Scholarship for a watercolor passion flower. Harriet Frances Newton of the Durham School of Art also wins a National Gilchrist Scholarship for a collection of drawings. Alice Hanslip's charcoal drawings win her a National Bronze Medal, a Queen's Scholarship, and a vacation prize. Emily Austin's oil of "a dead pigeon, a cabbage, some eggs, a bottle or two of pickles, etc." is very realistic and wins her a National Bronze Medal. Gertrude Hamilton and Rhoda Holmes win National Book Prizes. Emily May Wilks and Florence Thoresby win vacation prizes. Last year the Duchess of Edinburgh bought a flower painting from Helen Hancock, and this year she has commissioned one to go with it. Susan Ruth Canton was last year's National Gold Medal winner; she exhibits pen and ink sketches and designs for a fire screen.

562. "The Winter Exhibitions. Society of British Artists, Suffolk Street." *Art Journal* (February 1877): 53-54.

  With the Past is Mary S. Tovey's head study of an Italian by a wall with classic carvings. Henrietta Montalba sends *Landscape*, a picture of a girl, some geese, a pool, and some beech trees.

563. "The Winter Exhibitions. The Society of Painters in Water-Colours." *Art Journal* (February 1877): 54-55.

  The men [sic] such as Basil Bradley, Walter Duncan, and Clara Montalba... who exhibit their works as Associates of the Society of Painters in Water-Colours help maintain the continuing excellence of the gallery. Montalba's *Early Morning* and *Sunrise*, two Venetian scenes, attest to her continued progress with her work. *St. Mark's, Venice*, a picture of a monk walking down some steps, is "as manly a piece of work as any in the exhibition." Helen Allingham sends a "lovely" work titled *Spring Sketches*.

564. "The Winter Exhibitions. The Institute of Painters in Water-Colours." *Art Journal* (February 1877): 55-56.

Among the excellent landscapes in the exhibition is Marian Chase's painting of wild flowers and clover titled *In the Hayfield*. Mary L. Gow's *Fête-Dieu* is "a rather ambitious" but mostly successful painting of a procession of little girls dressed in white and carrying crosses and religious banners. Elizabeth Thompson's *Vintage Sketch in Tuscany* needs some restraint in its color, but her magnificent *Scots Greys Advancing* justifiably occupies one of the two places of honor in the gallery. Both pictures display her fine skills in figure painting. Henrietta Ward exhibits the sketch for her Royal Academy picture of last year, a scene featuring Mary Thérèse sketching her tower prison. Elizabeth Murray sends a picture of an old woman begging titled *Roman Orphan*. Mary Ann Duffield and Helen C. Angell both deserve mention for their fine flower paintings.

565. "The Guardi Gallery, Haymarket." *The Art Journal* (March 1877): 78.

Clara Montalba renders the boats in *View of Venice* with exceptional confidence and skill.

566. "The Dudley Gallery Water-Colours Exhibition." *Art Journal* (April 1877): 118.

Edith Martineau's portrait, *T. D. Webb, Esq.* and her drawing of a woman at an easel are both excellent. Louisa, Marchioness of Waterford's drawing of a *Boy's Head*, Elizabeth Westbrook's *Pretty Page*, and flower paintings by Helen C. Angell, Blanche Hanbury, Ellen Stone, Katharine M. Stocks, and Marie Spartali Stillman all deserve notice. Kate Greenaway's *Procession of Children with Flowers* is very good, but not as commendable as other efforts at decorative art in this exhibition of over 600 drawings.

567. "The Royal Hibernian Academy." *Art Journal* (May 1877): 135.

The Academy House in Dublin's forty-eighth exhibition features in its 500 exhibits the best collection in its history. One of the two best watercolors is Emma Oliver's *Scotch Landscape*. Works worth noticing are by excellent female artists Clara Montalba, M.D. Webb, Hannah Cooke, Ellen Connolly, Mary Julyan, E. Foster, L. Bowkett and Miss Law.

568. "Exhibition of the Institute of Painters in Water Colours." *Art Journal* (June 1877): 188.

Fruit and flower paintings are well represented in the work of Mrs. W. Duffield, Marian Chase and Helen Angell. Elizabeth Murray needs to work on proportion in her *Algerine Barber,* a picture of a little Arab boy getting his first haircut.

569. "Exhibition of the Society of Painters in Water Colours." *Art Journal* (June 1877): 187.

Among the excellent pictures upholding the reputation of this society are Helen Allingham's *The Old Men's Gardens, Chelsea Hospital* and Clara Montalba's *Street in Venice.*

570. "Minor Topics. Crystal Palace Picture Gallery." *Art Journal* (June 1877): 189.

A painting by Barbara Bodichon is among the works chosen in the Crystal Palace Picture Gallery to receive a gold medal.

571. "Minor Topics. Fine Art Society's Galleries, New Bond Street." *Art Journal* (June 1877): 190.

Together for the first time, Elizabeth Thompson's three paintings, *The Roll Call; Quatre Bras;* and *Balaclava* demonstrate the fidelity to spirit and detail that make them so justly famous.

572. "The Royal Academy Exhibition." *Art Journal* (June 1877): 185-186.

Louisa Starr's portrait of *Daughters of Robert Russell Carew, Esq.* shows the life-sized subjects dressed in white and is painted with unprecedented skill. Her portrait of *Mrs. J. E. Pfeiffer* is equally good. Kate Perugini's small *Impartial Audience* is "as full of quiet humour as it is of merit." Henrietta Ward has conveyed situation and feeling with her usual success in her picture of *Princess Charlotte of Wales* using her handkerchief to bandage the hand of a poor child.

573. "The Royal Academy Exhibition." *Art Journal* (July 1877): 197-200.

Eleanor S. Wood's study of grapes and oranges looks natural and succulent. Edith Elmore has two pictures, *Spring Flowers* and *A Study of Fruit and Flowers.* Her grapes lack translucence and plumpness, but next year's grapes will no doubt show "the courage and the patience" needed to paint such subjects. Kate Perugini has painted a small and excellent picture of a little girl and her dolls, which is titled *An Impartial Audience.* Edith Ballantyne's picture of a young girl showing her china to a friend is titled *Treasures.* Portraits by Louise Jopling titled *Colonel the Hon. Charles Lindsay* and by Janet Archer titled *Samuel Hanson, Esq.* are among the commendable works in this genre. Martha D. Mutrie's *Spring Flowers* and Annie Mutrie's *Wild Flowers of South America* lend "much life and light and colour" to the gallery.

574. "Art-Notes from the Provinces." *Art Journal* (August 1877): 235-236.

The Spring Exhibition of the Society of Water-Colour Painters in Liverpool features 244 drawings contributed by over 700 artists, of which only twenty-five are local. Miss Macgregor has two pictures, *Edge of the Pond* and *Way through the Churchyard*, both of which are "good and clever." Pauline Walker has sent exceptional studies of birds and flowers.

575. "The Black and White Exhibition at the Dudley Gallery." *Art Journal* (August 1877): 228.

Works in "charcoal, chalks, pencil and pen-and-ink" form one of the best black-and-white exhibitions ever. M. E. Staples' picture of a mother by a fireplace with her two children is titled *The Sweet Story of Old*. A pen-and-ink drawing of a young man fastening a necklace for a young woman is titled "The Finishing Touch." Mary L. Gow sends *Convalescent*, a picture of a little girl reading to a small friend. Rosa Bonheur sends a picture of sheep drawn on blue paper, and Kate Greenaway's drawing is titled *Spring is Come*.

576. "The Grosvenor Gallery." *Art Journal* (August 1877): 244.

Sir Coutts Lindsay's gallery is a fitting place for the fine works exhibited here, which include Lady Lindsay's portrait of *Miss Violet Lindsay*, and watercolors by Lady Louisa Charteris, Helen C. Angell, and Marie Spartali Stillman.

577. "The Royal Academy Exhibition." *Art Journal* (August 1877): 245-247.

Florence Bonneau sends *La Siesta*, a painting of a robed girl lying on a tiger skin. Miss M. Brooks' *Little Wisdom* is a picture of a girl in a lace-trimmed black dress with a red sash. Rosa and Georgina Koberwein must give their otherwise good pictures names, and not merely label them with quotations, but Georgina F. Koberwein does name her portrait *Miss Fraser*. Alice E. Donkin sends a portrait of *Mrs. J. Hartopp Nash* and Fanny Sutherland's portrait is of *Lady Romilly*. Kate Thompson's determination and hard work are admirably evident in the figure study of a hooded moor in *Entrance to the Hall of Las Dos Hermanas from the Court of Lions*. Other pictures to be noticed are Clementina Tompkins' *The Little Musician* and Blanche Jenkins' *A Little Sailor Boy*.

578. "The Royal Academy Exhibition." *Art Journal* (September 1877): 269-272.

Dreaming Awake, a picture of a girl in a hammock by Emily Mary Osborn, is more solidly painted than her landscape titled *Cemetery at*

Mazorbo, near Venice, but the two pictures are so different that one is able to admire Osborn's versatility. Unfortunately, M. Stuart Wortley's life-sized painting of a girl in red with a Japanese parasol is hung too near the ceiling to enable the viewer to appreciate its excellent feeling for color. Alice Havers does well with a girl and some geese titled *Eve of St. Michael*. Hilda Montalba's *Windy Day* shows a woman carrying a basket of freshly washed clothes. Helen Thornycroft's watercolor of *Saint Margaret* with a cross and a dove is simple but well done. *Roses and Lilies* shows how study with Madox Brown has matured Marie Spartali Stillman's excellent sense of color. Catherine Adelaide Sparkes has studied with her husband, whose training has helped her produce *Romola Pleading with Savonarola for the Life of Bernardo del Nero*, a painting which is not only Sparkes' best work to date, but is possibly the best work in the watercolor section. An equally notable oil, well designed and exhibiting "a classic chasteness," is *Parable of the Great Supper* by Theresa Thornycroft. In the exceptional handling of color Elizabeth S. Guiness excels her earlier works with *Sleeping Beauty*. Julia Pocock also shows increasing skill in her seven-part design *Ye Seven Ages*. Lady Coleridge's portrait of *John Henry Newman*, Annie Dixon's miniatures, Blanche Macarthur's small dressmaker in *Nearly Finished*, and Sophie Anderson's *The Proposal*, a picture of three girls reading a letter, deserve mention as well. Other women artists can only be mentioned by name, but their works have been discussed in other reviews.

579. "The Winter Exhibitions. The Suffolk Street Gallery." *Art Journal* (February 1878): 53-55.

Over 700 oils and water colors can be viewed at the Suffolk Gallery's last exhibition in its old building. Miss F. Martin's picture, *Student*, Margaret Backhouse's clever life-sized portrait titled *Girl in White Mob-Cap* and Beatrice Meyer's picture of a little girl and her family on her birthday deserve notice. Meyer needs to work on "a little more brightness and daylight." Other artists who should be named are E. M. Beresford, M. Clay and C. M. Noble.

580. "The Winter Exhibition. The Dudley Gallery Winter Exhibition." *Art Journal* (February 1878): 54-55.

Kate Thompson's excellent treatment of water in *Court of the Fish-pond* creates a remarkably pleasant picture. Alice Thornycroft is to be commended for her imagination with her white *Mona* seated on the rocks in the moonlight, and Theresa Thornycroft shows her power and talent with composition in *Infans Jesus com Passiflora*. The evening is captured nicely in *An Old Garden Wall* by Ellen Wilkinson. A woman arranging flowers in *Side Steps of St. Sulpice* shows Sophia Beale's talent for detail. *Study on the Cornish Coast* by Mrs. Val Bromley does well with its treatment of waves and rocks.

581. "The Winter Exhibition. Exhibition of the Water Colour Society." *Art Journal* (February 1878): 55.

Female members of The Society of Painters in Watercolours such as Mary Ann Alabaster Criddle, Margaret Gillies, and Maria Harrison have done it a great credit, and now the addition of Helen Allingham and Clara Montalba to the ranks promises to continue that tradition. Both Allingham and Montalba display "power with refinement" in their widely differing styles, and "there is nothing feminine but keen insight and consummate taste" in their work. In this exhibition, Clara Montalba's *Regatta; A Trabarcola; An Afterglow; A Summer Scirocco Day;* and *St. Mark's Column* demonstrate her talents very well. Allingham's equally gifted but quite different style is evident in *Cornfield, Margate; Scotch Street, St. Andrews; On the Sand, Eastbourne; Sussex Cottage;* and *Byre*.

582. "The Winter Exhibitions. Exhibition of the Institute of Painters in Water Colours." *Art Journal* (February 1878): 55-56.

Eliza Dundas Murray is "more than ordinarily strong this season." Her picture of an old woman, titled *Spanish Beggar*, and her study of an old *Arab Soldier* are quite good. *Muly Seedi Ben Ali*, a picture of an old man sitting on a stool, is the best of her three pictures. Mary L. Gow's *Convalescent*, a little girl with a doll being read to by a small friend is clever, but needs attention to texture and color. Flower and fruit pictures by Mary Ann Duffield and Marian Chase are very good.

583. "Institute of Painters in Watercolours." *Art Journal* (July 1878): 154.

Mary L. Gow does well with both people and trees in *Children's Garden Party*. Other works worth noticing are by Elizabeth Murray, Marian Chase, and Mary Ann Duffield.

584. "The Royal Academy Exhibition." *Art Journal* (July 1878): 145-148.

Rose Time, a picture of an elegant young woman beside a lily pool and carrying a basket of roses, is a credit to Louisa Starr's talent with color and modeling. *Psyche*, a figure in yellow and white by E. M. Busk illustrates lines from William Morris' poem "Earthly Paradise." Martha Mutrie's

White Lilac proves once again that nobody can paint flowers like the Mutrie sisters. Noteworthy among the portraits are Ethel Mortlock's *Right Hon. Robert Lowe, M.P.;* Louise Jopling's *Trixy, Daughter of John Hawton Philips,* and *Mrs. James Tomkinson;* and Maria Brooks' *Mrs. Welbury Mitton.*

585. "The Society of Painters in Water Colours." *Art Journal* (July 1878): 153.

The finest of Maria Harrison's four flower paintings is *A Sandy Bank with Harebells Growing.* Margaret Gillies, a popular artist with this gallery, has sent two figure paintings titled *In the Spring Time* and *A Mother and Child.* Eight drawings by Helen Allingham and five by Clara Montalba are "wonderfully artistic and masterly." Allingham's *London Flowers* calls attention to itself for its "tenderness"; Montalba's *Shipping--Venice* is remarkably strong.

586. "The Royal Academy Exhibition." *Art Journal* (August 1878): 165-168.

Henrietta Ward surpasses her already considerable talents at expressing "quiet subdued strength" in her paintings with her scene from the life of poet Robert Burns. In Ward's painting, a young woman dressed in white plays a spinet to help inspire Burns while he sits at a table composing with a quill pen the lines beginning "Oh, wert thou in the cauld blast...". The technical excellence of the painting is further imbued with feeling when one knows that these lines were some of Burns' last, that he was in fact dying. Clara Montalba's *Funeral in a Gondola in Venice* is beautiful and grand with its huge candles, banks of flowers, and priests in splendid vestments accompanying the "sacred freight" through "the silent ways of Venice."

587. "The Royal Academy Exhibition." *Art Journal* (September 1878): 177-180.

Helen Thornycroft excels at her previous works in a religious picture titled *Martyrdom of St. Luke.* A picture of a young mother with a baby by a flower-covered cottage is exhibited by Catherine Sparkes. Theresa Thornycroft maintains a "classic severity in figure study and a Vernonese-like" arrangement in her picture of Lazarus and the feasting Dives. Commendable works that must be mentioned include a picture of a little boy titled *In for a Scrape* by Kate Perugini; Louisa Starr's portrait of *Henry S. King, Esq;* two little girls walking together in a field in Alice Haver's *The Moon Is Up, but It Is Not Yet Night,* and *September;* Annie Beale's *Partisan of the Light Blues;* Sophy S. Warren's excellent watercolor titled *Early Morning, Exeter;* Helen Allingham's *The Bathing*

Place, Lynmouth; Purple Iris by Constance B. Philip; Anna Maria Guérin's *The Striped Azalea Tree;* Helen C. Angell's *Roses;* Emily Whymper's *Hollyhocks* and Edith Elmore's *Fruit and Still Life; Afternoon Tea* by Edith Ballantyne; Fanny Fildes' *Berkshire Cottage;* and a still life titled *Après le Déjeuner* by Kate Thompson.

588. "The Dudley Gallery, 1878." *Magazine of Art* 2 (1879): 18-21.

English Art seems to be acquiring the softer outlines and quieter tones that one might expect in good French art. Beatrice Meyer has sent *A Message,* which is not up to her usual quality, especially in the treatment of the hands. Color and draperies, however, are well done. Louise Jopling has done well with both *Portrait* and a sunny landscape, *From St. Aubin's Road, Jersey. Canal of San Giorgio, Venice,* by Clara Montalba, is a little too green to be true to nature, but her technique is so good that the color only adds interest and personality to her work. Hilda Montalba shows some eccentricity in her choices of colors for the sky in *A Quiet Morning.* While the sisters may use color that isn't true, they are incapable of using bad color.

589. "Pictures of the Year--I." *Magazine of Art* 2 (1879): 125- 128.

The 1842 massacre of General Elphinstone's army furnishes the subject of two paintings by Elizabeth Thompson Butler. *'Listed for the Connaught Rangers* depicts two young Irishmen regretfully leaving home for the military. The color and tone are intense and somewhat melancholy. *The Remnants of an Army* shows the tragic single survivor of the English army of 16,000. He and his horse stumble over a rocky plain; the expression on the subject's face makes the spectator feel that "he is in the presence of one of the tragedies of the world."

Reproductions (b/w):

Butler, Elizabeth Thompson: *The Remnants of an Army.*

590. "Pictures of the Year--II." *Magazine of Art* 2 (1879): 148- 152.

Lack of space in this review necessitates mentioning some important works by women at a later date. They deserve as much time from the reviewer as do the male artists because although the women suffer handicaps, they do exhibit in the Royal Academy with men, asking no favors, but demanding to be evaluated on like terms.

591. "Pictures of the Year--III." *Magazine of Art* 2 (1879): 161- 165.

The work of several female artists is considered together, not out of a wish to segregate them from works by the men, but for convenience only.

The Royal Academy and the Grosvenor Gallery both exhibit a Venetian picture by Clara Montalba. Her Grosvenor Gallery painting of Dominican friars is successful in its figure treatment, costume, and expression, and it possesses her usual brilliance at handling color. She does have a flaw in her handling of tree branches, however. In her Academy picture, a scene on a canal in Venice, she handles the water and the color of the crab baskets very well. Hilda Montalba's forest scene captures light with good effect. A portrait of *The Hon. Mrs. Romilly* by Louise Jopling is very lifelike and the blue-green background colors are "cleverly harmonized." Kate Perugini's *A Little Woman*, a profile of a small girl knitting, is both delicate and forceful, and the finish is exceptional. *Peasant Girls, Varengeville*, and *Stonepickers* are good indicators of Alice Haver's excellent talents. Christiana Thompson's garden scene, *Sunshine*, is flooded with brilliant light and considerable elegance. It hangs next to her daughter's painting of the Afghan campaign. Jessie Macgregor's *May Morning* depicts a bright processional.

Reproductions (b/w sketches):

Perugini, Kate: *A Little Woman*

Macgregor, Jessie: *May Morning*.

592. "Pictures of the Year--IV." *Magazine of Art* 2 (1879): 216- 220.

Lawrence Alma-Tadema's *A Hearty Welcome* is a portrait of himself, his wife Laura Epps Alma-Tadema and their two daughters in Roman dress. Henriette Browne exhibits a work that shows real excellence in both its drawing and its painting.

593. "Pictures of the Year--V." *Magazine of Art* 2 (1879): 240- 249.

Both the Paris Salon and London's Burlington house have exhibited Catherine Amyot's painting. *Return of the Penitent* is a well-organized, picturesque, and pleasantly-colored picture of a young woman, surrounded by a sympathetic family, on her knees asking an obdurate father for forgiveness. Henrietta Ward has painted a figure of a violin player in *Melody*. The picture is too simple; it cannot compare with her *Mrs. Fry Visiting Newgate*, the engraving of which has just been completed and dedicated to the Queen.

Reproductions (b/w engraving):

Amyot, Catherine (Englehart): *The Return of the Penitent*.

594. "Water-Colour Drawings at the Grosvenor Gallery." *Magazine of Art* (1879): 30-31.

No single style or technique dominates this exhibition's brilliant watercolors. Helen Allingham's style manages a combination of close detail with lightness and depth in *The Brown Girl; Near Titsey, Surrey;* and *Dangerous Ground.* Lady Lindsay's *Orchids* "are remarkably good for their force and colour." Clara Montalba shows her usual gifts for color, composition, and drawing. She studies nature in a way that is "close, humble, and unremitting."

595. "The Winter Exhibitions. The French Gallery." *Art Journal* (January 1879): 13.

Clara Montalba sends two "splendidly luminous" Venetian pictures; Hilda Montalba's *Returning from the Rialto* is nearly as good. Mrs. Val Bromley has two pictures of the Cornish coast. Mrs. B. W. Leader sends a picture titled *Asters in a Vase* and Linnie Watt exhibits a picture titled *On the Beach.*

596. "The Winter Exhibitions. The Maclean Gallery, Haymarket." *Art Journal* (January 1879): 13-14.

Helen Allingham and Helen Coleman Angell are among the many popular artists who exhibit at the Maclean Gallery. Rosa Bonheur sends *Sheep at Fontainebleau.*

597. "The Winter Exhibitions. Society for British Artists." *Art Journal* (February 1879): 33.

The best of the watercolor paintings are the "forcible and satisfactory" *Marigolds* by E. J. Jackson, and *Wallflowers* by C. E. Howell. Linnie Watts' *Chalky Beach* deserves mention, as does *A Legend,* a picture of people listening to a monk playing a guitar near a fountain.

598. "The Winter Exhibitions. Society of Painters in Water Colours." *Art Journal* (February 1879): 33-34.

Among Clara Montalba's numerous works in this exhibit are the "most unconventional and vigorous" *A Canal in Venice* and *The Grand Canal,* the latter remarkable for its brilliant depiction of daylight. Montalba, a "most virile artist" also exhibits in all the other galleries open at this time.

599. "The Winter Exhibitions. Institute of Painters in Water Colours." *Art Journal* (February 1879): 34-35.

A "more than ordinarily interesting" exhibition of over 300 works includes admirable examples of the work of Mary Ann Duffield, Emily Farmer, Mary L. Gow, Emma S. Oliver, and Elizabeth Murray.

600. "The Winter Exhibitions. Dudley Gallery." *Art Journal* (February 1879): 35-36.

> The Montalba sisters, Hilda and Clara, send *Quiet Morning* and *The Canal of San Giorgio*, both Venetian pictures of exceptional quality. Louisa Starr sends two female head studies, one wreathed in flowers, and both accompanied by lines from poetry.

601. "Art Notes from the Provinces. Bath." *Art Journal* (March 1879): 57.

> Among the well-known artists exhibiting painted china in the Paragon Art Studio exhibition are Elizabeth Cambridge Harbutt, Kate Earle and Charlotte Spiers. Only two of the pottery artists are male.

602. "The Female School of Art, Queen Square." *Art Journal* (March 1879): 44.

> The Female Art School mourns the loss of Naomi Burrell, one of its best teachers. This year's exhibition includes the National Gold Medal Winner, *Fighting Gladiator* by Katherine Benson. This painting has been purchased by the Department of Science and Art, which has also purchased Maud A. West's *Study of Mice*. Ida R. Lovering wins a National Silver Medal for the same subject. Alice Hanslip and Maud A. West receive National Bronze Medals. Ida Lovering, Ellen Ashwell, Edith Gibson and Florence Reason receive National Queen's prizes for their work. Flower drawings by Anne E. Hopkinson have been purchased by the Queen and awarded the Queen's Gold Medal. Scholarship winners include Elizabeth M. Lovell, Charlotte M. Havell, Harriett A. Payne, Catherine M. Wood and Florence Reason.

603. "Exhibition of Works by Modern Artists at the Royal Albert Hall." *Art Journal* (April 1879): 78.

> The upper galleries of the Royal Albert Hall contain an exhibition of over a thousand works by modern artists including Hilda Montalba, Theresa Thornycroft, and Lady Coutts Lindsay.

604. "An Hour with the Lady Artists: 48, Great Marlborough Street." *Englishwoman's Review* (15 April 1879): 156-159.

> The quality of pictures in this exhibition has improved year by year. Among the watercolorists, landscapes are a favorite subject and evoke charming images and pleasant memories. Among the oil paintings, Mrs. Campbell Cameron's copy of eighteenth-century artist Elizabeth Vegée Lebrun's self portrait demonstrates Cameron's ability to achieve good likenesses. Rebecca Coleman's china painting of a pretty face is not a success because one of the eyes is not where it should be. L. B. Swift's *Sambo* is a portrait of a charming, if not ugly, pug. Owners of these dogs

who would like to have them immortalized should arrange for portraits by this artist.

605. "General Exhibition of Water-Colour Drawings at the Dudley Gallery." *Art Journal* (May 1879): 91.

Catherine A. Sparkes has illustrated a fifth-century legend which tells of Judas Iscariot being allowed out of hell once a year to spend an hour on an iceberg as a reward for his once rendering compassion to a leper. Sparke's picture depicts St. Brendan in an "antique Norwegian boat" gazing at this spectacle with horror. In *Vanity Fair*, Elizabeth Walker shows a woman with a too-small face but in well-painted finery gazing into a mirror.

606. "The Royal Scottish Academy." *Art Journal* (May 1879): 89-90.

While over a thousand works are on exhibition at the Royal Scottish Academy, nearly that many were rejected. A very young artist, M. Hope, shows considerable promise in her picture *The Squire's Daughter* with its "nearly perfect" chiaroscuro. Excellent flower pictures include red and white poppies by Lily Blatherwick, and golden broom by Christina Ross.

607. "Royal Hibernian Academy." *Art Journal* (May 1879): 97.

Maria D. Webb's *Captive Maid* is one of the best figure paintings in this exhibition. Miss Allen, an Honorable Member of some years' standing, also sends some very good work.

608. "Exhibition of the Society of British Artists." *Art Journal* (June 1879): 115-116.

The British Artists' exhibition is one of the best it has had in some time. Among the many works deserving notice is Beatrice Meyer's picture, *A Nook by the Tiber*.

609. "The Royal Academy Exhibition. Introductory Notice." *Art Journal* (June 1879): 117.

Elizabeth Butler's *'Listed for the Connaught Rangers* and *The Remnants of an Army* are among the most impressive pictures to be seen. Clara Montalba's pictures also deserve notice.

610. "Society of Lady Artists." *Art Journal* (June 1879): 114-115.

Hilda Montalba's *Windy Day*, a picture of two girls carrying a basket of laundry is one of the best and most realistic of the paintings in this exhibition. Louise Jopling's *The Five Sisters of York* is an excellent illustration of a scene from *Nicholas Nickleby* in which women sit in a garden doing needlework. Ellen Montalba's picture, *At the Well*, also deserves praise for its color and composition. *Edelweiss* by Ellen Partridge is a life- sized portrait of a woman with a flower behind her ear. Partridge's *Seton, Son of Dr. Dycer Brown* and several small landscapes also merit notice. Louise B. Swift's *The Private View*, a picture of two dogs and a litter of puppies, and *Study of Fox Terrier's Head* and *Sambo*, a portrait of a pug, exemplify her skills at animal painting. Another animal painter, Margery May, shows promise in *Mare and Foal*. Emma Cooper's *Case of Fourteen Miniature Portraits on Ivory* is an exceptional revival of a vanishing skill. Amelia Mary Hicks' five pictures of *The Lunar Eclipse of August 23, 1877* have met with the approval of the Queen. Louise Rayner's *The Grass Market, Edinburgh* and Kate Edith Nichols' *The Town of Ifracombe* are good examples of cityscapes. Linnie Watts' picture of a girl in a blue dress, titled *Far Away* is very good, except that the subject's nose is too large.

611. "Minor Topics. The Brigand's Cave, by Camarano." *Art Journal* (July 1879): 141.

A life-sized painting of women and children taken prisoner by soldiers pursuing a fleeing band of robbers is on exhibition at the gallery of the Lady Artists. The painter, Michele Camarano, is a professor at the Academy of St. Luke in Rome. His work enjoys an international reputation.

612. "The Royal Academy Exhibition." *Art Journal* (July 1879): 125-128.

The best of the military pictures is Elizabeth Thompson Butler's *'Listed for the Connaught Rangers*, a realistic and moving scene from Ireland. Jessie Macgregor's best work yet can be seen in *May Morning*, a picture of flower-garlanded peasant girls. Macgregor's painting deserves its place on the line. Kate Perugini's *Little Woman* of a woman knitting and Edith Elmore's *Grapes and Chrysanthemums* are among the many excellent works in this exhibition.

613. "The Spring Exhibitions. Society of Painters in Water Colours." *Art Journal* (July 1879): 133-134.

A visit to the Society's pleasant gallery to see over 300 works by some of Britain's finest artists promises considerable rewards. Clara Montalba exemplifies "spontaneous suavity" with her *Canal of San Giorgio* and *Chioggia Fishing Boats*. Helen Allingham sends *Harvest Moon*, a picture of young reapers walking home in the moonlight. Helen C. Angell, a newly elected member, contributes fruit and flower pictures as "sweet and vigorous" as ever.

614. "The Spring Exhibitions. Institute of Painters in Watercolours." *Art Journal* (July 1879): 134-135.

The youngest member, Lady Lindsay of Balcarres, sends several works that place her among the best of figure painters. *Wintry Morning* is a life-sized head of "a dark-eyed, comely lady in a crimson bonnet looking full-face out of the picture." *The Dream Maiden* is a charming face with an emerald-green background in the French manner. Her humorously titled *An Exile From the South, and Some Chinese* is a large flower picture. The society has acquired a gifted associate in Lady Lindsay. Worthy of mention is Elizabeth Murray's painting of an Arab in white robes. Marian Chase and Mary Ann Duffield's flower and fruit paintings deserve notice.

615. "The Spring Exhibitions. The Grosvenor Gallery." *Art Journal* (July 1879): 135-136.

Two portraits by Lady Lindsay of Balcarres, *Charles C. Bethune, Esq.* and *Portrait of Signor Piatti* demonstrate her considerable skills with color and brush technique that will bring her "into the very front rank of women painters." Louisa Starr's portrait, *Ruth, Daughter of W. Wakefield, Esq.* is one of her best. Marie Spartali Stillman's *Night and Sleep* show the kinds of skills with color and fantasy associated with the work of Evelyn Pickering. A seascape by Mrs. Val Bromley and a landscape by Baroness Nathaniel de Rothschild complement the works sent by lady artists.

616. "Exhibition of Works in Black and White." *Art Journal* (August 1879): 161-162.

Among the most noticeable of the 586 "sketches and drawings in chalk, charcoal, pencil, sepia, and India ink" is Mary Stewart Wortley's *Pertida*, a "clever, careful pencil drawing."

617. "Painting on China by Lady Amateurs and Artists." *Art Journal* (August 1879): 164.

So popular has the art of painting on pottery become that Messers. Howell and James have had to build new galleries to house the growing numbers of exhibits which now rival in numbers those of the Royal Academy. In this year's exhibition, the Princess Alice Prize has been won by Edith S. Hall and the silver award has been won by Ada Beard. Lady Rawlinson has won the Countess of Warwick's Prize; Everett Green has won the Olive Guiness Prize. Linnie Watt, who has created fine pieces for Doulton, has won the silver medal. Helen Welby's *Head with Apple Blossoms*, Edith Robinson's *Puck*, and Everett Green's *Birds of a Feather* deserve special notice.

618. "The Royal Academy Exhibition. Third Notice." *Art Journal* (August 1879): 149-152.

    Maria Brooks shows her talent in *Cat's Cradle*, a painting of two young girls, one fair and one dark. Alice Havers also manages to make "the common place pictorial" in her picture *Peasant Girls* in which one girl sits on a bundle to remove something from her shoe. In the portrait gallery, Ethel Mortlock's *Portrait of a Lady* is among the meritorious works.

619. "The Royal Academy Exhibition. Fourth and Concluding Notice." *Art Journal* (September 1879): 173-175.

    Clara Montalba's *Canal, Venice* is among the best of the landscapes. Mr. R. C. Woodville's battle painting is of the high quality of Elizabeth Butler's work. Butler herself has a painting in Gallery VII depicting the sole survivor of a company of 16,000 as he and his horse struggle toward the gate of Jellalabad. Among the excellent collection of watercolors, Linnie Watt and Agnes E. MacWhirter's work deserves mention. While Henrietta Ward's picture, *Melody* is smaller in scale than most of her works, it is technically one of her best. Among the portraits, Louisa Starr's *Marguerite (Sissy), Daughter of W.R. Beverly, Esq.*, and Louise Jopling's *The Hon. Mrs. Romilly* are both excellent. Catherine A. Sparkes' *A Guerdon* is a good example of her work.

620. "The Australian Exhibitions." *Art Journal* (December 1879): 264.

    Included among the pictures on loan to Australia are engravings of *The Roll Call* and *Quatre Bras*, by Elizabeth Thompson. The engravings are sent by the Fine Art Society.

621. "Autumn Pictures of the Year." *Magazine of Art* 3 (1880): 80.

    Southwark Bridge and *Off Erith* show that Clara Montalba's handling of greys and shadows can turn foggy London into a veritable Venice. Hilda Montalba's *Parliament Buildings, Ottawa* shows a snow scene where the tints of sky and sunshine aren't quite successful.

622. "Grosvenor Gallery: Winter Exhibition." *Magazine of Art* 3 (1880): 163-165.

Clara Montalba does such fine work with her dark tones of *Greenhithe* and *Cannon Street Bridge* that she glorifies grime and soot.

623. "Pictures of the Year: The Dudley Gallery." *Magazine of Art* 3 (1880): 117-120.

Alice Havers paints sunshine well *In the Heat of the Day*, Beatrice Meyer abandons her usual somber mood for brilliant color *In Rome--Leading to the Campidoglio*. Kate Perugini's study of a little girl is very pretty. Louise Jopling's two portraits are quite life-like, and Hilda Montalba's *Crab Baskets* is attractive but overly simple. *Clavichord and Cither* by Edith Hipkins and *An Old Monk* by Henriette Corkran merit mentioning.

624. "Pictures of the Year--I." *Magazine of Art* 3 (1880): 276- 281.

Clara Montalba's *Hastings* is quite beautiful; Elizabeth Thompson Butler's *Defense of Rorke's Drift* is remarkable in its accuracy, detail, and expression.

625. "Pictures of the Year--II." *Magazine of Art* 3 (1880): 312- 317.

The *Santa Maria della Salute* is represented not only in Clara Montalba's superior handling of tones and color, but by her fine composition skills as well. Hilda Montalba's remarkable *Venetian Boy Unloading a Market-Boat* is perhaps a bit less than skillful in its drawing, but her treatment of light and color justifies its prominent place in the exhibition. The sea needs more warmth, however, and the boy's legs shouldn't be the same color as the object painted next to them.

Reproductions (b/w sketch):

Montalba, Clara: *Early Morning*.

626. "Pictures of the Year--III." *Magazine of Art* 3 (1880): 348- 352.

Kate Perugini's specialty is her excellent portrait studies of little girls. *Multiplication* is a relief from the too-clever pictures of a few other exhibitors.

627. "Pictures of the Year--IV." *Magazine of Art* 3 (1880): 396- 401.

The review in the last issue mentioned Kate Perugini's *Multiplication*, a sketch of which appears with this article. Mary Backhouse's well-finished and richly-colored *Eleanore* deserves commendation.

Reproduction (b/w sketch):

Perugini, Kate: *Multiplication*.

628. "Pictures of the Year--V." *Magazine of Art* 3 (1880): 436- 441.

Louise Jopling's two portraits are well painted and are excellent likenesses. The figure in Theresa Thornycroft's *The Feeding of the Multitudes* is not well drawn, and she has chosen to represent Christ as an Arab, while the Apostles are oriental in aspect and in drapery. The composition of the picture is excellent, but the color is "peculiarly pink and crude."

629. "Sketches and Studies of the Water-Colour Society." *Magazine of Art* 3 (1880): 158-161.

Court-yard of the Citadel, Quebec is one of a number of accurate and intelligent drawings of Canadian scenes exhibited by Princess Louise. Clara Montalba has abandoned Venice, which is well represented by other exhibitors, for the grey tones of fog-bound London in her study of the Thames.

630. "Society of British Artists--Winter Exhibition." *Magazine of Art* 3 (1880): 145-149.

The exhibition of the Society of British Artists fulfills all expectations for excellence and excels in its variety. A small painting by Mary Gow, *A Reverie,* is extremely competent and does credit to the artist and her family. *Ronda Capriccioso* is such a brilliant picture that it deserves reproduction with this article. It is firmly executed and richly colored.

Reproductions (b/w engraving):

Meyer, Beatrice: *Ronda Capriccioso*.

631. "The Maclean Gallery, Haymarket." *Art Journal* (January 1880): 28.

Helen Angell's brilliant flower pictures make up the largest group by a single contributor in this exhibition. Her brother, a painter of children, is also exhibiting. Of the animal paintings, one picture of sheep suggests the style of Rosa Bonheur.

632. "The Winter Exhibitions. The Dudley Gallery Winter Exhibition." *Art Journal* (February 1880): 45-46.

Alice Havers' *In the Heat of the Day*, a picture of a peasant girl carrying a child and trailed by another, is "full of nature." Mrs. J. M. Hopkins shows her knowledge of the "unconscious grotesqueries" in *Bathers Resting.*

633. "The Winter Exhibitions. The Institute of Art Exhibition." *Art Journal* (February 1880): 47.

    The Institute of Art was established as a means for women to sell their art and handiwork. In addition to the exhibits of lace, crewelwork, fire-screens, etc., some fine watercolors and oil paints are to be seen. The first prize for a watercolor painting is awarded to Sophia Beale for her landscape, *Bas Meudon*. Another smaller work, *Our Baby*, received honorable mention, but it is perhaps the better of Beale's two paintings. Miss Hooper's *Hillsborough* also received honorable mention. Beatrice Meyer's *Lady Gathering Grapes* deserved an award, although it didn't receive one, and Hortense Wood's *Sunset in Asia Minor* did not win first place only because it arrived too late to be considered for competition. Emily F. Jackson received first prize for her still life with "armour, ivory tankard with figures in relief, roses, &c."

634. "Exhibition of the Institute of Painters in Water Colours." *Art Journal* (March 1880): 73-74.

    Wide Awake, a picture of a little girl in a night dress, is not up to Lady Lindsay's usual skills. *Antonio,* a head study of a youthful Italian is interesting and well done. Elizabeth Murray's *An Arab Cavalry Officer*, a figure study of a sleeping soldier, is competent, but her choice of subject is better taken in a picture of a little "Algerine" girl carrying bread to the bakers on a board balanced upon her head. Curiously, the little girl from "Algeria" wears her skirts in the same impractical way as English girls, tied around their legs "in such a manner as to make them almost immovable." Marian Chase's fruit and Mary Ann Duffield's flowers keep them in the forefront of their fields, as does work by Emily Farmer, Emma Oliver and Mary L. Gow.

635. "Exhibition of the Society of Painters in Water Colours." *Art Journal* (March 1880): 74-75.

    Clara Montalba's *Blackfriars Bridge* exhibits her talent with light, detail and firmness; this work and Helen Allingham's *Sketches by the Sea* are the first pictures to attract the attention of a gallery visitor. Allingham displays her skills at figure drawing in *The Goat Carriage*; *Bluebells, near Sevenoaks; Hop-Tying, Kent;* and *Hanging out Clothes at Limpsfield, Surrey*. While the scenes are humble, Allingham's skill "exalts them and turns them into treasures." Princess Louise has recently returned from a visit to Canada and has sent paintings and drawings that record the people and customs she observed there. Some of the drawings, such as *Views from the Citadel of Quebec,* are true-to-life if somewhat amateurish in some respects. *Laril* and *View of Woods at Roseneath, Dumbartonshire* demonstrate considerable skill. Helen Angell's flower pictures, including *Study of Chrysanthemums;* Mary Ann Criddle's *Thoughtful Moment;* Margaret Gillies' *Study of a Little Girl with her Doll;* and Maria Harrison's *Purple Clematis* all merit attention. Criddle, Gillies and Harrison are associate members of this society, and while their work is not quite of the caliber of that of Montalba and Allingham, it is a familiar and consistent contribution.

636. "The Grosvenor Gallery." *Art Journal* (March 1880): 76.

Lady Violet Lindsay's pencil sketches are more indicative of her talent then her finished paintings. Her life-sized *Child of the South* is her best work.

637. "Minor Topics. Colonel Abuthnot's Pictures at the Bethnal Green Museum. Mdlle. Rosa Bonheur." *Art Journal* (March 1880): 94- 95.

The South Kensington museum exhibits about eighty excellent pictures by modern artists. The pictures, part of a collection loaned by Colonel Abuthnot, includes a small picture of cattle by Rosa Bonheur. In another note, Bonheur has been awarded a Commander's Cross of the "Royal Order of Isabella the Catholic" by the King of Spain. Bonheur is the first to receive this decoration.

638. "Water-Colour Drawings at the Old Bond-Street Gallery." *Art Journal* (March 1880): 93.

Among the best of the living artists represented in the Bond Street Gallery Exhibition are works by Helen Allingham and Helen C. Angell.

639. "Art Notes. Tapestry Painting." *Art Journal* (April 1880): 127.

Messers Howell and James's, Regent Street, have an exhibition of tapestry painting such as the enamel painting on satin of Mrs. Margaret Butterworth. The present interest in tapestries is "rather a revival than an invention" and gives an opportunity to exercise their artistic talents as well as to be "a source of remuneration."

640. "Dudley Gallery Spring Exhibition." *Art Journal* (May 1880): 155.

Nothing of "commanding excellence" is to be seen in this exhibition of nearly 700 paintings. A girl with a kitten, titled *Annie and Puck* by Edith Martineau is not her best, but her technique is careful and her artistic freedom evident. Martineau also sends *What Shall it Be?*, a picture of a woman in a red- figured dress, poised with a violin. E. V. B.'s two portraits of children are titled *Algernon Boyle* and *Isabella Boyle* and Charlotte Spiers' *Study of a Negro's Head* constitute careful drawing. Leigh Smith's *Dolomite Mountains from the Lido* and Kate Goodwin's *Only Landing Place at Balmacarra* deserve mention among the landscapes.

641. "Exhibition of the City of London Society of Artists." *Art Journal* (May 1880): 153.

This newly formed society eventually hopes to have its own gallery, but for now holds its exhibition in the hall of the Worshipful Company of Skinners at St. John's Wood. Since the time of the Medici, trade guilds have been associated with the arts, so this most recent association certainly has precedence. Nearly 400 oil and water color pictures can be seen in the current exhibition that enjoys the support of such well-known artists as Clara Montalba, Mary Ann Duffield and Ellen Connolly.

642. "Minor Topics. Messrs. Tooth's Gallery." *Art Journal* (May 1880): 159.

Among the works of British artists represented at Tooth's gallery is *Canal, Venice* by Clara Montalba.

643. "Society of Lady Artists, Great Marlborough Street." *Art Journal* (May 1880): 154-155.

About half of the 700 works are oils, and the other half are watercolors. While a lack of attention to the basics of drawing is still evident, the quality of the exhibition as a whole continues to improve. The best of the fruit pictures is *Peaches* by Eloise Stannard; equally praiseworthy is *Hazy Morning in the Harbour* by Kate Macaulay, and *The Cornish Shore* by Mrs. Val Bromley. Elizabeth Thompson Butler's mother, Christiana Thompson, sends small landscape studies that reveal her careful observation of nature. Figure paintings of note include *Francisca*, by Ellen Partridge; *Study*, by Hilda Montalba; *Dives and Lazarus* by Theresa Thornycroft; *Venetian Girl* by Mary Backhouse; *Daughter of Italy* by Florence Bonneau; *Portrait of a Bavarian Peasant*, by Theresa Schwartze; and *Head of an Indian* by Blanche Macarthur. Helen Thornycroft's *The Martyrdom of St Luke* is one of the most successful works.

644. "Exhibition of the Society of Painters in Water Colours." *Art Journal* (June 1880): 189-190.

The magnificent light in Clara Montalba's *Leaving Port, Venice* entitles the painting to a better placement in this exhibition. Helen Allingham's *The Lady of the Manor*, a picture of a woman in black talking to two children shows Allingham's skills at blending landscape and figure painting.

645. "Exhibition of the Institute of Painters in Water Colours." *Art Journal* (June 1880): 190.

The Princess Royal sends a fine life-sized portrait of an Italian boy in a blue jacket. The Princess is also a talented sculptor, a student of Mrs. Thornycroft. That the female members of the Institute "hold their own" in this exhibition is evidenced in work by Mary Ann Duffield, Mrs. W. Oliver, Lady Violet Lindsay, Marian Chase, Louisa Corbaux, and Elizabeth Murray.

646. "Grosvenor Gallery Exhibition." *Art Journal* (June 1880): 188-189.

Female sculptors hold their own in the works of Henrietta S. Montalba, Emma E. Phinney, Evelyn Pickering, and Alice M. Chaplin. Among the portrait paintings, Louisa Starr's *Portrait of Marguerita, Daughter of William Beverley* shows "refinement and delicacy." Also worthy of notice are Louise Jopling's *Portrait of A.J.R. Trendall* and a portrait of Jopling herself painted by J. E. Millais, R. A. Also pleasing is Evelyn Pickering's painting titled *Mater Dolorosa*. Lady Violet Lindsay's best is a picture of a girl titled *A Stitch in Time Saves Nine* and a seascape titled *The Harbour, Clovely, North Devon*. Mrs. Val Bromley's *Study on the Cornish Coast* is "happy and conscientious."

647. "The Royal Academy Exhibition." *Art Journal* (June 1880): 186-187.

Hilda Montalba's "usual force of brush and thorough comprehensiveness" is evident in *Venetian Boy Unloading a Market Boat*. In the humorous *Christmas Greeting*, Emily Mary Osborne shows a broad and firm treatment that has been lacking in her works lately. Among the excellent works in the portrait room are two works by Georgina Koberwein Terrel.

648. "Art Notes. Leeds Fine Art Exhibition." *Art Journal* (July 1880): 222.

Mrs. Marshall is among the local artists whose work can be seen in the first Exhibition of the Yorkshire Fine Art Society at Leeds.

649. "The Royal Academy Exhibition. Second Notice." *Art Journal* (July 1880): 219-221.

Among the portraits, Louisa Starr's *Elizabeth, Daughter of J. Ashton Boshtock, C.B.* and *Edith, Daughter of F. Algar* exemplify her skills, as does her life-like *Henry Pilleau*. Theresa G. Thornycroft paints a realistic crowd in *Feeding of the Multitude*. Noteworthy in the flower-painting category are *Roses* by Emily Pfeiffer and *Study of Fruit and Flowers* by Edith Elmore. Also commendable are Emily Mary Osborn's harmonious *Reflections;* Edith Ballantine's *Waiting; Where the Sea and River Meet* by Catherine Charlton; *The Morn in Russet Mantle Clad* by Fanny Duncan; *Shadow in the Home* by Ellen Clacy and *Blanchisseuses* by Alice Havers.

650. "Art Notes. The Black and White Exhibition." *Art Journal* (August 1880): 253.
    Helen Allingham's *Young Customers* is represented by an engraving by G. T. Stoddart.

651. "Art Notes. Sydney Exhibition." *Art Journal* (August 1880): 255.
    In the category of "Still Life and Ornaments," Annie F. Mutrie and Martha D. Mutrie receive mention.

652. "The Burlington Fine Arts Club." *Art Journal* (September 1880): 285.
    This exhibition of water colors at the Burlington Fine Arts Club recognizes painters who have died since the last exhibition, nine years ago. Mary P. Harrison, "the good lady who for forty years supported her family by art," is represented by *History of a Primrose*. Another artist, now deceased, represents bird and flower painting, a genre which is rarely seen now except in the work of Helen Angell. Drawings by flower painters Valentine Bartholomew and his wife, Anne Charlotte Bartholomew, are also in the collection.

653. "Provincial Art Exhibitions. The Royal Society of Artists, Birmingham." *Art Journal* (November 1880): 337.
    In the newly-opened gallery of the oldest art society in the provinces, the women exhibitors included Louise Jopling, Alice Havers, Emily Mary Osborn and Louise Rayner, among others. Flower paintings by Mrs. Westwood Whitfield are of her usual high quality.

654. "Art Notes." *Magazine of Art* 4 (1881): i-xlviii.
    The Walker Gallery at Liverpool exhibits the work of members and associates of the Royal Academy; works exhibited at Burlington House in spring and summer may appear in the Walker Gallery in the fall. Presently, one may view works by Helen Allingham, Louise Jopling, Clara Montalba, Kate Perugini and Alice Havers. Rosa Bonheur has been staying at St. Aubin-sur-Mer for her health; she has returned home and is working on some important pictures. Elizabeth Butler is painting at Plymouth. An exhibition at Liverpool of paintings by actresses and actors includes a work

by Genevieve Ward. Elizabeth Murray's eastern studies are realistic and truthful; her studio in Florence is a favorite Monday gathering place for art lovers. This year's exhibition of the Society of Lady Artists is easily the quality of any "minor exhibition...where the artist has, so to say no sex." Kate Macaulay and M. Freeman Kempson's seascapes deserve special mention, as do landscapes and still lifes by Mrs. Marrable and Edith Marrable, Mrs. Naftel and Maud Naftel, Ada Bell, Louisa Smith, Agnes Dundas, Emily Merrick, Anna Maria Guérin, Fanny Assembaum, May Izod Weld, Caroline Wright, Fanny Currey, Edith Hipkins, Emma Walter, and Emily F. Jackson. Christiana Thompson's *Out of a Suburban Window* is a humble subject painted with considerable skill. Louise Jopling has painted *Playtime*, with a little boy in a blue-green dress with a fur border. The subject faces the viewer with "charming gravity." Clara Montalba's *On the Grand Canal, Venice*, is "a fascinating little water-colour drawing." Hilda Montalba's *A Garden* is a love scene "brilliant with light." Miss Beresford would do well to study to improve her figure drawing. Salina Lyte has written a pamphlet, *Dreamland Painting*, published by Griffith and Farran, which offers suggestions for artists troubled for a subject. The Water-Colour Society exhibits drawings by Clara Montalba and Helen Allingham. Montalba "shows all her own inimitable refinement, luminosity, and effectiveness"; Allingham shows her "invariable exquisiteness." Rosa Bonheur's pictures at the Lefevre Gallery are not up to her usual standards. Deer are never as artistically interesting as horses. Engravings of her other works would make an exhibition by themselves. Louisa Fennell's twelve lithographs titled *The Life of St. Paul in Rome* may be interesting to students of St. Paul, but they are not very well done. Clara Montalba is back from Venice with many sketches. This fall she will devote her talents to the Thames in London. Anna Lea Merritt, a distinguished American artist living in England, is painting the portrait of the American minister, James Russell Lowell.

655. "The Black and White Exhibition of the Dudley Gallery." *Magazine of Art* 4 (1881): 410-414.

Many capable artists take up the challenge of painting in black oil, lamp black, sepia, charcoal, India ink, etc., which are the favored media for studies of form. Princess Louise, one of several artists in the Royal Family, has chosen the Dudley Gallery for her first public exhibition, a drawing of mountains and rocks titled *Mountain Gloom*. Another study, *Winter*, depicts snow and bare trees at Sandringham, the Princess' country residence.

656. "The Dudley Gallery." *Magazine of Art* 4 (1881): 342-343.

Since the Dudley Gallery admits work by artists not yet established, its exhibitions are sometimes uneven and ignored by critics; however, since younger artists have much to offer, the Dudley's exhibitions are always interesting. Marguerite Ludovici's *Tulips and Flowers* ranks as brilliant among the many good flower paintings exhibited by women. Louise Jopling's small drawing *On the Riviera* is pretty. Bertha Newcombe is too apt to use colors; she would be well advised to study M. Israel's use of restful greys. Bertha Newcombe's *Three Studies of Mère Morot* are intelligent drawings of an elderly peasant.

657. "Pictures for the Winter Exhibitions." *Magazine of Art* 4 (1881): 165-168.

This year's exhibition at the Dudley Gallery is not up to its usual quality, but some works, such as Letitia Parsons' painting of flowers and Beatrice Meyer's landscape, are worthy of mention.

658. "Pictures of the Year--I." *Magazine of Art* 4 (1881): 302- 307.

Elizabeth Thompson Butler has chosen as a subject *George II at the Battle of Dettingen* showing the little fat king leading his men on foot into smoke and flame. Last year Butler's *Rorke's Drift* was reviewed even though it had not been quite completed, but it is interesting now to compare it with another military painting of a French artist, M. de Neuville, whose style is more exuberant and less masculine than Butler's reserved and careful depiction of individual character and expression. It is in her Egyptian Hall exhibit, *Scotland Forever!* that Butler is at her best. There is no restraint in the head-on pose of men and grey horses just breaking from a trot to a gallop as they begin the charge at Waterloo. The power of color is evident in the subtle differences of shades of grey in the horses. Her skill at observation is obvious in the distinctive expression of each man and each animal.

659. "Pictures of the Year--III." *Magazine of Art* 4 (1881): 363- 367.

Clara Montalba has suppressed the color in her painting of St. Mark's Cathedral in order to present contrasts of light and shade. The front of the cathedral is flooded in light, while the sky is white and intensely luminous.

660. "Pictures of the Year--IV." *Magazine of Art* 4 (1881): 397- 400.

In his painting *Renouncing the Vanities by Order of Savanarola*, Mr. Topham introduces a tone of merriment and levity. Some years ago Jane Benham Hay painted the same subject with more severity and a "more Pre-Raphaelite spirit." Alice Havers dresses her subjects in eighteenth-century clothing as they assemble for a picnic in the woods in *The First Arrivals*. Elizabeth Pilsbury's *Fish Pond* and Kate Macaulay's *At Anchor* merit special notice.

661. "The Winter Exhibition at the Grosvenor Gallery." *Magazine of Art* 4 (1881): 177-182.

Evelyn Pickering's work is much like the style of Edward Burne-Jones; her two small Florentine landscapes evoke the work of "early Umbrian masters." Pickering's color treatment is excellent and she has a talent for adopting qualities of different styles of painting. *Love's Hiding Place* by Louise Jopling is as successful as her husband's flower paintings. Lady Lindsay's flower paintings are executed with her usual skill.

662. "Winter Exhibitions. French Gallery." *Art Journal* (January 1881): 29-30.

Henriette Browne has tried for difficult handling and succeeded in *Preparations for the Festival*, part of the exhibition at the French Gallery.

663. "Winter Exhibitions. The Dudley Gallery." *Art Journal* (January 1881): 29-30.

Rosa Brett, Helen Thornycroft, Helen Wirgman, and Mrs. Val Bromley exhibit pictures that excel as "Faithful Studies from Nature."

664. "Winter Exhibitions. The Maclean Gallery." *Art Journal* (January 1881): 29-30.

In an exhibition of foreign artists, the Maclean Gallery features some "capitally expressed" *Scotch Cattle* by Rosa Bonheur.

665. "Winter Exhibitions. The Society of Painters in Water Colours." *Art Journal* (January 1881): 29-30.

Helen Angell's *Zinnias* and *Chrysanthemums* excel over neighboring paintings with their strong treatment of color. Unfortunately, some members are changing their painting styles in flagrant imitation of a female artist whose work is "deservedly popular."

666. "Winter Exhibitions. The Water-Colour Societies." *Art Journal* (January 1881): 29-30.

There is very little new under the sun at either the Old Society or the Royal Society exhibitions. Clara Montalba is still painting Venice and Helen Allingham continues to turn out pictures of Surrey.

667. "Art Notes and Reviews. The Grosvenor Gallery." *Art Journal* (February 1881): 62-63.

Marie Spartali Stillman and Maud Naftel contribute flower paintings, and Evelyn Pickering sends "two pretty Tuscan landscapes," a change from her usual figure subjects.

668. "Art Notes and Reviews. The Institute of Painters in Water Colours." *Art Journal* (February 1881): 62-63.

Mary L. Gow's painting, *Beggar My Neighbor* deserves notice for its originality.

669. "Art Notes. The European Galleries." *Art Journal* (February 1881): 61-62.

Among the decorative art in the European Galleries are Mrs. Mallam's ceramic paintings and Clara Montalba's panel, *Funeral in Venice*.

670. "Art Notes and Reviews. Exhibition. An Exhibition of Paintings by Essex Artists at Chelmsford." *Art Journal* (March 1881): 93-94.

Ellen Wilkinson sends several pictures; among the best are *Feeding Pigeons; A Word of Advice; By the Old Gateway;* and *The Belle of the Market.* The exhibition of nearly 400 pictures did not do well because of bad weather.

671. "Art Notes and Reviews. The Dudley Gallery." *Art Journal* (April 1881): 125.

The somewhat seedy and neglected state of the Dudley Gallery is not improved much by the quality of the pictures exhibited there. Bertha Newcombe's *Three Studies of Mère Marat;* Gertrude Martineau's *Loch Pitvonlish;* Edith Martineau's *Meadow Sweet;* and Mary Foster's *A Village Garden* are exceptions with varying degrees of excellence.

672. "Art Notes and Reviews. Exhibitions. Society of Lady Artists." *Art Journal* (May 1881): 157.

The Society of Lady Artists deserves more public support than any other artistic institution. While much of what is exhibited lacks "true Art instinct," the same can be said of the work of these women's "sterner brethren." Among the 766 paintings at this exhibition, Louise Rayner deserves notice for her scene of a horse fair at *Foregate Street, Chester;* Kate Macaulay for *Evening on Loch Fyne;* Emma Cooper for *Wiseman's Bridge, Saundersfoot;* Emma Walter's *Fruit* and Emma Cooper's *Fruit Just Gathered.* Madeline Marrable's *Palm Trees on the Island of Capri* is excellent, and Mrs. Marrable's daughter, Edith, is close to excelling her with apple blossoms in *Decorative Panel.* Charlotte and Bessie Spiers have yet to reach their potential; they and Emily Lane are capable of doing better.

673. "Art Notes and Reviews. Exhibitions." *Art Journal* (June 1881): 189-191.

At the Grosvenor Gallery, a portrait of artist Kate Perugini painted by Mr. Millais bears the misquoted passage by Elizabeth Barrett Browning, "Sweetest Eyes Were Ever Seen." Mrs. John Collier sends a good portrait of a child and Louisa Starr exhibits a portrait of *Miss Shoobridge*. Evelyn Pickering handles color well but lacks drawing skills in *The Grey Sisters*, a painting in the style of Mr. Burne-Jones. In the Water-Colour Society's exhibition, Helen Allingham's *Chat over the Wall* is also excellent. At the Maclean Gallery, Rosa Bonheur exhibits scenes from her neighborhood at Fontainebleau. At the Tooth Gallery, another gem, an excellent interior by J. Hayllar who is reported to be "a lady, and still in her teens," shows much promise. Helen Angell's flower pictures rank among the best in their genre.

674. "The Royal Academy. The One Hundred and Thirteenth Exhibition, 1881." *Art Journal* (June 1881): 185-188.

Dawn at Bethlehem by Theresa Thornycroft represents a blue-mantled virgin and a sleeping child. Elizabeth Thompson Butler's *Rorke's Drift* is worthy of note because of its subject.

675. "Art Notes and Reviews. Animal Painting at the Royal Academy." *Art Journal* (July 1881): 221-222.

Artists attempting to represent animals and birds too often reveal a lack of understanding and familiarity with their subjects, often with incongruous or even ludicrous results. One of the few exceptions is Rose E. Stanton's *Hedgehogs*, to be found in the Water-Colour Room.

676. "The Royal Academy. The One Hundred and Thirteenth Exhibition, 1881." *Art Journal* (July 1881): 213-216.

Kate Perugini's *Little Nell: Old Curiosity Shop* is an interesting scene from one of her father's novels. *The First Arrivals*, a scene of greedy children at a picnic is a good picture by Alice Havers. Clara Montalba creates beautiful but improbable color in *St. Mark's, Venice*.

677. "Art Notes and Reviews. Art Exhibitions. Exhibitions of Paintings on China." *Art Journal* (August 1881): 253-254.

Two Royal Academicians juried this year's exhibition of painting on china, resulting in some improvement in quality over previous exhibitions. Everett Green and Marion Gemmel are among the winners of the most prestigious prizes donated and presented by royal patrons.

678. "The Royal Academy. The One Hundred and Thirteenth Exhibition." *Art Journal* (August 1881): 229-231.

      Jessie Macgregor's three pictures with a wedding theme, *The Mistletoe Bough*, do not merit their prestigious placement on the line. Elizabeth Thompson Butler's *The Defense of Rorke's Drift: January 22nd, 1879* has some excellent details, but taken as a whole, the composition is weak and the color "unpleasant." Sophie Anderson's classical theme is most successful in *The Song*. Jane Dealey's *Left Behind*, Mary Foster's *Richmond Castle* and a work by Henrietta Montalba merit notice.

679. "Art Notes and Reviews. Art Exhibitions." *Art Journal* (September 1881): 287.

      Kate Greenaway's "wearisome children" succumb to the more inspirational scenes of happy families and religious subjects of this year's exhibition of Christmas and New Year's Cards. Alice Havers, also known as Mrs. Morgan, has won the £200 first prize.

680. "Art Exhibitions and Art Notes." *Art Journal* (October 1881): 317-320.

      Elizabeth Butler's *Balaclava* is part of the exceptionally good exhibition at the Bolton New Infirmary. The Autumn Exhibition of the Glasgow Institute includes work by Henriette Ronner. Lady Violet Lindsay has done much to promote the Fine Art Association at Kirkaldy, Fife.

681. "Art Notes and Reviews. Art Exhibitions." *Art Journal* (November 1881): 349.

      An exhibition encouraging the citizens of Leicester to form a permanent art collection includes Elizabeth Butler's painting, *Quatre Bras*. Royal Academy members have not sent pictures to the Brighton Pavilion Gallery, but excellent local artists such as Emma Black, Mary Hurst, and Edith Smith are represented.

682. "Art Notes and Reviews. Winter Exhibitions." *Art Journal* (December 1881): 377.

      The best of the smaller works at the French Gallery include "adequate" paintings by women including Sophie Anderson, Mrs. Val Bromley, Clara Montalba and Hilda Montalba. Clara Montalba's thirteen Venetian pictures stand out at the Maclean Gallery exhibition. The Tooth Gallery exhibition contains fine examples of the distinctive interior scenes of Mary and Jessica Hayllar.

683. "Art Notes. At the Royal Pavilion, Brighton." *Magazine of Art* 5 (1882): ii.

      The Eighth Annual Exhibition of Modern Pictures in Oil which opened at the Brighton Pavilion in September features over 500 works.

One of the most eye-catching is *On the Lagoons, Venice,* a luminous work by Clara Montalba.

684. "Art Notes. Kirkcaldy." *Magazine of Art* 5, no. iii (1882).
    Although it is in a small town in a provincial locale, Kirkcaldy Fine Art Association offers a fine-arts club, prize money and respectable sales figures. The current tenth annual exhibition contains works by well-known artists such as Miss Montalba as well as "many promising works by local men."

685. "Art Notes. At the Exhibition of the Society of British Artists." *Magazine of Art* 5 (1882): ix-x.
    Edith Hipkin's *Blue Beards' Wives,* at the exhibition of the Society of British Artists contains "considerable power of colour and execution."

686. "Art Notes. The Winter Exhibition of the Dudley Gallery." *Magazine of Art* 5 (1882): x.
    The rumors of the impending closing of the Dudley Gallery add to the dismal air of a substandard exhibition. Among the many pictures of Venice, Hilda Montalba's work has a "pleasing sense of colour."

687. "Art Notes. The Second Exhibition of Tapestry Paintings." *Magazine of Art* 5 (1882): xiii.
    An exhibition review of tapestries at Howell and James's Galleries shows improvement in painting by women amateurs and artists. Mrs. Henry McDowell's copy of the *Europa* tapestry in Buckingham Palace and Elizabeth Chettle's copy of the Welbeck Abbey tapestry titled *Moses and Aaron before Pharaoh* are "the two largest and most striking" in the exhibition. The prize for the best original work by an amateur goes to Helen Jackson for screen painting with children. Eliza Turck's peacock panel intended for the back of a piano has also won a prize. Constance Fripp's copy of a Florentine tapestry is one of the best imitations.

688. "Art Notes. The Winter Exhibition of the Royal Society of Painters in Water Colours." *Magazine of Art* 5 (1882): xiii-xiv.
    Helen Allingham's drawings of women and children and Clara Montalba's studies of Venice can be seen at the excellent exhibition of the Royal Society of Painters in Water Colours.

689. "Art Notes. In the Exhibition of the Society of Lady Artists." *Magazine of Art* 5 (1882): xxvi.

Still lifes and flower pictures are good, but landscapes and figures are less than wonderful at the Exhibition of the Society of Lady Artists. Clara Montalba lacks drawing, color, and sentiment in *London Bridge*. Miss O'Hara does better with *White Wings;* Fanny Currey's *Carpenter's Cottage* contains excellent color and a skillful drawing of an elderly peasant woman. *Flirtation* by Bertha Newcombe is dull but well-painted, and Florence Reason's *Arab Chieftan* is ugly, but "well modelled and intelligent." Kate Macaulay's seascapes are pleasant but too "chalky." Linnie Watt, a "rising artist" does well with *The Back-Door* and *Spring Time*. *Mediterranean Fish* by Miss Anderson is not a particularly interesting work, but her treatment of the iridescent and brilliant colors of the fish make it one of the best works of the exhibition.

690. "Art Notes. The Spring Exhibition of Water-Colour Drawings." *Magazine of Art* 5 (1882): xxvi-xxvii.

Neither new nor established artists contributed anything memorable to the Dudley Gallery's spring exhibition. *Nasturtiums* by Edith Martineau is crisp and well-colored.

691. "Art Notes. The Exhibition of the Institute of Painters in Water-Colours." *Magazine of Art* 5 (1882): xxx.

Elizabeth Murray's *Boys School in Algeria* is worth noticing in a mediocre exhibition of the Institute of Painters in Water- Colours.

692. "Art Notes. The Royal Society of Painters in Water-Colours." *Magazine of Art* 5 (1882): xxxiii.

Constance Phillott's painting *Electra* and drawings by Clara Montalba are part of a good exhibition by the Royal Society of Painters in Water-Colours.

693. "An Exhibition of Christmas Cards." *Magazine of Art* 5 (1882): 30-32.

While the craze for "mortuary cards," valentines, and wedding cards has fortunately died out, the fairly recent custom of imposing "the tyranny of the Christmas Card" on "equally enslaved and reluctant friends and acquaintances" seems to be firmly in place. In an effort to at least improve the trite, garish and tasteless designs so popular with the public, the Suffolk Street and Dudley Galleries have held exhibitions and offered prizes for Christmas Card designs. Alice Havers takes the honors and a prize of £200; Victoria Dubourg's flower designs have received four prizes. Out of over a thousand drawings, most of them ugly and with such inappropriate subjects as smoke-belching Mississippi riverboats and illustrations from

Tennyson's poems, only about twenty cards are worthy contributions to a questionable genre.

694. "Winter Exhibitions. The Dudley Gallery." *Art Journal* (January 1882): 29-30.

Kate Perugini's portrait of *Edith, Daughter of Mrs. H. Merton* and Ada Tucker's *A Harmony in Black and Gold* are among the better pictures at the Dudley Gallery exhibition.

695. "Exhibitions. The Eighteenth Exhibition of Water-Colour Drawings." *Art Journal* (April 1882): 126.

The flower paintings especially rank as some of the best work at the Dudley Gallery. Maud Naftel and Ada Bell send *Flowers;* Victoria Dubourg sends *Summer Flowers* and Emily Jackson sends *Chrysanthemums,* a study in crimson, white and pink. Among the best drawings is Kate Macaulay's *A West Highland Fishing Town.* Kate Sadler's *Chrysanthemums* is also excellent.

696. "Exhibitions. Turner's Drawings." *Art Journal* (May 1882): 157-158.

In Mr. Ruskin's opinion, Miss Jay's copies of Turner's drawings are of better quality than most modern originals. Jay's work can be seen at Dowdeswell's Gallery in New Bond Street.

697. "Exhibitions. Grosvenor Gallery." *Art Journal* (June 1882): 189-191.

A portrait of a woman in black with azaleas and a cream background is an excellent painting by the Princess Louise. Rosa Corder sends a portrait of *F.R. Leyland, Esq.* Hilda Montalba also sends a good portrait worth noting.

698. "Exhibitions. The Water-Colour Societies." *Art Journal* (June 1882): 189-191.

The Children's Tea Party, a painting by Helen Allingham, is "unusual, important and delicate." Helen Angell uses the marble of a Venetian palace as a background for her wonderful *Chrysanthemums.* She also sends *Plate of Raspberries.*

699. "Exhibitions. Society of Lady Artists, Great Marlborough Street." *Art Journal* (June 1882): 189-191.

A number of exceptional pictures stand out in this "bright and pleasing exhibition." Louise Jopling exhibits skillful drawing in *Little Muriel,* as does Louise Rayner in *The Butter Cross, Salisbury.* Handling of color stands out in *Some Mediterranean Fish* by Sophie Anderson, and in several works by Mrs. Marrable. Pathos is exemplified in *Evangeline*, by Mrs. H. Champion; and in *The Last of the Brotherhood*, an aged monk skillfully portrayed by Kate Nichols. Her *The Valley of the Oaks* is also excellent, as is Kate Macaulay's *Fishing Boats on the West Coast;* Harriette Seymour's *On the Bar;* Madame Giampietri's *On Guard;* and Jane Deakin's *The Old Mill*.

700. "Exhibition. Liverpool Society of Painters in Water Colours." *Art Journal* (June 1882): 189-191.

Edith Martineau takes her inspiration from a poem by Woolner for her painting *My Beautiful Lady*. Her painting is among the attractions in the exhibition of over 300 works.

701. "The Exhibition of the Royal Academy." *Art Journal* (July 1882): 210-212.

Something Interesting is "a good little canvas dealing with children and storybooks" by Mary L. Gow. Anna Lea Merritt exhibits her portrait of *His Excellency the Hon. J. R. Lowell*, painted in his doctoral gown. Kate Perugini sends another illustration from Dickens in *The Doll's Dressmaker*. The color treatment in Elizabeth Butler's *Floreat Etona!* is crude, but the design is vigorous. Blanche Jenkins' lamp and firelight in *Nearly Bedtime* is realistically rendered.

702. "The Exhibition of the Royal Academy." *Art Journal* (August 1882): 237-239.

Hilda Montalba's *A Misty Day, Venice*, is "cleverly painted" but too big for its subject, and Edith Hayllar would have a good picture in *As Hungry as a Hunter* if she had omitted the "gentleman in 'pink.'" Blanche Jenkins' *The First Kiss* is charming and well done. This year's Constable Prize is awarded to *A Shady Lane* by Margaret Hickson. Necessarily unoriginal, the picture is exceptional in its treatment of light, shade, and impasto. Worthy of notice but hung too high is *A Coming Tragedian* by Mrs. John Collier. Kate Macaulay's *Scotch Herring Trawlers* also deserves attention. Composition suffers but design and color are good in Alice Haver's *Trouble*, a picture of suffering cottagers. Laura Alma-Tadema's treatment of a blue silk dress in *Asleep* shows that her skill is increasing.

703. "The Worcestershire Exhibition." *Art Journal* (August 1882): 253-254.

Elizabeth J. Binns, a well-known London exhibitor, shows her skills in Worcestershire with *That Wicked Weed--The Hop*. Mrs. Leader's flower pictures are commendable.

704. "Exhibitions. China Painting." *Art Journal* (October 1882): 318-319.

> At Howell and James's seventh exhibition of china paintings by lady amateurs, C. J. Barber, a pupil at the Lambeth School of Art, won a prize for her design of dog roses and bullfinches. Her plaque has been purchased by HRH the Grand Duke of Hesse.

705. "The Winter Exhibitions at the Smaller Galleries." *Art Journal* (December 1882): 378.

> The Fine Art Society's exhibition of Venetian scenes include work by Miss Montalba, whose exemplary handling of water and light make her paintings among the most notable in the exhibit. At the French Gallery at Pall Mall, Henriette Browne's *Alsace* does credit neither to her nor to her teacher. Bertha Newcombe's *Does it Rain?* is one of the better pictures at the Dudley Gallery.

706. "Art in April." *Magazine of Art* (1883): xxv-xxxiii.

> The Exhibition of Lady Artists still evidences some lack of skill and seriousness, but it continues to improve. Alice Havers' *Footsteps* is probably the most "ambitious" work shown. Clara Montalba's figure lacks life in *Sorting Crabs on the Venetian Lagoons*, but she has done well with tone and atmosphere. Bertha Newcombe has sent three works, all average for her, and too much influenced by "the preposterous mannerisms of a certain French School." *A Cottage Near Lismore* by Helen O'Hara has good color and atmosphere, but her other exhibit, *Throw Me a Rosy One* pictures a child in an orchard with light and life. *Fishing Boats of Chiozza* by Mrs. R. T. Wright deserves mention as does work by Linnie Watt, Charlotte Spiers, Kate Macaulay, Emily Merrick, and Grace Hastie. The Irish Fine Art Society's twentieth exhibition is the best in Dublin. Of the over 400 works, mostly watercolors, first place goes to Fanny Currey's clever *Modern Dutch Painter; Pansies;* and *Hawthorne;* Helen O'Hara, best known as an illustrator, deserves praise for *Kingfisher; Little Beggars; A Recitative* and a painting of primroses. J. J. Longfield's *A Wooded Glen* and *Mountain Road* deserve mention, as do works by Miss Keane, Rose Barton, Maud Peel, and Mary Fowler. The oils of Miss Webb and Sarah Purser are especially fine in their drawing.

707. "Art in May." *Magazine of Art* (1883): xxix-xxxii.

> The Institute of Painters in Water-Colours exhibition in Piccadilly includes Helen Maguire's *Orpheus*, which is original and pleasant. *Godmother* by Mary L. Gow is especially pleasing. The Royal Society of Painters in Water-Colours has an excellent exhibition, though it has little

to offer that is new. Clara Montalba's *The Convent Offering* has her usual skill with color, but "her palace seems astonished at its own perspective." The animals in Rosa Bonheur's exhibit at Lefèvere's Gallery are well detailed and technically competent, but they are still just animal portraits, not "pictures, in the right sense."

708. "Art Notes. The Royal Society of Painters in Water Colours." *Art Journal* (January 1883): 30.

The Old Water Colour Society has changed its name to The Society of Painters in Water Colours and many of its excellent members have died, but its galleries still contain excellent works by talented artists. HRH Princess Louise, Marchioness of Lorne, exhibits *Canoeing in the Cascapediae River, Canada* in which the figure of a young man and the surrounding landscape are rendered with a sure hand. Helen Allingham's *Dover Beach* is an excellent painting that departs from the artist's usual choice of subject, to her credit.

709. "Exhibitions and Art Notes. Some Spring Exhibitions." *Art Journal* (May 1883): 165-166.

On the whole, the exhibition of the Dudley Gallery Art Society is of good quality. Edith Martineau's *The Beautiful Lady* is not well drawn. Mrs. Cecil Lawson is content to stay with flower subjects and deserves commendation for her *Purple Poppies*. Kate Macaulay becomes too ambitious and is on the brink of "producing violent and too artificial shadows and reflections" in her water pictures. Bertha Newcombe's *Once Upon a Time* deserves mention. Few portraits can be seen at the Society of Painter-Etchers exhibition, but Anna Lea Merritt's portrait of James Russell Lowell is among the best. At the Society of Lady Artists' exhibition, Mary Forster, Kate Macaulay, and Bertha Newcombe contribute meritorious works. Hilda Montalba's *Sorting Crabs on the Venetian Lagoons* is a good example of fine treatment of air and light. E. M. Beresford's figures lack confident drawing of the kind found in the work of Edith Hipkins.

710. "The Exhibition of the Royal Academy." *Art Journal* (June 1883): 201-202.

Kate Perugini's *Bébelle* shows good handling of color in a head study of a "pretty wax-like face" with fair hair and violet head covering.

711. "The Grosvenor Gallery." *Art Journal* (June 1883): 203-204.

Miss Ellen Terry as Portia, a picture by Louise Jopling, harmonizes subject with color. Other works deserving mention are Evelyn Pickering's

By the Waters of Babylon, Clara Montalba's *Cement Works on the Thames* and a sculpture by Hilda Montalba.

712. "The Institute of Painters in Water Colors." *Art Journal* (June 1883): 193-196.
Evelyn Pickering demonstrates skill at painting drapery in *Deianeira*, but the figure is more suggestive of an Ariadne. Elizabeth A. Armstrong's "tenderly felt little studies" deserve attention; they are "little more than broad splashes of delicate color."

713. "Exhibition of the Royal Academy." *Art Journal* (July 1883): 217-220.
Anna Lea Merritt's *War* depicts a balcony "overcrowded with female figures" watching troops marching by. Clara Montalba's *Trabacolo* is a graceful rendering of a Venetian scene. *The New Gown* by Fanny Fildes depicts a young girl sitting in a garden finishing the details of the new dress she wears. Annie L. Robinson's portrait, *Fra Silvestro* is not nearly as good as the one she exhibited two years ago in Burlington House. Louisa Starr's *Lady Campbell* depicts a seated woman wearing a gauze scarf and a black velvet dress. Bertha Newcombe's *Evening* is a good landscape which, to the great discredit of the gallery, is poorly placed.

714. "The Royal Society of Painters in Water Colours." *Art Journal* (July 1883): 237.
Clara Montalba's picture *The Festival of St. John at Venice* is of brightly-clad figures in a narrow street. Helen Allingham's pictures titled *A Cottage Girl* and *Annie* are charming but not as good as *Girl Drying Clothes in a Sunny Garden*.

715. "The Triennian Salon of 1883." *Art Journal* (December 1883): 377-378.
The exhibit at the National Salon contains work by French artists only. Among the successful works in this somewhat disappointing collection are a seascape by Madame La Villette which has been hung too high; Madame Ayrton's still life, entitled *Fruits Secs;* and Madame Demont-Breton's *Plage*.

716. "Art in October." *Magazine of Art* (1884): i-iv.
A prestigious array of exhibitors at the Autumn Exhibition in Manchester includes Elizabeth Thompson Butler, Clara and Hilda Montalba, and Princess Louise. The Nottingham Autumn Exhibition includes over a thousand pictures, mostly watercolors. Clara Montalba's *A Hazy Winter Morning in Venice* and Bertha Newcombe's *French Peasant*

studies are "chief among the women's work." Mary Weatherhill's *St. Mark's* has already attracted attention at the Fine Art Society exhibition. Brighton's tenth exhibition is its best ever. Louise Jopling sends *Little Red Riding Hood*. Sophie Anderson's *Old Seaman* is very good; Alma Broadbridge's *Gossip on the Sands* is a bit cold, but "true and well-handled." Edith Heckstall Smith's flowers deserve mention. Perhaps the best still life in the exhibition is *A Little China Pot, with Ferns*, a School of Art medal winner by Marion A. Sterling.

717. "Art in November." *Magazine of Art* (1884): v-viii.

Some good work shows up in "the mass of rubbish at the Dudley." *Marshy Coast* by Hilda Montalba has good "color, tone, light and sentiment." Kate May's *Queen of the Night* is a well-painted and original flower picture. Mr. Wallis' exhibition is interesting, as is usual. Clara Montalba's *Venetian Boats Preparing to Anchor* does well with color, avoids mannerism, and may be her best work to date. The "utilitarian" exhibits at the Female School of Art include excellent designs for tiles, playing cards, and tapestries, as well as chalk studies and lithography. The school is about to ask the public for a new building.

718. "Art in December." *Magazine of Art* (1884): xi-xii.

Miss Montalba's watercolor, *Venice*, in the MacLean Gallery, shows a city that is "glowing, yet tempered with truth." The best Christmas books this season are Kate Greenaway's *Almanac, Calendars* and *Little Ann*. As familiar as Greenaway's drawings are, they never seem to become dull or tiresome.

719. "Art in January." *Magazine of Art* (1884): xiii-xvi.

The Royal Society of Painters in Water-Colours exhibition includes Allingham's charming *Stray Cat*. Miss Montalba handles color well in *Zwyndrecht*, a canal scene.

720. "Art in March." *Magazine of Art* (1884): xxi-xxiv.

Rosa Bonheur is feeling well enough to leave Paris for her country house. At the Dudley Gallery, Mrs. Cecil Lawson's *Purple Iris* is the best flower painting, but Mary Eley's *Gone* is a good effort wasted. It "lacks vitality and vigour."

721. "Art in April." *Magazine of Art* (1884): xxv-xxviii.

The death of Helen Cordelia Coleman Angell has been reported. She was a flower painter and belonged to the Society of Painters in Water Colours. The Royal Society of Painters in Water Colours has elected Mary Foster an Associate Member. The Melbourne Museum has acquired Elizabeth Thompson Butler's *Quatre Bras*. The Society of British Artists exhibition includes *Thochts Eerie* by Lizzie Reid. It is an original suggestion of the supernatural. The Society of Lady Artist's exhibition is disappointingly uninnovative. *Moonlight, Near the Thames* by Clara Montalba has power. Kate Macaulay's two works, *Sailing Out at Sunset*, and *The Golden Hour* show a good grasp of color, as does Bertha Newcombe's *Little Knitter*, which is also clever and well designed. Louise Jopling "has two pleasant studies of heads." *Swedish Landscape* by Hilda Montalba does well with figure and color treatment. A figure study, *From Damascus*, by Emily Merrick is strong and competent and Agnes Schenck's *Sad Memories* has "force and feeling." *Where the White Cloud Rests* by Annie Fraser is the best landscape in the exhibit. Emily Merrick's *Old Pots* is clever; Eugénie Simpson, Florence Bonneau, Eloise Stannard, and Florence Mann exhibit good fruit and flower pictures. Also of note are works by Mrs. Naftel, Mrs. Mirrable, and Helen O'Hara. The Irish Fine Art Exhibition contains excellent nature drawings by Fanny Currey and good bird studies by Helen O'Hara; Miss Barton's work is also worthy of notice.

722. "Art in May." *Magazine of Art* (1884): xxix-xxxii.

Except for the contributions of Evelyn Pickering and a few others, the Grosvenor Gallery exhibition is below average. Young artists have a good opportunity to be seen in the Fine Art Society's exhibit of "one hundred paintings and drawings by one hundred artists." Among the interesting works are Dorothy Tennant's picture of a baby titled *A Weight of Care*, and Bertha Newcombe's true-to-nature picture, *Through the Long Grass*. The two children in the picture are strongly rendered, but the light in the sky is somewhat weak. Mary L. Gow and Helen Allingham have good drawings. Rosa Bonheur's portrait of a bull titled *Monarch of the Herd* at Lefèvre's is one of her most powerful works.

723. "Art in June." *Magazine of Art* (1884): xxxiii-xxxvi.

Travellers, a picture by Maria Brooks of a weary woman by a roadside, is touching and impressive, although her use of impasto is unnecessarily heavy.

724. "Art in July." *Magazine of Art* (1884): vii-xl.

> Some time ago Mr. Ruskin rashly suggested that young ladies improve their art endeavors by copying Turner. The Turner exhibit at the National Gallery is now packed with busy females zealously copying Turner, "and what is worse...the copies will have to be sold."

725. "Art in September." *Magazine of Art* (1884): xlv-xlviii.

> Over 3,000 works in the annual exhibition of the Liverpool Corporation of Art Galleries combines art shown by seven major societies and exhibitions. Clara Montalba has some of her best known work in the "Old Society" room.

726. "Current Art. III." *Magazine of Art* 7 (1884): 397-401.

> Two landscapes worthy of close examination but so badly placed that they are impossible to study are Bertha Newcombe's *The Last Load* and Miss Robinson's "clever and sunny" picture titled *Don't.*

727. "Exhibitions. The Royal Society of Painters in Water- Colours." *Art Journal* (January 1884): 28-29.

> Helen Allingham's country scenes, *Surrey Sand Hills* and *Stray Pet* "smell more of the hearthside than of the studio." Clara Montalba has left the canals of Venice for the canals of Holland and the results are the very successful *Fish Market* and *Windmills.*

728. "The Institute of Painters in Oil Colours." *Art Journal* (February 1884): 62.

> *Children of the Night* by Evelyn Pickering contains imagination and skill, but ignores nature.

729. "Society of Lady Artists." *London Times* (12 March 1884): 4.

> The Society of Lady Artists' exhibition at the gallery at No. 48, Great Marlborough Street, consists of 550 watercolors and 200 oil pictures. As one might expect, flower pieces dominate the exhibition, which, since it is composed only of the work of amateurs, must be judged differently from the professional exhibits. Amy Scott's large watercolor study of dead game is without fault, except for the subject, which is unsuitable for a lady. Except for most of the oil paintings, which are "over- ambitious and poor," the exhibit displays thoughtful, careful work.

730. "Art Notes. The Lady Artists." *Art Journal* (May 1884): 158.

> Of the nearly 800 works exhibited at the Society of Lady Artists Gallery in Great Marlborough Street, about twenty show the kind of

painstaking effort to learn the basic skills so essential to the development of any good artist. The best work in the exhibition is probably Marian Croft's *No Partner.*

731. "Art Notes. The Royal Hibernian Academy." *Art Journal* (May 1884): 158-159.

Mediocre works and poor public attendance mark this year's exhibition of the Royal Hibernian Academy. Work by Miss P. A. Williams is among those worthy of mention.

732. "The Exhibition of the Royal Academy." *Art Journal* (June 1884): 177-179.

This year's Royal Academy Exhibition is dull, flat, and "dolefully depressing." Anna Pertz' *Still Life: Olives* is a quiet work of better quality than the "more ambitious works which surround it."

733. "London Spring Exhibitions. The Grosvenor and the Water-Colour Societies." *Art Journal* (June 1884): 184-191.

Among the Pre-Raphaelite pictures in the East Gallery is Evelyn Pickering's picture of sad lovers. Marie Spartali Stillman's *Madonna Pietra degli Schrovigni* is placed in a watercolor gallery, but with its strength and vivid colors it deserves to be placed with other Pre-Raphaelite paintings. Clara Montalba's watercolor, *A November Day, Middleberg* shows a canal, red-tiled roofs, and a grey sky. Mary Forster's *Morning on the Seine* exemplifies her talent at painting mist and haze. *Pat-a-Cake*, by Helen Allingham, is a charming domestic scene.

734. "The Royal Academy. (Fifth and Concluding Notice)." *The Athenaeum* (21 June 1884): 797-799.

The Last to Leave is one of the "most careful and brilliant" genre paintings in the exhibition. Jessica Hayllar has balanced humor with coolness in her original picture of guests who have stayed too long saying goodbye to a woman and her daughter; the scene is in the dawn light in a white room. Edith Hipkins has taken great care with detail in *Hickory, Dickory, Dock*, a woman holding a baby up to show it a clock. The woman looks a little stiff, her facial expression is not natural, and the blue color of her dress is rather crude, but overall the picture is skillfully done and deserves credit.

735. "Exhibition of the Royal Academy." *Art Journal* (July 1884): 209-212.

Among the best of the "pick of the portraits" in the Third Gallery is Emily Merrick's portrait of *J. Marshall, F.R.S.* Gallery IV contains

Kittens, by Mary K. Benson, a portrait of a little blonde girl with a white cat.

736. "The Exhibition of the Royal Academy." *Art Journal* (August 1884): 241-244.

The Last Load, a river scene by Bertha Newcombe, is hung so high that its colors and perspective cannot be appreciated. An otherwise excellent portrait of *Miss N. Huxley* by Marion Collier is spoiled by "disagreeable fleshtones and obtrusive background." *Danx,* a misprint for *Danae,* is a picture by Annie L. Robinson of a peasant girl framed by gold gorse blooms. Ethel S. Ring's chalk study of an old man's head has "rare quality of style." Laura Alma-Tadema sends one of her Dutch scenes, unusually large for her, titled *Saying Grace.*

737. "Art Notes. Sydney, New South Wales." *Art Journal* (October 1884): 319-320.

While it is a pity that the New South Wales Art Society's rules do not allow the selection committee to reject works by members, some works do deserve mention. Mrs. Stoddart sends "two charming portraits," Mrs. Williamson sends two fruit pictures, and Miss Combes sends some flower pictures. Miss Vinter should have limited entries to her two good studies, as her portrait of Sir Alfred Stephan is "very unsatisfactory."

738. "Autumn Exhibitions. The Walker Art Gallery, Liverpool." *Art Journal* (October 1884): 317.

Some of the best of Britain's art galleries and societies have sent paintings for exhibition at the Walker Art Gallery in Liverpool. The Grosvenor Gallery's contributions include work by Clara Montalba, whose paintings are also included from the Royal Society of Painters in Water Colours.

739. "Fine-Art Gossip." *The Athenaeum* (6 December 1884): 742-743.

More than 750 works, both good and bad, may be viewed at the Society of British Artists exhibition. Works by Jessica Hayllar and Louise Rayner have been contributed, and Edith Hipkin's *Old Volumes* deserves special mention.

740. "Art in November." *Magazine of Art* (1885): v-viii.

The "almost unrelieved mediocrity" at the Dudley Gallery has a few exceptions, including Helen Montalba's tenderly-colored Venetian pictures, Edith Berkeley's and Linnie Watts' landscapes, and Anna Weir's promising *Study of a Boy's Head.* Hildesheimer and Faulkner's prettiest Christmas cards this year are by Alice Havers. Helena Maguire's *Dogs* is pleasant but not novel.

741. "Art in December." *Magazine of Art* (1885): ix-xii.

Helen Allingham has "eight delightful drawings" in the Royal Society of Painters in Water-Colours' winter show. Messrs. Marcus Ward of London have published some miniature portfolios, among them "Sporting Sketches" by Georgina Bowers.

742. "Art in March." *Magazine of Art* (1885): xxi-xxiv.

The reviewer finds unusual quality in this year's exhibition of the Nineteenth Century Art Society. *Evil Intentions*, a dog picture by Fanny Moody, is amusing, lively, and accurate. *Eve*, by Janet Holloway, suffers with the hard drapery, but it has some charm and originality. *Fading and Falling* is an "amazing piece in still life" by Sophie D'Ouseley. The watercolor exhibit at Agnew's features *Spring Violets* by Ada Bell. It is unpretentious but "rich in effect." Bell also shows *Spring Violets* at the Dudley Gallery, where one can also see Mrs. Cecil Lawson's *Lily* and Kate Barnard's *Five O'Clock in the Morning*. Kate Macaulay's work shows great improvement this year. It is lighter and more original than her previous work.

743. "Art in April." *Magazine of Art* (1885): xxv-xxviii.

Trouble by Alice Havers and *Evening* by Bertha Newcombe are the most important works in this year's exhibition of the Society of Lady Artists. *Evening* is painted in greys and greens with a French influence. Field workers in the twilight convey a sense of sadness. Havers tells the story with "simplicity and force." Kate Macaulay does well with color and treatment in her study of Welsh bridges and several seascapes, the most notable of which is *Sailing Out at Sunset*. "Heavy atmosphere, breaking waves, and jubilant sea-gulls" set a satisfactory tone in *Wind and Waves* by Helen O'Hara. The hounds in Fanny Moody's *Fresh for a Run* are a welcome break from all the cats in the exhibition. Frances Eley's *A Wrong Stitch*, and Bertha Newcombe's *Gone Fishing* also merit attention. Louise Rayner's drawing and color are soundly executed in her study of an architectural interior.

744. "Art in May." *Magazine of Art* (1885): xxix-xxxii.

Constance Phillott's watercolors at the Royal Society's exhibition indicate that she is making good progress. An Academy gold medal winner, Emily M. Merrick, exhibits *Primrose Day* at the Shepherd Brothers' Gallery. The painting is shallow, sentimental and unoriginal, but technically correct; it will be etched and released to the public soon.

745. "Current Art. III." *Magazine of Art* 8 (1885): 428-434.

Mrs. Waller's *Little Snow-White* at the Grosvenor Gallery is a "spirited imitation" of the work of J. E. Millais.

746. W. E. H. "Current Art--I." *Magazine of Art* (1885): 346-352.

At the Grosvenor Gallery, Evelyn Pickering's *Dryad* reminds us of how dismal and uncomfortable are the wilds, "remote from Liberty's and the aesthetic teapot."

747. "The Society of Painters in Water Colours. (First Notice)." *The Athenaeum* (2 May 1885): 572-574.

A young woman in lavender carries *A Basket of Clothes* through a verdant cottage garden, enjoying the antics of a black kitten. The figure and the scene are elegant and spontaneous, the colors brilliant and true; the picture is a credit to artist Helen Allingham, who also sends *Lessons*, a school-room scene true to detail, colors, lights, composition, and perspective. Another of Allingham's exhibits, *Amelia*, deserves less mention. Mary Lofthouse's nature study, *Moonrise*, features moonlit trees and a river, painted mostly in tones of gray. It deserves favorable comparison with other fine works in this theme by well-known artists.

748. "The Royal Academy. (Second Notice)." *The Athenaeum* (16 May 1885): 635-637.

Apparently, the only excuse for Theseus' shameful treatment of Ariadne is to provide a subject for Henrietta Rae's painting, *Ariadne Deserted by Theseus*.

749. "The Royal Academy. (Third Notice)." *The Athenaeum* (23 May 1885): 666-668.

Anna Lea Merritt's *The Eve* has no business in its prominent place in this exhibition. A nude study, this picture is "dull and incompetent," and is an unfortunate advertisement for Merritt's shortcomings. Alice Havers' *Divided* is a little better. The two figures, a girl with a lamb, and a man with a fishing pole, are separated by a stream; it is not clear whether their eyes are meeting. The girl is well done, but the man looks "bilious" and the greens of the foliage are overdone. Sophie Anderson's *The Studio*, a study of a young Greek woman with children and an amphora is well-handled, especially in its treatment of sunlight. Anderson would do well to model her work after that of Lawrence Alma-Tadema, who could teach her some lessons about clarity and brilliance in light and color.

750. "Art in December." *Magazine of Art* (1886): ix-xii.

At the Dudley Exhibition, Ada Bell's flower paintings are "soft, fresh, and naturally coloured." The Royal Society of Painters in Water-Colours has some pleasing Dutch drawings by Clara Montalba. Caroline Paterson's illustrations for "Snow White," "Cinderella," and "Sleeping Beauty" make it one of this year's best Christmas books.

751. "Art in March." *Magazine of Art* (1886): xxi-xxiv.

Medal winners at the Female School of Art include Marion Ryden Henn, Emma Ada Newcomb, Hilda Lucy Bell, Bertha Jeffreys, Helen Louise Corder, Mary Harriet Fores, Ruth Harman, Charlotte Maria Alston, and Catherine Mary Howard. Some of the best portraits at the Nineteenth-Century exhibition are by Alice Miller. *A Studio Belle* is especially well done.

752. "Art in April." *Magazine of Art* (1886): xxv-xxviii.

Excellent watercolors at the Dudley include flowers by Ada Bell and *Battersea Bridge* by Kate Macaulay. At the Royal Academy, Miss Webb's *Net Mender* contains good color and drawing. Dorothy Tennant's two figure studies are not well placed. Miss Sharland's *Lyn Idwall* deserves notice, as does work by Marion Chase.

753. "Art in May." *Magazine of Art* (1886): xxix-xxxii.

Helen O'Hara's work is among the best of an excellent exhibition of the Royal Institute of Painters in Water Colours. The Society of British Artists' exhibition is not as good as in past years, but it still boasts some excellent work, including Miss Connell's *Waiting*. Clara Montalba lives up to her usual high standards in her Royal Society of Painters in Water Colours exhibition.

754. "Art in June." *Magazine of Art* (1886): xxxiii-xxxvi.

Portraits unusually good for the Nineteenth-Century Gallery exhibition are the work of Alice Miller and Ethel Rose. *Arthur Arnold, Esq.* by Lily Stackpoole has some faults in the drawing, but the color is unusually good. Black and white pictures on exhibition at Memorial Hall include excellent work by Clara Montalba, Alice Havers, and Mary Gow.

755. "Current Art. II." *Magazine of Art* 9 (1886): 353-359.

In *The Willow-Pattern Plate*, Mary L. Gow's painting at the Royal Institute, a woman tells the story of the willow pattern to a little girl, using the plate as a story book. Gow's composition, design, and color are so good that although the subject is a trite one, the picture avoids sentimentality.

Reproductions (b/w engraving):

Gow, Mary L: *The Willow-Pattern Plate.*

756. "Current Art. IV." *Magazine of Art* 9 (1886): 441-447.

In the Royal Academy's exhibition, *Minerals and Fossils* by Kate Whitley can be compared to the work of Holman Hunt in its "searching and careful detail."

757. Stevenson, R. A. M. "Art in Australia." *Magazine of Art* 9 (1886): 399-400.

Australian artists tend to emulate English and French schools when they should be expanding into a style of their own; nonetheless, several artists in Australia are producing paintings of merit. Miss E. Parson's watercolor landscape, *Red Bluff*, has good composition, and "the color is laid on in good broad washes." Mrs. Strawbridge paints excellent flower pictures, although they are a bit too much like "botanical specimens." The best figure picture in the Colonial Exhibition is Miss Panton's *Head of an Old Woman.*

Reproductions (b/w engraving):

Parsons, Miss E: *Red Bluff.*

758. "Art in October." *Magazine of Art* (1887): i-iv.

At the Nottingham Exhibition Louise Jopling exhibits a portrait titled *A Fair Venetian* which, as with most of the exhibit, is neither new nor distinguished. A. S. M. Fenn shows promise in the "domestic genre" but her work is too stiff.

759. "Art in November." *Magazine of Art* (1887): v-viii.

The Scottish Society of Water Colour Painters' exhibition in Glasgow includes two "richly tinted" scenes of Venice and a landscape of a Swedish stream by Clara Montalba. Anna Alma-Tadema's *My Sister's Room* treats detail with remarkable precision. In 1887, the exhibition of the Society of Lady Artists will be held in the Drawing-Room Gallery of the Egyptian Hall in Piccadilly. Louise Jopling's *Portrait of Sir J.E. Millais* will be reproduced by photogravure. The portrait was exhibited at the Grosvenor Gallery.

760. "Art in December." *Magazine of Art* (1887): ix-xii.

> In the Winter Exhibition of the Royal Society of Watercolours, Clara Montalba's work shows her usual ability to capture atmosphere, but lacks "sound and finished workmanship" that would add depth to her work.

761. "Art in February." *Magazine of Art* (1887): xv-xix.

> At the Dublin Art Club, as in most Irish exhibitions, the work by women artists excels. Sarah Purser's decorative panel, *The Captivity of St. Patrick* is quite powerful. It is to be placed at a hospital in Dublin. Miss Manning, Miss Armstrong and Mrs. Webb Robinson also send excellent examples of their work.

762. "Art in March." *Magazine of Art* (1887): xxi-xxiv.

> At the Manchester Academy exhibition, *Swans* by Isabel Dacre is a good picture of children. Florence Monkhouse's figure studies are remarkably interesting.

763. "Art in April." *Magazine of Art* (1887): xxv-xxviii.

> The lady artists have wisely rejected some 400 pictures in putting together their second exhibition at the Egyptian Hall. The quality of the exhibit is so good that it can be evaluated with no special considerations. *Alpen Rosen*, a study of a young girl by Ellen Partridge, is typical of the careful work one expects from this artist. Mrs. Cooper's ivory miniature is better than her *Farm Buildings*, which is good, but not her best. The best of Kate Macaulay's nine works is *A Bit of the Thames at Battersea*. A sophisticated treatment of perspective can be seen in Madeline Cockburn Marrable's *Rome, From the Old Covent Garden, Palatine Hill* and a *Side Street in Vienna*. Excellent technique is obvious in Kate Hastings' *A Maid of Araby;* Emily Barnard's *Blanche;* Maud Smith's *Marjory Daw;* Maud Naftel's *Green Grow the Rushes;* Lady Lindsay's *Red Roses;* Mrs. Cecil Lawson's *Spring Blossoms;* Eloise Stannard's *Alicants;* and Emma Walter's *Roses and Other Flowers.* Two peasant children create a successful combination in Miss Beresford's *Impromptu Loving Cup,* and Mary Waller's *Philip, Younger Son of Captain Noble, C.B.* is "honestly and largely treated." Other works worth "enthusiastic approval" are *Peggy* by Kate Perugini; *The Water Babies* illustration by Katherine Bywater; portraits by Annie L. Robinson; *Red Rose in White Rose Garden* and *The Young Widow* by Madame Schwartz; *Portrait of a Lady* by Blanche Jenkins; *Orchids* by Helen Thornycroft; *View on the Mole* by Bessie Spiers, and *A Bit of Monmouthshire* by Charlotte Spiers. Other artists who

are well known and have works in this exhibit are Madame Bisschop, Mrs. Val Bromley, the Marchioness of Waterford, Louise Jopling, Hilda Montalba, and Clara Montalba.

764. "Art in May." *Magazine of Art* (1887): xxix-xxxii.

Helen Allingham exhibits on "one small canvas in her characteristic style" and Clara Montalba sends two very good pictures, *Old Mill, Zaandam* and *Cannon Street Bridge* to the exhibition of the Royal Society of Painters in Watercolours. At the Royal Hibernian Academy in Dublin, the talented Sarah Purser has two portraits, *Miss Wynne* and *Dr. Salmon of Trinity*. The Irish Fine Arts Society exhibition is even better than usual, and most of the works are by women. Deserving of special mention, even among so much excellence, are *Marches of the Tideway* by Fanny Currey; *Thief on the Premises* by Helen O'Hara; Sophia Holmes' *Christmas Roses; Lonely Mere* by Miss Barton; and works by Marianne Stokes, Mrs. Naftel, and Mrs. Robinson.

765. "Art in July." *Magazine of Art* (1887): xxxvii-xl.

Cassell and Co., publishers, are exhibiting black and white drawings and engravings which illustrate some of their publications. Dorothy Tennant's "charming sketches of street Arabs" are "among the most interesting."

766. "Art in June." *Magazine of Art* (1887): xxxiii-xxxvi.

The Fine Art Society on Bond Street features an exhibition of Helen Allingham's work, titled *In the Country*. Allingham celebrates the beauties of the English countryside and its gardens, lanes and houses. Her treatment of the subject is delicate and charming; the overall effect is one of perfection. *Sandhills Common; Nightjar Lane; Banacle from Gray's Wood* and *Milking* are fine examples of her work. The Surrey landscape is exactly captured in *Under Hindhead*. The best of the exhibition is probably *Three Studies*. The Liverpool Jubilee Exhibition features several important paintings by Elizabeth Thompson Butler in its special section of battle scenes. Also to be seen is Jane Benham Hay's *A Florentine Procession*.

767. "Current Art. IV." *Magazine of Art* (1887): 376-384.

Henrietta Rae's Academy exhibition, *A Naiad*, is graceful of line and agreeable in color; her *Eurydice Sinking Back to Hades* is technically as good, but lacks the drama. Theodora Noyes' *Noonday* is weak in modeling but does well with drawing and color, and the landscape and figures compliment each other. In the watercolor section, Anna Alma-Tadema's *The Garden Studio* is complicated and technically excellent; it is the best watercolor in the exhibition. *The Eleventh of August* by Kate Hayllar is a "firm and harmonious" still life. Helen Thornycroft's *Peonies* deserve mention. Mrs. Lawson's *Azaleas* has merit, as do works by Miss Cook and Edith A. Stock. Hilda Montalba's pastel, *On Campden Hill* is one of the best of a mediocre class.

768. Forbes-Robertson, John. "Art at the Manchester Jubilee Exhibition." *Magazine of Art* (1887): 281-283.

   The collection of living masters of the Manchester Fine Arts exhibition includes Elizabeth Thompson Butler's *Connaught Rangers* and *Return from the Balaclava Charge*.

769. Philips, Claude. "The Americans at the Salon." *Magazine of Art* (1887): 421-426.

   The American artist, Elizabeth J. Gardener, imitates the style of one of her French art teachers just as well as Dorothy Tennant imitates her own teacher, M. Heener.

770. "Mrs. Anna Lea Merritt's Portraits and Pictures." *The Studio* (February 1887): 128-129.

   Most of Anna Lea Merritt's work exhibited at the Associated Artists consists of portraits. She is especially good at capturing the characters of children, but her portrait of James Russell Lowell has attracted much deserved admiration. She handles the two reds of his doctoral gown with a deep understanding of color and technique, and shows in Lowell's face all the character of a great poet and philosopher. *Camilla*, a life sized nude, is decidedly English in character. *St. Cecilia*, a picture in progress, is not in the exhibition, but deserves mention for its naturalness and sweetness. A painting of a bound Iphigenia waiting to be sacrificed is also unfinished and is intended for the Royal Academy exhibition. The picture excels in color and composition, avoids morbidity and projects a tone of optimism. Merritt's painting is criticized for its femininity and its English quality. It is true that her work lacks the firmness developed by years of hard study and struggle, but her sense of color is flawless and if she expresses her femininity there is certainly no harm done. Influences of other artists have no place in her paintings, which express "a strong individuality working out its problems in its own way."

771. "Chronicle of Art. Exhibitions of the Month." *Magazine of Art* (1888): viii.

The Maclean Gallery exhibits Rosa Bonheur's superb *Head of a Lioness*, a work so lifelike that it almost requires "iron bars...across the frame for the safety of the spectator." It is all the more remarkable that Bonheur should have produced one of her finest works at the age of sixty.

772. "Chronicle of Art. Exhibitions of the Month." *Magazine of Art* (1888): xxii-xxiii.

Almost a hundred drawings on exhibition at the Maclean Gallery show Clara Montalba's continued progress. Her best drawings are of Venice, and seen as a whole, her work can be appreciated more than has been previously possible. Work by Kate Macaulay and Miss Davidson help to raise the quality of the Nineteenth-Century Art Society exhibition.

773. "The Chronicle of Art. Exhibitions of the Month." *Magazine of Art* (1888): xxx-xxxi.

The Society of Lady Artists' exhibition is better than in previous years. Watercolors by Mrs. Naftel, Maud Naftel, Anna Lea Merritt, Alice Squire, Miss Spiers, Louise Rayner, Miss Kingdon, and Alice Havers "leaven the mass of mediocrity in the five hundred frames that cover the walls." Clara Montalba's *Dordrecht* and Hilda Montalba's *Tending the Rialto Shrine, Venice*, are both excellent works. Neither of the Montalbas is a member of the Society of Lady Artists. The exhibition as a whole makes the statement that lady artists express themselves better in watercolor than in oil. The Graves Gallery has an exhibition of Elizabeth Thompson Butler's best known paintings and some of her watercolor pictures of Egypt. The St. George Gallery has an exhibition of Irish pictures and sketches by Jane Inglis.

774. "Chronicle of Art. The Melbourne Art Gallery." *Magazine of Art* (1888): iii.

The Melbourne Art Gallery's grey-tinted walls admirably show off the red uniforms of the soldiers in Elizabeth Thompson Butler's *Quatre Bras*.

775. "Current Art." *Magazine of Art* (1888): 296-303.

Of the medieval-style painting tradition at the Grosvenor, only Evelyn Pickering and a few others remain. The trend at the Grosvenor is toward progress; this year the landscape selection is good, and Miss Montalba's exhibition is meritorious. At the New Gallery, Helen Hatton's portrait *Miss Mary Moore* is pleasing and promising. At the Royal Institute, Gertrude Hammond exhibits *Reverie*, which "contains some honest, careful work." Clara Montalba has freed herself from the canals of Venice and offers an excellent and most welcome change in *A Study, Ramsgate* and *Garden of the Hespirides, Cannes.* Both pictures can be seen in Pall Mall at the exhibition of the Old Water Colour Society. Helen Allingham sends a picture of two young women talking together over a wall.

776. "Monthly Record of American Art." *Magazine of Art* (1888): xxviii.
  The Union League Club of New York City has an exhibition of work by American women etchers. Anna Lea Merritt's method is "graceful, but rather weak."

777. "Monthly Record of American Art." *Magazine of Art* (1888): xxxvi.
  New York's Yandell Gallery has in its summer exhibition an interesting variety of modern and older works by American and European artists. Among the least admirable works is Anna Lea Merritt's *Portrait of Miss Marquand*, which is "pretentious" and "superficially effective."

778. Forbes-Robertson, John. "The City Art Gallery of Manchester." *Magazine of Art* (1888): 211-216.
  Henriette Browne is one of the foreign painters represented in the permanent collection of the City of Manchester. Browne has been a favorite of British art lovers since she exhibited here in 1862 at the International Exhibition. Her *Monk of the Brotherhood of Christian Instructors* was donated to the Manchester Gallery by R. N. Philips.

779. "Brighton Exhibition of Women's Arts and Industries." *Englishwoman's Review* 20, no. 91 (1889): 182-183.
  So successful was the 1887 Exhibition of Women's Arts and Industries that another one will be held at Brighton this year. There will be prizes for work by students in art schools, and for professional artists in such diverse areas as needlework, metalwork, wall decorations, titles, pottery, and furnishings.

780. "Chronicle of Art. The New Art Gallery at Leeds." *Magazine of Art* (1889): vi.
  A much-needed art gallery has been opened at a cost of £10,000; an exhibit of famous works loaned by private owners comprises the first exhibit. Elizabeth Thompson Butler's *Scotland Forever!* donated by Walter Harding, is the start of the gallery's permanent collection.

781. "The Chronicle of Art. Recent Exhibitions." *Magazine of Art* (1889): xxi-xxiii.

> The Bewick Club is one of the most successful art societies with very good exhibitions, the most recent of which features pictures by Louise Jopling-Rowe and Clara Montalba.

782. "The Chronicle of Art. Exhibitions of the Month." *Magazine of Art* (1889): xxix-xxxi.

> The Society of Lady Artists is an institution with "no school, no creed" and its only distinction lies in the fact that all of its exhibitors are female. Since women have always received fair treatment from galleries and societies, there is no reason for a female society, especially since the most recent exhibition, its thirty-fourth, has little to justify it. Clara Montalba exhibits a "dashing" landscape titled *Old Watchtower, Amsterdam*, and Hilda Montalba has two good sketches. *In the Orchard* by Bertha Newcombe is excellent but unfortunately too much influenced by the Newlyn School. Other works worthy of attention are *Free Seats* by Miss Kindon, drawings by Miss Naftel, Mrs. Naftel, and Florence Pash.

783. "Chronicle of Art. Art in November. Pastels at the Grosvenor Gallery." *Magazine of Art* (1889): v-viii.

> Elizabeth Armstrong Forbes sends *Hide and Seek*, a picture consistent with the qualities that distinguish her work.

784. "Current Art." *Magazine of Art* (1889): 120-124.

> Louise Jopling's portrait exhibit at the Institute of Painters in Oil Colours must be mentioned. At the Royal Society of Painters in Water Colours exhibition, nine drawings by Clara Montalba of the lakes and coast of Sweden indicate that she has made a timely escape from her usual Venice and Holland. All but one of her drawings, *The Market Place, Stockholm*, are "uncompromisingly grey" but her work demonstrates superior refinement and "subtle appreciation for atmospheric effect." In the landscapes, Helen Allingham's *Surrey Scene* is up to her usual standards. Maud Naftel has a "fresh little drawing" inscribed "the fields breathe sweet, the daisies kiss our feet."

785. "Exhibitions of the Month." *Magazine of Art* (1889): xxxiv- xxxv.

> Lefévre's Gallery features a painting of cattle by Rosa Bonheur. The animals are exceptional, but the landscape is unimaginative and the colors are dull. A collection of Helen Allingham's water colors titled "On the Surrey Border" has been at the Fine Arts Society Gallery. Allingham's pictures of cottages, flowers and pastoral scenes, including *Hillside*

Cottage; The End of the Day; and *Blackberrying,* display her talents with drawing and color, but her failure to explore other subjects leads to a sameness, which puts a limit on her abilities. Bertha Patmore's exhibit of neatly and exquisitely-rendered sketches of "butterflies, dormice, and feathers" and some title-page illustrations in fourteenth-century style are a triumph of decorative skill and taste.

786. "Lady Artists at the Royal Institute of Painters in Water Colours." *Englishwoman's Review* 20 (1889): 181.

Flowers are a favorite subject among the 119 female exhibitors; however, Louise Rayner and E. D'Oyley Rowe have contributed careful architectural studies. Many exhibits worthy of mention cannot all be named here, but Mrs. Duffield's *Roses* and Marian Chase's *In the Orchid House* are noteworthy. Some exhibits are already sold, including Miss Youngman's *The Queen of Flowers* and Edith Berkeley's *Gathering Wild Flowers.*

787. "Liverpool Autumn Exhibition." *Magazine of Art* (1889): xlvi.

Among over 600 water colors on exhibition, works by Marie Spartali Stillman number among the "leading attractions."

788. Didbin, E. Rimbault. "The Liverpool Corporation Collection. The Walker Art Gallery. II." *Magazine of Art* (1889): 50-56.

Louisa Starr's *Sintram* and Sophie Anderson's *Elaine* illustrate poetical subjects; Marie Spartali Stillman's exhibit numbers among the important landscapes.

789. "Chronicle of Art. Art in March. Recent Exhibitions." *Magazine of Art* (1890): xxi-xxiv.

The Royal Hibernian Academy exhibition in Dublin contains some exceptionally good portraits, including *Dorothy Nutting* by Mary Lemon Fowler.

790. "Chronicle of Art. Art in May. Recent Exhibitions." *Magazine of Art* (1890): xxix-xxxii.

Helen Law and Rose MacKay are among the artists whose work deserves a better gallery than the dark recesses of Humphrey's Mansions where the English Art Club has chosen to have its exhibition. Cassell's eighth Black-and-White Exhibition will feature work by many well-known artists, including Mary L. Gow, Alice Havers, and Dorothy Tennant.

791. "Chronicle of Art. Art in June. The Grosvenor and the New Galleries."
Magazine of Art. (1890): xxxiii-xxxvi.

Recently-issued statistics for the exhibitions at the Grosvenor and New
Galleries reveal that of the 283 artists exhibiting at the Grosvenor,
thirty-seven were women; of 164 artists exhibiting at the New Gallery,
twenty-one were women. Of artists exhibiting in both galleries, twenty-five
were women.

792. "Chronicle of Art. Art in June. Exhibitions." *Magazine of Art* (1890):
xxxiii-xxxvi.

Henriette Ronner's exhibition of paintings and drawings of kittens,
cats, and dogs at the Fine Art Society's Galleries is well worth visiting and
will be the subject of an article in this publication. Ronner's work contains
better "virility of execution" than animal paintings by Rosa Bonheur.

793. "Current Art." *Magazine of Art* (1890): 109-114.

The Royal Society of British Artists exhibition includes Hilda
Montalba's decorative paintings of Provence. Flora Reid's picture,
Grandfather, is reminiscent in style of that early work of J. R. Reid, but
lacks the garish colors that spoil his later painting. Helen Cridland's
unpleasant subject, a faithful dog with a drunken master, titled *Hero
Worship*, is energetically and technically exceptional and promises well for
Cridland's future in art. At the Royal Society of Painters in Water Colours
exhibition, Clara Montalba's sketches, especially *Torpedo Boats Entering
Portsmouth Harbour* are artistic and intelligent. Helen Allingham's
landscapes number among the "characteristic drawings." At the Institute
of Painters in Oil Colours, Marianne Stokes' study of a nude child sitting
by the fire is titled *Waiting for Santa Claus* and is an improvement over
her last year's academy picture.

794. Armstrong, Walter. "Current Art: The Grosvenor Gallery." *Magazine of Art*
(1890): 325-328.

Marianne Stokes has painted a madonna and child using the child as
a light source in the tradition of Rembrandt and others. *Light of Light* has
its own kind of originality and Stokes' treatment is sure.

Reproductions (b/w etching):
Stokes, Marianne: *Light of Light*.

795. Spielmannn, M. H. "Current Art. The Royal Academy--II." *Magazine of Art*
(1890): 253-260.

Henrietta Rae Normand's *Ophelia: "There's Rue for You"* is a "fairly novel version of the often-painted heroine." Elizabeth Armstrong Forbes' *Mignon* is worthy of her good reputation.

796. ---. "Current Art. The New Gallery." *Magazine of Art* (1890): 304-311.

In spite of its exalted reputation, the New Gallery has not achieved its usual sublimity in this year's exhibition. Still, the New Gallery's worst sets the standards for current art in Great Britain. Dorothy Tennant and Miss Alma-Tadema send pictures that justify their reputations. Laura Alma-Tadema's *Battledore and Shuttlecock* is "charming," but not exceptional. Among the portraits, Annie Swynnerton's *Sons of W. Herringham, Esq.* shows the influence of the Pre-Raphaelites. Blanche Jenkin's portrait of a little girl almost measures up to her Royal Academy painting.

797. "Exhibition of Mrs. Anna Lea Merritt's Portraits and Pictures." *The Studio* 10 (8 February 1890): 101.

Haseltine's Gallery in Philadelphia exhibits eight fine portraits, two subject paintings, and several etchings by Anna Lea Merritt. *Love Shut Out* [sic], a picture of a boy against a bolted door, is well drawn and truly colored, and will probably find popularity as an etching. Other etchings are *Eve* and *Irish Peasants Waiting for Mass.* Her portrait of Henry James presents its sitter in a more agreeable light than do his cynical literary works. The exhibit also features a portrait of Mrs. Holman Hunt and of Miss Marion Lea.

798. "The Royal Academy: First Notice." *London Times* (3 May 1890): 12.

Anna Lea Merritt's *Love Locked Out* is a praiseworthy work that seems to have been influenced by the style of George Watts.

799. Philips, Claude. "The Summer Exhibitions at Home and Abroad. II--The Royal Academy, the Grosvenor, and the New Gallery." *Art Journal* 10, no. 5 (June 1890): 161-174.

Evelyn Pickering de Morgan's *Medea* is one of the works of the Pre-Raphaelite School represented at the New Gallery. The picture tries to make up in strangeness what it fails to achieve in significance. Marie Spartali Stillman should know, as a follower of Rossetti, that she should not attempt subjects such as *The First Meeting of Dante and Beatrice* unless she can summon the measure of passion that the subjects and the Pre-Raphaelite school require. Laura Alma-Tadema's picture, *Battledore and Shuttlecock*, is her best work yet. Two little girls play while another little girl holding a baby watches them. The picture is rendered in delicate whites and greys with a neoclassical setting. Elizabeth Thompson Butler's Royal Academy picture, *Evicted*, is melodramatic, theatrical, and self-conscious. Grubby and energetic children play in Dorothy Tennant's New Gallery picture, *Street Arabs at Play*. The children are drawn very well, but the background is much less realistic. Marianne Stokes uses French models and evinces French influence in *Light of Light*, her Royal Academy picture that lacks the emotion essential for a representation of the infant Jesus and his devoted mother. Stokes' style does contain "much breadth."

800. "The Chronicle of Art. Art in October. Exhibitions." *Magazine of Art* (1891): i-iv.

    The Walker Gallery in Liverpool contains over a thousand paintings of modern artists. Henrietta Rae's *Ophelia* is one of four pictures selected to be part of the gallery's permanent collection. Emma Magnus' portrait of *Mr. Alderman Mark* in the Manchester Exhibition is not remarkable.

801. "The Chronicle of Art. Art in November. Exhibitions." *Magazine of Art* (1891): v-viii.

    The work of students at the Royal Female School of Art does credit to the teachers, who, however, should allow more freedom of expression. A chromo-lithographic studio offers works of graduates for sale.

802. "The Chronicle of Art. Art in January. Recent Exhibitions." *Magazine of Art* (1891): xiii-xvi.

    Mary Ann Stokes' portrait *Edelweiss* and Elizabeth Forbes' picture *The Witch* are among the most successful pictures by Newlyn painters at Dowdeswells' Gallery.

803. "The Chronicle of Art. Art in May. Recent Exhibitions." *Magazine of Art* (1891): xxix-xxxii.

    Clara Montalba's sketches are among the works that never change or vary the yearly exhibitions of the Royal Academy of Painters in Water-Colours.

804. "The Chronicle of Art. Art in June. Exhibitions." *Magazine of Art* (1891): xxxiii-xxxvi.

    Forming societies for works according to style and practice makes sense, but there is little reason to have a society founded strictly on gender, since the Royal Academy and other societies treat works by women with respect according to their due. The exhibition of the Society of Lady Artists at the Egyptian Gallery contains mostly mediocre works, since most competent female artists exhibit "in a more open field." Florence Pash's painting, *Lamplight,* is the best in the exhibition; Patty Townsend's sketches show more strength than can generally be seen in this exhibit.

805. Propert, J. Lumsden. "The English School of Miniature Art. With Special Reference to the Exhibition at the Burlington Fine Arts Club. From William Wood...to the Present Time." *Magazine of Art* (1891): 345-349.

Anne Folson Mee first exhibited a miniature portrait at the Royal Academy in 1815, but by the time of her death in 1851 miniatures were no longer fashionable. Although she is given credit for a miniature painting of the celebrated Emma Lyon Hamilton, it is doubtful that the work is correctly titled, since Hamilton died the same year Mee began exhibiting.

Reproductions (b/w):

Mee, Anna Foldsone: *Lady Hamilton* (so called).

806. Spielmann, M. H. "Current Art. The Royal Academy, 1891--II." *Magazine of Art* (1891): 253-263.

For the most part, this year's Royal Academy exhibition is over-crowded and confusing. A few pictures contribute to its success, including works by Henrietta Rae Normand. Annie L. Swynnerton's *Cupid and Psyche* lacks idealism, but excels in the rendering of flesh tones and "actually quivers with the pulsations of life." Elizabeth A. Armstrong Forbes' religious painting, *Hail, Mary!* displays the influence of the Munich School.

807. Wedmore, Frederick. "Current Art." *Magazine of Art* (1891): 109-114.

Among the scenes at the gallery in Pall Mall East can be seen Miss Montalba's picture of Venice in "pink and orange and lemon-greens."

808. "The Chronicle of Art. Art in March. Exhibitions." *Magazine of Art* (March 1891): xxi-xxiv.

Kate Greenaway and Hugh Thomson's work exhibited at the Fine Art Society makes up one of the best exhibitions of the season.

809. Elliot, Maude Howe ed. *Art and Handicraft in the Woman's Building of the World's Columbian Exposition, Chicago, 1893.* Paris and New York: Goupil and Co., 1893.

Essays by a variety of authors treat everything about women's activities from architecture to cottage industries, and from arts to science. Kate

Dickens Perugini's oil painting *Molly's Ball Dress* is the frontispiece for Edna Cheney's chapter on "Evolution of Women's Education in the United States" and a photo of a nude sculpture of *Diana* faces E. Crawford's chapter, "Great Britain--Art." Crawford begins with a summary of Englishwomen's long and distinguished history in the art world, and follows with a review of some of the forty-five women representing British artists at this American exposition. Laura Alma-Tadema, Marie and Lena Stillman, Kate Greenaway, and Mrs. G. Watts are mentioned. Annie Swynnerton's murals celebrating women in nursing, and Anna Lea Merritt's murals celebrating women's handicrafts and women's education decorate the vestibule of the Women's Building. Clara Montalba exhibits a picture of the poet Browning's palace in Venice; Hilda Montalba has sent *Market Woman of Dordrecht*, exhibited last year at the Royal Academy. Alice Grant and Kate Perugini send charming portraits of children; Helen Allingham's *The Sussex Cottage,* and Emmie Stewart Wood's landscape have been much admired. *Eurydice Sinking back into Hades* is a large, dramatic canvas by Henrietta Rae. E. Crawford's large watercolor of a Roman nun, a peasant woman, and a child uses new colors, especially reds, to create the striking picture exhibited in the Hall of Honor.

810. Merrill, J. S. ed. *Art Clippings from the Pen of Walter Cranston Larned and other Art Critics at the Fair*. United States: J. S. Merrill, 1893.

Under the heading "Merritt, Mrs. Anna Lee [sic], England," the reviewer marvels at the prominence of women and their works in the Chicago Exhibition. The "great army" of female artists is evidence that "If we are not yet in the full blaze of the woman's century we ...[have] emerged from the mists of its dawn." Merritt's mural is indicative of her great talent. The reviewer hopes she will send her exemplary portrait of *Mrs. Reginald De Koven. Love Locked Out* is in the exhibition.

811. Miller, Florence Fenwick. "Art in the Women's Section of the Chicago Exhibition." *The Art Journal (U.S.A.)* (1893): xiii-xvi.

Although the Women's Building at the 1893 world fair was designed by a woman and its construction supervised by a female architect, lack of funds made it disappointingly small, even stunted, when compared to large and lavish structures built for other exhibits. Still, it is a satisfaction to have a special building to house work by women. Anna Lea Merritt and Annie Swynnerton painted three entrance vestibule murals in England without knowing the inadequate size of the wall on which their canvasses would be displayed. Merritt's subject, *Needlework*, and Swynnerton's *Florence Nightingale in the Crimea* were designed to be viewed at a much greater distance than is possible in this space. While the best female artists preferred to exhibit in the general Fine Art category of male painters, some fine paintings by Englishwomen can still be seen in the Women's Building. Queen Victoria has sent landscapes and a few portraits of pets. Henrietta Rae's *Eurydice* is by far the most important piece in the exhibit. The largest painting is Elizabeth Thompson Butler's *To the Front*, which is somewhat affected; Alice Grant's *A Baby* shows promise; Clara Montalba's Venetian scene is lively and colorful; and Helen Allingham's *Sussex Cottage* is an example of her "sweet style." The work by English women is far behind what is exhibited by women from other countries.

Reproductions (b/w):

Allingham, Helen: *A Sussex Cottage*

Grant, Alice: *A Baby*

Merritt, Anna Lea: sketch of *Needlework*

Montalba, Clara: *Venice*

Rae, Henrietta, Rae: *Eurydice Caught* [sic] *Back to Hades.*

812. Henrotin, Ellen M. "An Outsider's View of the Women's Exhibit." *The Cosmopolitan* XV, no. 5 (September 1893): 560-566.

The women's exhibit at the Columbian exposition at the Philadelphia World's Fair is not only an international display of the works of female minds and hands, it is a statement of the advances women are making in the labor market and of their increasing importance in all phases of the arts. The Women's Building features murals by noted female artists; Anna Lea Merritt's entrance in the Women's Building will be judged on an equal basis with those of men, and the judges in the liberal arts include women.

813. Jopeslade, R. "An Australian Quartette." *The Magazine of Art* XVII (1895): 396.

The dealer engaged in engraving some of Henrietta Rae's paintings has put together an exhibit of her works which includes *Psyche at the Court of Venus*. This painting will look better in black and white because it will lose its "too sugary colour."

814. H. H. R. "Some Annual Exhibitions." *Englishwoman's Review* 28 (1897): 214-217.

Exhibitions were monotonous this year with the exception of Lucy Kemp-Welch's *Colt Hunting in New Forest* at Burlington House. This picture, the best of its kind since Landseer, has been chosen by trustees of the Chantrey Bequest and thus will be on permanent public display. Elizabeth Thompson Butler's *Steady the Drums and Fifes* shares honors with Welch's painting, although it is of a much different theme. The scene is depicted with such care for form, composition and detail that the tension and drama of war are made remarkably real. Annie Swynnerton, who is recognized as an excellent portrait painter, is exhibiting two landscapes that are proof of additional talents. A list of less successful paintings include Ursula Wood's *Children with a Puppy*, in which modern pessimism seems to have infected the very babies. Elizabeth Stanhope Forbes' *A Dream Princess* is "extremely ugly," and Laura Alma-Tadema's exhibit is spoiled by the figure's oversized hands.

815. "The New Gallery Summer Exhibition." *Art Journal* (1899): 185-188.

Laura Alma-Tadema's *Great Reward* possesses charm and realism. Miss Alma-Tadema has contributed a watercolor, *The Closing Door*, depicting, in subdued grey tones, an anxious woman sitting alone. Mr. Alma-Tadema has painted a charming portrait of a mother and daughter.

816. Wright, Melville E. "Philadelphia Art Exhibition." *Brush and Pencil* VII, no. 5 (February 1901): 257-276.

Women are well-represented at the seventieth annual exhibition of contemporary American artists at the Pennsylvania Academy of the Fine Arts. Anna Lea Merritt's *I Will Give You Rest* exemplifies the superior quality of the works on exhibition.

Reproduction (b/w):

Merritt, Anna Lea: *I Will Give You Rest.*

817. Bateman, Arthur Z. "The Fine Arts in Philadelphia." *Brush and Pencil* IX, no. 5 (February 1902): 318-319.

The annual exhibition of the Academy of Fine Arts in Philadelphia is the third oldest in the world, after the English Royal Academy and Salon of Paris. Its rigorous standards result in a smaller exhibition of works of exceptional quality. Among the portraits of famous people by famous artists (Celia Beau has painted Mrs. Stokes, Anna Klumpke exhibits a portrait of Rosa Bonheur) is Anna Lea Merritt's *Grandmother's Boa*, a portrait of a little girl that captures the essence of childish simplicity and may be the best picture in the gallery.

Reproductions (b/w):

Merritt, Anna Lea: *Grandmother's Boa.*

818. *Lady Alma-Tadema Memorial Exhibition: 1910.* London: Women's Printing Society, Ltd., 1910.

Laura Epps was a close friend of Catherine Madox Brown, studied art at the British Museum, and married Lawrence Alma-Tadema when she was nineteen. She is well known for her paintings of Dutch scenes, especially those containing children and babies. Her pictures are always fresh, different and lively; her landscapes are original and show her individuality in their perspective, light and detail. This exhibition catalogue contains a list of 130 works by and about her.

Reproductions (b/w):

Alma-Tadema, Laura: *Sigh No More Ladies; Love's Beginning; Trespassers; Always Welcome; Soon Ready; Looking Out o' Window; A Knock at the Door; Bright be Thy Noon; Fireside Fancies; Well Employed; The New Book; Love at the Mirror; Airs and Graces; A Mother's Pride*

Alma-Tadema, Laurence: *Portrait of Lady Alma-Tadema.*

819. Gibbs, Josephine. "Famous Women." *Art Digest* 18 (15 November 1943): 6.

The Feigl Gallery on Madison Avenue in New York City features an exhibition titled "Famous Women Painters" covering a range of 300 years and several centuries. Rosa Bonheur's small study of a cow is a remarkable contrast to her dramatic *Horse Fair*.

820. Nunn, Pamela Gerrish. "Rebecca Solomon." In *Solomon: A Family of Painters*, 19-23, 59-64. London: Geffrys Museum, 1965.

Rebecca Solomon's paintings of heterosexual couples seem to fit solidly into Victorian conventions of the courtship genre, but close examination reveals that Solomon, who never married, frequently presents, especially in her mature stages, less facile reading than is usual in similar pictures by her contemporaries. *The Governess*, one of her best-known works, conveys a message of human values through subtle facial expressions. (These subtleties were lost in an engraving of this painting used to illustrate Mrs. Cox's story "The Keepsake.") *Reading for Pluck* and *Reading for Honours* are subtle comments on male, rather than female morality. The animosity with which contemporary reviewers reacted to it indicates a personal rather than an artistic evaluation. The catalogue as a whole provides valuable background on the Solomon family as well as on the social and artistic position of Jews in England and in the English art world.

Reproductions (col):

Solomon, Rebecca: *The Governess*

Reproductions (b/w):

Solomon, Rebecca: *A Fashionable Couple; Reading for Pluck; Reading for Honours; The Governess.*

821. M. Newman Ltd. "A Selection of Paintings from our Exhibition of 19th Century Life." *Conoisseur* 158 (March 1965): xiv-xv.

An advertisement for an "Illustrated Catalogue...sold in aid of The Save the Children...and Youth Aliyah" features Gertrude Martineau's *The Broken Saucer* and Sophie Anderson's *Sweet Dreams.*

Reproductions (b/w):

Anderson, Sophie: *Sweet Dreams*

Martineau, Gertrude: *The Broken Saucer.*

822. *Women: A Historical Survey of Works by Women Artists.* Raleigh, N.C.: Salem Fine Arts Center and North Carolina Museum of Art, 1972.

Sophie Anderson's playful treatment of two girls and a dog, titled *Guess Again*, represents art by nineteenth-century British women.

Reproductions (b/w):

Anderson, Sophie: *Guess Again.*

823. Graves, Algernon. *The Royal Academy of Arts: A Complete Dictionary of Contributors and Their Work from Its Foundation in 1769 to 1904.* 1905-1906. Reprint. New York: Lenox Hill, 1972.

An alphabetical listing of Royal Academy contributors includes the year of each exhibit, its title, and the artist's address. Female exhibitors are listed by first and last name whenever possible. More often only the last name and the initials are given, and some women are listed by Mrs. and their husband's name, so that many female contributors remain virtually anonymous.

824. Bradshaw, Maurice. *Royal Society of British Artists: Members Exhibiting 1824-1892.* Leigh-on-Sea: F. Lewis, 1973.

Miss C. Adams exhibited architectural watercolors at the Royal Society of British Artists exhibitions in 1843 and 1844. Adams was "not listed as member" but her "name appears in heavy type" in the exhibition catalogue. Miss Heaphy exhibited portraits in 1824, was not on the members' list in the catalogue, but exhibited in 1825 after dropping her membership.

825. Findlay, Michael A. "Forbes Saves the Queen." *Arts Magazine* , no. 47 (February 1973): 26-30.

An exhibit titled "Victorian Painting, the Royal Academy 1837-1901, Revisited," shown at Princeton University, reflects the undergraduate project of Christopher Forbes, who, with the help of his art-collecting father, set out to acquire works by prominent Victorian artists, with the aim of giving them a place in a modern art world which has studiously ignored them. Findlay's account of Forbes' diligence, scholarship, imagination, insight and persistence in acquiring his collection is fascinating reading; less valuable are the rather breezy inaccuracies in the reviewer's summary of all Victorian art. Sophie Anderson's *Guess Again* is dismissed as "a lapse of taste," presumably because it is reproduced on the tops of chocolate boxes. Edith Hayllar's name is misspelled in the text, which ignores her art to speculate on the relationship of the four women and two men in her household. Students of Elizabeth Siddall will be surprised to learn that she died shortly after Millais' completion of *Ophelia* of pneumonia contracted from posing in the bathtub. One wishes Christopher Forbes had written this review.

Reproductions (b/w):

Hayllar, Edith: *A Summer Shower*.

826. Bradshaw, Maurice. *Royal Society of British Artists: Members Exhibiting 1893-1910*. Leigh-on-Sea: F. Lewis, 1975.

Members of the Royal Society of British Artists are listed alphabetically with address, title of painting, exhibition date, and sales amount.

827. Arts Council of Britain. *Great Victorian Pictures: Their Paths to Fame. An Arts Council Exhibition*. London: The Council, 1978.

Elizabeth Thompson Butler's *The Roll Call* and *Scotland Forever!*, Henrietta Ward's *Palissy the Potter*, and Henrietta Rae Normand's *Psyche Before the Throne of Venus* are included in the collection of paintings that drew enthusiastic responses from art-loving Victorians. Catalogue listings include modern commentary, a history of sales and exhibits, and excerpts from contemporary reviews.

Reproductions (b/w):

Butler, Elizabeth Thompson: *The Roll Call; Scotland Forever!*

Normand, Henrietta Rae: *Psyche Before the Throne of Venus*

Ward, Henrietta: *Palissy the Potter*.

828. Weimann, Jeanne Madeline. *The Fair Women*. Chicago: Academy Chicago, 1981.

An attempt to secure quality works by established artists for the Women's Building at the Columbian Exposition in Chicago in 1892 was only partly successful, mostly because female artists were divided on the subject of whether women should exhibit on their own turf or in mixed exhibits on equal footing with the men. Queen Victoria sent paintings of family dogs. Elizabeth Thompson Butler's *To the Front* was prominently exhibited in the rotunda. An exhibit titled "Etchings and Dry Point by Artists Now Living. English School" contained seventeen pieces. Anna Lee [sic] Merritt's etching, *Ophelia*, appears under the heading "American School."

829. Nunn, Pamela Gerrish. *Women Artists in the Nineteenth-Century. The Women's Art Show 1550-1970*. Nottingham Castle Museum: 1982.

The progress of women in the nineteenth century who wanted to be artists is remarkable, if hard won. At the beginning of Victoria's reign, only Margaret Carpenter had any degree of reputation. By the end of the nineteenth century several art schools, including the Royal Academy schools, were available to women, and women were pushing for further opportunities. Their progress was, and still is, impeded by pressure to conform to male standards in a male-defined world, but a significant number of women made a notable impact and deserve further study and inclusion into the study of art history.

Reproductions (b/w):
Anderson, Sophie: *Wait for Me*
Angell, Helen: *Azaleas*
Blunden, Anna: *The Seamstress*
Bodichon, Barbara: *Hastings Beach with Fishing Boats*
Bonheur, Rosa: *The Horse Fair*
Boyce, Joanna: *The Heather Gatherer, Hind Head*
Brett, Rosa: *The Old House at Farleigh*
Brown, Catherine Madox: *Ford Madox Brown*
Browne, Henrietta: *A Nun*
Brownlow, Emma King: *Riverside at Quimper*
Bunce, Kate: *The Chance Meeting*
Butler, Elizabeth Thompson: *Scotland Forever!*
Carpenter, Margaret: *A Spring Nosegay*
Dacre, Susan Isabel: *Italian Women in Church*
De Morgan, Evelyn: *Medea*
 Gillies, Margaret: *Trust*
Greenaway, Kate: *Mother Goose, or Old Nursery Rhymes*
Havers, Alice: *Mary Kept All These Things and Pondered Them*
Hayllar, Mary: *Lawn Tennis Season*

Jopling, Louise: *Phyllis*

King, Jessie M: *The Dance of the White Rose*

Macgregor, Jessie: *In the Reign of Terror*

McIan, Fanny: *After the Battle of Prestonpans*

Mackintosh, Margaret MacDonald: *Winter*

MacNair, Frances MacDonald: *Autumn*

Merritt, Anna Lea: *War*

Montalba, Clara: *Two Venetian Scenes*

Mutrie, Annie: *Flowers*

Mutrie, Martha: *Roses*

Nasmyth, Jane: *View of Strathearn*

Osborn, Emily Mary: *For the Last Time*

Pope, Clara Maria: *Composition of Flowers, in the Vase Presented to Edmund Kean*

Rae, Henrietta: *Death of Procris*

Rosenburg, Frances: *Flower; Study of Flowers in a Vase, with a Bird's Nest*

Sandys, Emma: *Portrait Study of a Lady in a Yellow Dress*

Setchell, Sarah: *The Momentous Question*

Severn, Mary: *Self-Portrait*

Sharples, Rolinda: *Village Gossips*

Siddall, Elizabeth: *Clerk Saunders*

Solomon, Rebecca: *The Mouse*

Spilsbury, Maria Taylor: *Confusion, or the Nursery in the Kitchen*

Stanhope-Forbes, Elizabeth: *The Edge of the Woods*

Stannard, Eloise: *Overturned Basket with Raspberries, White Currants and Roses*

Stannard, Emily: *Flowers in a Vase*

Stillman, Marie Spartali: *Messr Ansaldo Showing Diavola His Enchanted Garden*

Starr, Louisa: *Brian Hodgson*

Withers, Augusta Innes: *Botanical Drawing, Epidendrum Stamfordianum.*

830. Nochlin, Linda. "The Velvet Cage: Propriety and Passion in Victorian Art." *Vogue* 172 (May 1982): 54.

Two exhibitions now at the Yale Center for British Art show women's rules in Victorian England through the art of (male) artists who painted them. *The Substance and the Shadow: Images of Victorian Womanhood* focuses on images of women keeping the home as the nineteenth century felt it should be kept, and in a few instances, showing the consequences of failure in the sad fates of "fallen women." This exhibition also surprises with celebrations of the vamp and the sensuous *femme fatale*. The other exhibit, *The Great Exhibition: A Question of Taste*, has a more public side, as it catalogues the 1851 world exhibition of science and decorative arts for use in industry.

831. *Margaret Macdonald Mackintosh: 1864-1933. Exhibition of the Hunterian Art Gallery, 26 Nov. 1983-7 January 1984.* Glasgow: University of Glasgow, 1983.

It is difficult to classify or categorize Margaret Macdonald's work, since almost all of it is collaborative, and it is often impossible to separate her creations from those of her husband or her sister. Her marriage contributed to her accomplishments in that she produced her best work with her husband, who supported and admired her talent. On the other hand, she devoted much time and energy to Mackintosh's mental and physical well-being, and she was unable to work under stress. She was recognized as a genius in her lifetime; much of her work remains unique and unequaled in the art world. The exhibit is a testament to her tremendous originality and versatility.

Reproductions (b/w):

Macdonald, Margaret and Frances: Paintings, designs, jewelry, furniture, needlework, metal work, stained glass.

832. Rendell, Claire. "Art, The Pre-Raphaelites. Tate Gallery. 7 March-28 May, 1984." *Spare Rib* (1984): 42.

The Pre-Raphaelite brotherhood owes much to the "sisterhood" that provided them with models and inspiration; care should be taken in interpreting the paintings. Ford Madox Brown's *Take Your Son, Sir* is especially open to fresh critical approaches.

833. Truherz, Julian. *Hard Times: Social Realism in Victorian London.* Manchester: Lord Humphries/Manchester City Art Gallery, 1987.

An exhibit of paintings representing the Victorian efforts toward social conscience features paintings by Blunden, Havers, and Solomon of poor women—one overworked, one dead from overwork, and one with no work at all.

Reproductions (b/w):

Blunden, Anna: *For Only One Short Hour...(the Seamstress)*

Havers, Alice: *The End of her Journey*

Solomon, Rebecca: *The Friend in Need.*

834. Lee, David. "Painting Women: Victorian Women Artists: Rochdale Art Gallery Exhibit." *Art Review (London)* 39 (24 April 1987): 277.

The reviewer, who has neither read Deborah Cherry's catalogue for the Rochdale Gallery exhibition of Victorian Women Artists, nor seen the exhibit in its entirety, is impressed at the scope and quality of the exhibit and the works of the women it represents. He is especially impressed with Alice Havers' *The End of Her Journey*, the only painting in the exhibit that presents a feminine perspective independent of the male-established conventions. Alice Walker's *Wounded Feelings*, which falls into the male-established conventional courtship genre, bears an exhibition caption stating that the love-stricken young woman in the picture fits "within a phallic economy of desire." The reviewer grants the value of alternative ways of viewing art, but doubts that such phrases will contribute much to the cause of feminism and women's history.

Reproductions (b/w):

Forbes, Elizabeth Armstrong: *A Zaandvoort Fishergirl.*

835. *May Morris: 1862-1938. An Exhibition at the William Morris Gallery, 10 January--11 March, 1969.* London: William Morris Gallery, 1989.

May Morris' revival of embroidery as a serious art form, and her skills as a designer and craftswoman make her an important contributor to the turn-of-the-century Arts and Crafts Movement. The quality and variety of her work reflect a lifetime of energy, imagination, and talent.

Reproductions (col):

Morris, May: *Honeysuckle Wallpaper* (front cover)

Photos (b/w):

May Morris 1908; May Morris in her Tapestry Room; May Morris at her loom, 1934.

836. Pyle, Hillary and Martha Caldwell. "Review of Exhibit and Catalogue of Irish Women Artists: From the 18th Century to the Present Day." *Woman's Art Journal* II, no. 1 (March 1990): 44-49.

The exhibition is somewhat even in size and quality, but serves to bring to light some fine artists whose work has gone unnoticed for some time. Edith OEone Somerville's work shows the influence of continental training. Sarah Cecilia Harrison and Josephine Webb's portraits are singular. The catalogue for the exhibit includes a section on Anna Jameson and Margaret Stokes, both nineteenth-century Irish art historians. The catalogue also includes a section on the Irish Arts and Crafts Movement.

Reproductions (b/w):

Somerville, Edith OEone: *Retrospect.*

837. Casteras Susan P. "A Struggle for Fame: Victorian Women Artists and Authors." In *From Safe Havens to A Wide Sea of Notoriety.* New Haven, Connecticut: Yale Center for British Art, 1994.

The difficulties encountered by nineteenth-century women hindered their artistic and creative progress, but fostered close friendships and the formation of art societies and schools for women. Connections between artistic families and support groups fostered a significant network of "Critics, Mentors and Patrons" including a "matronage" of female art buyers.

Reproductions (b/w):

Claxton, Adelaide: *The Daily Governess; The Plain Sister; A Christmas Congregation; February--Ladies Gallery at the House of Commons; Christmas Belles*

Claxton, Florence (detail): *The Adventures of a Woman in Search of Her Rights; The Third Volume; Shopping; The Choice of Paris*

Alexander, Francesca: from *Roadside Songs of Tuscany*

Allingham, Helen: *Bluebells*

Butler, Elizabeth Thompson: *On the Morning of Waterloo*

Blunden, Anna: *The Song of the Shirt*

Wells, Joanna Boyce: *Portrait of a Mulatto Woman*

Boyle, Eleanor Vere: from *The Story Without an End*

Brickdale, Eleanor Fortesque: *The Introduction; In the Springtime...; Kilke, Ireland*

Darby, Mary: *Godesberg on the Rhine*

De Morgan, Evelyn Pickering: *Study of a Woman's Head*

Edwards, Mary Ellen: *Our Grandmothers*

Hayllar, Jessica: *Portrait of the Hon. Ethel Lopes; Castle Prior: Interior*

Hayllar, Kate: *A Thing of Beauty is a Joy Forever*

Hayllar, Mary: *For a Good Boy*

Osborn, Emily: *Where the Weary are at Rest; The Governess; November Noon, Hoveton; Sailing Barges in an Estuary*

Sandys, Emma: *Portrait of a Woman*

Solomon, Rebecca (engraving): *Peg Woffington's Visit to Triplet*

Stillman, Marie Spartali: *Orange Grove*

Siddall, Elizabeth: *Study of Two Figures*

Solomon, Rebecca: *A Fashionable Couple*

Queen Victoria: *Study of a Veiled Woman with a Hawk*

Princess Victoria: *An Italian Soldier Seated Outside a Tavern*

Walker, Alice: *Wounded Feelings*
Ward, Henrietta: *The Crown of the Feast.*

CHAPTER 3

Models

The Tyranny of the Ideal

In *A Room of One's Own*, Virginia Woolf wrote that "if women had no existence save in the fiction written by men, one would imagine her a person of the utmost importance; very various; heroic and mean; splendid and sordid, infinitely beautiful and hideous in the extreme; as great as a man, some think even greater." Further, Woolf observed that "imaginatively [woman] is of the highest importance; practically she is completely insignificant."[1] While Woolf was addressing the issue of women as fictional characters, her observations applied equally well to women aspiring to art careers as well as women who appear as fictional characters (i.e., not portraits) in paintings. A visit to an art museum provides the same impression of women as does a perusal of great literature. Women are everywhere--nude, clothed, heroic, splendid, sordid, mean--but the women themselves, both painters and models, remain largely unknown. The implications of women as art objects are complex, diverse, and much discussed--but equally intriguing and seldom addressed is the anonymity of those female art objects, and not just the nude ones. Reasearch into the lives and identities of these women grants them a rightful place in the history of art; it in no way devalues or detracts from the work of art itself. Seeing the models as human beings is yet another way of seeing art and of enriching one's appreciation of it.

During the nineteenth century, the interest in genre paintings included not only landscapes and flower scenes, but narrative scenes in which, as John Hadfield puts it, "every picture tells a story."[2] In an age where the public flocked to art galleries and public art exhibits much as people now go to movies, British art catered to middle-class tastes and reflected middle-class situations. But while Victorian painters often

---

[1] Virginia Woolf, *A Room of One's Own*, (New York: Harcourt, 1957), p. 45.
[2] John Hadfield, *Every Picture Tells a Story*, (London: Herbert Press, 1985).

enjoyed the interest of the public, little is known about the individuals who provided the models for their story-paintings--while, ironically, their faces appeared in prestigious galleries and as engravings on thousands of middle- and working-class walls.

A few models became almost as famous as the men who painted them--but our knowledge is mostly limited to their names and their faces. The Pre-Raphaelites, most enduring and controversial of the English Victorian painters, centered their work around the women they idealized, and in several cases, married. In her book *Pre-Raphaelites in Love*,[3] Gay Daly equated these women as "the equivalent of our goddesses caught on celluloid," yet in her quest to discover the people behind their famous faces she had to rely on what she could glean from a few letters, handwriting analyses, and second-hand accounts. The men who painted these women were "the equivalent of filmmakers in our world."[4] They themselves were much written about, wrote about themselves, and left enough of an impression that the histories of their models can be pieced together, albeit often in a fragmented and speculative way.

A few other models can be identified because they were friends or family members of the artists, or were artists themselves. Henrietta Ward included her children in many of her history paintings. The Hayllar family painted each other in the house they shared. Sir Lawrence Alma-Tadema often draped his wife, the painter Laura Epps Alma-Tadema, in a toga to model for his Roman scenes; many of his family paintings of "Victorians in togas" also included his two daughters. Dante Gabriel Rossetti's poet-sister Christina Rossetti modeled for John Everett Millais' *Mariana*, and possibly for the female figure in James Collinson's *A Mother and Child on the Isle of Wight*. Sophie and Alice Gray, sisters of Effie Millais, modeled for John Everett Millais' *Autumn Leaves*. Painter Rosa Corder modeled for James Whistler's *Arrangement in Black and Brown*. Marie Spartali Stillman, one of the best of the Pre-Raphaelite painters, modeled with Alexa Wilding in Rossetti's *The Bower Meadow*. Stillman also appears in Burne-Jones' *Danaë*. Stillman's sister, Christine Spartali modeled for Whistler's *Princess du Pays de la Porcelaine*, the central mural in his famous *Peacock Room*,

Recently the activist group Guerrilla Girls have asked "Do women have to be naked to get into the Met. Museum? Less than 5% of the artists in the Modern Art Sections are women, but 85% of the nudes are female."[5] The same might be said about nineteenth-century exhibitions, except that less than 1% of the artists were women, and perhaps 10% or 20% of the paintings were nudes or semi-nudes. The seeming contradiction between Victorian prudery and the popularity of female nudes

[3]Gay Daly, *Pre-Raphaelites in Love*, (New York: Ticknor, 1989), p. xviii. Hereafter cited as Daly.

[4] Daly, p. xviii.

[5] Guerrilla Girls, *Confessions of the Guerrilla Girls*, (New York: Harper Collins, 1995).

in Victorian art is a much-discussed subject. The only Victorian woman to make a vocation of painting nude women was Henrietta Rae, who was trained and certainly influenced by Sir Frederic Leighton, a Royal Academy president and renowned painter of nude female figures. Rae may have painted female nudes to demonstrate her considerable talent for painting flesh tones, or because she wanted to tap into the market which consisted mostly of male buyers, or even to make a statement about freedom from restrictive clothing and conventions. In any case, Victorian nudes are usually female. They avoid pornographic associations by being removed from the nineteenth century in rational, respectable classical settings, and almost always they demurely avoid eye contact with the viewer. Richard Jenkyns has observed that Victorian nudes almost always represent "woman as victim."[6] Thus, it may have been for reasons other than propriety that Lawrence Alma-Tadema painted his own wife and daughters clothed, and hired professional models for his numerous paintings featuring female nudes. Jenkyns reports some contemporary confusion over the propriety of this plethora of nudes.[7] Some of the more insightful Victorian critics thought Leighton's nudes were silly. Anotonia Cura, William Turner's "housekeeper," modeled for what must have been Leighton's silliest. Cura, in a Grecian garden setting, unclothed but for a sort of towel with no visible fastening around her hips, fixes her eyes on several balls which she juggles with casual intensity. Whatever the implications of Victorian nudes, one cannot imagine the great Leighton painting himself in such a situation, or the renowned Alma-Tadema in a self-portrait lounging all exposed in a Roman bath. The models for the Victorian nudes are not family members or female artists struggling to establish their social as well as their artistic standing. Leighton's favorite model, Ada Alice Pullan, who took the name Dorothy Dene, aspired to the stage, and with Leighton's financing and influence achieved some success.[8] She would no doubt be forgotten entirely had she not modeled for many of Leighton's classical (i.e., nude) paintings.

The names of some models have been preserved because a few artists mentioned them in their autobiographies. G. A. Storey, a nineteenth-century painter, remembers "Nelly M.," an Irish girl who modeled for his *Going to Church* and for John Ruskin's *A Good Resolve*. A woman named Muriel Newton was the model for Henrietta Rae's *Isabella and the Pot of Basil*, exhibited at the Royal Academy in 1897. Louise Jopling wrote "I asked my friend, Mrs. Williams. . . to sit for me for a picture I intended painting of 'Vashti,' a queen who always had a great attraction for me, as the originator and victim of 'Women's Rights.'"[9]

---

[6] Richard Jenkyns, *Dignity and Decadence*, (Cambridge: Harvard U. P., 1992). Hereafter cited as Jenkyns.

[7] Jenkyns, p. 126.

[8] Leone and Richard Ormond, *Lord Leighton*, (New Haven: Yale U. P., 1975). Hereafter cited as Ormond.

[9] Louise Jopling, *Twenty Years of My Life*, (London: John Lane, 1925).

One of the most enigmatic and interesting models is Constance (Connie) Gilchrist, one of the beautiful little girls photographed by Lewis Carroll, who took her to visit the Royal Academy so that she could see herself in Leighton's paintings. She became "Famous as a skipping-rope dancer at the Westminster Aquarium." She later posed with her skipping-rope for Whistler's *The Golden Girl.*[10]

Victorian models with identities, however, are an exception. Many more women whose figures and faces illustrate painted stories from history, literature, and popular Victorian culture remain uncelebrated and unidentified. Most often they were probably something like "meagre little Miss Churm," the professional model in Henry James' short story "The Real Thing." Churm, "only a freckled cockney, . . . could represent everything, from a fine lady to a shepherdess; . . . . She couldn't spell and she loved beer, but she had. . . practice, and a knack, and mother-wit, and a whimsical sensibility, and a love of theatre, and seven sisters, and not an ounce of respect, especially for the *h.*" Churm's value, writes Henry James' artist narrator, "resided precisely in the fact that she had no positive stamp, ..." Artist and author Anna Lea Merritt wrote that, in London, hundreds of people made their living as sitters for artists. "Some of them, who are particularly beautiful, are engaged every day in the year, and may earn from a dollar and a half to two dollars a day. They must keep still for hours, and often stand or kneel in tiresome positions. However, the models generally take a great interest in the pictures they sit for, and like to do their best for the artists who employ them."[11] In her memoirs, Henrietta Ward wrote that when her husband, Edward, was elected to the Royal Academy in 1857, the news came from one of his models, a man named Harrell, "who had come all the way from London to Slough to tell his employer. It has always been the custom for models to wait outside the Academy during the election of the Royal Academicians and directly the result becomes known to hasten to acquaint the new R. A. of the honour." Harrell, who had traveled a long way in the middle of the night with his news, and who was one of Edward Ward's favorite models, received "a handsome present, after a substantial supper" for his efforts.[12]

In an 1887 *Magazine of Art* article titled "Glimpses of Artist-Life: The Artist's Model," M. H. Spielman wrote that models may be full-time professionals, or they may model only long enough to get themselves out of financial difficulty. Models must look healthy, according to Spielman.[13] Art historians Deborah Cherry and Griselda Pollock have written of the contradiction between Victorian paintings of poor people and the undesirability of those real-life poor people as models. Dirty,

---

[10] Ormond, p. 67.

[11] Anna Lea Merritt, "A Talk About Painting," *St. Nicholas*, (Dec. 1884), pp. 85-92.

[12] Henrietta Ward, *Memories of Ninety Years*, Ed. Isabel McAllister, 2nd ed. (London: Hutchinson, 1924). Hereafter cited as Ward.

[13] M. H. Spielman, "Glimpses of Artist-Life: The Artist's Model," *Magazine of Art* (1887), pp. 136-141.

undernourished, and therefore ugly subjects were not in demand. Thus, many models came from the working-classes, since modeling was not a respectable occupation for a middle-class woman, but modeling opportunities were closed to paupers.[14]

Modeling offered an opportunity for working-class women to associate with the more fortunate classes. While their work may have been sporadic, wages were not bad, and while they might work long hours, the conditions in a studio were certainly better than were found in factories, mills, and seamstresses' attics. And as the history of the Pre-Raphaelites make clear, artists sometimes fell in love with their models and even married them. Henrietta Ward mentions four models who married Royal Academicians.[15] Spielman, too, wrote that, properly educated, a model could become a very good wife. Art history does not seem to record any cases of female artists marrying their male models.

A few models are fascinating because of a special air of mystery that surrounds them. Elizabeth Siddall, as Jan Marsh points out, has become a kind of cult figure endowed by succeeding generations with whatever was occupying them at the time: her passive, submissive exterior appealed to the Victorians, her laudanum addiction interested the 1960's drug-culture, and her apparent artistic talent overshadowed by Dante Gabriel Rossetti's career made her a victim for the feminist movement during the 1980's.[16] She has become a legend for all generations if only because she must be the only model whose grief-stricken artist-poet-husband placed his manuscript of poems in her coffin, only to have her body exhumed years later to recover what he very much wished to publish.

Another mysterious, and therefore fascinating model whose death broke the heart of her artist-lover, was Kathleen Newton, long the "dark lady" of French artist James Tissot, whose gorgeous paintings featured her again and again in breathtaking costumes. She died in 1882, at the age of twenty-eight, and Tissot was so stricken with grief that he spent years mourning her and attending seances in an effort to reach her through the spirit world. Wild stories circulated about her apparently mysterious death. A 1936 publication claimed that she had received a misdirected letter and hurled herself out of a bedroom window.[17] Rumors continued until in 1936 Marita Ross interviewed Newton's niece, Lilian Hervey, who supplied details about Newton's life that, if anything, made her story even more fascinating.[18] Raised in an Irish convent and put on a ship to India at sixteen to marry an older man chosen by

---

[14] Deborah Cherry and Griselda Pollock, "Patriarchal Power and the Pre-Raphaelites," *Art History* 7, No. 4 (Dec. 1984), pp. 480-495.

[15] Ward, p.284.

[16] Jan Marsh, "Imagining Elizabeth Siddall," *History Workshop Journal*, No. 25 (Spring 1988), pp. 64-82.

[17] James Laver, *Vulgar Society: The Romantic Career of James Tissot: 1836-1902*, (London: Constable, 1936).

[18] Marita Ross, "The Truth about Tissot," *Everybody's Weekly* (15 June 1946), pp. 6-7.

her father, Newton apparently was seduced by a man known as Captain Palliser, became pregnant, and when her new husband discovered her indiscretion he packed her back to England and divorced her. She gave birth to a daughter and later to a son, (paternity unknown, but probably not Tissot's child) and some time around 1876 she and her children went to live with Tissot. He and Newton seemed content to live unmarried and in seclusion while he painted her and the children in the idyllic gardens of their house at 17 Grove End Road, St. John's Wood, a fashionable London suburb. Newton was afflicted with tuberculosis--a major killer in the nineteenth-century--and Tissot's paintings of her seem to take on a somber note as her health deteriorated. A photograph of the pair taken in 1882, just before she died, shows her wrapped in shawls, smiling wistfully at something beyond the camera, while Tissot holds her hand and wraps a protective arm around her.[19] Since Newton's niece was only seven when her aunt died, and since Newton herself left no memoirs, Marita Ross' discoveries can be viewed as sketchy at best. What remains, as with Elizabeth Siddall, is a mysterious woman beloved by a talented man who immortalized his passion in his painting.

These models, the ones whose names we know and the ones whose identities are a mystery, remain anonymous behind their faces and figures, no matter how skillfully rendered by the artist. As Cherry and Pollock point out, the women in paintings are merely representative of whatever the artist wants to express.[20] In Victorian art especially, women were painted as submissive ideals. They represented the famous Victorian "angel in the house" so deplored by Virginia Woolf. Their personalities, desires, opinions, and personal lives were irrelevant in the scheme of art--thus the difference between a portrait of a woman and a painting of a woman. A good portrait may give the viewer a sense of the person behind the face, but a good painting uses the face and figure to convey feelings that are solely the artist's. Discovering even the names and at least fragments of information about the model's lives helps the modern scholar to compartmentalize social myths and human reality and thus to escape the persistent tyranny of the ideal. The female model is an actress, shaped by the artist's mind and brush into a role that may mask her social class, her personal experiences, and her values. What is presented on the canvas is, ironically, a social myth taken seriously by most art critics, as well as by most contemporary and modern viewers as the reality of the moment representing the pattern and fabric of women's history. If women are to separate themselves from imposed gender roles, they must have a

---

[19] David S. Brooke, "James Tissot and the *'ravissante Irlandaise,'*" *Connoisseur*, 168 (May 1968), pp. 55-59.

[20] Deborah Cherry and Griselda Pollock, "Woman as Sign in Pre-Raphaelite Literature: A Study of the Representation of Elizabeth Siddall," *Art History*, 7, No. 2 (June 1984), pp. 206-227.

history. The story behind the canvas must be considered separate from the story on the canvas, but it is no less important in its own right.[21]

Women seen and represented through the eyes and hands of other women are one step less removed from reality. The woman artist may be unconsciously reaffirming her own gender roles, or she may be subtly subverting them, but parts of herself are ineluctably a part of the subject before her both on the canvas and in the person of the female model. It is well to remember that models of blissful middle-class life are usually not middle-class, and in fact are working women, and the women who paint them in comfortable studios and homes are just as surely working too. A kind of double myth-making forms itself from women painting women: two classes of women work to represent idleness in a peaceful middle-class world. While searching for the identities and lives of the women in the paintings falls outside the traditional academic study of what is called art history, it fills in the gaps left by formal study, transcends the academic myths and poses another question: what was it really like for these women? This is in itself a serious step toward identifying women's social history, women's role in art history, and a re-evaluation that allows a place for women of all classes in the history of art.

---

838. Watts, Theodore. "Mr. D.G. Rossetti." *Athenaeum* (15 April 1882): 480-481.

Dante Gabriel Rossetti's late wife, the beautiful Elizabeth Siddall, served as a constant model and inspiration to the great poet and painter. After her death he temporarily lost interest in his work.

839. Spielman, M. H. "Glimpses of Artist Life. The Artist's Model." *Magazine of Art* (1887): 136-141.

Artist's models consist of individuals who are life-time professional posers and of others who work only occasionally when financial needs dictate. Female models tend to take care of their health, since healthy and well-formed individuals are most in demand. Artists frequently fall in love with their sitters, who, properly educated can become "model wives." Several Royal Academicians have married their models. Male models usually lack similar opportunities.

840. Millais, John Guille. *The Life and Letters of Sir John Everett Millais.* New York: F.A. Stokes, 1899.

---

[21] Elizabeth Langland, *Nobody's Angels: Middle-Class Women and Domestic Ideology in Victorian Culture,* (Ithaca: Cornell U. P., 1965). Langland asserts the importance of locating and identifying what she terms the "garbage" of history if women are to be freed from social myths in order to begin constructing a reality of self.

Walter Deverell's discovery of Elizabeth Siddall in a milliner's shop led to her posing for endless hours in a bathtub for his famous painting, *Ophelia*. Her resulting illness caused her to threaten legal action, but Millais paid her medical bills and Siddall recovered to pose again. Part of the success of his painting lay in his ability to capture Siddall's simplicity and purity.

841. Storey, G. A. *Sketches from Memory*. London: Chatto & Windus, 1899.

Nelly M., a girl from Dublin with a strong accent and a remarkably pretty face, modeled for Ruskin's painting *A Good Resolve,* for Storey's *Going to Church* and for Calderon's *Gloire de Dijon*.

Reproductions (b/w):

Storey, G.A.: *Nora.*

842. Sickert, Bernhard. "The Whistler Exhibition." *Burlington Magazine* (October 1904): 430-439.

James McNeil Whistler's portraits of such women as Rosa Corder and Connie Gilchrist reveal a disinterest in his models as personalities. It is a defect of his art that the people he paints are "mere patterns" in his compositions. The resulting portraits are unsympathetic, lifeless and reveal Whistler's self- centeredness.

Reproductions (b/w):

Whistler, James McNeil: *Connie Gilchrist Skipping.*

843. Staley, Edgecumbe. *Lord Leighton of Stretton, P.R.A.* London: Walter Scott Publishing, N.Y.: Charles Scribner's Sons, 1906.

Connie Gilchrist, Dorothy Dene, and Alice Smith were Sir Frederic Leighton's favorite models. Dene appears so frequently in Leighton's paintings that her personality emerges from the canvas.

844. Rothenstein, John. "Walter John Knewstub." *Artwork* VI, no. 22 (June 1930): 87.

Walter John Knewstub was Dante Gabriel Rossetti's only pupil, and most of his works are attributed to Rossetti. Knewstub married Emily Renshaw, who modeled for Rossetti. The Knewstubs had three daughters, two of whom, Alice Mary Knewstub Rothenstein and Grace Knewstub Orpen, married artists.

Reproductions (b/w):

Knewstub, Walter John: *Mrs. W. J. Knewstub and Her Daughter, Alice Mary.*

845. Rossetti, Dante Gabriel. *Dante Gabriel Rossetti's Letters to Fanny Cornforth*, ed. Paul Franklin Baum. Baltimore: Johns Hopkins University Press, 1940.

Dante Gabriel Rossetti's letters to Fanny Cornforth are full of warmth, affection, humor, and checks. It is clear from Rossetti's letters to her that she was a loyal friend who spared little effort in caring for his household and personal effects. A letter from her to an ailing Rossetti indicates she felt he was tired of her and that she was feeling injured by his friends' cruelty to her. While the nature of their relationship is still controversial, Cornforth has not been treated honestly by Rossetti's biographers, and she deserves credit for her devotion to Rossetti and for the inspiration she brought to his work.

Reproductions (b/w):

Rossetti, Dante Gabriel: *Crayon Study of Fanny; Lady with a Fan* (Fanny Cornforth as model).

846. Gaunt, William. *The Pre-Raphaelite Tragedy*. New York: Harcourt, 1942.

Elizabeth Siddall and even Fanny Cornforth were living props in the picture book of Dante Gabriel Rossetti's mind. Siddall's death was almost redundant; in her languid torpor she had been as good as dead for years. After her death she continued to serve as Rossetti's Beatrice in the form of a spiritual presence.

847. Ross, Marita. "The Truth about Tissot." *Everybody's Weekly* (15 June 1946): 6-7.

After publishing an article about artist James Tissot, Marita Ross was contacted by Lilian Hervey, a niece of Tissot's model and mistress, the mysterious Kathleen Newton. According to Hervey, Kathleen Newton was born Kathleen Irene Kelly, the daughter of an army officer serving in India. She was educated in England and France. At sixteen, she married a much older man, Dr. Newton, a wealthy physician. The marriage was unhappy, and Kathleen Newton returned to England two years later to live with her sister. Shortly after her arrival Kathleen gave birth to a daughter, who was raised with Lilian Hervey and Lilian's little brother and sister. These are the children that appear with Kathleen Newton in so many of Tissot's paintings. Tissot, who lived near Lilian Hervey's family, asked Kathleen to sit for him. They fell in love, and she and her two children went to live with him. Dr. Newton eventually divorced her, but since she and Tissot were Roman Catholic, they could not marry. They enjoyed friendships with James McNeil Whistler, Oscar and William Wilde, Henry Irving, and other literary and artistic notables. When Kathleen Newton died of consumption in 1882 at the age of twenty-eight, Tissot was inconsolable, left England and immersed himself in religion and spiritualism.

848. Hough, Graham. *The Last Romantics*. London: Duckworth, 1949.

Dante Gabriel Rossetti's vision of woman as mystical muse centered around Elizabeth Siddall in such a way that her death fulfilled his ideal of her.

849. Gaunt, William. *Victorian Olympus*. London: Jonathan Cape, 1952.

Victorian London is nearly as remarkable for its models as it is for the paintings they helped make possible. Professional models were shared among the artists, and they were comparatively well paid. Italian models were favored for their beauty and for their classical heritage, which, in the spirit of the Victorian love of classicism, gave them a kind of instinctive feel for the artistic. Leighton painted Antonia Cura as a juggler. His favorite model, Dorothy Dene, posed as Cassandra in a *tableau vivant*.

850. Mander, Rosalie. "Rossetti's Models." *Apollo* (July 1963): 18-22.

Jane Morris' sense of humor, Marie Spartali Stillman's intelligence and energy, and Alexa Wilding's generosity and affection are not evident in Dante Gabriel Rossetti's preoccupation with female beauty.

Reproductions (col):

Rossetti, Dante Gabriel: *La Boca Baciata* (portrait of Fanny Cornforth); *La Pia de' Tolomei* (portrait of Jane Morris)

Reproductions (b/w):

Rossetti, Dante Gabriel: *Rosalind, Countess of Carlisle; Elizabeth Siddal; Ruth Herbert; Head of Marie Spartali; Salutatio* (portraits of "Red Lion" Mary, Ruth Herbert and Fanny Cornforth); *La Ghirlandata* (portrait of Alexa Wilding).

851. Hunt, John Dixon. "'The Soul's Beauty': The Pre-Raphaelite Image of Woman." In *The Pre-Raphaelite Imagination: 1848-1900*. London: Routledge and Kegan, Paul, 1968: 177-210.

Dante Gabriel Rossetti's portraits of Elizabeth Siddall, Jane Morris, Fanny Cornforth, Marie Spartali and others all reflected the features of his feminine ideal with their pale faces, heavy, bent necks, droopy eyelids, small, full mouths, and masses of wavy hair. Whether his models actually possessed these features was immaterial to him. Rossetti was influenced by poets and painters of his own and earlier ages who saw the ideal woman as mysterious, supernatural, and somehow death-like and dangerous. The *femme fatale* image is evident in the work of other artists, including

Margaret Macdonald, who uses enigmatic and stylized female figures in many of her art nouveau designs.

Reproductions (b/w):

Elizabeth Siddall and Jane Morris as models in drawings and paintings

Macintosh, Margaret Macdonald: *Motherhood*

Photos (b/w):

Photo of Fanny Cornforth.

852. Brooke, David S. "James Tissot and the 'Ravissante Irlandaise': Reflections on an Exhibition at the Art Gallery of Ontario." *The Connoisseur* 168 (May 1968): 55-59.

The account of Kathleen Newton's niece Lilian Hervey may contain omissions or inaccurate information, since Hervey was only seven when Kathleen Newton died. Public records reveal that Isaac Newton married Kathleen Irene Ashburnham Kelly in India on 3 January, 1871, and filed for divorce in May of 1871. Kathleen Newton did not contest the divorce, which became final in July of 1872. Her daughter, Muriel Mary Violet, was born at Kathleen Newton's father's house in Yorkshire on 20 December, 1871. Kathleen had a son, Cecil George Newton, in March of 1876, naming Isaac Newton as the father. At this time she was living with her sister, Mary Hervey, in London. Kathleen Newton went to live with Tissot sometime in 1876 or 1877, and died there in November of 1882. Apparently Isaac Newton divorced Kathleen because she told him she had an affair with a Captain Palliser; later she wrote Newton that Palliser was Muriel Mary Violet's father. According to people who knew him, Tissot became involved with spiritualism in an attempt to reach Kathleen Newton after her death. His sketches, photos and paintings of her seem to record a premonition of her death, as the mood is often remote, even melancholy, and departure scenes are common.

Reproductions (b/w):

Photos, paintings and sketches of Kathleen Newton.

853. Hilton, Timothy. *The Pre-Raphaelites*. New York: Oxford University Press, 1970.

Dante Gabriel Rossetti's love for Elizabeth Siddall and his justifiable guilt over her untimely death inspired his masterpiece, *Beata Beatrice*. A posthumous portrait, the painting is both the earthly Siddall in its sexual overtones, and the artistic inspiration in its theme of Beatrice, the inspiration of Rossetti's poet namesake. Annie Miller and Fanny Cornforth, more lively, earthy, and less divine inspiration, marked his drug and drink-laden declining years, his passion for Jane Burden Morris redeeming him by its more idealistic affection and deeper friendship. Rossetti's paintings of her are so powerful and obsessive, Morris herself so private and reclusive, that it is impossible to discover her personality or to separate her reality from Rossetti's vision of her as the embodiment of beauty and artistic principles.

854. Wood, Christopher. "The Artistic Family Hayllar. Part I: James Hayllar." *Connoisseur* (April 1974): 266-273.

For his pictures known as "the Lily series" Hayllar employed a model named Mary Godsal who came from difficult circumstances but managed to educate herself and marry well. Hayllar also employed elderly villagers as models and frequently painted his own daughters. When they were old enough he gave them painting and drawing lessons. Jessica, who had been paralyzed in an accident, stayed with him and continued painting, but Kate gave up her painting to take care of her father in his old age.

Reproductions (b/w):

Hayllar, James: Portraits of Edith, Mary, Kate, and Jessica Hayllar and Mary Godsal.

855. Ormond, Leonée and Richard. *Lord Leighton*. New Haven: Yale University Press, 1975.

Connie Gilchrist posed for many of Frederic Leighton's paintings and was a photographic model and child friend for Lewis Carroll. Dorothy Dene, born Ada Alice Pullan, began modeling for Leighton as a young woman and later took the name Dorothy Dene when she began a career on the stage. She died at age thirty-nine of peritonitis. An entire chapter outlines her background, her work and her friendship with Leighton.

Reproductions (b/w):

Watts, G.F.: Portrait of Dorothy Dene

Paintings by Leighton with Dene and Gilchrist as models.

856. Casteras, Susan P. *The Double Vision in Portraiture: Dante Gabriel Rossetti and the Double Work of Art*. New Haven, Conn.: Yale University Art Gallery, 1976.

Dante Gabriel Rossetti's models provide subjects that themselves create an outlet for Rossetti's projection of himself into his art. His models fit a preconceived idea and are made to fit that idea--sometimes even using bits from different models: Marie Spartali's face, Jane Morris' neck, and Fanny Cornforth's hair, for example. Rossetti's portraits are more about himself than about his subjects.

Reproductions (b/w):

Rossetti, Dante Gabriel: *Fanny Cornforth* (sketches); *Annie Miller* (sketches); *Ruth Herbert* (sketches); *Elizabeth Siddall* (sketches); *The Return of Tibullus to Delia; Bonafazio's Mistress; Elizabeth Siddall* (sketches); *Bruna Brunelleschi; Mariana* (study from Jane Morris); *Silence* (study from Jane Morris); *Water Willow; The Day Dream.*

857. ---. "John Everett Millais' *Yes or No?*" *Yale University Art Gallery Bulletin* (September 1976): 18-20.

Artist Dorothy Tennant served as the model for the "No!" figure in John Everett Millais' 1875 painting of that title. The picture, now lost, was part of a series stemming from Millais' 1871 painting titled *Yes or No?*.

858. Dobbs, Brian and Judy. *Dante Gabriel Rossetti: An Alien Victorian*. London: MacDonald's and Jane's, 1977.

Separated by class differences from her real love, Walter Deverell, Elizabeth Siddall took refuge in depression and laudanum. Forced by Victorian conventions into the role of passive, pale maiden, she was by definition a fallen woman. Since he was the cause of her "ruin," Rossetti fell victim to remorse. They married because they were victims of the times and had little choice. She had no alternatives but marriage or prostitution; he had no honorable alternatives but to marry her and make her respectability a reality. Both took refuge in laudanum, ill health, and early deaths.

Reproduction (b/w):
Rossetti, Dante Gabriel: Two portraits of Elizabeth Siddall.

859. Battiscombe, Georgiana. *Christina Rossetti: A Divided Life*. London: Constable, 1981.

Elizabeth Siddall, whose depression is evident in her pictures and poems, was, in her quiet way, a valuable source of inspiration to Dante Gabriel Rossetti. Siddall and Christina Rossetti's relationship is not close, but Christina Rossetti's poem "In an Artist's Studio" shows that she saw Siddall in a sympathetic light. The poem implies that Dante Gabriel saw Siddall as an object, an idealized source of inspiration rather than as a woman. Christina Rossetti's poem, "Wife to Husband" seems to be about Siddall. The Rossetti family saw Dante Gabriel Rossetti's relationship with Jane Morris as platonic, and was delighted at William Rossetti's marriage to Lucy Madox Brown, although Lucy's disposition made it impossible for Christina to share a home with her brother and sister-in-law.

Reproductions (b/w):

Ford Madox Brown, Portrait of Lucy Madox Brown Rossetti and Her Daughter.

860. Pearsall, Ronald. *Tell Me, Pretty Maiden: The Victorian and Edwardian Nude.* Exeter, England: Webb & Bower, 1981.

Henrietta Rae rates two paragraphs which include her art training and the fact that her Royal Academy exhibits are evidence that "her brand of racy nudes" met the standards of the public and the art world. Antonia Cura and Marion Tatershall posed nude for Lawrence Alma-Tadema, who used his wife and daughters for clothed models. Connie Gilchrist was painted nude by Leighton and was photographed nude by Lewis Carroll. Dorothy Dene posed nude for Leighton and G.F. Watts.

861. Bell, Quentin. *A New and Noble School: The Pre-Raphaelites.* London: Macdonald, 1982.

Chatty and often catty, Bell describes the "Pygmalion Syndrome" of the Pre-Raphaelite men who found young women of working-class (or "worse") backgrounds, such as "the really dreadful Annie Miller" and attempted to refine, educate and marry them.

862. Marsh, Jan. "Pre-Raphaelite Women." *New Society* (23 February 1984): 279-282.

In Victorian times, the only way a woman could rise above her father's social class was to marry a man with superior wealth and status. Jane Burden Morris, Elizabeth Siddall, and Emma Hill Brown came from lower-class families and went through training and education to make them suitable wives for their gentleman-painter husbands. Annie Miller married into the upper class, but Fanny Cornforth was unable to shed her Cockney accent and remained, in effect, a prostitute. The Pre-Raphaelite painters not only changed the social identities of many of these women, but transformed their probably plain features by painting them as glamorous and sensual so that they became icons in the public eye. Photos and self-portraits show something nearer the truth. The women themselves, especially Jane Morris and Elizabeth Siddall, seem to have taken pains to hide their origins.

Reproductions (b/w):

Siddall, Elizabeth: *Self-Portrait*

paintings of Jane Morris, Effie Millais, Fanny Cornforth, Elizabeth Siddall, Rossetti and Millais

Photos (b/w):

Photo of Jane Morris.

863. Cherry, Deborah and Griselda Pollock. "Woman as Sign in Pre- Raphaelite Literature: A Study of the Representation of Elizabeth Siddall." *Art History* 7, no. 2 (June 1984): 206-227.

Elizabeth Siddall spelled her name with two "l's" but the men who appropriated her as a symbol of their artistic ideals not only changed her name spelling to "Siddal," but subverted her entire identity. Her art and poetry are seen only as they reflect Dante Gabriel Rossetti's tutelage and influence and are measured by male-established standards of excellence. Her family history consists of statistics contributing to a group classification rather than of statements of individual expression. The paintings in which she appears use her as a symbol of the established ideal of the female; none of the paintings are portraits attempting to capture the essence of her true self. Elizabeth Siddal is a representation and a symbol in art history and is not to be confused with Elizabeth Siddall, an individual in her own right.

864. ---. "Patriarchal Power and The Pre-Raphaelites." *Art History* 7, no. 4 (December 1984): 480-495.

A commercial exhibit of works of Pre-Raphaelites and the publication of the accompanying *Pre-Raphaelite Painters* continue the fictional mystique of nineteenth century male painters who are profit-centered purveyors of social propaganda perpetuating the middle-class vision of a tidy, well-regulated working class and a docile bourgeois female devoted to serving and pleasing a white male phallocentric power structure. Effie Millais' journal describes her search for suitable female models for her husband's paintings; the models for his *Autumn Leaves* include her sisters, Sophie and Alice Grey, who represent healthy, well-fed femininity; and Matilda Proudfoot and Isabella Nicholl, who represent working classes. Effie Millais describes the difficulty of finding models in the pauper's school who were not too ugly to be painted. The obvious differences in the healthy, well-fed Grey girls and the sallow, thin-haired paupers go beyond differences in clothing, but the painting is not offered as an appeal for humanitarian treatment of the poor.

865. Prideaux, Tom. "A French Artist's Victorian World of Tense Decorum." *Smithsonian* 15 (December 1984): 134-143.

The tension James Tissot felt over Kathleen Newton's fatal illness is evident in the darkness and shadows in his last portraits of her. After her death he painted the scene in which he had spoken with her spirit at a séance, but that picture is lost.

Reproductions (col):
Tissot, James: *Mme Newton à l'Ombrelle; En Plein Soleil*
Photos (b/w):
Kathleen Newton.

866. Matyjaszkiewicz, Krystyna. *James Tissot.* New York: Abbeville, 1985.

In the several essays treating Tissot's work, Kathleen Newton's background emerges with some interesting variations. In one version, she went to India to join her brother (rather than her father), being seduced along the way by a Captain Palliser, who was never mentioned in the account of Newton's niece, Lilian Hervey. She married Dr. Newton, ran away to return to Palliser, had four children (double the number in the Hervey version). After going to live with Tissot, she had a son (not mentioned in the Hervey account) who may or may not have been fathered by Tissot. One essay maintains that Tissot chose her clothes for his famous costume paintings; another writer maintains that Tissot's pictures changed as she began to assert her own taste in dress. It is probably safe to assert that Kathleen Newton remains an enigma.

867. Gaines, Charles. "Art: Those Victorian Ladies." *Architectural Digest* 41 (January 1985): 122-128.

Not an article about women artists, but illustrated with lush color photos of unnamed female models in classical dress and poses, painted by famous Victorian men.

868. Holman-Hunt, William. *A Pre-Raphaelite Friendship: The Correspondence of William Holman-Hunt and John Lucas Tupper*, ed.James H. Coombs. Ann Arbor: UMI Research Press, 1986.

Holman-Hunt's letters mention, mostly in passing, his marriage to Fanny Waugh, her death, his subsequent marriage to her younger sister, Edith, and the births of their children. Elizabeth Siddall appears briefly when Hunt apologizes to Tupper for having pretended that Siddall was his wife, hinting at her complicity as a "modest agreeable girl" who is "not a common model."

869. Wood, Christopher. *Tissot: The Life and Work of Jacques Joseph Tissot 1836-1902.* Boston: Little, Brown, 1986.

The mysterious figure of Kathleen Newton dominates much of Wood's narrative as she dominated much of Tissot's painting. A woman with a beautiful face and two illegitimate children, Newton was a *femme fatale*, a madonna, and a frail consumptive, all aspects that fascinated Victorians and dominated Victorian art. Her death at twenty-eight drove Tissot back to Paris where he took refuge in séances and Catholicism. Wood is careful to clear up old myths and to present what facts are known about Newton.

870. Beerbohm, Max. *Rossetti and His Circle*. New Haven, Conn.: Yale University Press, 1987.

    The women in the Pre-Raphaelite circle appear only casually in the text, but Beerbohm's caricatures of Elizabeth Siddall may be of interest to some.

    Reproductions (b/w):

    Beerbohm, Max: *Rossetti's Courtship, Chatham Place, 1850-1860; Swinburne, Elizabeth Siddal, and Rossetti.*

871. Casteras, Susan P. "Rossetti's Embowered Females in Art, or Love Enthroned 'The Lamps Shrine'." *Southeastern Nineteenth- Century Studies* 2 (1988): 27-56.

    Women alone on balconies and at windows are a frequent theme in nineteenth-century art by men; Dante Gabriel Rossetti was particularly fascinated by this image. Ellen Heaton and Fanny Cornforth were models for his *Regina Cordium, Fair Rosamund,* and *The Blue Bower,* three of his paintings in this genre. Alexa Wilding, Elizabeth Siddall and Jane Morris, three other women with whom he was obsessed during his life, also modeled for similar themes, suggesting his sexual obsession with the "embowered female." Perhaps as a complicated response to Siddall and her own work, Rossetti was increasingly concerned with this theme after Elizabeth Siddall's death in 1862.

872. Nochlin, Linda. "Lost and *Found:* Once More the Fallen Woman." In *Women, Art, and Power and Other Essays,* 57-85. New York: Harper, 1988.

    The term "fallen" has connotations of heroism for men and of sexual indiscretion for women. The Victorians were fascinated with the subject of women who deviated from the feminine ideal, and this fascination is reflected in the art and literature of the time. The theme had particular importance to Dante Gabriel Rossetti, whose models for *Found* were Fanny Cornforth and possibly Annie Miller. Hunt's *Awakening Conscience* may reflect deep personal conflicts about Annie Miller, the original model for the painting.

    Reproduction (b/w):

    Hunt, William Holman: *The Awakening Conscience; Found.*

873. Daly, Gay. *Pre-Raphaelites in Love*. New York: Ticknor and Fields, 1989.

The women whose faces made the reputations of the Pre-Raphaelite painters have become legend and myth. Since they left few or no records of their personal feelings and experiences, viewers see these women almost exclusively as the artists and their critics saw them. It is not possible to separate the personalities of the Pre-Raphaelite models from the men who painted them, but in re-examining the lives of the painters, much is revealed about their models that has been ignored, unnoticed, or censored by earlier biographical studies.

Reproductions (b/w):

Siddall, Elizabeth: *Self-Portrait; The Woeful Victory.*

874. Morris, Susan. "Saints, Sirens and Sinners. Piccadilly Gallery." *Arts Review* (24 March 1989): 229.

The Piccadilly Gallery exhibition of paintings of the female form begin with the Pre-Raphaelite females and continue into the 1930's. Some of the paintings reflect the artists' fear of women, some reflect no interest in individual character, and some manage to reveal the model's personality as well as her body.

875. Casteras, Susan P. "William Maw Egley's *The Talking Oak.*" *Detroit Institute of Arts Bulletin* (December 1990): 27-41.

Alfred, Lord Tennyson's poem "The Talking Oak" inspired William Maw Egley's painting of the same title, with Polly Egley serving as the model. Tennyson's poem also inspired Sophie Anderson.

876. ---. "Pre-Raphaelite Challenges to Victorian Canons of Beauty." *Huntington Library Quarterly* (December 1992): 13-35.

Nineteenth-century confidence in phrenology and similar methods of assessing character, coupled with firm notions of the duty of art to please the senses, brought critics' wrath upon Pre-Raphaelite painters for their realistic representations of peasants and women. Effie Millais' rough appearance in *The Order of Release* was particularly shocking since she belonged to the upper-middle class. Jane Burden Morris, considered outside the standards of beauty by many, subsequently became the idol of the Aesthetic Movement.

CHAPTER 4

Criticism, Art Schools, and Reviews

Integration and Commitment

During most of the nineteenth century, the art press shared a major concern with art schools: not *whether* women should or could become serious contributors to the art world, but *how* they should go about it. By mid-century it was obvious to nearly everyone that women must have decent, dignified employment, but few were willing to give up the persistent dream, born of the social reshuffling of the industrial revolution, of a domestic haven presided over by a devoted and selfless angel. The truth was that many women needed more intellectual and creative outlets and a great many women needed or wanted financial self-sufficiency. The conflicts arising from an ideal and a reality led to serious efforts at compromise, and art was seen as a possible money-maker for middle-class women for whom governessing was slavery, and for whom domestic employment or shopkeeping were deemed unacceptable. Painting, designing, and decorative work were ladylike, productive and dignified occupations, especially since they reflected qualities apparently gifted to women by nature. Further, middle-class girls were taught early on to draw a little, paint a little, and to find ways to make themselves and their surroundings pleasing and attractive. Turning these pursuits into genteel careers seemed an ideal compromise between necessity and respectability.

The two most immediate problems were the quality of production and the suitability of training. Galleries were flooded with work by women deemed by the academic community to have no notion of discipline, concentration, and intensive training necessary to compete in the art world. Not only could women not meet the established standards, but their work convinced the very people who could help them that women lacked the character, vision, and talent necessary to achieve excellence in art. Alarmed at what they saw as the poor quality of women's painting, the art journals concerned themselves with encouraging and evaluating traditional academic standards in women's art schools, keeping the public informed of women's progress, and directing women through formal training and education.

One of the earliest of these institutions, the Female School of Design, a kind of artistic trade school, suffered what amounted to persecution in an apparent effort to discourage students from attending. An 1849 letter to the *Art Union* protested these wrongs,[1] which according to an article published eleven years later in *Macmillan's Magazine* were still not corrected, mostly for lack of government funding.[2] A year later the *Art Journal* followed up with an article insisting on the school's practical value but also praising the achievements of its students and urging support from the government and from private donors.[3] The press continued to report the school's progress, regularly publishing names of high achievers, the medals and scholarships they had won--thus encouraging diligence and talent as well as keeping the school in the eyes and minds of the public, and of potential supporters and employers. The fact that the school and its students refused to give up in spite of poor conditions and sneaky politics is testimonial to their determination as well as a statement about the absolute necessity of the kind of training and employment the school offered to women.

In a three-part series published in the spring of 1872, the *Art Journal* outlined the necessity, the value, and the practicality of vocational art training for women. citing utilitarian justifications, bringing up popular objections (women abandon their training and jobs if they get a chance to marry), countering them (the married deserters will be quickly replaced by needy unmarrieds) and, perhaps most important, emphatically citing the fact that many girls and women possessed aptitude and a passion for learning. The *Art Journal* readers were not allowed the luxury of believing in the passive domestic angel--or at least they were confronted over and over with the bare fact that domesticity and passivity and fashionable indolence were not universal virtues. Neither could all women expect (or want) to be supported by others.[4]

But while the Female School of Design and much of the *Art Journal*'s efforts on its behalf were concerned with vocational training, other art schools, societies, and critics focused on women's progress in the fine arts. Although the prestigious British Royal Academy had two females among its founders and although nothing in its bylaws prohibited women from attending its schools, determined pressure from within kept women out until the second half of the century. The *Magazine of Art*

---

[1] "The Female School of Design," *Art Union*, (1 January 1849), p. 29.

[2] F. D. Maurice, "Female School of Art; Mrs Jameson," *Macmillan's Magazine* 2 (1860), pp. 227-235.

[3] Thomas Purnell, "Woman and Art. The Female School of Design," *Art Journal* 23 (1861), pp. 107-108.

[4] "Art Work for Women. I," (March 1872), pp. 65-66. "Art Work for Women. II," (April 1872), pp. 102-103. "Art Work for Women. III. How the Work May be Done," (May 1872), pp. 129-131.

consistently complained that the Royal Academy Schools were crowded with women, and leveled charges that women were "artistically weaker" and lacked the staying power to finish the school's course of studies.[5] The *Art Journal* consistently mentioned women's works in Royal Academy Exhibits and by 1890 the *Magazine of Art* grudgingly admitted that higher admission standards and access to undraped models would result in better quality work--an oblique admission that women were at least capable of producing decent art of an academic nature.[6] Within the Royal Academy school itself, the *Magazine of Art* reported angst in Eden--male students resented women's presence in their sacred space and women students found the males boorish and unsuitable for marriage.[7]

Meanwhile, competent and even superior training in the fine arts was available elsewhere for women. The prestigious Slade school attracted many talented women who wished to work and study side by side with male students, competing on an equal basis for scholarships and prizes. Accomplished and acclaimed professional artists such as Henrietta Ward and Louise Jopling opened schools. Women who could afford it and whose families allowed it went to Paris, Rome, and Munich to study alongside men and to have access to undraped models and continental art galleries. Many women eagerly read books and articles such as Alice Greene's *Magazine of Art* article "the Girl Student in Paris,"[8] Anna Mary Howitt's *An Art Student in Munich*,[9] Dinah Mulock Craik's "A Paris Atelier,"[10] and Charlotte Week's "Lady Artists in Munich,"[11] all of which encouraged study abroad where opportunities were good and prejudice much less of a problem.

Popular opinion remained divided on how integrated art students should be and whether a woman should take up art as a sideline or as a career, especially since the kind of dedication and labor involved in complete commitment was "unfeminine." Most female critics and art teachers insisted on total integration and expected that training for women would be as rigorous and disciplined as men's and that women's art would be judged by the same standards. Anna Lea Merritt announced at the 1900 International Congress of Women that those with a serious commitment to art must resist social pressures to marry or to serve as family drudges. Merritt always insisted

---

[5] "Chronicle of Art. Woman, and Her Chance as an Artist," *Magazine of Art* (1888), pp. xxv-xxvi. "Chronicle of Art: Women at the Royal Academy Schools," *Magazine of Art* (1889), p. xvii.

[6] "The Chronicle of Art. Art in March. Reform of the Royal Academy Schools," *Magazine of Art* (1890), pp. xxi-xxiv. "Chronicle of Art. Art in August. The New Rules at the Royal Academy Schools," *Magazine of Art* (1890), pp. xli-xliv.

[7] M. H. Spielman, "Glimpses of Artist-Life. The Royal Academy Schools," *Magazine of Art* (1888), pp. 55-60.

[8] Alice Greene, "The Girl Student in Paris," *Magazine of Art* (1883), pp. 286-287.

[9] Anna Mary Howitt, *An Art Student in Munich*, (London: Longman, 1853).

[10] Dinah Mulock Craik, "A Paris Atelier," in *About Money and Other Things*, (New York: Harper, 1887), pp. 183-197.

[11] Charlotte Weeks, "Lady Artists in Munich," *Magazine of Art* 4 (1881), pp. 343-347.

that women compete with men in schools and exhibitions so that they might achieve excellence through high standards and serious challenge.[12] A few critics, including Anna Jameson, took a "separate but equal" position, seeing women as somehow "clothed in moral beauty," to use the words of Sarah Stickney Ellis, a Victorian Phyllis Schlafly who wrote that custom had given Englishwomen "[t]he high and holy duty of cherishing and protecting the minor morals of life."[13] Many believed, along with John Ruskin, that this special moral sensibility would shine through anything a woman touched, including her paintings, to endow her art with a quality beyond the purview of men. This attitude provided a middle ground for those opposed in principle to women's leaving the hearthside to invade the world of men.

Ruskin's inability to see women's art clearly sent him from a "women can't paint" stand to a "nobody else can" attitude--both equally silly, but then Ruskin was often silly. Ironically it was Elizabeth Thompson's military painting, *Calling the Roll After an Engagement in the Crimea*, that sent him into such throes of enthusiasm. He was rather brutal to some women artists, including Anna Blunden, who sought his advice and asked for honest appraisals. Blunden's persistence, which so irritated Ruskin, would have seemed like dedication and admirable single-mindedness had she been an eager young male painter. Pamela Gerrish Nunn explains Ruskin's inconsistencies as a part of the larger controversy that was being waged around him.[14] Certainly the range of the public's ideas about women painters and women having careers was as extreme as Ruskin's opinions.

Modern critics often focus on nineteenth-century male condescension and persecution as a major cause of the difficulties encountered by women aspiring to professions in art. Undeniably, the English and American art worlds teemed with misogynistic males, "gatekeepers" with power and money determined to keep women out of business, education, art and the professions. But it would be grossly unfair to ignore the many males who used their power and influence to advance women's causes, just as it is unrealistic to ignore the Sarah Ellises and Eliza Lynn Lintons who made so much noise about women's divinely-imposed obligation to stay home and preserve family values. Queen Victoria herself, England's first lady of career women, deplored the women's movement even though she evidently saw no threat in the gentle art of painting. The truth is that the French Revolution, the industrial revolution, and the scientific revolution changed the world so quickly that the home seemed like a final refuge. Added to the millions of women without work, displaced

---

[12] *Women in Professions. Being the Professional Section of the International Congress of Women*, (London: T. Fisher Unwin, 1900).

[13] Sarah Stickney Ellis, *The Women of England: Their Social Duties and Domestic Habits*, (London: n.p., 1839).

[14] Pamela Gerrish Nunn, "Ruskin's Patronage of Women Artists," *Women's Art Journal*, No. 2 (September 1981), pp. 8-13.

from farms and cottage industries by big business, forced into idleness and into keeping the domestic world together, the result was a huge and complex, and most certainly fascinating, period of history where women entering the art world had a perfect opportunity, as the Victorians would say, to triumph over adversity and to become better persons for it. Without question, art and art history then and now benefit from women's considerable contributions and the diversity they brought to a once one-sided vision.

---

877. Jameson, Anna. *Memoirs and Essays Illustrative of Her Art, Literature and Social Morals*. New York: Wiley & Putnam, 1846.

Jameson's lucid prose style serves her well as she connects Titian's genius with Venice's mystery; analyzes Adelaide Kemble's sheer artistry and integrity on and off the stage; guides the British Museum visitor through the intricate Xanthian Marbles; points out the painful discrepancy between expectation and reality for working girls and women; and offers what must be the definitive word on the unfortunate, if not evil institution of governessing.

878. "The Female School of Design." *Art Union* (1 January 1849): 29.

A letter signed "The Guardian of a Pupil" protests the bad light, poor lodging and "innumerable petty annoyances" that the fifty or sixty women students of the Female School of Design must suffer. The editors reply that "some evil genius" seems bent on destroying the school, citing the mysterious removal of Mr. MacManus, who was doing a most satisfactory job and enjoyed considerable support from his pupils. His successor, Mr. Wilson, was responsible for MacManus' removal.

879. Jameson, Anna. "Some Thoughts on Art. Addressed to the Uninitiated." *Art Journal* (1 March 1849): 69-71; (1 April 1849): 103-105.

Art has become more than ever before a subject of interest and accessibility to the public, and as a consequence, the public is obligated to learn more about it. The rules of excellence were established by the Greeks and cannot be changed, but knowing something about what constitutes suitable materials, size, subject, and composition in sculpture, for example, is as essential for an educated person as knowledge about the sciences. Women, especially, are brought up to be cultural dilettantes, and "superficial knowledge of all kinds is the perdition of women." In all people, solid appreciation of art contributes toward individual and social well-being.

880. "One for the Ladies. The Old Water-Colour Society." *Art Journal* (June 1850): 192.

A Letter to the *Art Journal* signed "One for the Ladies" protests the demeaning title "Honorary Members" assigned to female exhibitors by the Arrangement Committee at the Old Water-Colour Society's exhibition. Further, there is no provision in the society's rules for such a designation; obviously the move was made by male members for the purpose of keeping women out of society membership. The editor, A.J., agrees with the letter. "This is not an age when the inferiority of women is to be maintained," and any effort to deny women's contributions to art and science is "miserable."

881. *Elegant Arts for Ladies*. London: Ward and Lock, 1856.

A section on oil painting assumes an ability to draw, provides assurance that painting in oils is neither dirty nor unhealthy, advises not to take the Pre-Raphaelites too seriously (they are "not likely to become popular in England"), and ends with a hope that the directions will lead the aspirant to "more advanced instruction." The preface points out that studying "elegant arts" is far from an idle diversion; the student will learn about colors, plants, animals, birds, and history.

882. "New Society of Female Artists." *London Times* (25 May 1857): 12.

The Society of Female Artists has been formed to aid women of all classes in exhibiting and selling their works. The society is not meant to compete with the Royal Academy, which has always had female exhibitors, but to offer women additional opportunities now necessarily closed to them by limited membership and original design. In addition, art lovers who cannot afford the prices of Royal Academy paintings will also find that the Society of Female Artists offers an opportunity to purchase good original artwork.

883. Maurice, F. D. "Female School of Art; Mrs. Jameson." *Macmillan's Magazine* 2 (1860): 227-235.

For Anna Jameson, nineteenth-century writer, critic, and advocate of human causes, the goal of women to be "integrated" into socially-productive participation is a psychological and a practical necessity. Many middle-class women, deprived of education and practical professional pursuits, find themselves not only stifled by enforced idleness, but hurt by male ridicule of their "silliness." Still other women desperately need the income to support themselves and dependents, but find that the professions are closed to them. The Female School of Design has proven its usefulness in the eight years since its founding, having trained women to work as teachers, as designers in factories, and as lithographers. The government has severely cut funding for the school; if it is to continue to contribute to the well-being of women in particular and the economy as a whole, as well as to a better balanced relationship between the sexes, it must have public recognition and support.

884. Purnell, Thomas. "Woman, and Art. The Female School of Design." *Art Journal* 23 (1861): 107-108.

Since lower-class women have always worked, and upper-class women don't need to work, it is middle-class women who must find suitable occupations when faced with the all-too-frequent necessity of feeding and clothing themselves when no husband or father is present to provide for them. The Female School of Design was founded with the aim of training middle-class, single women to work as teachers and designers in the arts. Its success is evident in its enrollment numbers, the medals and prizes won by its students, and in the success of its students in finding professions in which to support themselves. Although the school cannot be expected to pay for itself, the cost of running it is well within reason, especially considering its benefits. The threat of its being closed for lack of funding is to be taken seriously. The school may move to cheaper premises and may yet be saved by fund-raising activities, support of patrons (including the Queen herself) and donations from the public.

885. "Sisters in Art." *Illustrated Exhibitor and Magazine of Art* 2 (1862): 214-216, 238-240, 262-263, 286-288.

An accomplished and virtuous young orphan girl comes from the country to study art in drab London and to live with her snobbish aunt and miserly art-collector uncle. Even though she has progressed beyond the Female School of Design and she draws undraped models, Alice Law proves herself to be so good, charitable, and unaffected that she is able to soften the hearts of her elderly relatives and to rescue a poor girl from a future of child care and household drudgery by finding her a seventy-two-hour-a-week job and getting her enrolled in art classes.

886. Cobbe, Frances Power. *Women: Social and Moral Questions*. London: E. Faithfull, 1863.

Women cannot create great art and raise children at the same time, but they are definitely capable of great achievements. Women need education, access to books, leisure time, and stronger guidance in their formative years.

887. "Minor Topics of the Month: The Royal Academy." *Art Journal* (1 November 1863): 230.

An indefensible and irrational refusal of the Royal Academy Council against admitting women to the Academy schools is a discredit to the members "as artists and gentlemen." Some of the best works in Royal Academy exhibitions are from such notable artists as Henrietta Ward, Emily Osborn, Rebecca Solomon, and Annie and Martha Mutrie. The move is especially deplorable since women have made advances in other areas besides art; eventually the academy will have to be reformed, and then women will be admitted not only to the schools, but to the Royal Academy as full members.

888. "Female Art Students and the Royal Academy." *Art Journal* (1 May 1864): 154.

Twenty-three female art students have submitted a "memorial" to the Royal Academy protesting their exclusion from the Royal Academy schools. The academy closed its doors to female students last year, claiming lack of space, but the petitioners protest that this claim is groundless. They say that competition for space with male students will continue to be small, since there are far fewer females pursuing art careers; further, the female applicants compete for entrance on the same basis as males, which will not result in more students. The reviewer wholeheartedly supports the petition since there is considerable evidence of talent and genius in art by females. Women deserve the opportunity to improve their talent and to support themselves with it. "Justice, reason, public opinion, and gallantry" demand that the Royal Academy reconsider.

889. "Minor Topics of the Month." *Art Journal* (March 1870): 93-94.

Now that twenty-three females are enrolled at the Royal Academy schools with more deserving women no doubt on the way, the officials must arrange for separate facilities. It is "not seemly" that women should study nude models in the company of men, nor that an opportunity for flirtation be so openly available in the evening classes. At the School of Female Artists, women can study only "living and draped" models in safe, well-managed surroundings on Tuesdays and Fridays from twelve to four at three-and-a-half guineas for a three-month term.

890. Jeaffreson, John Cordy. "Female Artists and Art-Schools of England." *Art: Pictorial and Industrial: An Illustrated Magazine* 1, no. 1 (August 1870): 25-30.

Mary Moser and Angelica Kauffmann, the first female Royal Academicians, were not Englishwomen. Both were Swiss and both the daughters of artists. Both women were well established in their careers when the Royal Academy was founded, and not only did the Royal Academy have nothing to do with their success, but Moser's and Kauffman's signatures on the founding documents probably contributed significantly to the success of the Royal Academy. Female artists even in ancient Greece and Rome have been the children of artists, and thus owed their early artistic training not to art schools and academies, but to their relatives. The years following the success of Moser and Kauffmann reveal little more in the way of Royal Academy exhibits by women than "pieces of needlework and toys made of shells." The ratio of female to male representatives in the major exhibitions appears to have changed little over the decades, but allowances must be made for the facts that photography made the mostly female miniature painters obsolete, and that the academy has raised its standards. The current work by Henrietta Ward and Miss Mutrie is evidence of the progress toward excellence made by women painters. Still, no woman has achieved greatness in any professional field equal to the most famous man. Admittedly, rules and lack of educational opportunities have kept women out of science, the church, and the courts, but many women have had the advantage of domestic exposure to the masters of music and painting. One must consider the pressures of marriage, which "will always be the chief business of the best of womankind." Finally, male painters of the present day are less likely than the old masters to train and encourage female artistic endeavors.

891. "The Female School of Art." *Art Journal* (May 1871): 138.

Under the competent management of Louisa Gann, enrollment continues to rise at the Female School of Art and its students continue to carry off a creditable number of national prizes and scholarships. This year the Queen's gold medal is awarded to Emily Selous. Julia Pocock and Eliza Toulmin Smith have also distinguished themselves. Awards are also presented to Annie Elizabeth Hopkinson, Alice Locke, Ellen Isabella Hancock, Jeannie Moore, Christiana Powell, Ellen Ashwell, Jane Gibbons, and Charlotte Austen. While women will never abandon household duties which are their "privilege, pride, and reward," the accomplishments of students of the Female School of Art make it clear that in the study of art, at least, the campaigners for "Rights of Women" have a realistic aim.

892. "M. Yvon's ...School for Ladies." *Art Journal* (May 1871): 147.

> The recent upheaval in France has sent such talented figures as M. Yvon to England for refuge, giving students a rare opportunity to study with French teachers without going to Paris. M. Yvon will offer personal instructions to students working from a draped model. He will be assisted by one of his female students.

893. "Prizes to Superintendents of Schools of Art." *Art Journal* (February 1872): 57.

> Louisa Gann of Bloomsbury has received a prize of £40 in recognition of the excellence of her student's work at the Female School of Art. She is one of three second-place winners in a group of thirty-nine award recipients.

894. "Art Work for Women. I." *Art Journal* (March 1872): 65-66.

> Since well over half of the women in the United Kingdom must support themselves and sometimes have to provide for dependents as well, the aptitudes of many women and the willingness of manufacturers to employ them necessitates a careful assessment of work suitable, satisfying, and useful. Women can design Christmas, New Year's and Valentine's cards, color photographs, and paint and design china and pottery. Women can certainly succeed as art teachers, as has been demonstrated by Louisa Gann, who is rated second in her field. The National Art Training School at South Kensington accepts both male and female students with equal treatment. Teaching has "been the refuge for ladies incapable of other work," but with diligence it can be raised to the status of a respected profession.

895. "Art Work for Women. II." *Art Journal* (April 1872): 102-103.

> Women can hardly be expected to succeed in the arts as long as they are tied to domestic duties with their constant interruptions and demands, and as long as girls receive educations inferior to boys and are denied equal training in diligence and concentration. Girls with a passion for learning and knowledge are forced to sit idle; this is inexcusable because women outnumber men in England by nearly a million, and "three out of six" adult women are principal providers for dependents. Manufacturers are willing to hire women but complain that the best workers are the ones most likely to leave if they have an opportunity to marry. However, women who leave work to marry leave space for the other women who are forced to earn a living. Providing early training for women will make them better workers and give them "a resource in reserve for darker days."

896. "Art Work for Women. III. How the Work May be Done." *Art Journal* (May 1872): 129-131.

Extensive opportunities in art education are already open to women, and many women are working, but "it is not enough that a race-course should be open to all runners." Women frequently prove themselves to be unreliable employees who produce slipshod work. Technical schools, such as those in Scandinavia, should be opened in Britain to teach mathematics, chemistry, mechanics, economics, and business skills to women. Apprenticeships for females would also teach them the patience and diligence needed to reach excellence in art-related fields.

897. "Art Notes and Minor Topics. The Society of Lady Artists." *Art Journal* (February 1874): 61.

The Society of Lady Artists opens the doors of its new home at Number 48, Great Marlborough Street at the beginning of March. The society reorganized in 1865 and has been exhibiting regularly for about fifteen years. The new gallery has better light and more room than the old one. All art lovers are duty-bound to support this useful organization with its pleasant exhibitions.

898. "Art Publications." *Art Journal* (August 1876): 255-256.

While it is undeniably true that the art world has always been dominated by males, it is especially true that women have made invaluable contributions and deserve to be recognized. Ellen Clayton's book *English Female Artists*, published in two volumes by Tinsley Brothers, makes no attempt at art criticism, but it supplies a much-needed history of women artists in England from the time that Artemisia Gentileschi came with her father to paint portraits for Charles I. Clayton includes Frances Reynolds, a noted portrait painter of her time and sister of Sir Joshua Reynolds. Angelica Kauffmann, Mary Moser and Maria Cosway are included as founding members of the Royal Academy. The book concludes with Mary Harrison, Anna Maria Charretie, and Adelaide Macguire, all of whom died last year. It is difficult at times to obtain information about women artists who do not feel comfortable having attention called to themselves in print, but Clayton has done well with her compilation. She has, it is true, said more than necessary about some artists and not nearly enough about others, and she has omitted sculptors, but these shortcomings do not detract from the value of a highly commendable work.

899. "Art Publications." *Art Journal* (August 1876): 256.

>Anna Jameson numbers among the famous critics who comment on the theme of art inspired by Shakespeare's plays. The volume titled *Shakespeare Scenes and Characters*, published by Macmillan & Co. contains thirty-six engravings and essays on Shakespeare, his work, his inspiration, and his characters.

900. "Minor Topics. 'Pension' for Lady Artists in Rome." *Art Journal* (October 1877): 317.

>Another 500 pounds is needed to complete the sum of £1000 to establish a "pension," a home for young English women whose love of art drives them to study in Rome against all arguments of common sense. The proposed home will be self-supporting, and will provide "the comforts and protection of a home" as well as the best information to aid women in finding the best art instruction.

901. "Minor Topics. Earl Granville...Dover School of Art." *Art Journal* (December 1877): 273.

>Prizes awarded to women students at the Dover School of Art were accompanied by an address by Earl Granville, Lord Warden of the Cinque Ports, who feels that women in the past and in the present have benefitted considerably from their study in art schools. He did not mention the injustice of the Royal Academy's refusal to accept women.

902. Duffield, Mary Elizabeth Rosenberg. *The Art of Flower Painting*. New York: Putnam's, 1878.

>All a novice flower painter needs, from materials and techniques, to minute cautions and instructions, are carefully set out in an effort to encourage further advancement in what was once considered a standard feminine accomplishment. Modern improvements in watercolor media as well as new varieties of flowers make flower painting worth developing into serious art in the tradition of Rachel Ruysch, and more recently, Anne Bartholomew.

903. MacPherson, Geraldine. *Memoirs of Mrs. Jameson*. London: Longmans, 1878.

>Drawing from her aunt's letters, her own personal memories, and from family history, Geraldine MacPherson gives an account of Anna Jameson's life and final days. Included in an appendix are two of Anna Jameson's articles in the *Art Journal*: "John Gibson" and "Some Thoughts on Art, Addressed to the Uninitiated."

>Reproduction (b/w):

Jameson, Anna: *Anna Jameson at the Age of Sixteen from a Miniature by her Father.*

904. "Art Publications." *Art Journal* (November 1878): 235.

Anna Jameson's niece has published *The Life of Mrs. Jameson*, a biography of a woman remembered with considerable respect for her achievements in art criticism. Over twenty years after Jameson's death the book is a reminder of her *Art Journal* articles (reprinted in the appendix) as well as of the woman herself. Jameson was "perhaps more respected than loved"; she was somewhat cold, and she was "neither happy herself nor the cause of happiness in others." The book is too brief to give ample space to Jameson's full and productive career.

905. "Manchester Society of Women Artists." *Englishwoman's Review* 10, no. 79 (1879): 469-470.

Some Manchester women have formed The Manchester Society of Women Artists to provide life classes and to extend a broader course of training, experience and culture than what is presently available. The society provides classes in elementary drawing from the antique, and drawing and painting from live models. The committee forming the society includes artists who have exhibited at the Salon in Paris and at the Royal Academy. An exhibit of women painters is a possibility, and financial contributions are "earnestly requested."

906. Oldcastle, Alice. "Mrs. Jameson: A Biographical Sketch." *Magazine of Art* 2 (1879): 123-125.

Irish-born art critic Anna Jameson led a long and productive life in the company of women friends of literary repute such as Ottilie von Goethe, Harriet Martineau, and Lady Byron. She was especially good at interpreting the subjects in art for an audience of all classes and educational levels.

907. "Minor Topics. Mr. E.M. Ward, R.A." *Art Journal* (February 1879): 37.

Edward Ward has died under "melancholy circumstances."

908. "Minor Topics. Mrs. E.M. Ward." *Art Journal* (June 1879): 119.

Henrietta Ward has announced that her school will offer an extensive course of study to women wishing to increase their artistic skills. Each month the school will be visited by a prominent Royal Academician. Ward's address is No. 6, William Street, Lowndes Square.

909. "Minor Topics." *Art Journal* (November 1879): 254.

    As predicted, Henrietta Ward's art school is filling an urgent need and meeting with great success. Ward's school will begin a winter course of instruction soon.

910. Oldcastle, John. "Queen Victoria and Art." *Magazine of Art* 3 (1880): 283-288.

    Before the death of Prince Albert, Victoria regularly attended Royal Academy exhibitions. After Albert's death she continued her interest in art and artists. Purchases for her private collection include Elizabeth Thompson Butler's *The Roll Call*. Her own work, including some etchings, has been submitted to public exhibitions.

911. "Minor Topics." *Art Journal* (February 1880): 62.

    The Society for Promoting the Employment of Women is sponsoring classes in Kensington, taught by Frederica Moffat, to teach wood engraving "for ladies who are unfortunately compelled to labour for their maintenance."

912. "Minor Topics. Lady Royal Academicians." *Art Journal* (February 1880): 62.

    The Royal Academy has decided to consider for election in the future qualified women who will have the same privileges as male members except they will not be permitted to vote in Royal Academy elections nor to attend the annual banquet. The editors see no reason why elected female members should not vote, and it is fortunately no longer neither wise nor customary to exclude women from banquets.

913. "Old Masters at the Royal Academy." *Art Journal* (March 1880): 75.

    One of the pictures chosen as part of a loan exhibition is by the late James Ward, R.A., Henrietta Ward's grandfather.

    Reproductions (b/w):

    Queen Victoria: Two etchings of a little girl; *Favorite Dogs.*

914. "Minor Topics. The Royal Academy." *Art Journal* (June 1880): 191.

    The engraver, Frederick Stackpoole, has recently been elected as an associate of the Royal Academy on the strength of his work with such paintings as Elizabeth Thompson's *Roll Call* and *Quatre Bras.*

915. J.H.P. "Children in Painting and Sculpture." *Magazine of Art* 4 (1881): 286-289.

Children have been a popular subject of painters throughout the ages. Some of the world's greatest artists have met the challenge and experienced the delight of having children as subjects. For modern painters, children signify the beginning of the great mystery of human life as well as the joyous expression of innocence and purity.

Reproductions (b/w engraving):

Perugini, Kate: *Effie*.

916. Weeks, Charlotte J. "Lady Artists in Munich." *Magazine of Art* 4 (1881): 343-347.

Such a large number of English students studying in continental art schools suggests that something is lacking in opportunities for study at home. This is particularly true for women, who find academic study is closed to them, but that they are welcome in other countries. Of all the possible places for study, Munich offers the best instruction, the most opportunity for companionship with artists and students, and the most economical and hospitable living conditions. The female art student must pay for what the male students obtain free, but the Munich system where one works in a private studio visited regularly for individual instruction by an extremely competent professor is still a tremendous advantage.

Reproductions (b/w):

A Lady's Studio at Munich (artist not identified).

917. "Art Notes and Reviews. Art Notes." *Art Journal* (May 1881): 158-160.

A review in the French art journal *Le Moniteur des Arts* reveals not only a lack of accurate knowledge of English exhibitions, but also comments on the English prejudice and restrictions against female artists. Nearly all French artists, *Le Moniteur* proclaims, are attentive to women, while the English expect women to manage as best they can with the small things in life. At a recent election of the Society of Painters in Water Colours, only two out of fifty-three candidates were elected, revealing a "capricious exclusiveness." Two candidates, Mary Foster and Edith Martineau, received thirteen votes each of the twenty votes required for election.

918. "Art Notes. A Series of Winter Lectures." *Magazine of Art* 5 (1882): x.

Miss Bennet's College of Art for Ladies, South Wimbledon provides a moderately-priced home with excellent instructors and studios. In November, Mr. Sydney Hodges lectured on "Painting and Word Painting."

919. "Art Notes. The Inequalities Which Exist in the Royal Academy." *Magazine of Art* 5 (1882): xix.

Women and men study on an equal footing in the Royal Academy and government art schools until it is time to study figure drawing and painting which must be done from an undraped model. At this point the women are denied instruction; the results of their deprivation is clear in their advanced work. It is hardly necessary for men and women to work in the same room, but there is little sense in men being allowed to draw from undraped male and female models while women cannot study even female models. While many argue that lower standards are required of women artists, the opposite is true: women's work is judged more critically. An easy remedy could undo a severe injustice.

920. "Art Notes. It is Worthy of Note." *Magazine of Art* 5 (1882): xix.

The Slade School in London provides partially-draped models for both female and male students. One of the best and most promising students in the school is a female.

921. Cole, Sir Henry. *A Handbook for the Architecture, Sculpture, and Decorations of Westminster Abbey: with Fifty-Six Illustrations and Designs on Wood Engraved by Ladies.* London: Bell, 1882.

The preface credits the illustrations to Lady Calcott, Lady Palgrave, "and other art amateurs." The wood engravings, too, were rendered by females "to create an occupation for women."

Reproductions (b/w engravings):

Sketches of interior, decorations, and tombs.

922. De Mattos, Katharine. "Flowers and Flower Painters." *The Magazine of Art* (1883): 453-455.

It is not true that anyone can paint flowers, and it is certainly not true that just anyone *should* paint them. Women tend to believe that because they are women they have an affinity for flowers, but flowers are not a trivial subject; painting them requires careful study and an appreciation of their "haunting and soul-stirring power."

923. Greene, Alice. "The Girl Student in Paris." *Magazine in Art* (1883): 286-287.

The "École pour Dames" in Paris offers considerable advantages over similar institutions in London. The studio is centrally located in a Paris art district. The spirits of students, teachers and models are high. Students work with a live model and the master visits daily, spending ten to fifteen minutes with each student. Students enjoy ample opportunity to improve their French, attend operas and concerts, and visit art galleries which are open even on Sunday.

924.   Ruskin, John. *Realistic Schools of Painting. Lectures Given in Oxford.* Orpington, Kent: George Allen, 1883.

Only the hope of resurrection makes life's sorrows bearable. Artists with skill, imagination, sensitivity and attention to detail can capture this religious feeling and bring comfort into the homes and hearts of the bereaved and suffering. Women can, against all expectations, paint and draw capably; their artistic talents, together with the sympathy and goodness that is natural to women, equip them to render their subjects with sympathy and feeling.

925.   Weeks, Charlotte J. "Women at Work: The Slade Girls." *Magazine of Art* VI (1883): 324-328.

The generosity of Felix Slade has provided lectures in the fine arts at Oxford and Cambridge universities, and has established in London a school at which instruction is given by an artist-professor. The London Slade School is open to female as well as to male students; instruction and opportunities are available on an equal basis to both sexes. Female and male students compete for the same prizes, and they work from the same casts and models. Artistic instruction and academic instruction is careful, modern and thorough. Enrollment at present consists of an equal number of males and females, but females have won a significant number of scholarships and prizes. Among the distinguished students are Evelyn Pickering, Kate Greenaway, Hilda Montalba, Jessie Macgregor, and Edith Martineau.

Reproductions (b/w):
Burd, Miss A.P.: Sketches
King, Miss E.S.: Sketches.

926.   Scott, Leader. "Women at Work: Their Functions in Art." *Magazine of Art* (1884): 98-99.

Since art training from childhood is practically compulsory, and since too many women find themselves in need of something to do, either from economic need or a need to express themselves, walls and art galleries are crowded with bad pictures. Careful assessment will determine the difference between genius, talent and aptitude. The person with genius should be helped and encouraged to interpret life and nature in a way that only a woman can. The person with talent lacks the ability to interpret, and can only copy what she sees. She should not waste her time trying to paint pictures; she can earn a good living and make a positive contribution in the decorative and design field. The woman with a mere aptitude for art makes a priceless contribution at home, teaching her children, decorating their clothes and her walls and in general beautifying everyone's otherwise ordinary surroundings.

927. Somerville, E. Oenone. "An 'Atelier des Dames.'" *Magazine of Art* (1886): 152-157.

Since women are more content to work hard for very little, and to live quietly without frills, life in humble circumstances studying art in a Paris studio provides interest, freedom, and companionship that many women find quite agreeable. Every studio has its predictable situations, its personality types, its grim and its funny situations. Studying art in Paris is not easy, but a woman who has tried it will find the ordinary world "a very sorry empty place."

928. Craik, Dinah Maria (Mulock). "A Paris Atelier." In *About Money and Other Things*, 183-197. New York: Harper and Bros., 1887.

Women of all classes living together in simple lodgings and working hard for long hours present a model of modesty, industry, nobility, and mutual concern that puts the idle "butterfly" in proper perspective. Art is both a necessary and a suitable occupation for many women; these art students demonstrate that women without men can profit from being useful and industrious. If marriage does present itself, these women are not the worse for having worked, and should a single life be their lot, they will be better for having a busy and productive life.

929. "Chronicle of Art. Woman, and Her Chance as an Artist." *Magazine of Art* (1888): xxv-xxvi.

After the "first hot flush of youth and inspiration," it is obvious that women lack the staying power and the genius to succeed in serious art. The few women who have reached success in art, such as Lebrun and Kauffmann are exceptions that "emphasize the rule." Rosa Bonheur is as masculine in her art as she is in her face and in her dress. Female art students usually win a few minor awards before they "lose themselves in the Nirvana of obscurity." Art is the proving ground for the generally-accepted assumption that true creativity is beyond female abilities. The claim that women have been denied equal opportunities with men is merely an excuse for what is a natural lack of ability, and the sooner the Royal Academy adopts rules to discourage amateurs and china painters the better.

930. Spielmann, M. H. "Glimpses of Artist-Life. The Royal Academy Schools." *Magazine of Art* (1888): 55-60.

The male students resent the women's intrusion into a traditionally male institution, while the female students snub the men, whom they see as "selfish, noisy and ... ineligible." Women were admitted to the Royal Academy only through a "curious mistake," when a female aspirant pointed out that no written law in the Royal Academy rules specifically excluded women.

931. "The Chronicle of Art. Women at the Royal Academy Schools." *Magazine of Art* (1889): xvii.

An "extraordinary preponderance" of females admitted to the Royal Academy schools was reported last year. This year ten out of sixteen applicants are of the "artistically weaker sex." Women cannot justify their numbers since they seldom complete the course of studies and those who do complete them seldom produce anything but mediocre works. The level of skill required for academy admission involves nothing more demanding than studies of plaster casts, at which women excel. The Reform Committee of the Royal Academy must change the admission levels to correct this imbalance.

932. "The Chronicle of Art. Reviews." *Magazine of Art* (1889): xviii-xix.

Miss C. J. Ffloukes' *Handbook of the Italian Schools in the Dresden Gallery* published by W.H. Allen and Co. joins the vast number of ill-informed and largely plagiarized guide books already swamping an art-hungry public. Ffloukes is a "sincere dilettante" whose information is confused and jumbled, but she deserves praise for the comprehensiveness of her guidebook.

933. "Reviews." *Magazine of Art* (1889): xxxv.

Mrs. C. H. Strahan's carefully arranged and compendious *A History of French Painting,* published by Sampson Low and Co., contains "an extraordinary amount of information, collected and collated from scores of books and periodicals, and subdivided and arranged with rare intelligence and skill." As is usual with American writers, however, Strahan exhibits an ignorance of English art when she remarks that many English collect French art, while not much English art is to be found in France. Other lady-writers before her have mixed up "cause and effect," but this is a small defect. The book is a valuable addition to art history.

934. "The Chronicle of Art. Art in March. Reform of the Royal Academy Schools." *Magazine of Art* (1890): xxi-xxiv.

New admission standards, a more rigorous probationary period, and removal of the ban on undraped models for female students will result in a higher quality of graduates from the Royal Academy Schools.

935. "Chronicle of Art. Art in August. The New Rules at the Royal Academy Schools." *Magazine of Art* (1890): xli-xliv.

Changing the entrance requirements of the Royal Academy art schools has had the desired effect of dramatically lowering the number of women admitted. In addition, the age limitation of twenty-three years has excluded "petrified, middle-aged mediocrity" from the art schools.

936. Brown, Lucy Madox. "Ford Madox Brown." *Magazine of Art* (1890): 289-296.

Brown's biographical sketch about her father includes mention of his principal works.

937. "The Chronicle of Art. Art in March. Reviews." *Magazine of Art* (1891): xxi-xxiv.

Louise Jopling's book *Hints to Amateurs*, published by Chapman and Hall, unfortunately would lead amateur painters in watercolor to believe that a few tricks can substitute for hard work and experience. Jopling admits that she knows nothing about watercolor, but that she has interviewed experienced painters in that genre in order to gather hints. The book attempts to cover an extensive range which includes oil painting, photography, anatomy, and perspective. Jopling's superficial treatment is likely to send the amateur "spinning along the road to ruin."

938. "The Chronicle of Art. Art in May. Reviews." *Magazine of Art* (1891): xxix-xxxii.

Isabel Snow's novel *The School of Art*, published by Fisher Unwin, is an unconvincing and uninteresting novel about art schools, art students, art critics, a heroine who marries a Royal Academician and who, perhaps, "paints almost as well as her husband."

939. Fenwick-Miller, Florence. "The Ladies' Column." *Illustrated London News* (31 January 1891): 160.

Those interested in setting up and staging a tableau might wish to have professional help with arranging the lighting; care must be taken to choose pictures that do not require exhausting poses or unblinking countenances, and novices in particular should exercise caution in straining the nervous system by holding poses for more than a minute at a time. Ladies desiring to achieve excellence and recognition in the art world must not only work hard, but have the courage to act for themselves and to disregard public pressure to conform to standards of meekness and obedience. That thirteen of the twenty-one most recent candidates accepted to the Royal Academy schools were women is an indicator that women's work is improving and that opportunities are opening; still, women must work with diligence and courage, taking for examples the success of Anna Lea Merritt and Henrietta Rae. Both women were severely criticized a few years ago for exhibiting paintings of female nudes. Both women ignored public outcry and continued to paint what they felt was best for them. Their courage is now being rewarded with praise and recognition for their work.

940. "The Victoria Discussion Society." *Victoria Magazine* (3 August 1892): 320-338.

Dr. Zerffi's address to the society includes a catalogue of famous female artists from the ancient to the present time. He exhorts women to take advantage of increasing opportunities and to apply themselves to the arts for which they are so naturally suited. Emily Faithfull observes that the women who have made history in art are exceptions, and that women's artistic accomplishments do not match men's because women and girls have been at the mercy of domestic demands. Julia Ward Howe, a guest presider, remarks on the innate compatibility between domestic accomplishments and artistic endeavors.

941. MacKenzie, Tessa. *The Art Schools of London 1895: a Description of the Principal Art Schools in the London District*. London: Chapman & Hall, 1895.

At Mrs. Jopling's School, emphasis is on working from a live model, both clothed and nude. Still lifes, landscapes, and animal studies make up the balance. Jopling is frequently at the school checking students' progress, and will demonstrate her technique in head studies for a fee. At Mrs. Walker's school, students must learn correct drawing before they are allowed to work from a live model. Well-known visiting artists supplement the instruction. The Royal Family are among the patrons of Henrietta Ward's school, as are both serious students and hobbyists wanting to improve. Ward holds classes three days a week, and students work from casts, still life, and draped living models; animal painting is a specialty.

942. Hill, Georgiana. *Women in English Life from Medieval to Modern Times.* London: Richard Bentley, 1896.

After Sir Charles Eastlake's encouragement opened the Royal Academy schools to women in 1861, female artists found a gradual improvement in the number of art schools and the quality of instruction available to them. While the number of women recognized as great talents still remains low, their capabilities are becoming increasingly obvious. Their work has much to do with the improving standards of public taste.

943. *Women in Professions. Being the Professional Section of the International Congress of Women. London, July 1899.* London: T. Fisher Unwin, 1900.

The section on women in art is opened by a long address by Emily Sartain, of the Philadelphia School of Design for Women. Sartain provides an extensive list of American and English women distinguishing themselves in illustration, stained glass, murals, engraving, and picture and portrait painting. An architect and a sculptor assure women of their places in these fields. Barbara Hamley, a miniaturist from Great Britain, discusses her art, which she says is coming back into vogue. Anna Lea Merritt, representing the United States, insists that women have only themselves to blame if they do not succeed--it is not compulsory for them to marry or to exhaust themselves with overwork, and many successful male artists taught themselves to draw and to paint without the benefit of art schools. Merritt insists that women should compete on an equal basis with men, "avoiding the shows of women's work." Louisa Starr Canziani of Great Britain warns against the dangers of art for art's sake, nudes for nudes' sake, and the lack of discriminating taste typical in men; women with their "purer instinct" have the power and the duty to keep morality in art and advertising. Mrs. Montefiori Nicholls of Great Britain describes a program to improve the lives of London school children by exposing them to beautiful pictures. Finally, Miss Cridgett of Great Britain testifies that thanks to the effort of the National Vigiliant Society, public advertising is much improved.

944. Jopling, Louise. "On the Education of the Artistic Faculty. Education and Professions." In *The Women's Library, 1*, 102-172. London: Chapman & Hall, 1903.

Art can cure sickness, elevate the mind, develop powers of observation, strengthen the memory, "educate and refine the prosaic multitude," and provide myriad occupations for young women. Jopling gives advice on choosing an art school and preparing for admission. She advises artists on such subjects as drawing, studying anatomy, painting portraits and landscapes and arranging colors on a palette. She is emphatic on the subject of education for girls. Their educations should be taken seriously, and they should abandon needlework in favor of learning to cook for themselves.

945. Morris, May. "*Opus Anglicanum*. The Syon Cope." *Burlington Magazine* (October 1904): 278-284.

Ecclesiastical embroidery of the thirteenth and fourteenth centuries is rich in detail and sophisticated in design. Conventions in colors and stitching distinguish artists of different countries. This form of art deserves closer study by historians and artists.

946. ---. "*Opus Anglicanum* at the Burlington Fine Arts Club." *Burlington Magazine* VII, no. XXVIII (July 1905): 302-309.

The richness and sophistication of medieval English art does not end with cathedrals and manuscripts. English embroidery contains supreme examples of decorative detail, imaginative conception and design, and superlative technique. The public exhibition at the Burlington Fine Arts Club offers examples of "the versatility of the medieval genius at its best and happiest moments" as well as of its drama, character, and exuberance.

947. Bayliss, Wyke. *Olives: The Reminiscences of a President*. London: George Allen, 1906.

As president of the Royal Academy, Bayliss' speeches influenced the art world and reflected many of the academy's directions and attitudes. Bayliss presents a fresh and open attitude toward women in the art world, aside from his rather tiresome habit of speaking in classical parables. (In one of his stories, Minerva wishes to meet Lucy Kemp-Welch, whose portrait of Pegasus she admires; when Minerva finds that Kemp-Welch, Louise Jopling and Constance Smedley have gone off to the Lyceum Club, the muses and Minerva promptly follow them, presumably to talk about art). In an address to the Royal Society of British Artists in 1897, Bayliss admonishes art students that "there is a sisterhood as well as a brotherhood in art." Bayliss finds it strange that it has taken the art world so long to discover that women can paint. His appreciation of Anna Lea Merritt's *Love Locked Out* becomes a parable of Minerva (The Royal Academy) challenging Arachne (the female artist) to a picture-painting duel. Arachne wins, and Minerva beats her severely. But that was the case in the bad old times, according to Bayliss, because when Merritt sent *Love Locked Out* to the Royal Academy and she was not beaten, but honored as a genius.

948. James, Bartlett Burleigh. *Woman in All Ages and in All Countries.* Philadelphia: Rittenhouse, 1907.

The chapter titled "Women of the Nineteenth Century" contains a brief account of Laura Herford's artful admission into the Royal Academy School which then opened its doors for women. The chapter quotes Ellen Clayton's criticism of the Academy's willingness to leave female artists "to work in the cold shade of utter neglect."

949. Erskine, Mrs. Steuart., ed. *Anna Jameson. Letters and Friendships.* New York: Dutton, 1915.

Letters from and to Anna Jameson illuminate the career and personality of a woman from her first job as a penniless governess to her old age as a famous writer and art critic. Her friends and correspondents include Lady Byron, Ottilie von Goethe, Elizabeth Barrett Browning, Harriet Martineau, and Barbara Bodichon. Her letters reflect an observant, talented, intelligent, and unassuming woman.

950. Jameson, Anna. *Letters of Anna Jameson to Ottilie von Goethe.* London: Oxford University Press, 1939.

Anna Jameson's letters to her close friend Ottilie von Goethe contain references to books and women writers rather than to paintings and women artists. The letters present a frank and detailed record of Jameson's problematic marriage as well as of her close friendships with influential women of the day. The editor provides a useful introduction and index.

Reproductions (b/w):

Portrait of Anna Jameson

Specimen of Anna Jameson's handwriting.

951. Gardner, Albert Ten Eyck. "A Century of Women." *Bulletin of the Metropolitan Museum of Art* (1948): 110-118.

A short history of women in American art mentions Mrs. Ellet's *Women Artists in All Ages and Countries;* Ellet took most of her material from a German publication and added a few chapters of her own, the last three about Americans.

952. Bell, Quentin. *The Schools of Design.* London: Routledge, 1963.

The Female School of Design encountered problems because of the invasion of middle-class women looking for husbands; the school was intended to provide training for lower-class women who needed work. Further, the women also distracted male students and drawing masters. Women who were given training and education--even the plain ones--often married and their training was lost to manufacturing industries. The schools for women were overcrowded and plagued with politics and mismanagement by male administrators. Mrs. M'lan, who directed the school in London, insisted that all her pupils be serious students anxious to earn their own living.

953. Packer, Lona Mosk. *Christina Rossetti*. Berkeley: University of California Press, 1963.

While Christina Rossetti exemplified quiet, cloistered, frustrated femininity, Elizabeth Siddall was celebrated as a great beauty, her art encouraged and subsidized by Dante Gabriel Rossetti and his friends, including the great John Ruskin. Even the success of Christina Rossetti's *Goblin Market* was dampened by Elizabeth Siddall's death by a laudanum overdose and Dante Gabriel Rossetti's subsequent dramatic despair. The real and enduring talent, however, has been Christina Rossetti's.

954. Fredeman, William E. *Pre-Raphaelitism: A Bibliocritical Guide*. Cambridge: Harvard University Press, 1965.

Most of the references to women are incidental, but the thorough treatment and efficient organization of material make this a good source for researchers seeking locations of letters, paintings, and drawings in both public and private collections.

955. Thomas, Clara. *Love and Work Enough: The Life of Anna Jameson*. London: MacDonald, 1967.

This definitive biography of Anna Jameson contains excerpts from her letters and diaries, information about her marriage and short stay in Canada, as well as incisive and objective analysis of her life and works. A comprehensive bibliography includes a list of manuscript collections, works by Jameson, and general background information.

956. Hutchinson, Sidney C. *The History of the Royal Academy 1768-1968*. New York: Taplinger, 1968.

The "Instrument of Foundation" of the Royal Academy, signed in 1768 by thirty-eight men and two women, specified that all forty members must be artists of high reputation, residents of Great Britain, and "men of fair moral characters." While the two female founders, Angelica Kauffmann and Mary Moser, were undoubtedly women of fair moral character, the Academy chose in 1879 to exclude women regardless of their artistic achievement, standing in the art community, or their moral character. The election in 1936 of Laura Knight opened the Academy's doors to female members, but an exhibition of her work somewhat later is referred to as a "one-man show." Laura Ann Herford, who gained admission to the Academy's art school in 1860, had an easier time of it, since no one could find a gender-based exclusionary clause. A quota for female students was quickly imposed; Louisa Starr's winning the school's gold medal for painting in 1867 must have both justified the efforts of some and confirmed the worst fears of others.

957. Holman-Hunt, Diana. *My Grandmothers and I*. New York: Norton, 1969.

Diana Holman-Hunt's account of her childhood with her paternal grandparents and her maternal grandmother, Edith Holman-Hunt, tells a story of the Pre-Raphaelite circle that blends truth, fiction, history, and sheer Victorian dottiness.

958. Leslie, George F. *The Inner Life of the Royal Academy*. 1914. Reprint. New York: Benjamin Blom, 1971.

Under the chapter headings, "The Schools of the Royal Academy," one finds such sub-headings as "The invasion of the school by females" and "Pretty girl advantages"; within the text, however, one finds a quiet appreciation of the invaders. Leslie admires their diligence and appreciates the aesthetic contributions of their physical appearance. He worries that pretty female students possibly get preference over plain ones. He seems to harbor no grudge against Laura Herford for her part in opening the school to women; he makes it clear that her work was quite good and that she was not motivated by self-interest. A footnote describes Herford as a dedicated nurse during a cholera epidemic and regrets her death caused by an accidental overdose of chloroform.

959. Roget, John Lewis. *A History of the Old Water-Colour Society, Now the Royal Society of Painters in Water Colours*. 1891. Reprint. Clopton, U.K.: Antique Collector's Club, 1972.

This combination of history, biography, and criticism relies on records of the society as well as on information from Ellen Clayton's *English Female Artists*. The good news: lucid prose style, excellent organization and a good index. The bad news: no bibliography, and incomplete footnote citations.

960. Iskin, Ruth. "Sexual and Self-Imagery in Art--Male and Female." *Womanspace* (June 1973): 4-11.

Female nudes painted by men tend to reflect a passive idealism of male perfection capable of being possessed by the male owner/viewer. Women artists who paint female nudes encounter complex difficulties: they tend to paint copies of the male perspective and must at the same time confront their own sexuality. Nineteenth-century woman artists such as Rosa Bonheur and Mary Cassatt avoided the dilemma by avoiding the subject. Cassatt painted clothed women and Bonheur painted animals.

961. Wood, Christopher. *Victorian Panorama: Paintings of Victorian Life*. London: Faber, 1976.

Paintings by both female and male artists supply the illustrations for this book about Victorian experience. Three of Emma Brownlow's paintings provide especially valuable illustrations to a chapter titled "Foundlings." Since Brownlow was raised in a home for orphans, her personal experience coupled with artistic competence enabled her to paint detailed, unsentimental scenes of orphanage life.

Reproductions (col):

Brownlow, Emma: *The Family Restored to Its Mother*

Hayllar, Edith: *A Summer Shower*

Reproductions (b/w):

Blunden, Anna: *For Only One Short Hour*

Bowkett, Anna: *Preparing Tea*

Butler, Elizabeth Thompson: *The Roll Call; The Remnants of an Army*

Farmer, Mrs. Alexander: *An Anxious Hour; Reading Punch*

Osborn, Emily Mary: *For the Last Time; Nameless and Friendless.*

962. Cline, C. L., ed. *The Owl and the Rossettis: Letters of Charles A. Howell and Dante Gabriel, Christina and William Michael Rossetti*. University Park, Pennsylvania: Pennsylvania State University Press, 1978.

Reading others' mail tends to be tedious and confusing, since private correspondence contains much that is meaningful and useful only to the persons to whom they were written. While these letters mention Fanny Cornforth, Jane, Jenny and May Morris, Alexa Wilding, Elizabeth Siddall and Mary Zambaco, the references are mostly scattered, cryptic, superficial and as engrossing as a Victorian laundry list. Cline's footnotes and annotations provide some relief.

963. Greer, Germaine. *The Obstacle Race*. New York: Farrar Straus Giroux, 1979.

The chapter titled "The Nineteenth Century" maintains that male art teachers were condescending, bullying egomaniacs, and that the docility of their female students resulted in tame and derivative work. Since the art of such successful nineteenth-century artists as Anna Lea Merritt and Rosa

Bonheur are no longer considered important, women have still to come to terms with the complexities of gender and power in a social and artistic context.

Reproductions (b/w):

Bunce, Kate: *Musica*

De Morgan, Evelyn: *Love Which Moves the Sun and the Other Stars*

Merritt, Anna Lea: *War*

Nasmyth, Charlotte: *A Wooded Landscape with Travelers on a Path*

Nasmyth, Jane: *Forness Abbey with a Distant View of Morecambe Bay*

Osborn, Emily Mary: *Nameless and Friendless*

Thompson, Elizabeth: *Quatre Bras*

Reproductions (col):

Bonheur, Rosa: *The Horse Fair*

Butler, Elizabeth: *Scotland Forever!*

964. Thomas, Clara. "Anna Jameson: Art Historian and Critic." *Woman's Art Journal* (March 1980): 20-22.

Anna Jameson's art history and art criticism was meant to educate and refine the artistic taste of the middle classes. Sometimes opinionated and usually moralistic, Jameson's works were widely read (*Sacred and Legendary Art* went through 113 printings in about sixty years) on both sides of the Atlantic. Although her writing is no longer taken seriously, her positive influence and contributions to the study of art should not be overlooked.

965. Nunn, Pamela Gerrish. "Ruskin's Patronage of Women Artists." *Women's Art Journal* 2, no. 2 (September 1981): 8-13.

Ruskin's attitude toward female artists can best be described as inconsistent. He maintained that women could not paint and were not to be taken seriously, yet he encouraged quite a few women by buying their paintings and favoring them with private letters and public recognition. His ambivalence and lack of insight seems to be largely a reflection of his times.

Reproductions (b/w):

Alexander, Francisca: *Roadside Songs of Tuscany*

Boyce (Wells), Joanna: *Elgiva*

Butler, Elizabeth Thompson: *The Roll Call*

Louisa, Lady Waterford: *Looking Out to Sea.*

966. Casteras, Susan P. "Virgin Vows: The Early Victorian Artists' Portrayal of Nuns and Novices." *Victorian Studies* (December 1981): 157-184.

An appendix to this discussion of women's religious orders and Victorian artists' renditions of nuns includes a listing of works by Anna Blunden, Emma Brownlow, Mrs. Briane, and Emma Harriet Raimbach, among others.

967. Cherry, Deborah. "Picturing the Private Sphere." *Feminist Art News* 5 (1982): 8-11.

Domestic scenes painted by men tend to place women in the Victorian ideal of orderly, selfless creatures whose happiness manifests itself in devotion to husband, home, and children. Close examination of home scenes painted by women, however, suggests that happiness is more likely during male absence when the women and children relax together in cheerful disorder; other scenes clearly depict women alone, bored and trapped by enforced idleness. In some pictures, relationships between women are clearly more valuable than the dependent pair-bonding ideal pictured by male painters.

968. Bradley, Laurel. "The Substance or the Shadow: Images of Victorian Womanhood at the Yale Center for British Art." *Arts Magazine (U.S.A.)* 56, (June 1982): 125-129.

While the Yale Center exhibit emphasizes the roles of nineteenth-century women as reflected in paintings as social documents, it is equally important to explore the position of nineteenth-century women painters, and it is easy to forget, given the intensity of the subject matter, to consider the paintings as aesthetic objects. For example, Octavius Oakley's *A Student of Beauty* depicts a female art lover, but paintings by working artists Rebecca Solomon, Edith Hayllar, Henrietta Ward and Emily Mary Osborn can and should be compared artistically with the work of their male contemporaries. Viewed as a work of art, rather than as an example of social pathos, Rebecca Solomon's *The Governess* reveals problems with space that are compensated for by excellent handling of color and composition.

969. Holcomb, Adele M. "Anna Jameson: The First Professional English Art Historian." *Art History* 6, no. 2 (June 1983): 171-187.

Anna Jameson's career marks a point where the art historian who has traditionally been an artist writing for artists becomes a professional critic writing to educate a general audience. Jameson's work on religious imagery in Christian art and her view of historical periods as worthy of study without the desirability of revival are original and influential.

970. Maas, Jeremy. *Victorian Art World in Photographs*. New York: Universe Books, 1984.

In an age when the camera was still a novelty, thousands of Victorians were having their pictures taken by commercial photographers; the art world's ambivalence about the popularity and possibilities of photography is often visible in the pictures the artists had taken of themselves. They look self-conscious, uncomfortable, or appear studiously oblivious to the lens. The introductory material is an informative complement to the fascinating photographs. A separate chapter, "Models, Mistresses, Wives and Children" does not, alas, include husbands.

Reproduction (b/w photos):

Helen Allingham; Laura Alma-Tadema; Barbara Bodichon; Rosa Bonheur; Lucy Madox Brown; Jane Burden Morris; Georgiana Burne-Jones; Elizabeth Thompson Butler; Phoebe Newall Cookson; Fanny Cornforth; Evelyn de Morgan; Ada Forestier-Walker; Constance Gilchrist; Effie Gray Millais; Louisa Ruth Herbert; Catherine Madox Brown Hueffer; Edith Holman-Hunt; Fanny Holman Hunt; Sarah Hunt; Anna Jameson; Louise Jopling; Lucy Elizabeth Kemp-Welch; Annie Miller; May and Jennie Morris; Anna and Martha Mutrie; Marianne North; Henrietta Rae; Christina Rossetti; Elizabeth Siddall; Henrietta Ward; Anne, Eleanor and Mary Wardlow; Alexa Wilding.

971. Yeldham, Charlotte. *Women Artists in Nineteenth-Century France and England: Their Art Education, Exhibition Opportunities and Membership of Exhibiting Societies and Academies, with an Assessment of the Subject Matter of their Work and Summary Biographies*. New York: Garland, 1984.

In the best style of comprehensive doctoral dissertations, this work offers compilations of masses of information. It is not meant to entertain or to offer startling critical insights. The researcher will find useful overviews in the statistical tables and in the surveys of the sociology of Victorian female artists. The illustrations in the second volume are a useful source of works often difficult to locate in other printed sources. Quotations in French are not translated.

Reproductions (b/w):

Illustrations include works by both English and French artists; we list illustrations by English artists only, and we include watercolors and engravings.

Anderson, Sophie: *Elaine*

Blunden, Anna: *The Song of the Shirt; Vesuvius from Fochia*

Butler, Elizabeth Thompson: *Self Portrait; Calling the Roll After an Engagement, Crimea; The Return from Inkerman; 'Listed for the Connaught Rangers; The Remnants of an Army; Scotland Forever!; Floreat Etona!; The Camel Corps; Dawn of Waterloo*

Brown, Lucy Madox: *Romeo and Juliet; Après le Bal*

Brownlow, Emma: *The Foundling Restored to Its Mother*

Byrne, Anne Frances: *Grapes and Strawberries*

Carpenter, Margaret Sarah: *Richard Parkes Bonington; The Lacemaker; Self Portrait; Devotion; The Children in the Wood; The Spring Nosegay; Hon. Mrs. Henry Marshall*

Cookesley, Margaret Murray: *The Gambler's Wife*

Corbaux, Lisa: *Friends; Remembrances; The River of Yarrow; The Victim Bride*

Gillies, Margaret: *Trust; Harriet Martineau; William and Mary Wordsworth; Kate Southley; Portrait of Lady Charlotte Portal and Child; The End of the Pilgrimage, No.1; The End of the Pilgrimage, No.2; The End of the Pilgrimage, No.3*

Havers, Mary Alice: *The End of Her Journey*

Jopling, Louise: *Weary Waiting*

Macgregor, Jessie: *In the Reign of Terror; Arrested*

McIan, Fanny: *The Little Sick Scholar*

Merritt, Anna Lea: *Love Locked Out; War*

Osborn, Emily Mary: *The Escape of Lord Nithisdale from the Tower, 1716; Home Thoughts; Nameless and Friendless; Portrait of Madame Bodichon: A Golden Day-Dream; For the Last Time; God's Acre*

Pope, Clara Marie: *Composition of Flowers in the Vase Presented to Edmund Kean*

Rae, Henrietta: *Psyche Before the Throne of Venus; Apollo and Daphne*

Setchell, Sarah: *Ye Shall Walk in Silk Attire; The Momentous Question*

Sharpe, Eliza: *Eliza Sharpe and Her Sisters; Sketch of the Artist, Seated and Drawing Her Two Sisters, Louisa and Marianne; The Widowed Bride; Little Dunce; Miss Eliza Sharpe Presented with a Very Long Bill by a Remorseless Creditor*

Sharpe, Louisa: *The Wedding; The Unlooked for Return; Portrait of a Young Girl*

Siddall, Elizabeth: *The Eve of St. Agnes; Illustration to MacBeth*

Stillman, Marie Spartali: *Upon a Day Came Sorrow Unto Me*

Marchioness of Waterford, Stuart, Louisa: *Mentone Orange Woman; The Third Marquess of Waterford; Sleeping Disciples; Jesus Christ Among the Doctors; Relentless Time*

Ward, Henrietta Mary Ada: *Queen Mary Quitted Stirling Castle...; Palissy the Potter; The Maid of Orleans, or, Scene from the Childhood of Joan of Arc; The Princess in the Tower*

Wells, Joanna Mary Boyce: *Peep-Bo.*

972. Hadfield, John. *Every Picture Tells a Story: Images of Victorian Life with a Commentary by John Hadfield*. New York: Facts on File Publications, 1985.

A collection of narrative paintings with brief commentaries on each includes Sophie Anderson's *No Walk Today* as a work well known on both sides of the Atlantic, and which sold for less than £15 in the 1920's. *An Anxious Hour* is doubtfully attributed to Mrs. Alexander Farmer. Margaret Sarah Carpenter's *The Love Letter* exemplifies the poignancy and technical excellence seen in the works of many Victorian women painters. Hadfield sets the record straight on Anna Lea Merritt's allegorical *Love Locked Out:* the nude figure before the closed door of a tomb is not a symbol of forbidden love, but of Merritt's grief over the death that separated her from her husband.

973. Shefer, Elaine. "Deverell, Rossetti, Siddall, and 'The Bird in the Cage.'" *Art Bulletin (USA)* 47, pt. 3 (September 1985): 437-448.

Two of Walter Deverell's paintings of women with pet birds represent his strong feelings about Elizabeth Siddall, who had taken up with Dante Gabriel Rossetti shortly after Deverell had "discovered" her in a milliner's shop. Women and pet birds are a frequent motif in Victorian art and literature; Rossetti often used bird words in reference to Siddall, calling her his "dove" and referring to her as a "pigeon." In her poetry, Siddall sees herself as "a bird with a broken wing" and Rossetti's painting, *Beata Beatrix*, which he saw as a memorial to Elizabeth Siddall, shows her being visited by a red dove that brings death in the form of a poppy.

Reproductions (b/w):

Goodman, Maude: *Fantastical Figures*

Siddall, Elizabeth: *The Lady of Shalott; Sister Helen; Lady Claire; Self-Portrait.*

974. Nunn, Pamela Gerrish. *Canvassing: Recollections by Six Victorian Women Artists*. London: Camden Press, 1986.

Nunn's text is a compilation of excerpts from biographies and memoirs of Anna Mary Howitt, Anna Lea Merritt, Elizabeth Thompson Butler, Henrietta Ward, Louise Jopling, and Estella Canziana. An introduction, chapter prefaces and notes provide lucid and informative background information and supplement the material written by the artists.

Reproductions (b/w):

Butler, Elizabeth Thompson: *Calling the Roll after an Engagement, Crimea*

Canziana, Estella: *The Pipes of Dreams*

Canziani, Louisa Starr: *Brian Hodgson; Sintram; The Alien*

Howitt, Anna Mary: *The Sensitive Plant (The Lady); The School of Life*

Jopling, Louise: *Self-portrait*

Merritt, Anna Lea: *Love Locked Out*

Ward, Henrietta: *Queen Victoria; Palissy the Potter*

Photographs (b/w):

Elizabeth Thompson Butler

Henrietta Ward.

975. Bell, Quentin. "The Pre-Raphaelite Sisterhood." *Burlington Magazine* 128 (January 1986): 47.

Jan Marsh's book, *The Pre-Raphaelite Sisterhood*, about the women in the lives of the Pre-Raphaelite painters, is more a contribution to feminist study than a book about Pre-Raphaelite art. Emma Madox Brown, Elizabeth Siddall, Annie Miller, Fanny Cornforth, Jane Morris and Georgiana Burne-Jones are sympathetically portrayed, although a more complete treatment of Brown seems called for. Marsh neglects the poet Christina Rossetti, who, as the female sibling of Dante Gabriel Rossetti, is the only real Pre-Raphaelite sister.

976. Shefer, Elaine. "Women's Mission: Theme of Woman as Comforter in Victorian Painting." *Woman's Art Journal* 7, no. 1 (March 1986): 8-12.

The popularity of the Victorian ideal of "woman as comforter" is evident in the plethora of paintings dealing with this theme. Emily Mary Osborn's *Escape of Lord Nithisdale from the Tower, 1717* appears to reverse the theme, but since Nithisdale, albeit disguised in female garb, leans against his female rescuer, the painting is actually showing a female in a supporting role. The woman in Jane Bowkett's *Preparing for Dinner* is not only supporting her husband by keeping his home, she is also training the two small girls in the painting to do likewise: one is fetching slippers, the other tends the hearth fire. Margaret Dicksee's illustration represents a cherished Victorian social ideal and artist's theme.

977. Casteras, Susan P. *Images of Victorian Womanhood in English Art.* Rutherford, N.J.: 1987.

A sociological study of the images of women from virginity and purity, (as represented by the modern madonna or the nun), to sexual degradation (as represented by the modern Magdalene or prostitute), is coupled with a study of paintings, since Victorian art is concerned with the narrative and with images of women.

Reproductions (b/w):

Anderson, Sophie: *No Walk Today*

Osborn, Emily: *Nameless and Friendless; Home Thoughts; The Cornish Bâl Maidens Going to Work in the Mines*

Solomon, Rebecca: *The Governess*

Stillman, Marie Spartali: *The Convent Lily.*

978. Corn, Wanda M. "Women Building History." *American Women Artists 1830-1930*, 26-34. Washington, D.C.: National Museum for Women in Arts Catalogue, 1987.

The Philadelphia Women's Pavilion and the Columbian Exposition Women's Building were the first large-scale exhibitions in history dedicated solely to women's accomplishments. The Columbian Exposition gave such artists as Mary Cassatt and Mary MacMonnies their most important commissions, and included works by recognized artists such as Anna Lea Merritt and Rosa Bonheur. The exhibitions were prototypes of the National Museum of Women in the Arts in Washington, D.C.

979. Heller, Nancy. *Women Artists: An Illustrated History.* New York: Abbeville, 1987.

Rolinda Sharples, Sophie Anderson, Emily Mary Osborn, and Lady Elizabeth Thompson Butler had successful careers and exhibited in the Royal Academy, overcoming limited access to education, training, and nude male models.

Reproductions (col):

Anderson, Sophie: *No Walk Today*

Butler, Elizabeth Thompson: *Calling the Roll After an Engagement, Crimea*

Osborn, Emily Mary: *Nameless and Friendless*

Sharples, Rolinda: *Cloakroom in the Clifton Assembly Room.*

980. Marsh, Jan. *Pre-Raphaelite Women: Images of Femininity*. New York: Harmony Books, 1987.

Under the classification of paintings of women, a series of sub- genres emerge with such headings as "Holy virgins," "Fallen Magdalenes," "Sorceresses," and "Pale Ladies of Death." In addition to being a reflection of male fear and desire, these genres reveal profound social changes as the patriarchy topples and the industrial revolution restructures the work force and the family unit. A readable, informative, and richly-illustrated text with a disappointingly scant bibliography.

Reproductions (col):

Bunce, Kate Elizabeth: *Melody*

De Morgan, Evelyn: *Queen Eleanor and Fair Rosamund; The Hour Glass; Study of the Head of Jane Morris in Old Age; The Captives; The Gilded Cage*

Morris, Jane and Burden, Elizabeth: *Hyppolyta* (full-page color photo of embroidery)

Siddall, Elizabeth: *Self-Portrait; The Ladies Lament; Lady Affixing a Pennon to a Knight's Spear*

Stillman, Marie Spartali: *Convent Lily*

Wells, Joanna Mary: *Gretchen*

Reproductions (col):

Fortesque-Brickdale, Eleanor: *Guenevere*

Siddall, Elizabeth: *Sister Helen; Clerk Saunders*

Solomon, Rebecca: *The Wounded Dove*.

981. Spurling, John. "Bullfighters. Rev. of *Painting Women*, Camden Arts Centre...*Victorian Women Artists*, by Pamela Gerrish Nunn...*Art for the City*, Lloyd's of London...*New Statesman*." *New Statesman* 114 (25 September 1987): 26-27.

The exhibition of paintings by Victorian women at the Camden Arts Centre is limited by its small size, lack of quality, and the fact that art of the period by either sex tended to be unremarkable. The exhibit is further hampered by commentary by Deborah Cherry who is determined to use the paintings to air her political views. A more neutral treatment is provided by Pamela Gerrish Nunn in her book *Victorian Women Artists*. Nunn describes the artists' working and social conditions and provides detailed information about five of the artists.

982. Nead, Lynda. *Women's Mission to Women in Myths of Sexuality: Representations of Women in Victorian Britain*. N.Y.: Blackwell, 1988.

Rebecca Solomon's *A Friend in Need*, exhibited at the Royal Academy in 1856, documents the emerging philanthropy of the middle-class woman serving as a kind of social mother. These women, represented in Solomon's painting by the well-dressed matron staying the pompous patriarchal hand of the beadle, indicate a responsiveness to the plight of the prostitute as a sister who has fallen out of the ideal sphere of home and family. Women's involvement in philanthropy served as a rehabilitation rather than a regulatory or punitive effort; since this movement was in its beginning stages in the 1850's, Solomon's painting served to carry the idea into the Royal Academy and before the eyes of the public.

Reproductions (b/w):

Solomon, Rebecca: *A Friend in Need*.

983. Parry, Linda. *Textiles of the Arts and Crafts Movement London*. London: Thames and Hudson, 1988.

Women who contributed designs and who expressed their artistic talent in embroidery play a significant part in the Arts and Crafts Movement.

984. Pollock, Griselda. "Woman as Sign in Pre-Raphaelite Literature: the Representation of Elizabeth Siddall." In *Vision and Difference: Femininity, Feminism and Histories of Art*, 91-117. New York: Routledge, 1988.

Since art history has traditionally been a male-oriented system in which ideals of women and femininity and men and masculinity are identified and defined, and since the archives have been male-determined, the female model is not historically represented as herself, but as she reflects masculine sexuality and desire. Thus, Dante Gabriel Rossetti's portraits of Elizabeth Siddall are not Siddall at all; she serves as a model to reflect his fascination with suffering, death-like women who represent fragility, passivity, and inactivity.

985. ---. "Woman as Sign: Psychoanalytic Readings." In *Vision and Difference: Femininity, Feminism and Histories of Art*, 120-154. New York: Routledge, 1988.

The Pre-Raphaelite paintings are images of women who ignore sexuality or are unaware of it and who ignore the presence of the viewer/voyeur, who is thus not challenged to respond. Since manliness is measured by self-control, these women can inspire sexuality by representing male desires, and control sexuality by inspiring restraint. Pre-

Raphaelite paintings are not representations of actual women, but expressions of the male ideal of female sexuality.

986. Denvir, Bernard. "Injustice Collectors." *Artist*, no. 103 (August 1988): 5.

Recent books about women in nineteenth-century painting seem to be obsessed with the theme of social and physical oppression of women by sadistic, egotistical males. While many of the claims are valid, modern feminist art historians dwell on the negative, overlooking the positive accomplishments, attitudes, and progress of talented and successful artists such as Mary Cassatt, Rosa Bonheur, Elizabeth Butler, and many other women who were well- represented in art schools and galleries of the nineteenth century and earlier. The trend among feminist art historians to make accusations of male persecution seems to be a kind of reversal of the historical witch hunt. The modern accusers are just as inaccurate and politically motivated as their male prototypes.

987. Holcomb, Adele M. "Anna Jameson on Women Artists." *Woman's Art Journal* (September 1988): 15-24.

Anna Jameson's art criticism is important not only for its precedence in the field of art history, but for its clear approach to art by women as separate from, but equal to art by men. Jameson maintains that women's approach to life, far from being a weakness, can add dimensions not possible for men in the realm of subject painting. Holcomb's lucid commentary compliments an extended quoted passage by Jameson.

Reproductions (b/w):

Sharpe, Louisa: *The Unlooked-for Return; Exercise with Ma Tante, Exercise without Ma Tante*

Vogelstein, Karl von: *Portrait of Anna Jameson.*

988. Kestner, Joseph. *Mythology and Misogyny: The Social Discourse of Nineteenth Century British Classical Subject Painting.* Madison: University of Wisconsin Press, 1989.

Classical subjects contributed significantly to the disempowerment of women. Henrietta Rae is an adherent of the stereotypes of her time, depicting women as dangerous or helpless; at the same time, she celebrates the female nude with no apologies. Rae's representations of women are consistent with the male-centered vision of the feminine ideal.

989. Marsh, Jan and Pamela Gerrish Nunn. *Women Artists and the Pre-Raphaelite Movement.* London: Virago, 1989.

The women who were influenced by, and contributed to the Pre-Raphaelite movement from its inception through the Art Nouveau period have been dropped from the art history canon. Restoring them, rather than apologizing for them or defending them, is the aim of this major contribution to art history scholarship.

990. Edwards, Lee M. "Rev. of *Pre-Raphaelite Women: Images of Victorian Femininity* by Jan Marsh." *Victorian Studies* 32, no. 3 (March 1989): 431-432.

Jan Marsh's *Pre-Raphaelite Women: Images of Victorian Femininity* contains perceptive arguments that the artists of the Pre- Raphaelite school created women to meet an ideal. She presents valuable insights in her usual clear style that reflects knowledge and enthusiasm in her subject.

991. Rezelman, Betsy Cogger. "Review of *Images of Victorian Womanhood* in English Art, by Susan P. Casteras and *Victorian Women Artists* by Pamela Gerrish Nunn." *Victorian Studies* 32, no. 3 (March 1989): 429-431.

Casteras' *Images of Victorian Womanhood* uses art as a cultural reflection of middle-class nineteenth-century women, and spends little time on the artists themselves. Casteras also fails to explain why the art of the period ignored women in the roles of servants and domestic supervisors. She is clearly knowledgeable and provides perceptive views. Nunn's *Victorian Women Artists* provides valuable information, especially on Rosa Brett and Emma Brownlow. Nunn's resourceful academic sleuthing unearths materials owned by the artists' descendants and she provides illustrations of hard-to-find and previously unpublished paintings. Both books are valuable contributions to nineteenth- century women's studies.

992. Casteras, Susan P. "Review of *Myths of Sexuality: Representations of Women in Victorian Britain* by Linda Nead, and *Victorian Women Artists*, by Pamela Gerrish Nunn." *Woman's Art Journal* (September 1989): 35-38.

Linda Nead has valuable ideas about how Victorian art illustrated and reinforced nineteenth-century notions of social propriety. Unfortunately, her prose style is so jargon-ridden and enslaved by the political rhetoric of male semioticians that the reader has a difficult time following her arguments. Pamela Gerrish Nunn provides much that is new and insightful in her book while avoiding the ponderous Marxist moralizing that hinders Nead.

Reproductions (b/w engraving):
Solomon, Rebecca: *A Friend in Need.*

993. Gillett, Paula. *Worlds of Art: Painters in Victorian Society.* New Brunswick, N.J.: Rutgers University Press, 1990.

The social, economic, and cultural situations of people making a living in the nineteenth-century art world present a dimension that goes far beyond what is evident on the finished canvas. Two chapters, "Painting and the Independent Woman" and "Progress and Obstacles: Women Painters from Mid-Century to the Close of the Victorian Era," trace the progress of women seeking careers as professional painters, and show the differences between their worlds and the paths of their male contemporaries.

Reproductions (col):

Butler, Elizabeth Thompson: *The Roll Call*

Osborn, Emily Mary (b/w): *Portrait of Barbara Leigh Smith Bodichon*

Queen Victoria: Etchings

Photos:

Elizabeth Thompson Butler Painting at Dover Castle

Anna Lea Merritt

Louise Jopling

Female School of Art, Queen's Square: The Life Class (illustration from the *Illustrated London News)*

Female School of Art (cartoon from *Punch*).

994. "World of Drawings and Water Colours [Advertisement]. Ellen G. Hill (fl. 1864-93) 'An Artist's Early Day in Paris. '" *Apollo* (January 1990): 30.

Reproductions (b/w drawing):

Hill, Ellen G: *An Artist's Early Day in Paris.*

995. Mancoff, Debra N. "Review of *Images of Victorian Womanhood in English Art* by Susan P. Casteras." *Woman's Art Journal* 11, no. 1 (March 1990): 42-45.

As an iconologist, Casteras reads some subtle subtexts in Victorian subject painting. Sophie Anderson's picture of a little girl behind a window, *No Walk Today*, says much about the nineteenth-century view of the fragile imprisoned female, while Emily Osbourne's *Nameless and Friendless* fails to show the difficulties female art students faced in their need for training. Casteras' sound scholarship and her academic distance from her subject provide valuable insights as well as a solid example for other feminist scholars.

996. Norris, Pamela ed. *Sound the Deep Waters: Women's Romantic Poetry in the Victorian Age*. Boston: Little, Brown and Company, 1991.

Poems by Victorian women such as Alice Meynell, Edith Nesbit, Christina Rossetti, and Anne Brontë are illustrated by works from contemporary artists, both female and male. The editor includes an introduction by the editor and brief biographical sketches of the poets.

Reproductions (b/w):

Anderson, Sophie: *Young Girl with a Garden of Marguerites; Peek-A-Boo!; Head of a Nymph*

Canziani, Louisa Starr: *Undine*

Corbet, Edith Ellenborough: *The Sleeping Girl*

De Morgan, Evelyn: *Queen Eleanor and Fair Rosamund; Port after Stormy Seas; Love's Passing; Lux in Tenebris; The Storm Spirits; The Prisoner; Flora; The Valley of Shadows; The Worship of Mammon; Hope in the Prison of Despair; Night and Sleep*

Fortesque-Brickdale, Eleanor: *The Lover's World*

Kate, Elizabeth Bunce: *The Chance Meeting; The Keepsake; Meloda (Musica); A Knight*

Merritt, Anna Lea: *War*

Rossetti, Dante Gabriel: *Portrait of May Morris*

Sandys, Emma: *A Necklace of Wildflowers*

Spartali Stillman, Marie: *Jolie Coeur; The Rose from Armida's Garden; By a Clear Well, Within a Little Field*

Swynnerton, Annie: *The Sense of Sight; Cupid and Psyche*.

997. Faxon, Alicia Craig. *"Birds, Cages and Women in Victorian and Pre-Raphaelite Art* by Elaine Shefer." *Woman's Art Journal* 12, no. 2 (September 1991): 35.

Shefer's book offers contributions through its studies of the Pre-Raphaelite adoption of free-flowing women's clothing that eliminated the restricted movement dictated by the rigid traditional dress of the time, and in her analysis of the motif of nineteenth-century females as caged birds and captive pets. Shefer errs in making unsubstantiated assumptions about the identity of models and their relationships with the male artists. There is, for example, no basis for assuming that Christina Rossetti was the real subject of Walter Deverell's painting, *The Pet*, for which his sister modeled. Shefer's editors have produced a book containing numerous typographical errors, an outdated bibliography, and poor arrangement of illustrations.

Reproductions (b/w):

Bunce, Kate: *Melody (Musica)*.

998. Ludley, David A. "Anna Jameson and Dante Gabriel Rossetti: His Use of Her Histories." *Woman's Art Journal* 12 (September 1991): 29-33.

A comparison of several of Anna Jameson's sketches illustrating her *Sacred and Legendary Art* with several of Rossetti's works reveals a clear influence. Rossetti owned a copy of *Sacred and Legendary Art* as well as Jameson's *Commonplace Book of Thoughts, Memories, and Fancies*. John Ruskin, who was probably jealous of Jameson's reputation as an art critic, would have been appalled at the extent of her influence on his protege.

Reproductions (b/w sketches):

Jameson, Anna: *St. Cecelia; Laus Deo; The Birth of Mary*.

999. Casteras, Susan P. "Excluding Women: The Cult of Male Genius in Victorian Painting." In *Revisiting the Victorians: Theory, History and the Politics of Gender*, 116-146. ed. Linda Shires. New York: Routledge, 1992.

The abundance of Victorian paintings of scenes from boyhoods of famous men served to identify genius as a male attribute and to relegate female creativity to domestic roles. Famous women do not seem to be depicted as geniuses and in the instance of Margaret Dicksee's *Angelica Kauffmann, Introduced by Lady Wentworth, Visits Mr. Reynold's Studio*, the female artist appears as a subservient interloper in a male domain.

1000. Morris, Edward and Amanda McKay. "British Art Students in Paris 1814-1819." *Apollo* (February 1992): 78-84.

Paris attracted considerable numbers of nineteenth-century students of art because women were allowed to study nude models and could work in rooms set aside for them, or even, in some studios, alongside male artists. Women paid more for their instruction but they enjoyed a freer and more welcoming atmosphere in Paris than in Britain or America.

1001. "A Struggle for Fame. Victorian Women Artists and Writers Celebrated at the Yale Center." *Victoria Magazine* 8, no. 4 (April 1994): 16-17.

The Yale Center for British Art features an exhibition titled "A Struggle for Fame: Victorian Women Artists and Authors" from March 1 through May 8. Curator Susan Casteras observes that Victorian women authors are still read as literature, but Victorian women artists have virtually disappeared to the point where finding out anything about them is extremely difficult.

1002. Cherry, Deborah. "Women Artists and the Politics of Feminism, 1850-1900."
In *Women in the Victorian Art World*, 49-69. ed.Clarissa Campbell Orr.
New York: Manchester University Press, 1995.

The myth of the lonely struggling artist does not apply to Victorian
women who, especially after the middle of the century, worked together
for social reform. The term "feminism" was not used in England before
the end of the century, and women then, as now, often disagreed on
women's social roles and on the type and degree of social reform required.
The desire of women artists for equity in training and exhibition
opportunities is reflected in their work, particularly in history paintings
such as Anna Mary Howitt's *Boadicea Brooding Over Her Wrongs*
(1856) and Louise Jopling's *Queen Vashti Refusing to Show Herself to the
People* (1872). Women artists' portraits of each other are especially
significant because they represent female ideals of woman for a female
audience and thereby reflect neither male ideals of the female face and
form nor pander to the male-controlled market for art consumption.

Reproductions (b/w):

Bodichon, Barbara: *Ye Newe Generation; B.R.P.* (drawing of Bessie
Rayner Parkes)

Dacre, Susan: *Portrait of Lydia Becker*

Gillies: *Portrait of Mary Howitt*

Osborn, Emily Mary: Sketch after a portrait of Barbara Bodichon

Swynnerton, Annie Robinson: *Portrait of Susan Isabel Dacre.*

1003. Dodd, Sara M. "Art Education for Women in the 1860s: a Decade of Debate."
In *Women in the Victorian Art World*, 187-200. ed Clarissa Campbell Orr.
New York: Manchester University Press, 1995.

Victorians in the 1860s agonized over such seemingly insurmountable
problems as training women artists to draw the human figure (which
involved more questions of nudity, propriety, and "separate but equal"
facilities) and the establishment of schools to train women in artistic
professions. During the 1860's the Women's Art School at South
Kensington won support and approval, and the Royal Academy finally
accepted female students.

1004. Nunn, Pamela Gerrish. "Critically Speaking." In *Women in the Victorian Art
World*, 107-124. ed. Clarissa Campbell Orr. New York: Manchester
University Press, 1995.

The necessity of freeing art history from the hide-bound confines of
male-established conventions must extend to identifying the work of

female art critics. Since the Victorian art critic's voice was almost exclusively a male voice, women artists were deprived of the clear judgment and unbiased evaluation of educated women with a critical eye. The search for female art criticism must extend not only to the published work of Victorian women, but to diaries, biographies, autobiographies, letters and works of fiction for their cultural commentary and artistic insight.

Reproductions (b/w):

Hay, Jane Benham: *The Florentine Procession (The Burning of the Vanities)*

Trevelyan, Lady Paulian and L.G. Loft: *Portrait of Lady Emilia Frances Dilke.*

Index of Names and Dates

This list includes artists, models and critics listed in the citations index. We include births, deaths, and exhibition dates when available. Exhibition dates are approximate. Duplications are unavoidable because women often changed their names when they married, used their husband's names with "Mrs.," or used only their last names and "Miss," "Mrs.," or "Lady." Some women used variations of their own names, occasionally using their middle names or nicknames. Katherine can be "Catherine" or "Kate" or all three, and Matilda and Frances sometimes become "Maud" or "Fanny." The press compounds the problem with its own abbreviations. "The three Miss Walkers," "The Miss Mutries," and "The Montalba sisters" present interesting ambiguities. Spelling errors are sometimes obvious as when the press refers to Adelaide and Florence Claxton as "Caxton," but a reference to Miss Aldridge may mean either Emily or Maude Allridge, and Florence E. Greenish may be the same woman as "Emma Greedish" and "Emma Greenish." We have made corrections and clarifications where possible and listed all possibilities when in doubt.

We have chosen to use the abbreviation "exh." for "exhibited" rather than the more usual abbreviation "fl," since Victorian women artists did not always "flourish" in the usual sense. The foremother whose moment was a Royal Academy exhibit that has been passed along in the family, or who is a family legend, is of supreme importance to individuals and families, if not to art in its old set of standards. We do not attempt to judge art, but rather to offer up what we have found in hopes of contributing to the redefinitions that began in the nineteenth century and which are still in progress.

We list only those names which appear in this bibliography. For additional listings and biographical information, we suggest Chris Petteys' *Dictionary of Women Artists: An International Dictionary of Women Born Before 1900* (Boston: Hall, 1985), Elizabeth Ellett's *Women Artists in all Ages and Countries* (1859), and Eleanor Tuft's *Our Hidden Heritage: Five Centuries of Women Artists* (N.Y.: Paddington, 1874).

A. L., exh. 1873
Acland, A., exh. 1875
Acraman, Edith, exh. 1847-1852
Adams, Caroline, 1830-1837
Adams, Charlotte, exh. 1829-1844
Adie, Edith Helena, exh. 1892-1930
Aitken, Janet Macdonald, 1873-1941
Alabasta, Palacia, exh. 1872
Alabaster, Mary Ann *(see* Criddle)
Alford, M.A., exh. 1849

Allen, Miss, exh. 1879
Allingham, Helen Paterson, 1848-1926
Allridge, Emily, exh. 1880
Allridge, F. Maude, exh. 1876
Alma-Tadema, Anna, 1865-1943, exh. 1885-1903
Alma-Tadema, Laura Theresa (Epps), 1852-1909
Alston, Charlotte Maria, exh.1887-

1888

Amyot, Catherine, exh. 1879-1890

Anderson, S., exh. 1856-1872

Anderson, Sophie Gengembre, 1823-1903

Angell, Helen Cordelia (see Coleman)

Angell, Maude, exh. 1889-1904

Angus, Christine, exh. 1899-1900

Anstey, Mrs Chisholm, exh. 1858

Archer, Janet, exh. 1873-1893

Arden, Margaret Elizabeth, 1769-1851

Armstrong, Elizabeth A. (see Forbes)

Arnold, Harriet Gouldsmith, exh. 1848-1849

Ashwell, Ellen, exh. 1871-1879

Ashworth, Miss, exh. 1872

Assembaum, Fanny, exh. 1871-1881

Atkins, G., exh. 1849-1850

Attwell, Mabel Lucie (m. Earnshaw), 1897-?

Austen, Charlotte Amelia, exh. 1871-1875

Austin, Emily, exh. 1872-1877

Ayrton, Annie, exh. 1879-1886

Babb, Charlotte, exh. 1866-1880

Backhouse, Margaret (m. Holden), 1818- ?, exh. 1846-1882

Backhouse, Mary (m. Miller), exh. 1870-1893

Baker, Alice E. J., exh. 1875-1882

Baker, Annie, exh. 1890-1898

Baker, Mary, exh 1842-1856

Ballantyne, Edith, exh. 1866-1884

Banks, Miss, exh. 1868

Barber, C.J., exh. 1881-1882

Barker, Lucette Elizabeth, 1816-1905, exh. 1870

Barnard, Catherine, exh. 1888-1902

Barnard, Emily, exh. 1887

Barraud, Miss, exh. 1881

Barret, Harriet, exh. 1861

Barrett, Elizabeth, exh. 1875

Barrett, Marianne (Foster), exh. 1872-1884

Bartholomew, Anna Maria (see Fitz James)

Bartholomew, Anne Charlotte Fayerman (Mrs. Valentine B.), 1800-1862

Barton, Rose, 1856-1929

Bauerlé, Amelia, exh. 1894-1907

Baxter, Louisa, exh. 1872

Bayfield, Fanny Jane, exh. 1872-1897

Beal, Annie L., exh. 1878-1888

Beale, Sarah Sophia, exh. 1863-1888

Beard, Ada, exh. 1879-1896

Beard, Katherine, exh. 1885-1890

Bearne, Catherine (see Charlton)

Behenna, Kathleen, exh. 1897

Belcher, Lady, exh. 1858-1861

Belford, Kate, exh. 1879

Bell, Ada, exh. 1880-1903

Bell, Lucy Hilda, exh. 1886-1901

Benham, Jane E. (m. Hay), exh. 1848-1881

Benson, K., exh. 1878

Benson, Charlotte, exh. 1875-1907

Benson, Mary Katherine, exh. 1877-1884

Beresford, E. M., exh. 1866-1887

Berkeley, Edith, exh. 1884-1891

Bert, F., exh. 1879

Bewick, Jane, 1787-1881

Biffin, Sarah, 1784-1850

Binns, Elizabeth J. exh., 1879-1895

Bird, Hannah (see Essex)

Bishop, C. E., exh. 1872

Bisschop, Kate, exh. 1872

Bisschop, Louise *(see* Swift)

Black, Emma L. (m. Mahomed), exh. 1880-1894

Blackburne, Jemima Wedderburn, 1823-1909

Blackmore, Isabel, exh. 1836-1853

Blaine, Mrs. Robertson, exh. 1858-1866

Blake, Fanny, ?-1851

Blake, Louisa, exh. 1885

Blake, Miss, exh. 1849-1858

Blandy, L.V., exh. 1879

Blatherwick, Lily, exh. 1879-1904

Bleaden, Mary, exh. 1853-1880

Blunden, Anna (m. Martino), 1829-1915, exh. 1856-1867

Blunt, Lady Anne, exh. 1880

Bodé, Otille, exh. 1881

Bodichon, Barbara Leigh Smith, exh. 1866-1872

Bogardus, J., exh. 1839

Bone, Louisa, exh. 1844

Bonheur, Juliette Peyrol, ?-1891, exh. 1864-1870

Bonheur, Marie Rosa, 1822-1899, exh. 1857-1883

Boot, C., exh. 1847

Boothby, F., exh. 1849

Bosanquet, Charlotte, 1790-1852

Bouteiller *(see* Browne, Henriette)

Bouvier, Agnes Rose (m. Nicholl), exh. 1863-1882

Bowditch, Sarah Wallis, 1791-1865

Bowers, Georgiana (Mrs. Bowers-Edwards,) 1836-?, exh. 1866-1886

Bowkett, Eliza Martha, 1840-?

Bowkett, Jane Maria (m. Stuart), 1838-1891, exh. 1860-1885

Bowkett, Leila, 1853-?, exh. 1877

Boyce, Joanna Mary (m. Wells), 1831-1861, exh. 1855-1860

Boyd, Alice, exh. 1895

Boyd, Janet A., exh. 1875-1899

Boyd, The Hon. Mrs. *(see* Boyle, Eleanor)

Boyle, Eleanor Vere Gordon, 1825-1916, exh. 1865-1880

Bradley, Dora, exh. 1878

Bradley, Gertrude M., exh. 1893-1902

Branfil, Miss, exh. 1881

Brebner, Elizabeth M., exh. 1896-1897

Bremer, Frederica, exh. 1858

Brett, Rosa 1829-1881, exh. 1858-1875

Brewer, Mary, exh. 1848-1853

Briane, Mrs., exh. 1835

Brickdale, Eleanor *(see* Fortescue-Brickdale)

Bridell, Eliza Florence *(see* Fox)

Brimmer, Anne, exh. 1846-1857

Bromley, Mrs. Val, exh. 1878-1887

Brooks, Maria Burnham, exh. 1873-1890

Brown, Alberta, exh. 1870-1872

Brown, Catherine Madox (m. Hueffer), 1850-1927

Brown, Helen Paxton, exh. 1886-1903

Brown, Mrs. J. B., exh. 1861

Brown, Mrs J. W., exh. 1864-1873

Brown, Lucy Madox (m. W. M. Rossetti), 1843-1894

Browne, Henriette (pseud. of Bouteiller, m. de Saux), 1829-1901

Brownlow, Emma (King), 1832-1905, exh. 1857-1873

Brunner, Anne, exh. 1846-1857

Bryne, Mary (m. Green), exh. 1795-1845

Buckingham, Ethel, exh. 1893-1901

Bunce, Kate Elizabeth, 1858-1927

Bunce, Myra L., exh. 1891-1893

Burd, A.P., exh. 1883

Burden, Jane *(see* Morris)

Burgess, Adelaide, exh. 1857-1886

Burgess, Ethel K., exh. 1896-1907

Burgess, Jane Amelia, exh. 1843-1848

Burgess, Mrs. W., exh. 1873

Burleigh, Averil Mary, ?-1949

Burney, Mary Anne, exh. 1877

Burr, Mrs. Higford (Margaretta), exh. 1858-1861

Burrow, A. E., exh. 1873

Burrows, Miss, exh. 1858

Bushby, Lady Frances, 1838-1925

Burt, Maria E. (m. Simpson), exh. 1872-1880

Busk, E. M., exh. 1873-1889

Buss, Mrs. Alfred J., exh. 1858

Butler, Christiana, exh. 1880

Butler, Elizabeth Thompson, 1846-1933

Butler, Mildred Anne, 1858-1941

Butterworth, Margaret, exh. 1880-1894

Byrne, Anne Frances, 1775-1837

Bywater, Elizabeth, exh. 1879-1888

Bywater, Katherine D. M., exh. 1884-1890

Cadogan, Augusta, exh. 1849-1850

Cadogan, F., exh. 1849

Calvert, Edith, exh. 1886-1907

Cameron, Katharine, 1874-1965

Cameron, Mrs. Campbell, exh. 1879-1882

Campion, Serai M., exh. 1880

Canning, Viscountess, exh. 1849

Cantello, Ellen, exh. 1859-1867

Canton, Susan Ruth, exh. 1872

Canziani, Estella, 1887-1964

Canziani, Louisa *(see* Starr)

Carpenter, Margaret Sarah Geddes, 1793-1873

Carpenter, Mrs. W., exh. 1855

Carrington, M.A., exh. 1858

Carter, Amelia, exh. 1879

Carter, Mrs. J. H., exh. 1839-1869

Caxton *(see* Claxton)

Cazin, Marie, exh. 1874-1878

Chalon, Maria A. (m. Moseley), exh. 1841-1860

Champion, Mrs. H., exh. 1879-1882

Chaplin, Alice, exh. 1880

Charlton, Catherine (m. Bearne), exh. 1878-1880

Charretie, Anna Maria Kenwell, 1819-1875, exh. 1870-1875

Charteris, Lady Louisa, exh. 1877-1880

Chase, Marion, 1844-1905, exh. 1866-1893

Chettle, Elizabeth M., exh. 1882-1904

Cheviot, Lilian, exh. 1894-1902

Childers, Milly, exh. 1894-1904

Childs, Julia, exh. 1852-1859

Christison, Mary *(see* Tovey)

Clacy, Ellen, exh. 1872-1900

Clarke, Harriet Ludlow, exh. 1849

Clarke, Julia, exh. 1873-1874

Claxton, Adelaide (m. Turner), 1858-1905, exh. 1864-1875

Claxton, Florence A., 1855-1879, exh. 1859-1875

Clay, M., exh. 1878

Clemones, Miss, exh. 1864

Clive, Miss, exh. 1849

Clow, Florence, exh. 1884

Coffey, Miss, exh. 1872

Cole, Augusta (m. Samwell), exh. 1835-1860

Cole, Ellen, exh. 1841-1858

Cole, Hannah, exh. 1873

Cole, Mary Ann, exh. 1841-1858

Coleman, Helen Cordelia (m. Angell), 1847-1884, exh. 1875-1878

Coleman, Rebecca, exh. 1867-1882

Coleridge, Maud, exh. 1873-1901

Colkett, Victoria S. (m. Hine), exh. 1870-1872

Collier, Marion (see Huxley)

Collier, Mrs. John, exh. 1881-1888

Collinson, Eliza, exh. 1856-1868

Colville, E., exh. 1884

Combe, E., exh. 1834-1840

Combermere, Viscountess, exh. 1849

Combes, Miss, exh. 1884

Conder, Helen Louise, exh. 1886-1901

Connell, M. Christine, exh. 1885-1907

Conolly, Ellen, exh. 1873-1885

Coode, Helen Hoppner, exh. 1859-1882

Cook, Eliza, exh. 1882

Cook, Jane E., exh. 1880

Cook, Miss, exh. 1887

Cooke, Hannah, exh. 1877

Cooksley, Margaret Murray, ?-1927, exh. 1884-1902

Cooper, Mrs. Alexander Davis, exh. 1854-1868

Cooper, Emma Wren, exh. 1875-1884

Cooper, Florence M., 1874-1935, exh. 1889-1901

Cooper, Louisa, exh. 1879

Corbaux, Louisa, 1808-?, exh. 1857-1880

Corbaux, Marie Françoise (Fanny), 1812-1883, exh. 1848-1876

Corbet, Edith Ellenborough (Mrs. Arthur Marsh), exh. 1892-1903

Corbett, F., exh. 1875

Corcoran, Jessie, exh. 1873-1875

Corder, Rosa, exh. 1879-1882

Corkran, Henriette L., exh. 1880-1903

Cornelissen, Marie (m. Lucas), 1855-1921, exh. 1877-1904

Coutts-Lindsay, Lady, exh. 1879

Cowham, Hilda G., 1873-1964, exh. 1898-1901

Cox, Louisa E. C., 1850-1910, exh. 1874-1888

Coxeler, Miss, exh. 1891

Cramm, Baroness Helga von, exh. 1879-1880

Crawford, Emily Aldridge, exh. 1869-1877

Criddle, Mary Ann (Alabaster), exh. 1849-1878

Cridland, Helen, exh. 1888-1901

Crockett, Victoria (m. Hine), exh. 1876-1880

Croft, Marian, exh. 1869-1884

Crombie, Elizabeth E., exh. 1881-1894

Cruickshank, Grace, exh. 1860-1894

Cumming, Constance H., exh. 1895-1898

Currey, Fanny W., exh. 1881-1897

Cust, F., exh. 1849

Dacre, Lady, exh. 1849

Dacre, Susan Isabel, 1844-1933, exh. 1887

Dalziel, Margaret Jane, 1819-1894

Daniel, A.S.W., exh. 1824-1845

Davidson, Mrs., exh. 1849

Davies, Miss, exh.1860

Davis, C. S., exh. 1879

Davis, F., exh. 1876

Davis, Sara, exh. 1846-1854

Davison, Miss, exh. 1888

Dawson, Elizabeth *(see* Rumley)

Day, Frances S., exh. 1838-1858

Day, Mrs. W.C., exh. 1847

Deakin, Jane, exh. 1870-1880

Dealy, Jane, exh. 1861-1884

Dealy, Jane M., exh. 1881-1903

Dealy, M. Lewis, ?-1939

Dean, Stansmore, 1866-1944

Dear, Mary E., exh. 1848-1867

Deffell, Justina, exh. 1867

Defries, Sara, exh. 1879

De Gûe, Madame, exh. 1864

Dell, Etheldine Eva, exh. 1855-1923

Demont-Breton, Madame, exh. 1883

De Montmorency, Lily, exh. 1895-
1906

De Morgan, Evelyn Pickering,1850-
1919

Denley, Mary, exh. 1879

Dewar, De Courcy, 1878-1959

Dewar, Mrs., exh. 1850

Dicksee, Margaret Isabel, 1858-1903

Diddeman, Florence *(see* Tiddeman)

Dixon, Annie, exh. 1844-1893

Dixon, Ella Hepworth, exh. 1879-
1881

Dixon, Emily, exh. 1885-1886

Dixon, Mrs. F., exh. 1875

Dixwell, Miss, exh. 1885

Domett, Susan C., exh. 1873

Donkin, Alice E., exh. 1871-1900

Dorrington, Elizabeth A., exh. 1872

Douglas, Miss, exh. 1834-1841

D'Ouseley, Sophie, exh. 1885

Dowling, Mary, exh. 1845-1846

D'Oyley, Rowe E., exh. 1889

Drew, Mary, exh. 1879-1901

Drummond, Eliza, exh. 1820-1837

Drummond, F. Ellen, exh. 1838-
1860

Drummond, Rose Emma, exh. 1815-
1835

Drummond, Rose Myra, exh. 1833-
1849

Dubourg, Victoria, exh. 1882-1896

Duff, Jane, exh. 1874

Duffield, C. M., exh. 1976

Duffield, E., exh. 1855

Duffield, Mrs. William (Mary Ann
Rosenberg), 1819-1914, exh.
1848-1893

Dunbar, Lady Sophia, ?-1909, exh.
1863-1875

Duncan, Fanny, exh. 1876-1889

Dundas, Agnes, exh. 1864-1873

Dundas, Alice, exh. 1876

Dunn, Edith, exh. 1862-1906

Durant, Susan, exh. 1850-1873

Durell, Amy, exh. 1890-1891

Durrant, Miss, exh. 1881

Dutton, Miss, exh. 1830-1856

E.V.B. *(see* Boyle, Eleanor Vere)

Earl, Maud, ?-1943, exh. 1884-1901

Earle, Kate, exh. 1890-1903

Earnshaw, Mabel *(see* Attwell)

Earnshaw, Mary Harriot, exh. 1896

Eastlake, Elizabeth R., exh. 1871-
1883

Edmonds, Anna Maria, (m. Guérin),
exh. 1867-1878,

Edwards, Catherine Adelaide (m.
Sparkes), exh. 1866-1879

Edwards, Ellen. E., exh. 1865-1868

Edwards, J. A., exh. 1875

Edwards, Kate, exh. 1865-1879

Edwards, Mary Ellen (m. Freer, m. Staples), 1839-?, exh. 1862-1903

Egerton, Jane Sophia, exh. 1844-1856

Eley, Frances, exh. 1885-1890

Eley, Mary, exh. 1876-1897

Elias, Annette, exh. 1881-1904

Ellis, Miss, exh. 1872

Ellison, Edith, exh. 1884-1888

Elmore, Edith, exh. 1877-1887

Enfield, Mary P. C., 1860-1920, exh. 1892-1901

Epps, Ellen (m. Gosse), exh. 1879

Epps, Laura *(see* Alma-Tadema)

Erichson, Nelly, exh. 1883-1901

Errington, Isabella, exh. 1846-1850

Escombe, Anne, exh. 1869-1875

Escombe, Jane, exh. 1869-1877

Essex, Hannah (m. Bird), exh. 1854-1855

Eustace, Mrs. Wilson, exh. 1865

Faed, Susan Bell, 1827-1909, exh. 1866-1868

Fahey, Palacia E., exh. 1865

Fanner, Alice Maude (m. Taite), 1865-1930

Farmer, Mrs. Alexander, exh. 1855-1867

Farmer, Emily, exh. 1847-1880

Farmiloe, Edith, exh. 1898

Farnall, Miss, exh. 1881

Farquahar, Elizabeth, exh. 1872-1902

Fawcett, Emily Addia, exh. 1874-1896

Fayerman *(see* Bartholomew)

Fenessey, Emily, exh. 1871-1872

Fenton, Annie Grace, exh. 1876-1885

Fenwick-Miller, Florence (late 19th cent. art critic)

Ffloukes, C.J., exh. 1889

Finch, E., exh. 1849

Finch, F., exh. 1849

Fitz James, Anna Maria Bartholomew, exh. 1848-1879

Flack, Edith Mary, exh. 1889-1891

Florence, Mary Sargant, 1857-1954

Folkard, Elizabeth F., exh. 1877-1881

Folkard, Julia Bracewell, exh. 1872-1902

Follingsby, Mrs., exh. 1863

Forbes, Elizabeth Armstrong (Mrs. Stanhope-Forbes), 1859-1912, exh. 1877-1891

Forbes-Cockburn, Charlotte, exh. 1876

Ford, Emily S., exh. 1894

Ford, G. M., exh. 1879

Fores, Mary Harriet, exh. 1886-1888

Forest, B., exh. 1855

Forester, Mary (m. Lofthouse), 1853-1885, exh. 1876-1883

Forster, Mary, exh. 1883-1884

Fortescue-Brickdale, Eleanor 1871-1945

Foster, A. H., exh. 1884

Foster, E., exh. 1877

Foster, Marianne *(see* Barrett)

Foster, Mary, exh. 1880

Fowkner, F., exh. 1877

Fowler, Mary Lemon, exh. 1883-1890

Fowler, Mrs., exh. 1845-1852

Fox, Eliza Florence (m. Bridell, m. Fox), ?-1904, exh.1847-1894

Frank, Mrs. Gustav, exh. 1873

Fraser, Annie, exh. 1861-1884

Freer, Mary Ellen *(see* Edwards)

French, Annie, 1872-1965

Frere, Miss, exh. 1880

Frier, Jessie, exh. 1874-1879

Fripp, Constance L., exh. 1882-1887

Furnell, C., exh. 1843

Fussey, Ada E., c. 1840-1910

Gamble, Louisa, exh. 1842

Gardner, Elizabeth J., exh. 1879-1887

Gastineau, Maria A., ?-1890, exh. 1855-1889

Gay, Susan Elizabeth, exh. 1874-1876

Gayleard, Sophia, exh. 1839-1846

Geddes, Margaret (see Carpenter)

Geefs, Madame G. (Fanny), exh. 1847-1849

Gemmell, Mary, exh. 1883-1894

Gent, Mrs., exh. 1832-1845

Giampietri, Madame, exh. 1882

Gibbons, Jane, exh. 1871

Gibbs, Miss, exh. 1845

Gibson, Edith, exh. 1879-1886

Gibson, Edith M., exh. 1891

Gilbert, Annie Laurie, 1848-1941

Gilbert, Ellen, exh. 1875-1878

Giles, Miss, exh. 1891

Gillies, Margaret, 1803-1887, exh. 1832-1878

Gilmour, Margaret, 1860-1942

Gilmour, Mary, 1872-1938

Gloag, Isabel Lilian, 1865-1917

Goodall, Eliza (m. Wild), exh. 1846-1855

Goodman, Matilda (Maude?) exh. 1874

Goodman, Maude (m. Scanes), ?-1938, exh. 1874-1901

Goodman, Mrs., exh. 1866

Goodman, Mrs. L., exh. 1879

Goodwin, Kate Malleson, exh. 1873-1893

Gordon, Julia Isabella Levinia, 1772-1867

Gordon, Lady, exh. 1879

Gordon, Miss, exh. 1849

Gosse, Mrs. (see Epps, Ellen)

Gotch, Caroline Burland Yates, exh. 1890-1895

Gouldsmith, Harriet (m. Arnold), 1787-1867

Gow, Kate, exh. 1877

Gow, Mary L. (m. S. C. Hall), 1851-1929

Grace, Elizabeth, exh. 1878

Grant, Alice, exh. 1879-1904

Gray, Alice, exh. 1891-1892

Gray, Lady, exh. 1849

Gray, Norah Neilson, 1882-1931

Greedish, Emma (see Greenish)

Green, Everett, exh. 1879

Green, Mary Byrne, exh. 1805-1845

Greenaway, Kate, 1846-1901, exh. 1876-1895

Greener, Mary Ann, exh. 1845-1853

Greenish, Emma, exh. 1874-1875

Griffith, Kate, exh. 1879-1885

Griffiths, Bertha, exh. 1877

Grose, Milicent S., exh. 1882-1884

Grote, Harriet Lewin, exh. 1858

Gubbons, H., exh. 1843-1849

Guérin, Anna Maria (see Edmonds)

Guillod, Bessie, exh. 1873

Guiness, Elizabeth Sarah Smith, exh. 1874-1887

Hadden, Nellie, exh. 1885-1920

Hake, Miss, exh. 1891

Hale, Ellen D., exh. 1882

Hall, Ann Ashley, exh. 1873

Hall, Edith S., exh. 1879

Hall, Fannie Hoseason, exh. 1861

Hall, Mary *(see* Gow)

Halle, Elinor, exh. 1885

Hallward, Adelaide Bloxham, exh. 1888-1922

Hamberger, Helen Augusta 1836-1919

Hamilton, Gertrude, exh. 1873-1876

Hamilton, Maggie, 1867-1952

Hamley, Barbara, exh. 1895-1896

Hammond, Gertrude Demain, 1862-1953, exh. 1888-1890

Hammond, Kate (m. Shepherd), exh. 1879-1899

Hanbury, Ada, exh. 1875-1881

Hanbury, Blanche, exh. 1876-1882

Hancock, Ellen Isabella, exh. 1871-1875

Hankey, Mabel, exh. 1898-1904

Hannay, Mrs. W., exh. 1866

Hanslip, Alice, exh. 1872-1879

Harbutt, Elizabeth, exh. 1879-1895

Hardcastle, Charlotte, exh. 1855-1866

Harding, Emily J., exh. 1877-1902

Hardy, Ruth, exh. 1895-1898

Harman, Ruth, exh. 1886

Harris, Frances Elizabeth Louisa *(see* Rosenberg)

Harrison, Annie Jane, exh. 1888-1904

Harrison, Harriet, exh. 1855-1880

Harrison, Maria, exh. 1845-1883

Harrison, Mary P. (Mrs. Harrison, née Rossiter), 1788-1875, exh. 1831-1875

Harrison, Sarah Cecilia, exh. 1889-1902

Hart, Dorothy, exh. 1897

Haseler, Margaret, exh. 1878

Hastie, Grace H., exh. 1874-1903

Hastings, Kate Carr, exh. 1880-1887

Hatton, Helen Howard (m. Maretson), 1860-?, exh. 1885-1894

Havell, Charlotte M., exh. 1879

Havers, Alice Mary (m. Morgan), 1850-1890

Hay, Emily, exh. 1879

Hay, Jane *(see* Benham)

Haycraft, Lillie Stackpoole, exh. 1896

Hayllar, Edith, 1860-1948

Hayllar, Jessica, 1858-1940

Hayllar, Kate, exh. 1885-1898

Hayllar, Mary (m. Wells), exh. 1880-1887

Hayward, Emily L., exh. 1887

Heamans, Felicia, exh. 1882

Heaphy, Elizabeth (m. Murray), exh. 1834-1882

Heaphy, M. A. (m. Musgrave), exh. 1821-1847

Hegg, Teresa, exh. 1871-1879

Heming, Matilda Lowery, 1808-1855, exh. 1847-1855

Hemming Mrs. W. B., exh. 1856-1859

Henn, Marion Ryden, exh. 1886-1899

Hentsch, Emily, exh. 1873

Herford, Laura, ?-1870, exh. 1861-1869

Herring, Mrs. G. E., exh. 1840-1858

Herring, Mrs. J. F., exh. 1866-1873

Hewitt, Beatrice M., exh. 1888-1902

Hewitt, F., exh. 1860-1861

Hewitt, Sarah F., exh. 1857

Hicks, Amelia Mary, exh. 1879

Hickson, Margaret, exh. 1882-1900

Hill, Ellen G., exh. 1864-1893

Hill, Kate E., exh. 1874-1897

Hindes, Mrs. B.L., exh. 1875-1879

Hine, Victoria *(see* Crockett)
Hipkins, Edith, exh. 1874-1898
Hobson, Alice M., 1860-1954, exh.
    1879
Hodge, Elizabeth, exh. 1872-1873
Holden, Evelyn B., 1877-1968
Holden, Louisa Jane, exh. 1840-
    1843
Holliday, Lily, exh. 1879
Holloway, Janet, exh. 1885-1897
Holmes, Rhoda Carleton, exh.
    1876-1881
Holmes, Sophia, exh. 1887-1889
Hooper, Miss, exh. 1879
Hope, M., exh. 1879
Hopkins, Edith, exh. 1871-1880
Hopkins, Mrs. J. M., exh. 1880
Hopkinson, Anne Elizabeth, exh.
    1871-1887
Houlton, Miss, exh. 1849
Howard, Catherine, exh. 1886-1888
Howard, Sarah T., exh. 1840-1851
Howell, C. E., exh. 1879
Howitt, Anna Mary (m. A. A.
    Watts), exh. 1855-1858
Hueffer, Catherine *(see* Brown)
Hueffer, Mrs. F., exh. 1876
Hulme, Alice L., exh. 1879-1890
Humphrey, K. Maude, exh. 1883-
    1894
Humphreys, J. K., exh. 1866-1876
Hunter, Elizabeth, exh. 1854-1883
Hunter, Mary Young, 1878-1936
Hurlstone, Mrs., exh. 1848
Hurst, Mary, exh. 1881
Hussey, Mrs., exh. 1865
Huxley, Marion, exh. 1882-1897
Ierson, Agnes, exh. 1872-1874
Inglis, Jane, exh. 1859-1903
J.B. *(see* Bewick)
Jackson, E. J., exh. 1879

Jackson, Emily E., exh. 1882-1884
Jackson, Emily F., exh. 1878-1884
Jackson, Helen, exh. 1882-1904
James, Charlotte Isa, exh. 1867-
    1881
James, Edith, exh. 1886-1896
James, Miss, exh. 1860-1864
Jay, J. Isabella Lee, exh. 1882-1896
Jeffreys, Bertha, exh. 1886
Jekyll, Gertrude, exh. 1867-1870
Jenkins, Blanche, exh. 1872-1915
Jennings, Emma M., exh. 1880
Jerichau-Bauman, Elizabeth Marie
    Anna, exh. 1859-1876
Jerson, Agnes, exh. 1873-1875
Jevons, Louisa E., exh. 1893-1901
Jobling, Isa M., ?-1926, exh. 1892-
    1900
Johnson, M.H., exh. 1843-1848
Johnston, Mrs., exh. 1881
Johnstone, J., exh. 1874
Johnstone, Mrs. (M.A. Wheeler),
    exh. 1838-1843
Jones, Anna M., exh. 1868-1884
Jones, Charlotte, exh. 1866
Jones, Eliza, exh. 1807-1852
Jones, Isabella, exh. 1866
Jones, Matilda, exh. 1825-1843
Jones, Sarah, exh. 1873
Jopling, Louise Goode (m. Romer),
    1843-1933
José, Juliana, exh. 1876
Julyan, Mary E., exh. 1863-1877
Kays, Miss, exh. 1879
Keary, Miss, exh. 1891
Keating, Mrs. Colonel, exh. 1860-
    1863
Kelly, Mrs. Tom, exh. 1890
Kemp, Emily, exh. 1885
Kempson, Miss, exh. 1871-1881
Kempson, Mrs. Freeman, exh.

1868-1879

Kemp-Welch, Lucy Elizabeth, 1869-1958

Kendrick, Emma Eleanora, 1788-1871

Kettle, Clara E. F., exh. 1845-1872

Keys, Frances M., exh. 1856-1880

King, Ethel Slade, exh. 1884-1896

King, Jessie, 1876-1949

Kingdon, M.E., 1879-1904, exh. 1888

Kingsford, Florence, exh. 1899-1903

Kipling, Mary, exh. 1843-1846

Kirkman, Miss, exh. 1881

Kirschner, Mary Louisa, exh. 1876

Knapping, Miss, exh. 1880

Knight, Laura Armstrong (m. Johnson, pseud. Orovida), 1877-1970

Knip, Henriette (m. Ronner), exh. 1882

Knowles, Leonora C. E., exh. 1844

Koberwein, Georgina F. *(see* Terrell)

Koberwein, Rosa, exh. 1876-1882

Laird, Alicia H., exh. 1846-1865

La Jeune, Elizabeth, exh. 1844

Lamb, Miss, exh. 1872

La Monte, Elish, 1800-1870, exh. 1856-1859

Lance, E., exh. 1859-1861

Landseer, Emma (m. MacKenzie), exh. 1857-1865

Landseer, Jessica, 1807-1880, exh. 1865-1870

Lane, Clara S., exh. 1856-1859

Lane, Emily, exh. 1873-1881

Lane, Miss, exh. 1864-1873

Lansdell, Elizabeth, exh. 1847

Lauder, I. Scott, exh. 1875

LaVillette, Madame, exh. 1883

Law, Helen, exh. 1890

Law, Miss, exh. 1877

Lawford, Mrs. Rowland, exh. 1880

Lawrence, Mary (m. Kearse), exh. 1807

Lawson, Mrs. Cecil, exh. 1880-1887

Leader, Mrs. B.W., exh. 1879-1882

Leavers, Lucy Ann, 1845-1915, exh. 1882

Le Breton, Rosa, exh. 1857-1865

Leckie, Mary Mulready (m. Stone), exh. 1840-1844

Ledsam, Miss, exh. 1877

Lefroy, Miss, exh. 1864-1865

Legge, C., exh. 1849

Legge, M.A., exh. 1849

Lejeune, Elizabeth, exh. 1844

Lemann, E.A., exh. 1878-1889

Lennox, A., exh. 1876-1879

Leod, Miss, exh. 1878

Levy, Alice, exh.1879

Lewis, Grace R., exh. 1900

Lewis, Jane M. *(see* Dealy)

Lewis, Mabel T., exh. 1899

Lewis, Madeleine, exh. 1898

Lewis, Mary, exh. 1895-1900

Lindsay, Lady Caroline Blanche, 1844-1912

Lindsay, Mary (m. Holford), exh. 1851

Lindsay, Violet (m. Manners) (Marchioness of Granby), exh. 1879-1899

Linnell, Mary, exh. 1858

Linnell, Mrs. J. T., exh. 1861

Linnell, Sarah, exh. 1858

Locke, Alice, exh. 1871-1875

Locking, Kitty, exh. 1879

Lofthouse, Mary *(see* Forster)

Longfield, J.J., exh. 1874

Lovel, Martha, exh. 1874

Lovell, Elizabeth M., exh. 1879

Lovering, Ida, exh. 1876-1903

Lowther, Mrs., exh. 1867

Lucas, Marie *(see* Cornelissen)

Ludovici, Marguerite, exh. 1887-
1896

Luker, Mrs., exh. 1867

Lundgren, Mme., exh. 1863

Lyons, Agatha, exh. 1875

M.E.E. *(see* Edwards, Mary Ellen)

Macandrew, Miss, exh. 1867

Macarthur, Blanche F., exh. 1870-
1883

Macaulay, Kate, exh. 1876-1887

Macdonald, Frances (m. MacNair),
1874-1921

Macdonald, Margaret (m.
Macintosh), 1865-1933

Macgregor, Jessie, 1853-1919, exh.
1874-1877

Macguire, Helena, exh. 1883-1885

Macintosh, Margaret *(see*
Macdonald)

Macirone, Emily, exh. 1846-1873

Mackenzie, Isabella, exh. 1843-1846

Mackreth, Harriet F.S., exh. 1828-
1842

MacLeod, Jessie, exh. 1845-1875

MacNicol, Bessie, exh. 1893

MacWhirter, Agnes Eliza, exh.
1870-1879

Magnus, Emma, exh. 1884-1901

Maguire, Adelaide A., 1852-1875

Maguire, Helen, exh. 1879

Mahomed, Emma L. *(see* Black)

Mallison, Mrs., exh. 1858

Manby, E.A., exh. 1870

Manly, Alice, exh. 1875-1897

Manly, Eleanor E., exh. 1888-1898

Mann, Fenn (Florence), exh. 1884-
1886

Mannin, Mrs. Millington, ?-1864,

exh. 1829-1857

Manning, Eliza F., exh. 1880-1887

Mansell, Marianne, exh. 1887-1900

Margetson, Maria, exh. 1858-1860

Margetts, Mary, exh. 1841-1875

Marrable, Edith, exh. 1876

Marrable, Madeline Cockburn, exh.
1864-1903

Marsh, Catherine, exh. 1849

Marshall, Angela Mary, exh. 1877

Marshall, Mrs., exh. 1880

Martin, Florence, exh. 1879-1884

Martineau, Edith, 1842-1909, exh.
1877-1883

Martineau, Gertrude, exh. 1862-
1894

Martino, Anna *(see* Blunden)

Massey, Gertrude, exh. 1898-1904

Mathews, Minnie, exh. 1886-1896

Matthews, Winifred, ?-1896

Mawson, Elizabeth Cameron, 1849-
1939, exh. 1889-1891

May, Kate, exh. 1876-1884

May, Margery, exh. 1879

Mayer, B., exh. 1879

Maynard, Mrs E., exh. 1865

McCrossan, Mary, ?-1834

McDowell, Mrs. Henry, exh. 1882

McIan, Frances Mathilda Whitaker,
(Fanny), 1814-1897, exh.
1836-1849

McKay, Rose, exh. 1894-1899

McKenzie, Emma *(see* Landseer)

Meakin, Mary L., exh. 1843-1862

Mearns, Lois, exh. 1878-1879

Mee, Anne Folson, ?-1851, exh.
1804-1837

Merrick, Emily M., exh. 1880-1899

Merrifield, Mrs., exh. 1851

Merritt, Anna Lea, 1844-1930

Merrylees, Annie R., exh. 1894-

1900
Meyer, Beatrice, exh. 1878-1888
Meyer, Henrietta, exh. 1874
Miles, Helen, exh. 1882
Miller, Alice, exh. 1885-1896
Mills, E., exh. 1875
Mills, Eliza, exh. 1858
Minns, F.M., exh. 1881
Mitchell, Clara, exh. 1864-1865
Mitchell, Mrs., exh. 1866
Moberly, Mariquita Jenny, exh. 1855-1903
Moffatt, Frederica, exh. 1874
Mohl, Mary, 1793-1883
Möller, Mrs. Nils, exh. 1865
Monkhouse, Mary F., exh. 1884-1891
Montalba, Clara, 1842-1929, exh. 1866-1895
Montalba, Ellen, exh. 1872-1902
Montalba, Henrietta Skerrett, exh. 1875-1893
Montalba, Hilda, ?-1919, exh. 1873-1903
Montmorency, Lily de, exh. 1898
Moody, Fannie, 1861-1897, exh. 1885-1897
Moore, Jennie (Jeannie) exh. 1871-1900
Morgan, Alice (see Havers)
Morgan, Jane, exh. 1884
Morice, A.A., exh. 1871-1885
Morris, Jane Burden, 1840-1914
Morris, May, 1844-1930
Morris, Mrs. Best (neé Sharpe), exh. 1822-1841
Mortlock, Ethel, exh. 1878-1904
Morton, Maria, exh. 1839-1851
Moseley, Maria A. (see Chalon), exh. 1841-1866
Mothersole, Jessie, exh. 1901

Murray, Eliza Dundas, exh. 1860-1878
Murray, Elizabeth (see Heaphy)
Mutrie, Annie Feray, 1826-1893
Mutrie, Martha Darley, 1824-1885/6
Mylne, H., exh. 1879
Naftel, Isabel Oakley, exh. 1862-1889
Naftel, Maude, 1856-1890, exh. 1879-1881
Naftel, Mrs. Paul, exh. 1875-1884
Nasmyth, Anne Gibson, 1798-?
Nasmyth, Barbara, 1790-1870
Nasmyth, Charlotte, 1804-1884, exh. 1840-1862
Nasmyth, Elizabeth, 1793-?
Nasmyth, Jane, 1793-1866, exh. 1850
Nasmyth, Margaret, 1791-1869
Neilson, Ellen, exh. 1879
Nesbitt, Frances E., 1864-1934, exh. 1896
Newberry, Jessie Rowat, 1864-1948
Newcomb, Emma Ada, exh. 1886
Newcombe, Bertha, exh. 1882-1904
Newell, S., exh. 1819-1838
Newenham, Lady H., exh. 1875
Newill, Mary J., exh. 1884-1925
Newton, Harriet Frances, exh. 1876
Newton, Mary (see Severn)
Nicholl, Agnes Rose (see Bouvier)
Nicholls, Rhoda Holmes, 1858-?, exh. 1884
Nichols, Catherine Maud, exh. 1871-1891
Nichols, Kate Edith, exh. 1879
Nichols, Mary Anne, exh. 1840-1850
Nicholson, Alice M., exh. 1884-1888

Nicholson, Lady Sarah Elizabeth, exh. 1879-1880

Nisbet, Ethel C., exh. 1881-1903

Nixon, Minna, exh. 1865-1904

Noa, Madame Jessie, exh. 1858-1867

Noble, C. M., exh. 1877-1878

Nordgren, Anna, exh. 1887-1899

North, Marianne, 1831-?

Norton, Miss, exh. 1891

Nottage, (Nottidge) Caroline, exh. 1874

Nourse, Elizabeth, exh. 1892-1893

Noyes, Theodora F., 1882-1887

Nutter, Katherine M., exh. 1883-1890

Oakes, Miss, exh. 1879

Oakley, A.L., exh. 1865

Oakley, Isabel *(see* Naftel)

Oakley, L., exh. 1850

O'Connell, Madame, exh. 1861

OEnone, Edith Somerville, 1858-1949

Offor, Beatrice (m. Littler), exh. 1887-1904

Offord, Gertrude Elizabeth, 1860/61-1903

O'Hara, Miss, exh. 1882-1867

Oliver, Emma S. Eburne (m. Sedgwick), exh. 1842-1880

Orovida (pseud. Laura Knight)

Osborn, Emily Mary, 1834-1908, exh. 1851-1908

Osbourne, Harriet, exh. 1875

Overbury, Louisa, exh. 1873

Paget, Elise, exh. 1878-1888

Palmer, Charity, exh. 1849-1858

Palmer, Hannah Linnell, 1818-1893, exh. 1840-1842

Paris, Louisa Catherine, 1813/14-1875

Parkes, Bessie, exh. 1865-1867

Parnell, G., exh. 1846-1856

Parsons, Beatrice E., exh. 1889-1899

Parsons, Letitia Margaret (m. Keith), exh. 1881

Parsons, Miss E., exh. 1886

Partridge, Ellen, exh. 1844-1893

Pash, Florence, exh. 1891-1903

Pasmore, Mrs. John F., exh. 1842-1865

Paterson, Caroline (m. Sharpe), ?-1919

Paterson, Caroline, exh. 1880-1887

Paterson, Emily Murray, 1855-1934

Paterson, Helen *(see* Allingham)

Patmore, Bertha G., exh. 1876-1903

Paulson, Ann, exh. 1848

Payne, Harriett A., exh. 1879

Pearson, Mary Martha Dutton, 1799-1871

Peel, Florence, exh. 1858-1863

Peel, Maude, 1880-1885

Percy, Miss E., exh. 1870

Pertz, Anna J., exh. 1884-1897

Perugini, Kate Dickens, 1839-1929, exh. 1877-1883

Pfeiffer, J. Emily, exh. 1876-1881

Pfeiffer, Mrs., exh. 1865

Philip, Constance B. (m. Lawson), exh. 1874-1879

Phillips, Mrs., exh. 1850

Phillott, Constance, exh. 1868-1885

Phinney, Emma E., exh. 1880

Picken, Eleanor E., exh. 1842

Pickering *(see* De Morgan)

Pickerman, Mary Ann, exh. 1872

Pickersgill, M.A., exh. 1834-1838

Pierrepont, C., exh. 1876

Pilsbury, Elizabeth, exh. 1879-1881

Pitman, Janetta R. A., c. 1850-1910, exh. 1880-1901

Pitman, Rosie M. M., 1883-1907, exh. 1894-1897

Pocock, Julia, exh. 1870-1903

Pohlmann, Charlotte, c. 1860-1920, exh. 1888

Poole, Louisa E., exh. 1875

Pope, Clara Maria Leigh (m. Wheatley, m. Pope), 1750-1838, exh. 1808-1838

Potter, Helen Beatrix, 1866-1946

Powell, Christiana, exh. 1871

Pratten, Mrs., exh. 1875

Preindlsberger, Marianne (see Stokes)

Princep, Emily Rebecca, 1798-1860

Princess Louise, Duchess of Argyll, exh. 1880-84

Pringle, Agnes, exh. 1884-1893

Proctor, Adelaide, exh. 1882

Purdie, Mrs., exh. 1881

Purser, Sarah H., 1848-1943 exh. 1885-1887

Pyne, Eva (M.E.A. Pyne), exh. 1866-1903

Queen Victoria, 1824-1901

Rae, Henrietta (m. Normand), 1859-1928

Raeburn, Agnes Middleton, 1872-1955

Raeburn, Lucy, 1869-1952

Raimbach, Emma Harriett, exh. 1835-1855

Raphael, Mary F., exh. 1889-1902

Rawlinson, Lady, exh. 1879

Rayner, Frances (Fanny), exh. 1866

Rayner, Louise, 1829-1924, exh. 1860-1880

Rayner, Margaret, exh. 1864-1881

Rayner, Nancy, 1827-1855

Rayner, Rose, exh. 1821-1866

Reason, Florence, 1896-1914 exh. 1875-1903

Redgrave, Evelyn Leslie, exh. 1876-1887

Redgrave, Frances M., exh. 1864-1882

Reid, A. M., exh. 1880

Reid, Flora MacDonald, exh. 1879-1929

Reid, Lizzie, exh. 1884-1886

Renshaw, Alice, exh. 1875

Renshaw, Emily (see Knewstub)

Reynolds, Miss, exh. 1891

Ribbing, S., exh. 1873-1875

Richards, Emma Gaggiotti, exh. 1850-1854

Richardson, Agnes E., exh. 1896

Richardson, Mrs. Charles, exh. 1846

Richter, Henrietta S., exh. 1842-1849

Rickerby, Eliza G., exh. 1840-1844

Rimer, Louisa Serena, exh. 1856-1874

Ring, Ethel S., exh. 1884

Riviére, Annette L., exh. 1870-1887

Riviere, Mary Alice Dobell, exh. 1869-1870

Robbinson, Margaret (neé Stage), 1831-1879, exh. 1854-1870

Roberts, F. M., exh. 1879

Roberts, Katherine May, exh. 1900-1901

Roberts, Louisa, exh. 1851-1855

Robertson, Mrs. James (Saunders), exh. 1823-1848

Robinson, Annie Louisa (see Swynnerton)

Robinson, Edith Brearey, exh. 1879-1894

Robinson, Emily, exh. 1880

Robinson, Maria D. Webb, exh. 1877-1901

Robinson, Maud, exh. 1877

Rogers, Jane Masters, exh. 1847-1870

Romer, Louisa Goode *(see* Jopling)

Ronner, Madame Henriette (neé Kemp), exh. 1881-1903

Rose, H. Ethel, exh. 1885-1888

Rosenberg, Ethel, exh. 1883-1901

Rosenberg, Frances, (Fanny, m. Harris), 1822-1872, exh. 1845-1850

Rosenberg, Mary Ann *(see* Duffield)

Rosenberg, Mrs. F. (also listed as T. Rosenberg), exh. 1857

Ross, Christina P., exh. 1874-1897

Ross, Magdalene (m. Dalton), exh. 1820-1841

Rossiter, Frances Fripp Seares, exh. 1866-1882

Rossiter, Mary P. *(see* Harrison)

Royal, Miss, exh. 1866

Rumley, Elizabeth (m. Dawson), exh. 1859-1876

Rushout, Hon. Anne, 1768-1849

Ryder, Emily, exh. 1870

Sadler, Kate, exh. 1879-1889

Sainsbury, Grace E., exh. 1891-1904

Salaman, Kate, exh. 1841-1856

Salter, Anne, exh. 1867-1885

Samwell, Augusta *(see* Cole)

Samworth, Joanna, exh. 1867-1881

Sandys, Emma, 1843-1877, exh. 1868-1874

Sargant, Florence Mary, 1857-1954

Sarjent, Emily, exh. 1845-1864

Savill, Josephine, exh. 1863-1884

Schenck, Agnes, exh. 1884

Schute, Mrs. E.L., exh. 1891

Schwartze, Theresa, exh. 1880-1887

Scott, Alice M. exh. 1880-1889

Scott, Amy, exh. 1883-1900

Scott, Caroline Lucy, 1784-1857

Scott, Emily, exh. 1836-1855

Scott, Emily Anne (m. Seymour), exh. 1844-1855

Scott, Janet Mary, exh. 1896-1903

Scott, Katharine, exh. 1879-1890

Scott, Miss, exh. 1851

Sedgwick, Emma *(see* Oliver)

Seeley, E. L., exh. 1873-1875

Selous, Emily *(see* Fenessey)

Setchell, Elizabeth, exh. 1832-1845

Setchell, Sarah, 1803-1894

Severn, Anna Mary (m. Newton), 1832-1866

Sewell, Miss, exh. 1858

Seyffarth, Agnes E., exh. 1850

Seyffarth, Louisa *(see* Sharpe)

Seymour, Harriette Anne, exh. 1866

Sharland, Miss, exh. 1846

Sharp, Dorothea, exh. 1901-1904

Sharp, Mary, exh. 1880-1884

Sharp, R.E.A., exh. 1880

Sharpe, Caroline *(see* Paterson)

Sharpe, Charlotte B. ?-1849, exh. 1838-1842

Sharpe, Eliza, 1795/6-1874, exh. 1847-1873

Sharpe, Louisa (m. Seyffarth), 1843-1898

Sharpe, Mary Anne, ?-1867, exh. 1819-1863

Sharples, Rolinda, 1794-1838

Shirley, Mrs. A. S., exh. 1858

Shute, Mrs. E. L., 1883-1907

Siddal, Elizabeth Eleanor (m. D.G. Rossetti), 1829-1862

Simpson, Agnes, exh. 1827-1848

Simpson, Eugénie, exh. 1883-1888

Simpson, J., exh. 1876

Simpson, Maria E. *(see* Burt)

Simpson, Mary, exh. 1849-1858

Small, Florence, 1860-1933 exh.,
1881-1901

Smirke, Mary, 1779-1853

Smith, Alice Percival, exh. 1875

Smith, Barbara Leigh *(see*
Bodichon)

Smith, Bradshaw (Miss) exh. 1865

Smith, Mrs. Clifford. H., exh. 1839-
1875

Smith, Edith Heckstall, exh. 1881-
1890

Smith, Eliza Toulmin, exh. 1871

Smith, Julia Cecelia A., exh. 1872

Smith, Louisa, exh. 1881-1884

Smith, Mrs. E.J., exh. 1881

Smyth, Dorothy Carleton, exh.
1901-1925

Sneyd, E., exh. 1849

Sneyd, M. E., exh. 1849

Sohden, Susannah, exh. 1867-1890

Solomon, Rebecca, 1832-1903, exh.
1857-1874

Somers, Countess, exh. 1849

Sparkes, Catherine Adelaide *(see*
Edwards)

Spartali, Marie *(see* Stillman)

Spiers, Bessie J., exh. 1886-1895

Spiers, Charlotte H., exh. 1879-1901

Spilsbury, Maria *(see* Taylor)

Spooner, Minnie Dibden, exh. 1893-
1927

Squire, Alice, 1840-1936, exh. 1888

Squire, Emma, exh. 1872-1901

Stacks, Katherine, exh. 1879

Stackpoole, Lily, exh. 1886

Stacy, Ellen, exh. 1877

Stanhope-Forbes, Elizabeth *(see*
Forbes)

Stanley, Mrs. E., exh. 1849-1858

Stanley, Lady Henry M. (Dorothy
Tennant), ?-1926, exh. 1852-

1909

Stanley, Sara, exh. 1895-1902

Stannard, Anna Marie, exh. 1859

Stannard, Eloise Harriet, 1829-1915,
exh. 1855-1893

Stannard, Emily Coppin, 1803-1885

Stannard, Lilian, 1877-1944

Stannard, Maude H., exh. 1856-1860

Stanton, Rose Emily, exh. 1875-
1896

Staples, Mary Ellen Edwards *(see*
Edwards)

Starr, Louisa (m. Canziani) 1845-
1909, exh. 1863-1884

Steele, Madame Louise, exh. 1875-
1877

Steers, Fanny, exh. 1849-54

Sterling, Marion A., exh. 1884

Stern, Louise, exh. 1871

Stevens, Miss, exh. 1880

Stewart, Mrs. Charles *(see* Bowkett,
Jane)

Stigand, Helen M., exh. 1868-1876

Stillman, Marie, 1844-1927, exh.
1873-1877

Stocks, Katherine M., exh. 1880-
1889

Stoddart, Frances, exh. 1837-1840

Stoddart, Mrs., exh. 1884

Stokes, Marianne Preindlsberger,
1855-1927, exh. 1885-1904

Stone, Ellen, exh. 1874-1877

Stone, Marianne, exh. 1858

Strahan, Mrs. C. H., exh. 1889

Stratton, Helen, exh. 1892-1925

Strawbridge, Mrs., exh. 1886

Stuart, G.E., exh. 1848

Stuart, Jane Maria *(see* Bowkett)

Stuart, Louisa (Lady Waterford),
1818-1891

Stuart, Miss, exh. 1858

Sturch, Mrs., exh. 1861

Sumner, Margaret, exh. 1880-1914

Surenne, Mary H., exh. 1879

Surtees, Mrs., exh. 1877-1880

Sutcliffe, Harriette F. A., exh. 1881-1922

Sutherland, Fanny, exh. 1877-1883

Swainston, Laura, exh. 1870-1894

Swan, Mary E., exh. 1889-1898

Swift, Georgina, exh. 1859-1874

Swift, Catherine (Kate) Seaton, exh. 1858-1866

Swift, L. Burgess, exh. 1880

Swift, Louise Bisschop, exh. 1860-1887

Swift, Mrs. W. B., exh. 1835-1860

Swinburne, Miss, exh. 1849

Swynnerton, Annie Louisa (m. Robinson), 1844-1933

Sykes, Marianne, exh. 1855-1891

Sykes, Mrs., exh. 1840-1859

Talbot, Mrs., exh. 1849

Tammage, Madge, exh. 1879,

Tarbotton, Jessie, exh. 1873

Tatham, Helen S., exh. 1878-1891

Taylor, Maria (m. Spilsbury), 1777-1820

Taylor, S. M. Louisa, exh. 1867-1873

Tegetmeier, Edith, exh. 1872

Tekusch, Margaret, exh. 1845-1888

Tennant, Dorothy (afterwards Lady Stanley), ?-1926, exh. 1874-1890

Terrell, Georgina F. (Koberwein), exh. 1876-1880

Terrere, Miss Townsend, exh. 1866

Teulon, Flora, exh. 1872

Thicke, Charlotte, exh. 1802-1844

Thomas, Margaret, exh. 1868-1877

Thomas, Miss, exh. 1860

Thomas, Miss F., exh. 1877

Thompson, Christiana, exh. 1881

Thompson, Elizabeth (see Butler)

Thompson, Isa (see Jobling)

Thompson, Kate, exh. 1877-1882

Thompson, L. Beatrice, exh. 1885

Thompson, Mrs. T.J., exh. 1858

Thoresby, Florence, exh. 1876

Thornton, C., exh. 1880

Thornycroft, Alyce M., exh. 1864-1892

Thornycroft, Helen, exh. 1864-1904

Thornycroft, Theresa G., exh. 1875-1883

Tiddeman, Florence, exh. 1875-1876

Tillotson, Mary, exh. 1839-1844

Tilt, Georgiana, exh. 1879

Tompkins, Clementina, exh. 1877

Tothill, Mary D., exh. 1874-1875

Tovey, Mary Simpson (m. Christison), ?-1879, exh. 1872-1877

Townsend, Mary, exh. 1845-1848

Townsend, Miss, exh. 1866-1877

Townsend, Patty (m. Johnson), exh. 1881-1892

Trevelyan, Pauline Jermyn, 1816-1866

Trevor, Helen Mabel, 1831-1900, exh. 1881-1895

Troubridge, Laura, exh. 1882

Turck, Eliza, ?-1832, exh. 1851-1886

Turnbull, Anne Charlotte Fayerman (see Bartholomew)

Turner, Adelaide (see Claxton)

Turner, Elizabeth, exh. 1841

Turner, Miss, exh. 1872-1881

Twining, Louisa 1820-1900

Upton, Florence K., ?-1922

Vertue, Rosamund, exh. 1847

Vigers, Miss, exh. 1881

Vinter, Harriet Emily, exh. 1879

Vivian, Elizabeth Baly *(see* Farquahar)

Walker, Alice, exh. 1858-1862

Walker, Cordelia, exh. 1863

Walker, Emma, exh. 1858

Walker, Elizabeth, exh. 1846-1863

Walker, Ethel, exh. 1898-1899

Walker, Marcella, exh. 1876-1901

Walker, Pauline, exh. 1877-1879

Walker ("The Three Miss Walkers"), exh. 1877

Walker, Wilhelmina Augusta, exh. 1876-1900

Waller, Eliza, exh. 1828-1838

Waller, Mary Lemon Fowler (m. Edmund), ?-1931, exh. 1871-1916

Wallis, Sarah *(see* Bowditch)

Walters, Emma, exh. 1855-1887

Walton, Constance, exh. 1886-1887

Ward, Eva M., exh. 1873-1879

Ward, Flora E. S., exh. 1872-1875

Ward, Henrietta Mary Ada (m. E. M. Ward), 1832-1924, exh. 1849-1904

Ward, Mary *(see* Webb)

Ward, Mrs. George Raphael, exh. 1860

Wardlow, Annie, exh. 1887-1891

Wardlow, Mary Alexandra, exh. 1885-1892

Warren, Miss, exh. 1864-1871

Warren, Sophy S., exh. 1869-1878

Waterford, Louisa, Marchioness of , 1818-1891, exh. 1849-1887

Watkins, Kate, exh. 1850-1888

Watson, Rosalie M., exh. 1872-1887

Watt, Linnie, exh. 1875-1908

Watts, Jane, 1792-1826

Watts, Louisa Margaret Hughes, exh. 1884-1900

Weatherill, Mary, exh. 1884

Webb, Josephine, 1853-1924

Webb, Maria D. *(see* Robinson)

Webb, Mary Whiteman, exh. 1872

Webb, Miss, exh. 1871-1886

Wedderburne, Jemima (m. Blackburn), exh. 1848-1849

Weekes, Charlotte, exh. 1876-1890

Weigall, Julia (m. Capes), exh. 1848-1864

Weir, Anna, exh. 1884-1885

Welby, Helen, exh. 1879

Weld, Mary Izod, exh. 1881

Weller, Augusta, exh. 1839

Wells, Augusta, exh. 1864-1879

Wells, E., exh. 1854

Wells, Joanna Mary *(see* Boyce)

Wells, Mary *(see* Hayllar)

Wells, Mrs. H. T., exh. 1860

Wendon, Miss, exh. 1881

West, Alice L., exh. 1891-1904

West, Maud, Astley, 1879-1961

West, Miss, exh. 1872

Westbrook, Elizabeth T., exh. 1870-1880

Westbrook, Miss, exh. 1876

Westcott, Lottie, exh. 1879

Wheeler, M.A. *(see* Johnstone)

Whitaker, Frances Mathilda *(see* McIan)

White, Florence, exh. 1881-1904

Whitehead, Mary, exh. 1874

Whiteside, R. Cordelia, exh. 1892-1904

Whitfield, Mrs. Westwood, exh. 1880

Whitley, Kate Mary, exh. 1884-1892

Whymper, Emily, exh. 1877-1878

Wilkes, Sarah, exh. 1860-1869
Wilkinson, Ellen, exh. 1875-1878
Wilkinson, Maude I., exh. 1899-
1904
Wilkinson, Miss, exh. 1861
Wilks, Emily May, exh. 1876
Willcocks, Mabel, exh. 1899-1904
Williams, Caroline Fanny, 1836-
1921, exh. 1858-1890
Williams, Emily Epps, exh. 1881-
1889
Williams, P. A., exh. 1884
Williams, S. H., exh. 1849
Willis, Miss, exh. 1839-1843
Wilmot, Florence N. Freeman, exh.
1883-1909
Wilson, Marion Henderson, 1869-
1956
Wilson, Mrs. R., exh. 1873
Wirgman, Helen, exh. 1881
Wise, Miss, exh. 1872
Withers, Augusta Innes, 1829-1875,
exh. 1855-1873
Wood, Catherine M. (m. Wright),
exh. 1879-1904
Wood, Eleanor Stuart, exh. 1876-
1886
Wood, Emmie Stewart, exh. 1888-
1904
Wood, Hortense, exh. 1872-1880
Wood, Lady, exh. 1881
Wood, Ursula, 1868-?, exh. 1890-
1901
Woods, Ellen M., exh. 1875-1881
Woods, Fanny (m. Fildes), exh.
1878-1873
Woodward, Alice Bolingbroke, exh.
1890-1900
Woodward, Mary, exh. 1890-1914
Wortley, Mary Caroline Stuart (also
Lady Wentworth), exh. 1875-

1879
Wren, Louisa, exh. 1876-1898
Wright, Caroline, exh. 1881
Wright, Meg, exh. 1891-1899
Wright, Miss, exh. 1881
Wright, Mrs. R. T., exh. 1883
Wylie, Mrs., exh. 1879

Index of Annotations

Numbers refer to citation numbers throughout the book.

Ballantyne, Edith, 573, 587, 649
Banks, Miss, 498
Barber, C. J., 677, 704
Barker, Leila, 396
Barker, Lucette Elizabeth, 336, 503
Barker, Octavia, 396
Barnard, Catherine, 742
Barnard, Emily, 763
Barret, Harriet, 380
Barrett, Elizabeth, 547
Barrett, Marianne Foster, 533
Barrington, Emilie, 1004
Barrow, Janet Ross, 157
Bartholomew, Anne Charlotte
      Fayerman, 15, 246, 358, 396,
      410, 415, 420, 424, 429, 432,
      442, 444, 446, 448, 459, 469,
      652
Barton, Rose, 321, 380, 388, 706,
      721, 764, 1000
Bater, Nellie, 314
Bates, Jessey Fairfax, 373
Bauerlé, Amelia, 321
Baxter, Louisa, 35
Bayes, Jessie, 203
Bayfield, Fanny Jane, 388, 396
Beal, Annie L., 587
Beale, Ellen, 396
Beale, Lucette, 396
Beale, Sarah Sophia, 396, 509, 580,
      633
Beard, Ada, 617
Beckett, Jane, 396
Begg, Annie, 376
Begg, Grace, 376
Begg, Isabella, 376
Begg, Jean, 376
Begg, Mary S., 376
Behenna, Kathleen, 814
Belcher, Lady, 459, 469
Belford, Kate, 604

Belinaye, Miss de la, 49
Bell, Ada, 643, 654, 695, 729, 742,
      750, 752
Bell, Lucy Hilda, 751
Benham, Jane (see Hay)
Bennett, Isabel, 543
Benson, Charlotte, 321
Benson, Katherine, 70, 72, 602
Benson, Mary Katherine, 321, 735,
      836
Beresford, E. M., 490, 579, 643, 654,
      709, 729, 763
Berkeley, Edith, 740, 786
Bert, F., 604
Best, Mary Ellen, 396
Bewick, Jane, 101, 201, 304
Biffin, Sarah, 8, 246
Binns, Elizabeth J., 610, 703
Bishop, C. E., 513
Bisschop, Kate, 513, 546, 763
Black, Emma L., 75, 681
Blackburne, Jemima Wedderburn,
      336, 321, 358, 403
Blackmore, Isabel, 246
Blaine, Mrs. Robertson, 434, 455,
      458, 459, 469, 484, 490
Blake, Miss, 418, 459
Blandy, L. V., 615
Blatherwick, Lily, 376, 606
Bleaden, Mary, 640
Blunden, Anna, 9, 140, 302, 305,
      336, 358, 377, 379, 390, 396,
      448, 455, 458, 459, 461, 485,
      497, 829, 833, 837, 966,
      1002
Blunden, Emma, 459
Blunt, Lady Anne, 646
Bodé, Otille, 99
Bodichon, Barbara Leigh Smith, 140,
      244, 260, 270, 272, 297, 300,
      325, 334, 336, 337, 346, 357,

358, 379, 382, 390, 396, 400,
402, 403, 404, 455, 458, 490,
503, 507, 518, 525, 553, 570,
697, 829, 837, 993, 1000,
1002, 1003
Bogardus, J., 246
Bone, Louisa, 246
Bonheur, Juliette Peyrol, 503
Bonheur, Rosa, 68, 85, 97, 100, 103,
104, 105, 113, 116, 131, 180,
181, 201, 203, 214, 245, 260,
299, 315, 332, 336, 358, 390,
397, 399, 402, 454, 495, 496,
500, 502, 503, 544, 551, 575,
596, 631, 637, 654, 664, 673,
707, 720, 722, 771, 785, 792,
819, 829, 960, 978, 986, 993
Bonneau, Florence, 577, 643, 721,
729
Boot, C., 246
Boothby, F., 418
Bosanquet, Charlotte, 396
Bouvier, Agnes Rose, 396, 434, 488,
490, 503, 507, 610, 689
Bowditch, Sarah Wallis, 380
Bowers, Georgiana, 140, 142, 182,
321, 503, 741
Bowkett, Eliza, 396
Bowkett, Jane, 278, 336, 358, 379,
391, 396, 967, 976
Bowkett, Jessie, 396
Bowkett, Leila, 396, 567
Boyce, Joanna Mary, 14, 201, 267,
336, 358, 379, 390, 396, 468,
475, 478, 829, 837, 993,
1000
Boyd, Alice, 51, 260, 267, 305, 314,
400
Boyd, Janet A., 304
Boyle, Eleanor Vere, 321, 336, 357,
364, 380, 488, 507, 525, 640,

646, 837
Bradley, Dora, 72
Bradley, Gertrude, 321
Branfill, Miss, 670
Bremer, Frederica, 459
Brett, John, 336
Brett, Rosa, 130, 305, 336, 343, 358,
388, 390, 391, 396, 400, 509,
522, 545, 663, 829
Brewer, Mary, 246
Briane, Mrs., 966
Bridell, Eliza *(see* Fox)
Bridell, Louisa F., 509
Bridell, Mrs. Lee, 494
Brimmer, Anne, 410
Broadridge, Alma, 716
Bromley, Mrs. Val, 580, 595, 615,
643, 646, 663, 672, 682, 763
Brooks, Maria Burnham, 542, 545,
546, 558, 577, 578, 584, 618,
723
Brown, Alberta, 396, 503, 513
Brown, Catherine, 140, 147, 196,
260, 336, 358, 390, 396, 400,
552, 697, 829
Brown, Eleanor, 396
Brown, Emma Hill, 273, 400, 862,
997
Brown, Hannah, 260
Brown, Helen Paxton, 396
Brown, Lucy, 140, 191, 195, 196,
260, 280, 336, 358, 379, 390,
396, 400, 524, 697, 829, 936
Brown, Mrs. J. B., 469
Brown, Mrs. J. W., 459, 484, 518
Browne, Henriette, 34, 71, 87, 93, 97,
105, 201, 336, 358, 495, 511,
515, 517, 544, 545, 662, 705,
778, 829
Brownlow, Emma, 336, 358, 450,
469, 473, 484, 485, 488, 494,

Cartwright, Julia, 358
Cassatt, Mary, 960, 986
Cazin, Marie, 533
Chalon, Maria A., 246
Champion, Mrs. H., 610, 672, 699
Chaplin, Alice M., 646
Charlton, Catherine, 649
Charretie, Anna Maria, 58, 246, 336,
        358, 396, 503, 505, 507, 523,
        525, 542, 543, 546
Charteris, Lady Louisa, 576, 646
Chase, Marian, 358, 540, 544, 551,
        556, 564, 568, 582, 583, 614,
        634, 645, 729, 752
Chettle, Elizabeth, 687
Childers, Milly, 396
Childs, Julia, 432
Clacy, Ellen, 396, 649
Clarke, Harriet Ludlow, 358, 418
Clarke, Julia, 39, 49
Clarke, Mary Constance, 1004
Clarke, Miss, 418
Claxton, Adelaide, 12, 25, 140, 182,
        249, 283, 321, 336, 358, 391,
        518, 837
Claxton, Florence, 13, 249, 283, 321,
        336, 358, 391, 396, 455, 458,
        490, 503, 507, 518, 837,
        1002
Claxton, M., 552
Claxton, Miss, 543
Clay, M., 579
Clayton, Ellen, 396, 898, 1004
Clemones, M., 484
Clive, Miss, 418
Clow, Florence, 729, 730
Coffey, Miss, 32
Cole, Augusta, 246, 413, 426
Cole, Ellen, 405, 459
Cole, Hannah, 39
Cole, Mary Ann, 405, 413, 459

Coleman, Helen Cordelia, 336, 388,
        537, 540, 551, 554
Coleman, Rebecca, 107, 396, 503,
        507, 518, 525, 604, 643
Coleridge, Maud, 518, 522, 547, 578
Colkett, Victoria, 336, 513
Collier, Mrs. John, 154, 673, 702
Collinson, Eliza, 472
Colville, E., 729
Combe, E., 246
Combermere, Viscountess, 418
Combes, Miss, 737
Conder, Helen Louise, 751
Connell, M. Christine, 321, 753
Conolly, Ellen, 521, 567, 641
Coode, Helen Hoppner, 321, 484
Cook, Eliza, 106
Cook, Jane E., 89
Cook, Miss, 767
Cooke, Hannah, 567
Cooper, Emma Wren, 396, 537, 542,
        553, 578, 610, 640, 643, 672,
        729
Cooper, Florence M., 321
Cooper, Louisa, 41
Cooper, Mrs. Davis, 459, 763
Corbeaux, Louisa, 321, 396, 451,
        556, 645, 506
Corbeaux, Marie Françoise (Fanny),
        245, 274, 336, 358, 396, 409,
        419, 421, 425, 426, 440, 447,
        556
Corbett, F., 542
Corcoran, Jessie, 39, 52, 738
Corder, Rosa, 118, 258, 280, 697,
        697, 842
Corkran, Henriette, 623
Cornelissen, Marie, 211, 358
Cornforth, Fanny, 259, 260, 273, 280,
        296, 400, 697, 845, 846, 850,
        851, 856, 858, 861, 862, 871,

Drummond, Eliza D., 246
Drummond, F. Ellen, 246
Drummond, Jane, 246
Drummond, Rose Emma, 156, 157, 246
Drummond, Rose Myra, 246
Dubourg, Victoria, 693, 695, 729
Duff, Isabella, 49
Duff, Jane, 49
Duffield, C. M., 553
Duffield, E., 444
Duffield, Mary Ann Rosenberg, 336, 358, 432, 499, 502, 504, 506, 508, 520, 524, 544, 551, 556, 564, 568, 582, 583, 599, 614, 634, 641, 645, 786
Duffield, Mary Elizabeth, 373, 388, 396, 902
Dunbar, Lady Sophia, 490, 494
Duncan, Fanny, 649
Dundas, Agnes, 484, 488, 490, 654
Dundas, Alice, 553
Dunn, Edith, 321, 336
Dunnell, Miss, 801
Durant, Susan, 358, 670, 1000
Dutton, Miss, 246
E. V. B. *(see* Boyle, Eleanor)
Earl, Maud, 193, 379, 396
Earle, Kate, 601
Earnshaw, Mary Harriot, 179
Eastlake, Caroline, 336
Eastlake, Elizabeth R., 358, 507, 640, 1004
Edmonds, Anna Maria Guérin, 542, 587, 610, 654
Edwards, Catherine Adelaide *(see* Sparkes)
Edwards, Ellen, 152, 473, 489
Edwards, J. A., 543
Edwards, Kate, 321, 336
Edwards, Marian, 604

Edwards, Mary Ann, 511
Edwards, Mary Ellen, 140, 142, 249, 321, 336, 358, 396, 493, 497, 505, 521, 525, 545, 546, 552, 575, 837
Egerton, Jane Sophia, 246, 336, 409, 419, 440
Egley, Polly, 875
Eley, Frances, 743
Eley, Mary, 553, 720
Elias, Annette, 193
Ellet, Elisabeth Fries, 358, 951
Ellis, Alice B., 35, 37, 39, 512
Ellis, Miss, 32
Elmore, Edith, 573, 587, 612, 649
Emilia, Lady Dilke, 1004
Enfield, Mary P., 277
Epps, Ellen (Nellie), 140, 188, 257, 396, 615
Epps, Laura *(see* Alma-Tadema)
Erichson, Nelly, 321, 388
Errington, Isabella, 304
Escombe, Anne, 500
Escombe, Jane, 577
Essex, Hannah, 446
Eustace, Mrs. Wilson, 488
Faed, Susan Bell, 335, 493
Fahey, Palacia E., 488
Fairbairn, Hilda, 321
Farmer, A., 493
Farmer, Emily, 246, 336, 358, 460, 486, 492, 495, 496, 499, 502, 506, 599, 634
Farmiloe, Edith, 321
Farnall, Miss, 677
Farquahar, Elizabeth Baly, 33
Farquahar, Maria, 1004
Faser, Annie, 469
Fawcett, Emily, 41
Fellowes, Caroline, 336
Fenn, A. S. M., 721, 758

Fennell, Louisa, 654
Fenton, Annie Grace, 552
Fenwick-Miller, Florence, 358, 1004
Ffloukes, C. J., 932
Finch, E., 418
Finch, F., 418
Finnessey, Mrs. E. (Selous), 37
Fitz James, Anna Maria, 396, 484, 488, 490, 503, 507, 518, 553, 610, 1002,
Flack, Edith Mary, 801
Flake, Fanny, 380
Florence, Mary Sargant, 321, 370, 1000
Folkard, Elizabeth F., 578, 640
Folkard, Julia Bracewell, 31, 578
Follingsby, Mrs., 434
Forbes, Elizabeth Armstrong (Mrs. Stanhope Forbes), 174, 193, 195, 321, 345, 358, 370, 380, 388, 396, 783, 795, 802, 806, 814
Forbes-Cockburn, Charlotte, 553
Ford, Emily Susan, 396
Ford, G. M., 604
Fores, Mary Harriet, 751
Forster, Mary, 128, 133, 709, 730, 733, 747
Fortescue-Brickdale, Eleanor, 211, 227, 230, 303, 321, 326, 338, 357, 370, 390, 837,
Fortesque, Henrietta Anne, 380
Foster, A. H., 729
Foster, E., 567
Foster, Mary, 643, 671, 678, 721, 917
Foster, Mrs., 1004
Foster, Mrs. W., 277
Fowkner, F., 688
Fowler, Mary Lemon, 706, 789
Fowler, Mrs., 246
Fox, Eliza Florence, 140, 336, 358,

390, 404, 455, 458, 459, 468, 469, 485, 489, 498, 503, 513, 553, 604, 610, 993, 1002
Fox, Miss, 415, 424, 426, 442
Frank, Mrs. Gustav, 518
Fraser, Annie, 484, 721
Freer, Mary Ellen *(see* Edwards)
Freer, Miss, 498
French, Annie, 326, 376, 831
Frere, Miss, 643
Frier, Jessie, 523, 604, 610
Fripp, Constance, 687
Furnell, C., 246
Fussell, Alice E., 277
Fussey, Ada E., 277
Gamble, Louisa, 246
Gann, Louisa, 32, 35, 37, 49, 52, 70, 358, 687, 891, 893, 894, 896, 1003
Gardener, Elizabeth J., 769
Gartside, Mary, 403
Gastineau, Maria A., 336, 380, 484, 488, 490, 494, 503, 518, 542, 610, 672
Gay, Susan Elizabeth, 396
Gayleard, Sophia, 246
Geefs, Fanny, 246, 336, 405
Gemmel, Mary, 677
Gent, Mrs., 246
Giampietri, Madame, 699
Gibbons, Jane, 891
Gibbs, Miss, 246
Gibson, Edith, 602
Gilbert, Annie Laurie, 277
Gilbert, Ellen, 543
Gilbert, Kate Elizabeth, 316, 396
Gilchrist, Constance, 842, 843, 855, 860
Giles, Miss, 801
Gillies, L., 428
Gillies, Margaret, 45, 140, 156, 246,

260, 276, 336, 358, 396, 413,
420, 426, 433, 434, 441, 445,
447, 459, 462, 464, 467, 469,
471, 474, 482, 484, 487, 488,
510, 550, 581, 585, 613, 615,
635, 644, 829, 1000, 1002
Gilmour, Margaret, 376, 396
Gilmour, Mary, 396
Gloag, Isobel Lilian, 321, 1000
Godsal, Mary, 854
Goodall, Eliza, 396, 405, 413, 420,
426, 427, 430, 433, 442
Goodman, Matilda, 41
Goodman, Maude, 388, 391
Goodman, Mrs., 488, 490
Goodman, Mrs L., 610
Goodwin, Kate, 640
Gordon, Julia Isabella, 380
Gordon, Miss, 418
Gosse, Ellen *(see* Epps)
Gosse, Sylvia, 239, 396
Gotch, Caroline Burland Yates, 396,
1000
Gouldsmith, Harriet, 336, 358
Gow, Kate, 688
Gow, Mary, 230, 321, 336, 358, 540,
544, 556, 575, 630, 668, 701,
707, 754, 967
Gow, Mary L., 125, 136, 396, 564,
582, 583, 599, 634, 722, 755,
790
Gow, Miss, 211
Grace, Elizabeth, 72
Grant, Alice, 193, 809
Grant, Mary, 358, 1000
Gray, Norah Neilson, 376
Greedish, Emma *(see* Greenish)
Green, Elizabeth Shippen, 326
Green, Everett, 617, 677
Green, Mary Byrne, 246
Greenaway, Kate, 92, 108, 135, 142,

148, 149, 173, 203, 223, 230,
245, 277, 315, 321, 350, 357,
358, 364, 388, 396, 549, 566,
575, 605, 679, 718, 808, 809,
829, 837, 1003
Greene, Alice, 1000
Greener, Mary Ann, 246
Greenish, Emma, 41, 52
Grey, Alice, 864
Grey, Euphemia (Effie), 224, 293,
861, 864
Grey, Lady, 418
Grey, Sophie, 864
Griffith, Kate, 610
Griffiths, Bertha, 688
Grose, Milicent, 729
Grote, Harriet Lewin, 358, 459, 993
Gubbons, H., 246
Guérin, Anna Maria *(see* Edmonds)
Guillod, Bessie, 39
Guiness, Elizabeth Sarah Smith, 41,
43, 578
Hadden, Nellie, 388
Hake, Miss, 801
Hale, Ellen D., 555
Hall, Ann Ashley, 518
Hall, Edith S., 617
Hall, Fannie Hoseason, 469
Hall, Marguerite Bernadine, 1000
Halle, Elinor, 828
Hallward, Adelaide Bloxam, 321
Hamilton, Gertrude, 39, 561
Hamilton, Maggie, 376
Hamilton, Mrs. L. Vereker, 828
Hamley, Barbara, 943
Hammond, Gertrude, 166, 775
Hammond, Kate, 617
Hanbury, Ada, 560, 617
Hanbury, Blanche, 566
Hancock, Ellen Isabella, 49, 35, 37,
39, 52, 561, 738, 891

Hankey, Mabel, 826
Hannay, Mrs. W., 490
Hanslip, Alice, 35, 39, 52, 70, 512,
        561, 602, 687, 738
Hanslip, Emily, 49
Harbutt, Elizabeth, 601
Hardcastle, Charlotte, 459
Harding, Emily, 321
Hardy, Ruth, 321
Harman, Ruth, 751
Harris, Fanny *(see* Rosenberg,
        Frances)
Harrison, Harriet, 396, 488, 553
Harrison, Jane, 143
Harrison, Maria, 358, 396, 406, 411,
        417, 441, 445, 462, 550, 581,
        585, 613, 635
Harrison, Mary P. Rossiter, 45, 57,
        59, 336, 358, 396, 407, 409,
        410, 419, 420, 422, 425, 429,
        432, 447, 448, 502, 503, 518,
        542, 544, 551, 652
Harrison, Mrs. Charles, 413
Harrison, Mrs. H., 490
Harrison, Mrs. M., 410
Harrison, Sarah Cecilia, 828, 836
Hart, Dorothy, 321
Haseler, Margaret, 72
Hastie, Grace H., 549, 604, 643, 699,
        706, 729
Hastings, Kate Carr, 640, 763
Hatton, Helen Howard, 321, 775
Havell, Charlotte M., 602
Havers, Alice Mary, 137, 138, 139,
        142, 145, 152, 153, 159, 170,
        171, 177, 321, 358, 396, 546,
        578, 587, 591, 618, 623, 632,
        649, 653, 654, 660, 676, 679,
        693, 702, 706, 740, 743, 749,
        754, 773, 790, 829, 833,
        1000

Haweis, Miss, 140
Hay, Emily, 610
Hay, Jane Benham, 193, 321, 336,
        358, 396, 400, 404, 413, 463,
        473, 476, 478, 503, 507, 518,
        553, 660, 670, 1004
Haycraft, Lillie Stackpoole, 396
Hayllar, Edith, 310, 313, 358, 379,
        391, 396, 702, 825, 854, 967
Hayllar, Jessica, 310, 313, 358, 379,
        391, 396, 673, 682, 734, 739,
        837, 854, 967, 968
Hayllar, Kate, 313, 358, 388, 391,
        767, 837, 854
Hayllar, Mary, 313, 358, 391, 396,
        682, 829, 837, 854
Hayward, Emily, 235
Heaphy, Elizabeth *(see* Murray)
Heaphy, Miss, 824
Heaton, Ellen, 871
Hegg, Theresa, 507, 513, 542, 553,
        610
Hemans, Felicia, 106
Heming, Matilda, 246, 321
Hemming, Mrs., 459, 488
Henderson, E. M., 239
Henn, Marion Ryden, 751
Hentsch, Emily, 39
Herbert, Ruth, 850, 856, 858
Herford, Laura, 27, 230, 336, 358,
        396, 837, 896, 956, 1002,
        1003
Herring, Mrs. G.E., 433, 442
Herring, Mrs. J.F., 490, 503, 518
Hewitt, Mrs., 469
Hewitt, Sarah, 488
Hicks, Amelia Mary, 604, 610
Hickson, Margaret, 94, 702
Hill, Ellen G., 522, 533, 640, 994
Hill, Emma Brown, 260
Hill, Kate, 41, 52

Hindes, Mrs. B.L., 542, 610

Hine, Victoria *(see* Crockett)

Hipkins, Edith, 41, 623, 654, 685,
709, 734, 739

Hobson, Alice, 605

Hodge, Elizabeth, 35, 39

Holden, Edith, 321

Holden, Evelyn B., 321

Holden, Louisa Jane, 246

Holliday, Lilly, 610

Holloway, Janet, 742

Holmes, Rhoda Carleton, 70, 561

Holmes, Sophia, 764

Hooper, Miss, 633

Hope, M., 606

Hopkins, Edith, 511, 640

Hopkins, Mrs. J. M., 632

Hopkinson, Anne Elizabeth, 35, 39,
49, 70, 80, 602, 891

Hopkinson, Edith, 602

Hopkinson, Miss, 512

Houlton, Miss, 418

Howard, Catherine Mary, 751

Howard, Sarah T., 246

Howell, C. E., 597

Howitt, Anna Mary, 10, 162, 260,
276, 336, 358, 379, 382, 389,
390, 396, 397, 400, 402, 404,
437, 455, 458, 697, 837, 993,
1002, 1004

Hueffer, Catherine *(see* Brown)

Hulme, Alice L., 610

Humphrey, Maude, 321

Humphreys, J. K., 490

Hunt, Diana, 957

Hunt, Edith, 224, 868, 957

Hunt, Fanny Waugh, 282, 868

Hunt, Violet, 697

Hunter, Elizabeth, 336, 436, 518

Hunter, Mary Young, 206

Hurlstone, Mrs., 415

Hurst, Mary, 681

Hussey, Mrs., 488

Huxley, Marion Collier, 110, 193,
396, 736,

Ierson, Agnes, 32, 35, 49

Ingelow, Jean, 404

Inglis, Jane, 472, 773

Irvine, Anna Forbes, 403

Jackson, E.J., 597

Jackson, Emily E., 654, 695

Jackson, Emily F., 633

Jackson, Helen, 687

James, Charlotte Isa, 494, 503, 507,
515, 604, 610, 672

James, Edith, 1000

James, Miss, 484

Jameson, Anna, 358, 389, 390, 836,
877, 879, 883, 899, 903, 904,
906, 949, 950, 955, 964, 969,
987, 993, 998, 1002, 1004

Jay, Isabella Lee, 109, 336, 696

Jeffreys, Bertha, 751

Jekyll, Gertrude, 396, 494, 503, 983

Jenkins, Blanche, 193, 545, 577, 701,
702, 796, 809

Jennings, Emma M., 643

Jerichau-Bauman, Elizabeth Marie,
30, 38, 336, 358, 434, 466,
481, 493, 498, 500, 513, 552

Jerson, Agnes, 39

Jerson, Miss, 52

Jevons, Louisa E., 304

Jobling, Isa, 304, 388

Johnson, M. H., 246

Johnston, Mrs., 670

Johnstone, J., 523

Jones, Anna M., 729

Jones, Charlotte, 490

Jones, Eliza, 246

Jones, Isabella, 490

Jones, Matilda, 246

Jones, Sarah, 39

Jopling, Louise, 87, 140, 144, 230, 243, 336, 358, 396, 397, 521, 522, 525, 530, 531, 542, 544, 545, 552, 553, 558, 573, 584, 588, 610, 615, 619, 623, 628, 646, 653, 654, 656, 661, 672, 699, 711, 716, 721, 758, 759, 763, 781, 784, 826, 829, 837, 937, 941, 944, 967, 993, 1000, 1002

José, Juliana, 552

Julyan, Mary, 567

Kauffmann, Angelica, 890

Kays, Miss, 604

Keary, Miss, 801

Keating, Mrs. Col., 434, 469

Kelly, Mrs., 167

Kemp, Emily, 828

Kempson, Miss, 507, 518, 553, 604, 672

Kempson, Mrs. Freeman, 503, 513, 610, 654

Kemp-Welch, Lucy, 206, 211, 230, 274, 279, 317, 358, 388, 396, 826

Kendrick, Emma Eleanora, 246

Kettle, Clara E. F., 246, 413, 424, 429, 432, 444, 448, 469, 488, 513

Keys, Frances M., 513, 643

King, Emma *(see* Brownlow)

King, Jessie M., 216, 314, 321, 326, 329, 374, 376, 390, 394, 396, 829, 983

Kingdon, Miss, 773, 782

Kingsford, Florence, 321

Kingsley, Jessie, 396

Kipling, Mary, 246

Kirkman, Miss, 677

Kirschner, Mary Louisa, 553, 1000

Knapping, Miss, 633

Knewstub, Emily Renshaw, 844

Knight, Laura, 203, 279, 286, 289, 381, 391, 396, 956, 993

Knowles, Leonora C. E., 246

Koberwein, Georgina *(see* Terrell)

Koberwein, Rosa, 577, 640

Kruger, Barbara, 376

L.A., 518

La Jeune, Elizabeth, 246

La Villette, Madame, 715

Laird, Alicia H., 336, 405, 469

Lamb, Miss, 512

LaMonte, Elish, 321, 336, 448

Lance, Mrs. E., 469

Landseer, Emma, 358, 488

Landseer, Jessica, 358, 488, 503, 837

Landseer, Miss, 494

Lane, Clara S., 336

Lane, Emily, 518, 643, 672

Lane, Miss, 484, 503, 507, 516, 518

Lansdell, Elizabeth, 246

Lauder, I. Scott, 541

Law, Helen, 790

Law, Miss, 567

Lawford, Mrs. Rowland, 640

Lawrence, Mary, 380

Lawson, Mrs. Cecil, 640, 695, 709, 720, 742, 763, 767

Le Breton, Rosa, 321

Leader, Mrs. B.W., 595, 703

Leavers, Lucy Ann, 119, 277

Leckie, Mary Mulready, 246

Ledsam, Miss, 688

Lee, Vernon, 1004

Lefroy, Miss, 484, 488

Legge, C., 418

Legge, M.A., 418

Lemann, E.A., 321

Lennox, A., 542, 553

Leod, Miss, 72

Marrables, 542

Marsh, Catherine, 5

Marshall, Angela Mary, 70

Marshall, Mrs., 648

Martin, Florence, 124, 579

Martineau, Edith, 155, 244, 336, 358,
511, 537, 546, 566, 578, 640,
671, 690, 700, 709, 917

Martineau, Gertrude, 244, 524, 600,
605, 671, 821

Martineau, Harriet, 358

Martineau, Miss, 521, 522

Martino, Anna *(see* Blunden)

Massey, Gertrude, 379

Mathews, Minnie, 321

Matthews, Winifred, 321

Mawson, Elizabeth Cameron, 304

May, Kate, 61, 717

May, Margery, 610

Mayer, B., 597

Maynard, Mrs. E., 488

McCrossan, Mary, 1000

McDowell, Mrs. Henry, 687

McIan, Fanny, 358, 389, 396, 405,
431, 829, 993

McKay, Rose, 790

McKenzie, Emma *(see* Landseer)

Mearns, Lois, 336

Mee, Anne Foldsone, 246, 264, 805

Merrick, Edith, 654

Merrick, Emily M., 706, 721, 729,
735, 744

Merrifield, Mary P., 1004

Merrifield, Mrs., 429

Merritt, Anna Lea, 73, 81, 86, 132,
140, 141, 150, 151, 158, 176,
192, 198, 203, 215, 232, 234,
255, 256, 323, 333, 358, 369,
379, 396, 397, 545, 555, 559,
615, 654, 701, 709, 713, 749,
770, 773, 776, 777, 797, 798,
809, 810, 811, 812, 816, 817,
826, 828, 829, 837, 939, 943,
947, 978, 993

Meyer, Beatrice, 579, 588, 608, 623,
630, 633, 657

Meyer, Henrietta, 41

Meynell, Alice, 1004

Miles, Helen, 107

Millais, Effie *(see* Grey, Euphemia)

Miller, Alice, 133, 751, 754

Miller, Annie, 260, 273, 296, 856,
862, 872, 993, 997

Miller, Florence *(see* Fenwick-Miller)

Miller, Josephine Haswell, 376

Mills, Eliza, 455, 458, 459

Minns, F.M., 677

Mitchell, Clara, 484, 488

Mitchell, Mrs., 490

Moberly, Mariquita Jenny, 388

Moffatt, Frederica, 41, 911

Mohl, Mary, 1000

Möller, Mrs. Nils, 488

Monkhouse, Mary Florence, 762

Montalba, Clara, 45, 146, 193, 195,
227, 230, 251, 336, 358, 396,
525, 538, 542, 546, 548, 550,
552, 563, 565, 567, 569, 581,
585, 586, 588, 591, 594, 595,
598, 600, 609, 613, 619, 621,
622, 624, 625, 629, 641, 642,
644, 654, 659, 666, 669, 676,
682, 683, 688, 689, 692, 706,
707, 711, 713, 714, 716, 717,
721, 725, 727, 729, 733, 738,
753, 754, 759, 760, 763, 764,
772, 773, 775, 781, 782, 784,
793, 803, 809, 811, 829

Montalba, Ellen, 396, 521, 530, 558,
610, 740

Montalba, Henrietta Skerrett, 193,
358, 553, 562, 646, 678

Montalba, Hilda, 41, 118, 358, 549, 553, 577, 578, 588, 591, 595, 600, 603, 604, 610, 615, 621, 623, 625, 632, 643, 647, 672, 682, 686, 697, 702, 709, 711, 716, 717, 729, 763, 767, 773, 782, 793

Montalba, Mary, 1000

Montalba, Miss, 45, 48, 64, 684, 705, 718, 719, 775, 796, 807

Montmorency, Lily de, 321

Moody, Fannie, 321, 742, 743

Moore, Eleanor Allen, 376

Moore, Jeannie, 35, 53, 55, 75, 605, 891

Morgan, Alice *(see* Havers)

Morgan, Jane, 730

Morice, A. A., 507

Morris, Jane Burden, 258, 260, 267, 273, 280, 296, 298, 307, 326, 352, 353, 357, 361, 375, 390, 400, 850, 851, 853, 856, 858, 862, 876

Morris, May, 236, 237, 294, 326, 352, 361, 393, 835, 871, 945, 946, 983

Morris, Miss, 983

Morris, Mrs. Best, 246

Mortimer, Alice, 235

Mortlock, Ethel, 193, 584, 618

Morton, Maria, 246

Moseley, Maria A., 413, 442, 446, 459

Moser, Mary, 890

Mothersole, Jessie, 235

Mullam, Miss, 669

Mulready, Elizabeth Varle, 130

Mulready, Mary, 246

Murray, Eliza Dundas, 459, 484, 488, 507, 582

Murray, Elizabeth Heaphy, 246, 336, 358, 455, 458, 459, 469, 486, 492, 495, 496, 504, 551, 556, 564, 568, 583, 599, 614, 645, 654, 691

Murray, Miss, 442

Muthesuis, Anna, 376

Mutrie, Annie Feray, 9, 44, 66, 201, 336, 358, 396, 438, 442, 443, 446, 448, 452, 455, 456, 461, 463, 466, 470, 475, 476, 477, 481, 497, 500, 505, 511, 519, 533, 560, 573, 651, 829, 887, 993, 1002

Mutrie, Martha Darley, 9, 44, 66, 143, 201, 336, 358, 396, 438, 442, 446, 448, 455, 463, 470, 476, 481, 497, 546, 560, 573, 584, 651, 829, 887, 993, 1002

Mutrie, Miss, 447, 450, 466, 531

Mylne, H., 610

Naftel, Isabel Oakley, 396

Naftel, Maude, 169, 358, 388, 396, 610, 654, 667, 695, 721, 763, 773, 782, 784, 1000

Naftel, Miss, 729

Naftel, Mrs. P. J., 518, 542, 553, 604, 605, 610, 654, 672, 721, 729, 764, 773, 782

Nasmyth, Anne Gibson, 336, 396

Nasmyth, Barbara, 319, 396

Nasmyth, Charlotte, 3, 314, 319, 396, 415, 429

Nasmyth, Elizabeth, 396

Nasmyth, Jane, 314, 319, 336, 396, 423, 829

Nasmyth, Margaret, 319, 336, 396

Neale, Maud, 396

Neilson, Ellen, 75

Nesbitt, Frances, 321

Newberry, Jessie Rowat , 308, 326, 376, 396, 831

Newcomb, Emma Ada, 751

Newcombe, Bertha, 656, 671, 689,
    705, 706, 709, 713, 716, 721,
    722, 726, 729, 736, 743, 782

Newell, S., 246

Newenham, Lady H., 534

Newill, Mary, 321, 390, 983

Newton, Harriet Frances, 561

Newton, Kathleen Irene, 265, 847,
    852, 865, 866, 869

Newton, Mary (see Severn)

Nicholl, Agnes Rose (see Bouvier)

Nicholl, Isabella, 864

Nichols, Catherine Maud, 507, 828

Nichols, Kate Edith, 610, 699

Nichols, Mary Anne, 246, 410, 413,
    420, 423

Nichols, Miss, 730

Nicholson, Alice M., 304

Nicholson, Lady Sarah, 617

Nisbet, Edith, 99

Nisbet, Ethel C., 119

Nixon, Minna, 542

Nixon, Mrs., 488

Noa, Madame Jessie, 494

Noble, C.M., 579

Nordgren, Anna, 193

Normand, Henrietta (see Rae)

North, Marianne, 112, 331, 336, 354,
    395

Norton, Miss, 801

Nottage, Caroline, 41, 43, 610

Noyes, Theodora F., 94, 767

Oakes, Miss, 604

Oakley, A.L. , 488

Oakley L., 246

O'Connell, Madame, 469

OEnone, Edith (see Somerville)

Offord, Gertrude Elizabeth, 396

O'Hara, Helen, 689, 706, 721, 743,
    753, 764

Oliver, Emma S. Eburne, 336, 358,
    396, 408, 425, 428, 434, 459,
    469, 484, 524, 544, 556, 567,
    599, 634, 645

Orovida (see Knight, Laura)

Orpen, Grace Knewstub, 844

Osborn, Emily Mary, 16, 21, 336,
    358, 379, 391, 396, 446, 452,
    468, 470, 476, 478, 485, 489,
    497, 505, 509, 511, 522, 539,
    546, 548, 553, 578, 647, 649,
    653, 809, 829, 837, 887, 968,
    976, 993, 995, 1002

Osbourne, Harriet, 1000

Osbourne, Mary, 1000

Overbury, Louisa, 39

Paget, Elise, 396

Paget, Violet, 1004

Palmer, Charity, 418

Palmer, Hannah Linell, 294, 380

Paris, Louisa Catherine, 396

Parker, Agnes Miller, 376

Parkes, Bessie Rayner, 260, 358, 402,
    488, 494, 1002

Parnell, G., 246

Parris, Mary Ann, 405

Parson, Beatrice E., 757

Parsons, Letitia Margaret, 657

Partridge, Ellen, 434, 448, 463, 469,
    484, 507, 513, 518, 542, 604,
    610, 643, 672, 763

Partridge, Emily, 542

Pash, Florence, 782, 804

Pasmore, Mrs. J.F., 336

Paterson, Caroline, 149, 388, 396,
    640, 750

Paterson, Emily Murray, 1000

Paterson, Mary Viola, 376

Patison, Emily, 396

Patmore, Bertha G., 785

Paton (Hill), Amelia, 336, 358

Paulson, Ann, 408
Paulson, Mrs., 412
Payne, Harriett A., 602
Pearson, Mary Martha Dutton, 29
Peel, Florence, 459, 469
Peel, Maude, 706
Pell, Florence, 434
Percy, Miss E., 503
Pertz, Anna J., 732
Perugini, Kate Dickens, 186, 254,
        269, 336, 358, 396, 572, 573,
        587, 591, 612, 626, 627, 654,
        673, 676, 694, 701, 710, 763,
        809, 915
Peyrol, Juliette Bonheur, 178, 484
Pfeiffer, J. Emily, 649, 667
Pfeiffer, Mrs., 488
Philip, Constance B., 41, 587
Phillips, Mrs., 422
Phillott, Constance, 117, 396, 511,
        523, 524, 640, 692, 744
Phinney, Emma E., 646
Picken Eleanor E., 246
Pickering (see De Morgan)
Pickerman, Mary Ann, 35
Pickersgill, M.A., 246
Pierrepont, C., 553
Pilsbury, Elizabeth, 660
Pitman, Janetta R.A., 277
Pitmann, Rosie M.M., 321
Pocock, Julia, 32, 35, 37, 503, 507,
        512, 513, 542, 578, 626, 891
Pohlman, Charlotte, 277
Poole, Louisa E., 52
Pope, Clara Maria, 246, 829
Potter, Beatrix, 380, 392, 837
Powell, Christiana, 891
Poynter, Agnes, 284
Pratten, Mrs., 537
Preindlsberger, Marianne (see
        Stokes)

Princep, Emily Rebecca, 380
Princess Beatrice, 106
Princess Louise, 118, 292, 629, 635,
        655, 697, 708, 716
Princess Victoria (see Queen Victoria)
Pringle, Agnes, 304
Proctor, Adelaide, 106, 400, 404
Proudfoot, Matilda, 864
Purdie, Mrs., 677
Purser, Sarah H., 706, 761, 764, 836,
        1000
Pusey, Clara, 336
Pyne, Eva E., 490
Queen Victoria, 209, 210, 292, 314,
        327, 811, 828, 837, 910
Quesne, Rose Le, 321
Rae, Henrietta (Normand), 32, 187,
        190, 192, 193, 195, 202, 211,
        213, 221, 230, 250, 279, 289,
        306, 330, 358, 388, 396, 748,
        767, 795, 800, 809, 811, 813,
        827, 829, 860, 939, 988, 993,
        1000
Raeburn, Agnes Middleton, 326, 376,
        396
Raeburn, Lucy, 376, 831
Raimbach, Emma Harriet, 966
Raimbach, Miss, 446
Raphael, Mary, 193, 200
Rawlinson, Lady, 617
Rayner, Frances (Fanny), 358, 396,
        490
Rayner, Louise J., 336, 358, 380,
        388, 396, 442, 469, 488, 490,
        513, 516, 518, 524, 546, 578,
        610, 643, 653, 672, 699, 739,
        743, 773, 786
Rayner, Margaret, 358, 380, 396,
        484, 490, 494, 503, 672
Rayner, Miss, 484
Rayner, Nancy, 358, 396, 408

Rayner, Rose , 358, 396, 490

Reason, Florence, 99, 321, 561, 602, 689, 738

Redgrave, Ellen, 578

Redgrave, Evelyn, 396

Redgrave, Frances M., 396, 509

Reid, A.M., 643

Reid, Flora MacDonald, 358, 396, 793

Reid, Lizzie, 721

Reid, May, 376

Reid, Miss, 193

Renshaw, Alice, 542

Reynolds, Miss, 801

Ribbing, Miss, 522

Ribbing, S., 531

Richards, Emma Gaggiotti, 396

Richardson, Agnes Edith, 304

Richardson, Mrs. Charles, 304

Richter, Henrietta, 246

Rickerby, Eliza G., 246

Rigby, Elizabeth, 1004

Rimer, Louisa Serena, 456, 459

Ring, Ethel S., 736

Riviére, Miss, 505

Robbinson, Margaret Stage, 358, 452, 459, 461, 463, 468, 473, 493, 498, 505, 514, 764

Roberts, F.M., 610

Roberts, Katherine May , 828

Roberts, Louisa, 444

Robertson, Mrs., 246, 408, 416

Robinson, Annie Louisa (see Swynnerton)

Robinson, Edith Brearey, 617

Robinson, Emily, 396, 643

Robinson, Maria D. Webb, 761

Robinson, Maud, 688

Robinson, Miss, 726

Robinson, Mrs., 455, 458

Rogers, Jane Masters, 246, 446

Romer, Louisa (see Jopling)

Ronner, Hénriette, 111, 183, 680, 792

Rose, H. Ethel, 754

Roseberg, Frances, 396

Rosenberg, Ellen Mary, 336, 396

Rosenberg, Ethel, 396

Rosenberg, Frances Elizabeth Harris, 396, 425, 451, 460, 508, 829

Rosenberg, Gertrude, 396

Rosenberg, Mary Ann (see Duffield)

Ross, Christina P., 523, 606

Ross, Magdalene, 246

Rossetti, Christina, 953

Rossetti, Lucy (see Brown)

Rothenstein, Alice Mary K., 844

Rowe, E. D'Oyley, 786

Royal, Miss, 490

Rumley, Elizabeth, 560

Rushout, Anne, 380

Ryder, Emily, 503

Sadler, Kate, 107, 605, 640, 695

Sainsbury, Grace, 388

Salaman, Kate, 246, 446

Salter, Anne, 604

Samworth, Joanna, 396, 537, 1000

Sandys, Emma, 336, 358, 390, 396, 525, 533, 829, 837

Sargant, Florence Mary, 281

Sarjent, Emily, 246

Savill, Josephine, 730

Schenck, Agnes, 721

Schute, Mrs. E.L., 167

Schwartze, Theresa, 643, 763

Scott, Alice M. , 235

Scott, Amy, 729

Scott, Caroline Lucy, 380

Scott, Emily, 246

Scott, Emily Ann (see Seymour)

Scott, Katherine, 543

Scott, Mary, 396

Scott, Miss, 429

Seeley, E. L., 321

Selous, Emily Fenessey, 35, 512, 891

Setchell, Elizabeth, 396

Setchell, Sarah , 336, 358, 396, 409,
419, 425, 440, 829

Severn, Mary, 223, 271, 285, 336,
358, 396, 481, 829, 1000

Sewell, Miss, 459

Seyffarth, Agnes E., 246

Seymour, Emily Anne, 246, 490

Seymour, Harriette Anne, 488, 503,
643, 699

Sharland, Miss, 752

Sharp, Dorothea, 826

Sharp, Eliza, 518

Sharp, Mary, 640, 730

Sharp, R.E.A., 643

Sharpe, Charlotte B., 987

Sharpe, Eliza, 50, 336, 358, 406, 987

Sharpe, Louisa Saffarth, 246, 357,
987

Sharples, Rolinda, 301, 336, 358, 829

Shirley, Mrs. A.S., 459

Shute, Mrs. E.L., 321

Siddall, Elizabeth Eleanor, 4, 147,
162, 163, 164, 165, 218, 224,
249, 252, 259, 260, 261, 266,
267, 270, 273, 275, 276, 280,
294, 295, 298, 307, 318, 322,
328, 336, 338, 344, 358, 366,
367, 372, 377, 382, 383, 385,
390, 391, 396, 400, 404, 453,
454, 697, 829, 837, 838, 840,
846, 848, 850, 851, 853, 856,
858, 859, 861, 862, 863, 868,
870, 871, 973, 993, 997

Sillett, Emma, 396

Simpson, Agnes, 246

Simpson, Eugénie, 721

Simpson, J., 552

Simpson, Maria E. *(see* Burt)

Simpson, Mary, 246

Small, Florence, 277

Smirke, Mary, 380

Smith, Alice Percival, 542, 843

Smith, Barbara Leigh *(see* Bodichon)

Smith, Bradshaw, 488

Smith, Dorothy Carleton, 396

Smith, Edith Heckstall, 388, 681, 716

Smith, Eliza Toulmin, 891

Smith, Julia Cecelia A., 31

Smith, Louisa, 654, 729

Smith, Mrs. Clifford, 246

Smith, Mrs. E.J., 677

Smyth, Dorothy Carleton, 321, 376

Smyth, Olive Carleton, 376

Smythe, Emma, 290

Sneyd, M. E., 418

Sohden, Susannah, 537

Solomon, Dorothy, 475

Solomon, Rebecca, 11, 249, 321, 336,
348, 349, 358, 368, 379, 388,
391, 396, 438, 442, 452, 466,
468, 472, 473, 476, 477, 478,
480, 481, 489, 525, 820, 829,
833, 837, 887, 968, 982,
1002

Somers, Countess, 418

Somerville, Edith, 1000

Somerville, Edith OEnone, 321, 836

Sparkes, Catherine Adelaide, 130,
396, 578, 587, 605

Sparkes, Mrs. , 640

Spartali, Christine, 342

Spartali, Marie *(see* Stillman)

Spiers, Bessie J., 610, 672, 763

Spiers, Charlotte H., 601, 617, 640,
672, 706

Spiers, Miss, 773

Spilsbury, Maria *(see* Taylor)

Spooner, Minnie Dibden, 321

Spurlin, Miss, 670

Squire, Alice, 396, 773
Squire, Emma, 396
Stacks, Katherine, 610
Stackpoole, Lily, 754
Stacy, Ellen, 578
Stanhope, Elizabeth *(see* Forbes)
Stanley, Eleanor, 418
Stanley, Lady *(see* Dorothy Tennant)
Stanley, Mrs., 193
Stanley, Mrs. E., 459
Stannard, Anna Marie, 396
Stannard, Eloise, 233, 309, 336, 358, 396, 443, 456, 465, 481, 483, 485, 503, 507, 518, 542, 553, 643, 672, 721, 763, 829
Stannard, Emily Coppin, 388, 396, 829
Stannard, Maude H., 448
Stanton, Emily Rose, 542
Stanton, Rose E., 675
Staples, Mary Ellen *(see* Edwards)
Starr, Louisa, 22, 28, 193, 268, 336, 358, 396, 497, 498, 501, 505, 507, 516, 521, 530, 533, 539, 546, 560, 572, 584, 587, 600, 615, 619, 646, 649, 673, 713, 788, 829, 943, 956, 993
Steele, Louise, 547, 578
Steers, Fanny, 358, 419
Sterling, Marion A., 716
Stern, Louise, 507
Stevens, Miss, 90
Stiers, Fanny, 440
Stigand, Helen M., 503
Stillman, Marie Spartali, 54, 140, 193, 227, 247, 258, 287, 295, 338, 342, 358, 370, 375, 390, 396, 537, 546, 552, 566, 576, 578, 615, 667, 733, 764, 787, 788, 799, 829, 837, 850, 851
Stillman, Lisa, 809

Stocks, Katherine M., 566, 640
Stoddart, Frances, 423, 459
Stoddart, Mrs., 737
Stokes, Catherine A., 619
Stokes, Margaret, 836
Stokes, Marianne Preindlsberger, 174, 192, 207, 208, 212, 321, 396, 764, 793, 794, 799, 802, 829, 1000
Stokes, Mrs. Adrian, 195
Stone, Ellen, 396, 531, 566
Stone, Marianne, 459
Strahan, Mrs. C.H., 933
Stratton, Helen, 321
Strawbridge, Mrs., 757
Stuart, Amelia, 396
Stuart, G.E., 396
Stuart, Lady Louisa *(see* Waterford)
Stuart, Miss, 459
Stuart, Theresa Fanny, 396
Sturch, Mrs., 469
Sumner, Margaret L., 321, 643
Surenne, Mary H., 83
Surtees, Mrs., 578, 640
Sutcliffe, Harriet, 388
Sutherland, Fanny, 577, 640
Swainston, Laura, 304
Swan, Mary, 321
Swift, Georgina, 434, 484, 488, 542
Swift, Kate (Catherine), 336, 358, 434, 459, 483, 484, 490, 493
Swift, L. Burgess, 604, 643
Swift, Louise Bisschop, 396, 498, 507, 513, 518, 542, 553, 604, 610, 672
Swift, Miss, 488
Swinburne, Miss, 418
Swynnerton, Annie Louisa, 193, 269, 274, 279, 358, 396, 713, 736, 763, 796, 806, 809, 811, 814, 829, 1000,

1002

Sykes, Marianne, 446

Sykes, Mrs., 246

Talbot, Mrs., 418

Tammadge, Madge, 610

Tarbotton, Jessie, 39

Tatershall, Marion, 860

Tatham, Helen S., 321, 640

Taylor, Rose, 336

Taylor, Maria, 829

Taylor, S.M. Louisa, 518

Tegetmeier, Edith, 35

Tekusch, Margaret, 246, 336, 396, 455, 458, 459, 547

Tennant, Lady Dorothy Stanley, 49, 144, 321, 396, 752, 765, 769, 790, 796, 799, 857, 1000

Terrell, Georgina Koberwein, 577, 647

Terrere, Miss Townsend, 490

Teulon, Flora, 33

Thicke, Charlotte, 246

Thomas, Florence Elizabeth, 396

Thomas, Margaret, 321, 578

Thomas, Miss F., 67

Thompson, Christiana, 654

Thompson, Elizabeth (see Butler)

Thompson, Isa (see Jobling)

Thompson, Kate, 577, 580, 587

Thompson, L. Beatrice, 828

Thompson, Mrs. T.J., 459

Thoresby, Florence, 561

Thornton, C., 640

Thornycroft, Alice, 580

Thornycroft, Alyce M., 501, 503, 507, 513, 516, 518, 525, 542, 552

Thornycroft, Helen, 396, 507, 518, 537, 542, 549, 552, 553, 578, 605, 610, 640, 643, 663, 672, 763, 767

Thornycroft, Mary, 336, 829, 1002

Thornycroft, Miss, 498, 503, 547

Thornycroft, Mrs., 336, 469

Thornycroft, Theresa G., 396, 546, 552, 578, 580, 587, 600, 603, 628, 643, 649, 674

Tiddeman, Florence, 545, 552, 558

Tillotson, Mary, 246

Tilt, Georgiana, 610

Tompkins, Clementina, 577

Tothill, Mary, 41

Tothill, Mary D., 52

Tovey, Mary Simpson, 84, 396, 542, 543, 545, 553, 562

Townsend, Mary, 405

Townsend, Miss, 688

Townsend, Patty, 804

Traquair, Phoebe Anna Moss, 204, 326, 370, 390, 983

Trevelyan, Lady Pauline Jermyn, 304

Trevor, Helen Mabel, 836, 1000

Trotter, Lilian, 358

Troubridge, Laura, 107

Trywhitt, Ursula, 358

Turck, Eliza, 9, 76, 140, 358, 380, 396, 429, 452, 687, 993

Turnbull, Anna (see Bartholomew)

Turner, Ada, 694

Turner, Adelaide (see Claxton)

Turner, Elizabeth, 246

Turner, Miss, 33, 670

Twining, Louisa, 321

Underwood, Annie, 826

Upton, Florence, 321

Van Eyck, Margaret, 358

Vernon, Ellen, 396

Vernon, Florence, 396

Vernon, Mary, 396

Vernon, Norah, 396

Vertue, Rosamund, 405

Vigers, Miss, 677

Vinter, Miss, 737

Vivian, Elizabeth *(see* Farquahar)

Walker, Alice, 336, 379, 396, 459, 837

Walker, Augusta, 396

Walker, Cordelia, 396, 434

Walker, Edith, 358, 381

Walker, Eliza, 434

Walker, Elizabeth, 246, 605

Walker, Marcella, 649

Walker, Pauline, 574, 605

Waller, Eliza, 246

Waller, Mary Lemon Fowler, 192, 388, 396, 745, 763

Walters, Emma, 358, 396, 434, 446, 459, 469, 484, 488, 490, 503, 507, 518, 542, 553, 610, 654, 672

Walton, Constance, 376, 396

Walton, Hanna, 396

Ward, Edward, 907

Ward, Eva, 396, 507, 513, 522, 545

Ward, Flora, 396, 507, 513, 516, 521, 533

Ward, Flora E.S., 542

Ward, Genevieve, 654

Ward, Henrietta, 17, 18, 19, 23, 24, 26, 44, 63, 66, 81, 82, 140, 185, 201, 260, 324, 336, 358, 379, 388, 389, 391, 396, 426, 438, 442, 448, 452, 455, 458, 459, 461, 463, 468, 473, 475, 476, 477, 478, 479, 481, 485, 491, 493, 497, 498, 500, 507, 509, 513, 514, 516, 518, 531, 533, 542, 557, 558, 572, 573, 586, 593, 619, 827, 829, 837, 887, 908, 909, 913, 941, 968, 993, 1003

Ward, Henriette, 517

Ward, Mary, 246

Ward, Mary Webb, 396

Ward, Mrs., 242

Warren, Miss, 484, 507

Warren, Sophy S., 336, 488, 490, 503, 513, 518, 553, 554, 587

Waterford, Louisa Marchioness, 184, 193, 194, 304, 321, 336, 358, 380, 396, 403, 418, 566, 615, 646, 763, 829, 837, 993

Watkins, Kate, 304

Watson, Rosalie M., 35, 39, 615

Watt, Linnie, 595, 604, 617, 643, 689, 729

Watt, Louise, 672

Watts, Jane, 304

Watts, Linnie, 597, 610, 740

Watts, Louisa Margaret, 321

Watts, Mrs. G., 809

Waugh, Edna, 358

Wayne, Lilian, 235

Weatherhill, Mary, 716

Webb, Josephine, 836

Webb, Maria D., 567, 607

Webb, Mary, 32

Webb, Mary W., 512

Webb, Mary Whiteman, 35

Webb, Miss, 507, 706, 752

Wedderburne, Jemima, 418, 420

Weeks, Charlotte J., 916, 925

Weigall, E., 448

Weigall, Julia, 246

Weir, Anna, 740

Welby, Helen, 617

Welch, Lucy Kemp, 193, 217, 311, 814

Weld, Mary Izod, 654

Weller, Augusta, 246

Wells, Augusta, 396, 516, 546

Wells, E., 436

Wells, Joanna *(see* Boyce)

West, A. Maud, 602

West, Alice, 159

West, Maud Astley, 321
West, Miss, 32
Westbrook, Elizabeth, 542, 566
Westbrook, Miss, 552
Westcott, Lottie, 610
Whitehead, Mary, 49
Whiteside, Miss, 801
Whitfield, Mrs. G. , 79
Whitfield, Mrs. Westwood, 653
Whitley, Kate, 756
Whymper, Emily, 587
Wilcox-Smith, Jessie, 326
Wilding, Alexa, 296, 338, 850, 856, 871
Wilkes, Sarah, 484
Wilkinson, Ellen, 536, 580, 670
Wilkinson, Miss, 469
Wilks, Emily May, 561
Williams, Caroline Fanny, 316, 336, 396, 484, 488, 490, 507, 513, 610
Williams, Emily Epps, 396
Williams, Miss, 434, 494
Williams, Miss P.A., 731
Williams, Mrs., 941
Williams, S.H., 418
Williamson, Mrs., 737
Willis, Miss, 246
Wilson, Marion Henderson, 376
Wilson, Miss, 35, 49
Wilson, Mrs. R., 521
Wirgham, Helen, 663
Wise, Miss, 512
Withers, Augusta Innes, 336, 518, 829
Withers, Mrs., 444, 459, 469, 484, 518
Wood, Catherine M., 99, 602
Wood, Eleanor Stuart, 560, 573
Wood, Emmie Stewart, 809
Wood, Hortense, 513, 633

Wood, Lady, 670
Wood, Ursula, 814
Woods, Ellen, 52
Woods, Fanny, 87, 587, 713
Woodward, Alice, 321
Woodward, Mary, 321
Woolard, D., 239
Wortley, Mary C. Stuart, 545, 558, 578, 615, 616
Wren, Louisa, 553
Wright, Caroline, 654
Wright, Margaret, 376
Wright, Mary Ellen, 983
Wright, Miss, 677
Wright, Mrs. R.T., 706
Wylie, Mrs., 615
Wyon, Mrs., 246
Yetts, Miss, 459
Younger, Jane, 376
Youngman, Annie Marie, 380, 610
Zambaco, Maria, 357, 378
Zimmern, Helen, 358
Zornlin, Georgiana Margaretta, 321